RAF BOMBER
COMMAND
Reflections of War

Other volumes in this series

RAF BOMBER COMMAND: REFLECTIONS OF WAR

Volume 1: Cover of Darkness (1939–May 1942)
Volume 3: Battleground Berlin (July 1943–March 1944)
Volume 4: Battles With the *Nachtjagd* (30/31 March–September 1944)
Volume 5: Armageddon (27 September 1944–May 1945)

RAF BOMBER COMMAND
Reflections of War

Volume 2
Live to Die Another Day
(June 1942–Summer 1943)

Martin W Bowman

Pen & Sword
AVIATION

First Published in Great Britain in 2012 by
Pen & Sword Aviation
an imprint of
Pen & Sword Books Ltd
47 Church Street, Barnsley, South Yorkshire S70 2AS

ISBN 978-1-84884-493-3

A CIP catalogue record for this book is
available from the British Library.

Typeset in 10/12pt Palatino by
Concept, Huddersfield

Printed and bound in England by
CPI Group (UK) Ltd, Croydon, CRO 4YY

Pen & Sword Books Ltd incorporates the Imprints of Pen & Sword
Aviation, Pen & Sword Family History, Pen & Sword Maritime, Pen & Sword
Military, Pen & Sword Discovery, Wharncliffe Local History, Wharncliffe
True Crime, Wharncliffe Transport, Pen & Sword Select, Pen & Sword
Military Classics, Leo Cooper, The Praetorian Press, Remember When,
Seaforth Publishing and Frontline Publishing.

For a complete list of Pen & Sword titles please contact
PEN & SWORD BOOKS LIMITED
47 Church Street, Barnsley, South Yorkshire, S70 2AS, England
E-mail: enquiries@pen-and-sword.co.uk
Website: www.pen-and-sword.co.uk

Contents

Acknowledgements vi

Chapter 1   *'Terrorangriff'*   1

Chapter 2   Italy Blitz 53

Chapter 3   Through the Storm 79

Chapter 4   'Juggling with Jesus' – 'Gambling with God' 111

Chapter 5   Whoever It Happens To, It Won't Be Me 149

Chapter 6   Mary of the Golden Hair 193

Index 236

Acknowledgements

Gebhard Aders; Harry Andrews DFC; Frau Anneliese Autenrieth; Mrs Dorothy Bain; Günther Bahr; Charlie 'Jock' Baird; Harry Barker; Irene Barrett-Locke; Raymond V Base; Don Bateman; Steve Beale; A D 'Don' Beatty; Jack Bennett; Andrew Bird; Peter Bone; Alfons Borgmeier; Jack Bosomworth; Len Browning; Don Bruce; George Burton; Jim Burtt-Smith; Maurice Butt; Philip J Camp DFM; City of Norwich Aviation Museum (CONAM); Bob Collis; Jim Coman; B G Cook; John Cook DFM; Rupert 'Tiny' Cooling; Dennis Cooper; Ray Corbett; Coen Cornelissen; Leslie Cromarty DFM; Tom Cushing; Hans-Peter Dabrowski; Rob de Visser; Dr. Karl Dörscheln; J Alan Edwards; Wolfgang Falck; David G Fellowes; Elwyn D Fieldson DFC; Karl Fischer; Søren C Flensted; Vitek Formanek; Stanley Freestone; Ian Frimston; Prof. Dr Ing. Otto H Fries; Air Vice Marshal D J Furner CBE DFC AFC; Ken Gaulton; Jim George; Margery Griffiths, Chairman, 218 Gold Coast Squadron Association; Group Captain J R 'Benny' Goodman DFC* AFC AE; Alex H Gould DFC; Hans Grohmann; Charles Hall; Steve Hall; Jack F Hamilton; Eric Hammel; Erich Handke; James Harding; Frank Harper; Leslie Hay; Gerhard Heilig; Bob Hilliard; Peter C Hinchliffe; Neville Hockaday RNZAF; Werner 'Red' Hoffmann; Ted Howes DFC; Air Commodore Peter Hughes DFC; John Anderson Hurst; Zdeněk Hurt; Ab A Jansen; Karl-Ludwig Johanssen; Wilhelm 'Wim' Johnen; Arthur 'Johnnie' Johnson; John B Johnson; Graham B Jones; Hans-Jürgen Jürgens; Erich Kayser; George Kelsey DFC; Les King; Christian Kirsch; Hans Krause; Reg Lawton; J R Lisgo; Chas Lockyer; Günther Lomberg; Peter Loncke; George Luke; Ian McLachlan; Nigel McTeer; B L Eric Mallett RCAF; Len Manning; The Honourable Terence Mansfield; Eric Masters; Bernard 'Max' Meyer DFC; Cyril Miles; Colin Moir; Frank Mouritz; Friedrich Ostheimer; Maurice S Paff; Simon Parry; Path Finder Association; Wing Commander David Penman DSO OBE DFC; Richard Perkins; Peter Petrick; Karl-Georg Pfeiffer; Eric Phillips; Vic Poppa; John Price; Stan Reed; Ernie Reynolds; Peter Richard; Albert E Robinson; Heinz Rökker; Squadron Leader Geoff Rothwell DFC;

Fritz Rumpelhardt; David M Russell; Kees Rijken; Eric Sanderson; Klaus J Scheer; Dr. Dieter Schmidt-Barbo; Karl-Heinz Schoenemann; Jerry Scutts; Johan Schuurman; Group Captain Jack Short; Leslie R Sidwell; Don L Simpkin; SAAF Assn; Albert Spelthahn; Dr Ing. Klaus Th. Spies; Dick Starkey; Squadron Leader Hughie Stiles; Mike 'Taff' Stimson; Ted Strange DFC; Maurice Stoneman; Ken Sweatman; Paul Todd; Fred Tunstall DFC; Hille van Dieren; George Vantilt; Bob Van Wick; Andreas Wachtel; Georg Walser; David Waters; H Wilde; John Williams; H J Wilson; Henk Wilson; Geoffrey and Nick Willatt; Dennis Wiltshire; Louis Patrick Wooldridge DFC; Fred Young DFM; Cal Younger.

I am particularly grateful to my friend and colleague Theo Boiten, with whom I have collaborated on several books, for all of the information on the *Nachtjagd* or German night fighter forces contained herein. And, aviation historians everywhere owe a deep sense of gratitude to his and all the other valuable sources of reference listed in the end notes; in particular, those by the incomparable W R 'Bill' Chorley, Martin Middlebrook and Chris Everitt and Oliver Clutton-Brock. Finally, all of the late authors' books, as listed, who are beyond compare. This book and its companion volumes are dedicated to their memory.

CHAPTER 1

'Terrorangriff'

It is improbable that any terrorisation of the civil population which could be achieved by air attack could compel the Government of a great nation to surrender ... In our own case, we have seen the combative spirit of the people roused and not quelled by the German air raids. Nothing that we have learned of the capacity of the German population to endure suffering justifies us in assuming that they could be cowed into submission by such methods, or indeed that they would not be rendered more desperately resolved by them.

Winston Churchill, Minister for Munitions, 1917

What shouts of victory would arise if a Commando wrecked the entire Renault factory in a night, with a loss of seven men! What credible assumptions of an early end to the war would follow upon the destruction of a third of Cologne in an hour and a half by some swift moving mechanised force which, with but 200 casualties, withdrew and was ready to repeat the operation 24 hours later! What acclaim would greet the virtual destruction of Rostock and the Heinkel main and subsidiary factories by a Naval bombardment. All this and far more, has been achieved by Bomber Command: yet there are many who still avert their gaze, pass by on the other side and question whether the 30 Squadrons of night bombers make any worthwhile contribution to the war.

So said Sir Arthur Harris to Winston Churchill and the War Cabinet on 28 June 1942. Always there were doubts in certain quarters about the success or otherwise of area bombing raids on German cities but Harris never wavered. However, for three months – June, July and August – it was on only one night that 'Bomber' Harris was able to put into the air a force exceeding 500 aircraft. His wish to mount two or three raids each month of the order of 700 to 1,000 sorties was defeated by the weather, the rising casualties and the losses suffered by the OTUs. Despite the

1

obvious harm that was being done to the training organization Harris used OTU aircraft and crews on four more operations to Germany. On three of these raids OTU aircraft and crews made up about a third of the force and on two of them the training units suffered a higher rate of losses than the squadrons. When OTU aircraft were included raids were mounted by between 400 and 650 crews, but in general Harris was compelled by the uncertain weather conditions to use only his operational squadrons. With these he achieved a high rate of effort, dispatching forces of the order of 200 aircraft ten times in June. A record 147 Bomber Command aircraft were destroyed by *Nachtjagd* that month. From then until the introduction of *Window* in July 1943, German night fighters inflicted heavy losses on the bomber force (*Window* consisted of strips of silver paper, which were picked up by German radar and produced thousands of returns covering the whole of their screens, preventing the operators from picking out individual aircraft).

On the night of 27/28 June when 144 aircraft visited Bremen again, 119 aircraft bombed blindly through cloud after obtaining *Gee* fixes. It was believed that the raid was successful. Nine aircraft, four of them Wellingtons, two Halifaxes and two Lancasters and a Stirling were lost. *P-Peter*, the Stirling flown by Sergeant Frank Griggs RAAF on 214 Squadron successfully bombed the objective but over the target area the aircraft sustained much damage from anti-aircraft fire. One of the starboard engines was hit and put out of action. Shortly afterwards *P-Peter* was subjected to an attack by an enemy fighter, fire from which, caused further damage. Sergeant Horace Arthur William Sewell, the rear-gunner, who was from Eastbourne was killed in his turret in the initial attack. Almost immediately a second fighter opened fire and Sergeant Bill Wildey, the first wireless operator, was wounded in the arm. The first fighter then returned to the attack but was met with a long and vicious burst from Flight Sergeant Jim Waddicar's guns, which sent the enemy aircraft spinning towards the ground, where it exploded on impact. Sometime later, after crossing Holland, Sergeant Arthur O'Hara, the navigator observed two enemy fighters closing in. A few minutes later another fighter appeared, opening fire with a long burst, but Waddicar's return fire caused it to break off the engagement. Sergeant Ronald Watson, who was tending the injured wireless operator, immediately attempted to man his turret but it was jammed. With the assistance of O'Hara, who held his legs, he managed to reach his guns and deliver an effective burst at the leading fighter, which caused it to dive towards the sea completely out of control. Meanwhile, Waddicar, with commendable ingenuity, had temporarily repaired one of his guns which had failed and opened fire at the second aircraft from close range. The attacker dived away and exploded before hitting the water. The Stirling was not yet out of danger, being subjected to machine gun fire from the sea. Sergeant Griggs, displaying fine airmanship, eventually flew his severely damaged bomber safely back to Stradishall for a successful wheels-up landing.[1]

On the night of 29/30 June Bomber Command dispatched 253 aircraft to Bremen and 184 aircraft, relying only on their *Gee* fixes, released their bombs within 23 minutes. This was the highest rate of concentration yet achieved. Fire caused extensive damage to five important war industries including the Focke-Wulf factory and the AG Weser *U-boat* construction yard. Eleven aircraft failed to return. Warrant Officer Len Collins RAAF was a Stirling gunner on 149 Squadron at Lakenheath who had completed his tour and was awaiting a posting to an EFTS (Empire Flying Training Station) to train as a pilot. He had volunteered to stand in for the mid-upper-gunner, who was ill, on the crew of Squadron Leader George William Alexander, who would be flying *Q-Queenie*. Collins recalls:

It was my 33rd trip. Other than the second pilot, Flying Officer [William George] Barnes DFC on his first trip to gain experience, the remainder of the crew were on their thirtieth. All were RAF. I was the only Aussie. The trip to Bremen was uneventful. Conversing with the squadron leader I found that he was most interested with the pyrotechnic display from the flak and the colours of the searchlights as we crossed the enemy coast. I predicted we were in for trouble when a blue one slid off our wing tip. However, either our doctored IFF did not work or the Germans were given a tip-off. Over Bremen we received a direct hit from flak on our inner starboard engine, killing Alexander and Pilot Officer [Cyril William] Dellow, observer, and injuring Sergeant D S Hickley the WOp. The bombs were dropped live, a photo taken and we headed for home on three engines. Over the Zuider Zee a night fighter appeared.[2] I can still recall the flash of his windscreen in the darkness as he opened fire. As I was speaking to the rear gunner, Sergeant [Richard Thomas Patrick] Gallagher, he was blown out of his turret. I was ringed with cannon shells and injured in the leg by shrapnel. Owing to the electrical cut out which protected the tail of the aircraft from the mid-upper guns, I was unable to fire on the fighter attacking us. Fortunately, the turret became jammed in the rear position, allowing me to vacate it. Forward, the aircraft was burning like a torch. I could not contact any crewmember. The position was hopeless. I felt I had no option but to leave the aircraft. My parachute was not in its storage holder. I found it under the legs of the mid-upper turret with a cannon shell burn in it. I removed the rear escape hatch, clipped on the parachute and sat on the edge of the hatch. I pulled the ripcord and tumbled out. The parachute, having several holes from the shell burn, 'candle-sticked' (twirled) as I descended and I landed in a canal. I was apprehended the following day and was taken to Leeuwarden airfield for interrogation. Here I met the pilot of the

Messerschmitt 110 who claimed to have shot us down. I abused him in good Australian. He understood, having spent three years at Oxford University.[3]

Despite a brush with a Ju 88, Sergeant Neville Hockaday RNZAF in a Wellington on 75 Squadron RNZAF returned safely to Feltwell on what was his first trip with his own crew, having flown as a 'second dickey' on the Essen raid of 2 June.[4]

On 2/3 July the target was again Bremen to follow up the con- siderable damage reported as having been done to the Focke-Wulf factory last time. We got in sight of the Dutch coast when Bruce [Sergeant Bruce Philip RNZAF, rear gunner] reported a sick stomach getting worse. Not wishing to risk combat with night fighters with a sick rear gunner we returned to base after jettisoning our 'Cookie' into the sea set 'safe'. On 7/8 July we were *Gardening* off Nordeney where we placed two mines without incident, the whole trip of four hours flown at 2,000 feet or below. Our next trip on 8/9 July was to the naval dockyard at Wilhelmshaven, a heavily defended target, which I decided to attack from 11,000 feet – low enough to avoid the night fighters, which would be after the four-engined bombers at greater heights. We got a fairly hot reception and dropped our 'Cookie' against the outer wall of the dockyard and made our escape. However, all was not yet over and we were harassed by flak ships off Emden and Borkum. We landed after five hours and 15 minutes. The next two nights' operations were cancelled because of weather.

Two weeks earlier 83 Squadron crews at Scampton had assembled in the big station headquarters room used for briefings. 'Something' was in the wind. Seated alongside the CO, Wing Commander 'Mary' Tudor, and the station commander, was an unidentified officer, who, judging from the quality and thickness of the rings on his cuff could only have been from Group. The CO was first on his feet. The babble died away. 'First of all, let me tell you that nothing, absolutely nothing of what I have to say must be repeated outside this room.' Any enemy agent worth his pay could have gleamed much from simply hanging around the pubs of Lincoln any night of the war. The 'Saracen's Head' in Lincoln was known to one and all as the 'Snake Pit' or the 'Briefing Room'. It was firmly believed throughout 5 Group that if one wanted to know if ops were on that night one had but to enquire of the barmaid in that opulent lounge bar and thus save a telephone call to Scampton or Waddington, Skellingthorpe or Swinderby. 'If any case comes to my notice of anyone breaking this instruction, the offender will be court martialled.' Crews listened in silence. 'Firstly, 83 Squadron is stood down from operations for at least the next two weeks.' 'Mary' Tudor let that sink in and smiled at the ironic cheers. Then the CO added: 'Before you start celebrating, you had better know that in those two weeks you are going to do more flying and training than you have ever done before on this squadron. Yes, you are scheduled for what I will call a "special operation"; and it will be in daylight.'

On 11 July 'Shepp' the grey-haired intelligence officer at Scampton drew back the curtain covering the large map on one wall and revealed what crews had waited a fortnight to find out. He must have savoured the gasp of astonishment when the unveiling revealed that the target was Danzig (now Gdansk) a major *U-boat* repair and construction base far up on the Baltic, further even than Augsburg (when on 17 April seven out of the twelve Lancasters did not return).[5]

John Bushby wrote:

Briefing over we dispersed buzzing with excitement ... It suddenly became very important to observe all the little personal idiosyncrasies and superstitions of pre-flight preparation. In my case the left flying-boot always had to be donned before the right. Why? Because that was the way I had always done it and so far I had come back.

Later, it would become unalterable custom for Bushby and Lambert, the mid-upper gunner, a thin sandy-haired Londoner with a scrubby moustache, to bid each other a solemn good-night before each climbed into his turret before take-off. Lambert had been one of the new members to join the crew when they had converted from the Manchester. His mother was French and he spoke French like a native, which he considered would be most useful if the crew were shot down over France. 'And you can get stuffed to begin with,' was Williams' first reaction to this show of bravado. None of the original crew really wanted to see or hear much of Lambert off duty but he was competent and cool in the air. The cockney Skipper always wore his famous good-luck charm, a scarf. At least five feet long; it consisted of varying colours, knitted with loving care by one of his aunts and was always wound once round his neck and tucked into the Irvine jacket front just before take-off. The Lancaster did not carry a second pilot but instead a flight engineer to manage engine and fuel systems. Flight Sergeant Thomas Rodham 'Tommy' Armstrong, a gentle soul from Northumberland, not long out of Halton apprentices' school, was an expert on the Merlin engine. He played patience during his off duty moments. Flight Sergeant Crawley, the wireless operator, was a cheerful Liverpudlian they called Charley. Flight Sergeant 'Davey' Davies was considered the best navigator on the squadron, precise and accurate in his job, unflurried and unruffled under fire and easy to get along with on the ground. Pilot Officer George 'Bish' Bishop the Canadian bomb aimer, was, like most of his trade, an ex-wireless operator given a quick course on bombs and bomb aiming and mustered to this new category.

Forty-four Lancaster crews had been briefed for the 'special operation': a round trip of 1,500 miles.

John Bushby wrote:

Right from the start there was a comic air about the whole thing. At 5 o'clock on that fine Saturday afternoon the sky two or three thousand feet above Skegness was a mass of Lancasters, all solemnly circling round, for all the world like a pack of stray dogs meeting in the street. Occasionally, when someone though he identified the letter on someone else's machine, an aircraft would break across the circle, sniff tentatively at another and then fall in beside it or, disappointed, cast around elsewhere.

The force flew at low level and in formation over the North Sea before splitting up and flying independently across the Jutland peninsula, then south before swinging due east across southern Sweden to emerge over the Baltic heading south-east to Danzig. Crews had been promised blue skies all the way, which was an open invitation for fighters, especially when crossing Denmark, but none appeared. The target as expected was clear of cloud and the Lancasters bombed the *U-boat* yards from normal bombing heights just before dusk. *L-London*, Bill Williams' faithful Lancaster, was hit by one solitary heavy flak burst which knocked out the intercom. The return to England was made during darkness. Above the clouds the stars were clear and frosty. John Bushby swung the rear turret from side to side:

[We] recognised constellations as the suburban commuter, hardly glancing up from his newspaper, recognises stations. Deneb, Vega, Altair, Betelgeuse, Polaris ... Mitch, Tooting, Clapham Common, Waterloo, Leicester Square. Through a gap in the cloud over Sweden we saw the lights of a town. It was a novel, remarkable and surprising sight after three years of blackout and we marvelled.

'First time since I left Canada' remarked Bish.

'First time since 1939' said someone else.[6]

Unlike the daylight to Augsburg the plan worked well although some Lancasters were late in identifying Danzig and had to bomb the general town area in darkness. Twenty-four Lancasters bombed at Danzig and returned. Two more were shot down at the target.[7]

Sergeant Neville Hockaday recalls:

On 13/14 July, the target was Duisburg and this proved to be the first of four visits to that city during the next twelve nights, by which time we had named ourselves The Happy Valley Express, a great understatement for the Ruhr was anything but a happy place for Bomber Command. To reach it we crossed the North Sea and then Holland which held a network of radar units operating in co-operation with night fighters. Next there were radar controlled searchlights in which, a blue master light sought out the bomber and because of its blue colour it was almost impossible to spot it before it made contact when the first warning was a blue glare full in the face. Then half a dozen white beams would cone the aircraft. All these combined threats added up to a chastening experience! Over the Ruhr itself the night fighters were the most audacious anywhere and would think nothing of flying amongst their own anti-aircraft fire. After bombing, the gauntlet had to be run again in reverse. A visit to the Ruhr involved two and a half hours of strain that it is almost impossible to describe. We made nine operational visits and came out unscathed, a fact at which I still marvel. On return from the first of these the greatest risk was faced on return to base where the cloud base had fallen to 300 feet.

The next night we went Gardening again, this time to Terschelling without incident. The weather was unfit for operations for the next week or so but the next moon period was coming up and on 21 July The Happy Valley Express set off for its second excursion. We followed a direct route from Southwold to Duisburg, passing south of Rotterdam and to the north of the night fighter base on the island of Walcheren. Using our usual technique of seeking a gap in the flak ahead we found it near the island of Goeree, crossing the coast and keeping north of Tilburg we arrived unimpeded at the outer defences of the Ruhr. The searchlights and night fighters were showing their usual ferocity but somehow we got through without being intercepted. Duisburg lay on the east bank of the Rhine a few miles north of a sharp bend in the river. There were many dummy fires on the west bank but the bright full moon and silvery ribbon of water led us directly to our target. We dropped our 'Cookie' on some marshalling yards and turned for Geldern before returning, again crossing the Dutch coast near Goeree and again left alone by the defences. Two nights later we went there again and followed almost the same route but this time the aiming point was obscured by cloud and we had to make a *Gee* bombing run from the last visible 'fix'. The cloud also hampered the defences and we were not intercepted.

On this, the second raid on Duisburg that same week, the flares dropped by the leading aircraft were scattered so many of the 215 aircraft did not hit the aiming point. Those bombs that did fall in Duisburg caused some housing damage and 65 people were killed. Three Wellingtons and two Stirlings failed to return, and at Bottesford *N-Nan* on 207 Squadron was one of the two Lancasters that were missing. *Nan*'s pilot was Flight Sergeant 'Bill' Hawes from Cootamundra in New South Wales who, lonely for reminders of Australia, crossed the mud at the Leicestershire station to see again *Forty Thousand Horsemen* in the station cinema just to hear them singing 'Waltzing Matilda'. And he had written home asking for a copy of Banjo Patterson's poems. On leave in London a little over a fortnight earlier he and Bill Smith, his rear-gunner, a Londoner, had visited Australia House in the Strand, checked on promotion and then Bill had shown his antipodean pilot the sights. They saw a show and next day Hawes watched the changing of the guard at Buckingham Palace; he thought it was 'spectacular' but 'a lot of bull'.[8]

Nan did not return. At 00.48 hours in the dawn of the new day Hawes and Smith and four other crew were lost without trace somewhere in the bleak North Sea. The only body given up was that of Flight Sergeant Timothy Clayton Blair RCAF who was laid to rest at Amsterdam New Eastern Cemetery. At Bottesford, Hawes' Canadian buddy 'Bob' Weatherall made arrangements for his buddy's effects to be sent home to Cootamundra. Weatherall hung on to the Aussie pilot's diary so that he could post it from Canada and avoid the censors but when he too was killed, in May 1944, a kind-hearted English lady rescued it and she returned it to Cootamundra after the war.[9]

On 25/26 July Sergeant Neville Hockaday of 75 Squadron RNZAF and the crew of the *Happy Valley Express* made it four in a row by setting course for Duisburg yet again, this time crossing the Dutch coast and setting off as if for Düsseldorf where some diversionary marker flares had been dropped. Just past Krefeld to their port, Hockaday turned sharply north-east and headed once more for the tell-tale bend in the Rhine. Incredibly, after three raids on Duisburg, surprise was achieved and they saw their 'Cookie' blow up in the middle of a large factory fire. They brought back a very good photograph to prove it. The next night, again in full moonlight, the target was Hamburg. In all, 403 bombers were dispatched. Twin-engined types like the Wellington and to a lesser extent the Hampden still formed the backbone of Bomber Command. Air Marshal Harris was gradually building up his numbers of four-engined types and the 181 Wellingtons and 33 Hampdens were joined on the raid by 77 Lancasters, 73 Halifaxes and 39 Stirlings. Sergeant Neville Hockaday recalls:

> The plan was to make a long sea crossing wide of Heligoland, as though bound for the Baltic via Jutland before turning south east below Rendsburg to fly down the Elbe estuary to our target. All went well until crossing the Kiel Canal when without warning we developed a fault in the intercom. We flew in wide circles while Sergeant Mike Hughes, WOp/AG frantically tried to locate the fault.

After ten minutes we began to run out of time on the target and not wishing to take on the defences all alone decided to go for the secondary target of Rendsburg, selecting the submarine pens as our aiming point. Communication was extremely difficult, everything having to be said several times to be heard over the static. The bombing run was done using hand signals for 'left', 'right' or 'steady'. Just as we were on the bombing run Mike found the fault and corrected it so the run was completed normally and the 'Cookie' fell in the shipyard on the canal. We cleared the area out to sea and descended to 200 feet to frustrate the radar screens at Heligoland, another fighter base that was considered a regular hornet's nest.

At Marham at around 22.00 hours, 115 Squadron had put up 14 Wellingtons and crews. Wing Commander Frank Dixon-Wright DFC, the 31-year-old CO popular with his crews and who had already completed a tour of operations, led the briefing. Some members of his crew of Wellington *G-George* were second tour men. They too were well respected. Normally this crew would fly with Squadron Leader Cousens, CO 'A' Flight but Cousens was on stand down. Twenty-year-old Sergeant Baden Feredey, an experienced pilot with 15 operational flights, captained another 'A' Flight crew on *K-King*. Not every crew flying to Hamburg was as experienced as these. Sergeant Jim Howells RNZAF had completed five operations as a second pilot with other crews and he was given captaincy of a new crew in 'A' Flight. He was to fly his first operation as an aircraft captain on *L-Leather*. There had been recent criticism of the squadron for failing to obtain suitable photographs of the target so the New Zealander decided that his crew would bring back a superb photograph. Sergeant Jim Burtt-Smith and crew had been with the squadron for just over a month. They had been allocated to 'A' Flight. Having overcome their operational teething problems, including writing off a Wellington when returning from a raid, they were now settled in to completing a tour of 30 operations flying *B-Bear*. Hamburg would be their ninth operational flight.

Howells, the novice captain, had managed to coax his Wellington up to 14,000 feet by the time he reached Hamburg. He was carrying a mixed load of high explosive and incendiary bombs. Despite the opposition from the defences he was still determined to obtain a good photograph of his bomb bursts. Reaching the aiming point his bomb aimer released the bombs. This action automatically opened the shutter on the fixed camera and released the flash bomb. All the pilot had to do was fly a straight and level course until the flash functioned. The photograph would then be taken. More experienced, perhaps more prudent pilots would have had greater concern for the immediate safety of their aircraft than bringing back a photograph for the planners at base to study. The flak at Hamburg was accurate and intense. In such situations following the release of the bombs it was usual to stick the nose down in a shallow dive, build up speed and corkscrew like hell away from the target. Howells was resolute. Following a straight and level course he flew blissfully on. It was a golden opportunity for the flak batteries and one they could not ignore.

Almost immediately the Wellington was ranged. Flak hit the port engine. It may have damaged the propeller as well as the engine, as intense vibration began to rack the airframe. Howells quickly feathered the propeller and switched off the engine. To his dismay the aircraft began to lose height. He managed to weave away from the target with no further damage to the bomber. Rapidly losing height he crossed the German coastline in an attempt to fly back over the comparative safety of the North Sea. It was all to no avail. The Wellington would not stay in the air. Below he could see clearly the tops of the breaking waves. He issued orders for ditching. The observer collected all the survival apparatus including the Very pistol and cartridges and placed them in a bag. As the bomber hit the sea a wall of water cascaded through the fuselage and tore the bag from the observer's hand. When they clambered into the dinghy they found the marine signals stowed aboard had perished. They were adrift in the North Sea with no Very pistol or any means of attracting the attention of a passing ship or aircraft. They were to drift like this for three days. On the first day a Beaufighter came close to them but did not see them. That night they drifted within earshot of a fierce naval battle, presumably between German *E-boats* and a convoy. On the second day two Spitfires flew over without seeing them. On the third day a German seaplane from Nordeney rescued them and took them off to captivity.

B-Bear and Sergeant Burtt-Smith's crew arrived in the target area about the same time as Howells. Fortunately for them the defences were pre-occupied with another aircraft and they quickly made their way to the aiming point, released their bombs and set course for the German coast-line. Jim Burtt-Smith continues:

We were on course, homeward bound and flying between Bremer-haven and Wilhelmshaven, when New Zealander 'Frizzo' Frizzell piped up from the rear turret, 'What about a bloody drink? I'm gasping.' Sergeant Jack French, the WOp/AG was just about to hand me a cup of coffee when, BANG! We were hit in the port engine. The smoke and havoc was appalling. I feathered the port engine and managed to bring her head round. Fortunately, no one was hurt. The bomb aimer, Sergeant Lionel 'Len' Harcus, came out of the front turret to hang on to the rudder bar to try to help counter the violent swing to port. I took stock of the situation and tried to increase boost and revs on the starboard engine but to no avail. By this time we were losing height. I got Barney D'Ath-Weston, my New Zealander navigator, to give me a new course for home. Heavy ack-ack was still pounding away. We were heading for the open sea and try as I might, I could not gain any height. As we headed over the coast the searchlights pointed our way to the fighters. We were now down to 1,000 feet. I told Jack to let out the 60-foot trailing aerial. We were having a terrible time trying to keep the aircraft straight and level. The drag of the dead engine was pulling us to port. I applied full rudder bias and Len hung onto the rudder for dear life. It was impossible to set a straight course. I gave instructions, 90 miles out over the North Sea, to take positions and prepare for ditching. It was as black as a November fog; no moon, no nothing.

As Jack and Len left the cockpit I jettisoned the fuel, shut off the remaining engine and turned towards England. I had no idea of height because when the port engine failed, so did the lights and instruments. Jack clamped the Morse key down so our people could get a fix on us.[10] I told him to give me a shout when the aerial touched the water so I knew I had 60 feet of height left. I had to keep playing with the stick to keep her airborne, letting the nose go down then pulling her up a bit, just like a bloody glider. I prayed for a moon, knowing full well that if I couldn't see to judge which way to land we would plunge straight in and down. (One had to land towards the oncoming waves; any other way would be disastrous.)

The bomb aimer and the wireless operator retreated to their ditching stations. Jim Burtt-Smith shut off the starboard engine and began to glide, repeatedly dropping the nose and then pulling up gently.

Jack shouted out, '*Sixty feet!*' and there we were, wallowing about like a sick cow. I shouted to the lads to hold tight, we were going in. 'Frizzo' turned his turret to starboard so that he could get out when we crashed. This was it! Prepare to meet thy doom. Suddenly, the moon shone and, thank God, I could see the sea. The moonbeams were like a gigantic flare-path. We actually flew down them. We were practically down in the drink when I saw we were flying the wrong way. I lugged *B-Bear* around, head-on to the waves. I hauled back on the stick and there was one almighty crash. We were down! It was 03.00 hours.

The water closed over my head and my Mae West brought me to the top. I got my head out of the escape hatch and there we were, wallowing in the sea. Then the moon went in! It was again as black as it could be. Len helped me out of the cockpit. Jack popped out of the astro hatch carrying the emergency kit, followed by D'Ath-Weston, who had stayed to destroy the *Gee* box and papers. 'Frizzo' scuttled along the fuselage and we all scrambled into the dinghy, which had popped out of the engine nacelle and was inflating in the water, still attached to the Wimpy, which was sinking fast. D'Ath-Weston slashed the rope and we pulled away as best we could before we got sucked under.

At 09.30 hours a German seaplane from Nordeney picked up the crew of *B-Bear* and they all finished the war as PoWs.

Sergeant Baden Feredey and the crew of *K-King* had reached Hamburg without incident. The outward journey was relatively calm and there were no interceptions from night fighters. The inward flight was near Borkum and Feredey flew down the side of the river to Hamburg. Sergeant Frank Skelley, the youngest member on the crew at 19, jokingly remarked that his Skipper wouldn't be able to find the aiming-point, as the only part of Hamburg he knew from his Merchant Navy days was the red light district. (Fereday had joined the Merchant Navy as a boy and after war broke out he had transferred to the RAF to train as aircrew.) Skelley acted as bomb aimer and he manned the front turret. *King* carried a 4,000lb bomb, a huge weapon not designed for delivery by a Wellington aircraft. Modifications to the bomb bay were necessary, including the removal of the bomb bay doors. Most of the flotation bags, which gave the aircraft buoyancy in the event of a ditching, also had to be removed. Once the bomb was dropped the open space of the bomb bay would cause considerable drag.

Feredey wrote:

I approached Hamburg at about 13,000 feet. The place was well alight and the bombing was causing plenty of havoc on the ground and many searchlights illuminated the darkness. I bombed and flew around to take photographs. (There was some rivalry amongst the crews on the squadron to get good photos of our attacks. On a previous raid on Duisburg I had a photo of my bomb hitting the target and the photo was put on display on the Squadron for all to see). I flew over Hamburg taking pictures with the aid of other flash bombs exploding and then asked my navigator [Sergeant 'Harry' Lindley] for a course to fly home on. He told me that in two minutes we should be crossing the German coast. Suddenly all hell broke out. North of Bremen a blue master searchlight pinpointed me and 20–30 other white searchlights coned me. At the same time ack-ack poured through to the aircraft and the first shell burst a few inches away from my face. I could smell the cordite from the explosion, which blew the fuel lines to the instruments, causing them all to go to zero. The oil from the burst pipes came down on the compass, blanking it out and making it impossible to use. The only thing working was the altimeter: I was at 12,000 feet. Both turrets were u/s and the guns were of no use. I was in this situation for three-quarters of an hour, diving and turning to try to get out of the glare of the searchlights. At the same time the guns were giving me hell from the ground. I went down to 8,000 feet. Later the crew told me the aircraft was peppered with holes, through which you could map-read below. I gave instructions to Sergeant Glafkos Clerides [the wireless operator, who was in the astrodome] to come forward to destroy the paperwork and secret codings. At this point a piece of shrapnel caught him in the leg and caused him to collapse on the floor. His intercom plug came out of its socket. When he came to he was talking into a dead mike. He thought we had bailed out so he decided to jump out through the rear escape hatch. Two searchlights followed him down to the ground. The Germans must have thought we were going to follow him or we were all dead as all the lights went out and the ack-ack guns were silent.[11]

When I got out of the searchlights I found I was heading back to Hamburg so I decided to go home the same way I had entered Germany. The wheels and flaps had come down causing drag. I climbed to 14,000 feet and re-crossed the coast over Borkum where again the Germans shot at me. Then all was quiet. I checked the fuel gauge and found I had lost 200 gallons in 20 minutes. The rear gunner [Sergeant Kelvin Hewer Shoesmith, a 21-year-old Australian] had to tell me if and when I was turning, as I had no instruments to fly on. (While we had been in the dilemma of ack-ack and searchlights the rear gunner had been shot in his side. However badly I never knew but subsequently it hastened his death). I instructed Skelley to radio our troubles to base. (As my wireless operator had bailed out, it meant that the front gunner was now sending out radio messages to warn the Squadron what was happening to us). All the time I was losing height and I went down to 1,500 feet. Lindley put the nacelle tanks on so I estimated I had about one hours' fuel left. I was down to 500 feet by this time. Then the starboard engine started to cough and splutter. I sent out a Mayday on the radio. This was becoming the final phase in the drama. I told the crew to prepare for ditching. First the starboard engine and then the port engine stopped. I suddenly realized that the escape hatch over my head was still closed but I managed to get it open. As all this was going on I had turned away from the moonlight and was heading into total blackness for a ditching. My speed was about 140 mph. I had to land tail first to help slow the speed down.

Finally we went into the sea. I wasn't strapped in so my head went through the windscreen. I may have been temporarily knocked out but the cold water soon brought my senses back. I was up to my waist in water with water pouring in through the escape hatch over my head. I wrenched my helmet off to release me to get out; I also lost one flying boot as I got out of the aircraft, which was already going under with the tail in the air. After getting onto the port wing I was chest deep in water. By this time the front gunner and navigator had made their escape via the astrodome. Shoesmith jumped out of the rear turret but he got entangled with the trailing aerial and he shouted that the rapidly sinking bomber was dragging him under. [Frank Skelley and Harry Lindley swam over and released him. They all worked hard on the dinghy to inflate it but it was riddled with shrapnel holes. Their task was impossible]. The four of us managed to get hold of a loose wooden box, which one stood on to look out of the astrodome, that had floated out of the open hatch just before the aircraft sank. We each grabbed a corner with one hand and the other hand held on to the adjacent crewmember. We drifted with the waves breaking over us continually. All we had to keep us afloat were our Mae Wests. We were able to talk to each other and we tried to estimate how far from land we were. Shoesmith told us he had been wounded in his side but we were unable to ascertain his injuries. His Mae West was deflating so Harry Lindley had to blow it up with his mouth to keep him afloat. [The shrapnel, which had pierced his side, had also penetrated his Mae West]. At times we were up to our lips in water; this was causing us to swallow some of the salt water. The harrowing part of this tale was when Lindley began to pray and asked God to save us. When I tried to reassure him that we would be saved, he rubbed his hand down the back of my head and said that he was grateful for cheering him up. It seemed pretty hopeless at the time, as the water was up to our mouths as we floated around.

After a few hours Shoesmith, who was directly opposite me, suddenly went quiet. He opened his eyes and they seemed to turn around. Some white foam came from his nose and mouth. At this point Skelley was unconscious. I tried to lift him on to the box to keep his head out of the water but minutes later he too died very quietly, again with white foam coming from his nose and mouth. He hadn't been injured but later I realized that he was pretty near to death. When the front and rear gunners died we let them go but they continued to drift near us. After six hours in the sea only two of us were alive. Then in the distance I saw a German seaplane flying towards us. I tried to attract the attention of the crew and Lindley started blowing his whistle. I kept telling him they couldn't hear him but his mind had gone blank. They circled around and the chap in the gun turret turned his gun towards us. I honestly thought he was going to shoot us. However he lifted his hand and saluted. Thank God, what a relief that we weren't going to die in this way. The seaplane landed and taxied towards us with its two engines ticking over but they were too fast to grab us as they passed. They returned on just one engine with crew on the floats holding boat hooks. I managed to grab hold but they had to hook Lindley by his jacket to stop him going past. They lifted me on to the float and tied a rope around my waist to lift me into the aircraft where I was laid on the floor and a blanket placed over me. Lindley was then brought in. Although they must have seen that the two gunners were dead the Germans did not stop to pick them up and they allowed them to continue floating in the sea. Shivering with cold I motioned to one of the crew for a drink but instead of a hot drink or a brandy they gave me soda water! I fell asleep as we took off for Nordeney where we landed and were lifted out of the water onto the beach. I was helped to my feet and out of the plane into the daylight where an ambulance waited to take us to hospital. The German crew came with us. At the hospital I thanked the crew for picking us up and I asked the pilot what time he had started searching for us. He told me it was 03.40; the exact time I crashed in the sea. Lindley remembered nothing of the rescue or his journey to hospital and it was six pm that evening when he recovered sufficiently to be taken into custody.[12]

In all, 115 Squadron lost four Wellingtons on the night of 26/27 July. At 02.35 hours *Hauptmann* Helmut 'Bubi' Lent of II./NJG1 was patrolling over the North Sea in a Bf 110 night fighter when he brought down Halifax *H-Harry*, which crashed in the North Sea north west of Vlieland.[13] Four minutes later a dark shape loomed into his line of sight. Quickly closing the gap between himself and the other aircraft he perceived the unmistakable bulky outline to be a Wellington bomber. Not wishing to overshoot and lose the enemy aircraft in the darkness Lent eased back on his throttles. Wing Commander Frank Dixon-Wright and his crew were doomed. Their aircraft crashed into the sea near the crash position of Lent's Halifax victim at 02.39 hours. The only body recovered from the water was that of 25-year-old Pilot Officer George Whittaker DFM, the WOp/AG.

Night fighters were active this night because of the clear moonlight conditions along most of the route and over the target flak was accurate. 115 Squadron's four missing Wellingtons were among 29 bombers shot down.[14] Many of the missing aircraft came down off the north-west German coast, in the northern part of The Netherlands and in the Friesian Islands area. Others, like the Wellington of 75 Squadron RNZAF that was flown by Flying Officer Ian James Shepherd RNZAF, was coned and heavily hit by flak over the target. According to Sergeant John Dixon the rear gunner and the only Englishman in the otherwise all New Zealand crew, his Skipper and Sergeant James Francis Winstanley the bomb aimer/front gunner did 'a grand job' getting the bombs away:

Sudden evasive action was taken with a stall turn down the blinding cone of searchlights. Roaring over the city rooftops, we were caught in a murderous, brilliant barrage of light ack-ack. The front gunner and I got in a few bursts at the searchlights as we sped away. Our battle-scarred Wimpy, now at tree-top height, took quite a battering as we ran the long gauntlet. But finally, with our gun turrets out of action we were overwhelmed and crashed in a meadow near the village of Dose, ten miles west of Wilhelmshaven. After getting out of the wreckage in which my right leg had been jammed, I was captured by civilians and handed over to a soldier. He dragged me away saying that I was to be shot. There was no doubt, by his aggressive manner, that he meant it. He had a rifle with him. However, another soldier, 19-year-old Heinrich Dirks, with real courage, wrestled me free and insisted that I was a prisoner of war and an airman and had a right to be interrogated by the Luftwaffe. I was then taken to a local pub and from there moved to Wilhelmshaven naval hospital.[15]

Hamburg suffered its most severe air raid to date and widespread damage was caused, mostly in the housing and semi-commercial districts. The fire department was overwhelmed and forced to seek outside assistance for the first time. Some 337 people lost their lives, 1,027 were injured and 14,000 people were made homeless. Damage amounted to the equivalent of £25,000,000.

Bomber Command was stood down on 27/28 July but this was the full moon period and on the night following, a return to Hamburg was announced at briefings when crews were told that the raid would be on a far bigger scale than two nights before. At Feltwell Sergeant Neville Hockaday, who was not to be denied his trip to Hamburg, which his crew had failed to reach on 26/27 July, heard that nearly 800 bombers were planned to bomb the devastated town. At Oakington, Pilot Officer Leslie Sidwell, the rear-turret gunner on 23-year-old Flight Lieutenant Douglas Whiteman's crew of Stirling *B-Beer* of 7 Squadron, made a note that said it was another 'Thousand Raid'. He surmised, correctly, that the number was again being made up with OTU crews:

Out at dispersal we got everything finally checked and ready in the sweltering heat inside the aircraft before climbing out into the oh-so-welcome cool night air. It was lovely to relax outside on the grass and smoke casually before reluctantly putting on the flying kit which I knew would be badly needed for the cold later on, after the muck-sweat had gone. I donned flying kit, regretfully and knowing full well it would be freezing at height was soon in another sweat in the aircraft. We took off at 22.29 hours. The weather was good. We passed over Cromer and out over the North Sea. I spent the time taking the usual sightings from my rear turret on flame-floats we'd dropped to check drift for the navigator. We'd been briefed to cross the German coast north of the Elbe estuary, then to turn south 20 miles north of Hamburg to run up to the target.

Sergeant Neville Hockaday continues:

We made the sea crossing at 200 feet and planned to bomb from 8,000 feet, which would be just below the forecast cloudbase. This was a dangerous place to be, as one would be silhouetted against the cloud background but flying above it would expose us similarly to fighters. There was plenty of activity around Heligoland as we passed safely five miles to seaward and taking advantage of the confusion crossed the coast without interference and began the long climb to bombing height, levelling out as we crossed the Kiel Canal near Rendsburg. Twice I had to break away to avoid interception by searchlights and began a time and distance run as a precaution against the target being obscured by cloud. Ten minutes from the target there was much activity ahead: more ferocious than I had expected. There were about six groups of searchlights; each of which held a bomber in a cone, the flak concentrating on each. At one time I saw five aircraft going down in flames. The cloud was barely 8,000 feet and solid, having the effect of trapping the searchlight beams below it and turning the sky over Hamburg into a vast mirror. I could see that it would be no trouble identifying the aiming point if we could get to it! Just as I was preparing for the bombing run an FW 190 came out of the target area, having flown through his own flak and we narrowly missed a head-on collision. He was almost on top of us before he spotted us and he sheered off as Bruce opened fire on him. A few seconds before Drew [Sergeant Alfie Drew RNZAF, front gunner/bomb aimer] released our bomb a blue master search-light fastened on us and just as 'bomb gone' was called we were coned in about half a dozen searchlight beams. Standing on the rudder pedals I threw *F-Freddie* into a stall turn to port, the most violent turn I had ever made. With the engines screaming the Wimpy went down in a spiral dive, speed rising to 250 mph until, eventually, we broke free from the lights. Heading north westerly away from the target the vibration of the airframe and the over-revving of the engines died down and we regained level flight at 400 feet.

Leslie Sidwell in the rear turret of Whiteman's *B-Beer* continues:

There was heavy flak and we were hit just before the run up. Just after we'd bombed, someone on the intercom reported tracer coming up from below and we were hit by night fighter attack from under-neath. I reported a decoy headlight out on the starboard quarter and searched around for other fighters. I reported one coming in from above on the port side and told the Skipper to turn to port. I think I hit him with a burst before my power went off. A fighter came in again from the rear and continued firing. My turret was shattered and we seemed to be in a steady dive. The Skipper gave the emergency bail-out order, quickly followed by what sounded like his cries of pain. Then the intercom abruptly cut off and we were on fire.

When my turret power had failed I'd been left partly on the beam. I started to operate the dead man's handle (emergency winding gear) to centralize my turret so that I could get back into the fuselage to grab my parachute and bail out. ('Chutes could not be stored in the rear turret as one did in earlier two-engined jobs, which were dead easy for rear gunners to quit in a hurry). I wound away like mad at the hand-winding gear behind me, very conscious that we were losing precious height. As if in a dream, I saw a Me 110 closing in from astern with his guns blazing away. I wound away as I watched him through the shattered Perspex. My painfully slow progress was like a nightmare. I was conscious of the EBO order given in what seemed some time ago ... Would I be in time? He was extremely close to me when he eventually broke away and I finally managed to move the turret sufficiently to fall back hurriedly into the fuselage. I grabbed my 'chute from the stowage outside the turret doors, forced open the nearby emergency exit door and as quickly as I could, jumped out into space. In those seconds I was conscious of flame and smoke up front in the fuselage. I gave no thought at all to any dangers of bailing out, or that I'd had no practice in jumping. I just concentrated in getting out of a doomed aircraft. In my haste to get out I banged my head on something as I quit poor old *B-Beer*, partly knocking myself out. I pulled the ripcord without counting as you were normally told to do. I must have done the right thing because I came to swinging in the air. I could see the waters of the Elbe shining below, with the full moon bright towards the south.

After all the turmoil I was now swinging gently in a strangely contrasting silence, floating down and rather higher than I'd expected. This peace was suddenly interrupted by a dazzling searchlight, which probed around as if looking for me. It held me in its blinding beam. I felt naked, vulnerable and powerless hanging there, not knowing what to expect. I raised my arms and wondered, '*Is this It?*' But it soon switched off, as if satisfied that I'd been located and I was left to watch the Elbe more clearly as I lost height and to worry about landing in the wide waters. I'd never fancied coming down in the water and I pulled the rigging lines as instructed, hoping to spill air from the 'chute to alter my course. Probably more by luck than anything else, the Elbe disappeared and I braced myself for a landing, south of the river. The ground seemed to loom up very quickly in the moonlight and it wasn't possible to judge my first parachute landing expertly. I landed rather clumsily and hurt my right ankle on the hard ground but tall growing crops helped to cushion me. My watch showed 01.10 hours just after landing. I remembered that my first duty was to hide my chute. As I struggled to gather it all up I thought I'd have a good view of a big 'Thousand Raid' but I was surprised. Little was seen or heard and I wondered, 'Where are they?'[16]

Sergeant Neville Hockaday meanwhile crossed the Kiel Canal at 2,000 feet when he saw tracer fire coming up over the port wing from behind.

I called Mike who replied that it was from a chap on top of a building. Bruce had just fired back and all had gone quiet; he thought he had got him. Later I checked to find that we had wandered over Meldorf and the building was probably the local barracks. We went well out to sea to avoid Heligoland and just as I ordered, 'Watch out for "flak ships"' one opened up at us but we were too fast for him and were soon out of range. Mike said that not all our aircraft had reported to base after bombing and as we approached Cromer we were all diverted to Methwold. We assumed that someone was in trouble and that Feltwell was being kept clear for him. It was six am by the time we walked into debriefing to learn that of the 14 aircraft of our squadron only eight had returned. We then learned that far from there being 800 aircraft on the raid there had been only 165 as a late forecast had predicted bad weather on return and all except 3 Group had cancelled. If only we had been told we could have revised our tactics to meet the new situation.[17]

Huia Russell on 149 Squadron in 3 Group recalled:

It was a bit disconcerting when sitting at the navigator's table to hear ice breaking off the propellers and thumping the fuselage of the Stirling. Ice could be a hazard at many heights and this was the worst experience of icing that I had. There was thick cloud to about 2,000 feet but though all groups except 3 Group were scrubbed and the OTU aircraft were recalled we tried climbing through the cloud once we were over the North Sea. However, we had not climbed very high when we iced up and began losing height. Eventually we tried jettisoning our load of 4lb incendiaries gradually. It was not until we had released most of our bomb load that we were able to maintain height at under 2,000 feet. We then returned home after this unnerving experience.

No. 3 Group lost nine out of 71 Stirlings and 16 out of 94 Wellingtons and
a Stirling crashed at RAF Coltishall. Four OTU Wellingtons, including a
101 Squadron Wimpy at Bourn, which was involved in a collision with
a 101 CF Stirling at Oakington were lost. The Stirling crashed near
Cottenham in Cambridgeshire. There were no injuries to the crew but
all five on the Wellington died. A 10 OTU Whitley ditched in the sea
ten miles south-east of Tynemouth.

Neville Hockaday continues:

We had all lost many good friends and our morale was temporarily
very low but at about 3pm we were advised that we were 'on'
tonight, briefing at 6pm. We snapped out of it, every survivor of the
night's debacle wishing nothing more than the chance to 'get back at
the bastards'. Morale rocketed. We had had very little sleep but this
did not dampen our determination. The target was Saarbrücken, a
town that had not been raided since November 1940. Before briefing
began the Station Commander said that the C-in-C appreciated that
we had taken a beating last night and that anyone who did not feel
up to it could withdraw from tonight's operation without any blame.
All ten captains stood and said as one man, 'Tell Butch Harris we'll
bloody well go.'

'Thank you, gentlemen', said the CO. 'I told the AOC I was sure
that would be your answer.'

Clearly this operation was intended as a morale booster for our
Group after the trauma of yesterday, as Saarbrücken would be taken
by surprise after two years unmolested. Only four heavy flak guns
were believed to be there and if early arrivals could put them and
the searchlights out of action the remainder would go in low for
accuracy – although with a cookie we were limited to 5,000 feet
because of the enormous blast, which would be felt to that height.
The planned route was Beachy Head, Le Treport and then direct
to the target returning via Le Cretoy and Brighton. There was much
searchlight activity and a heavy barrage from Dieppe to Calais so
searching for a gap I found it in the Somme Estuary. We avoided
Abbeville and also Amiens where we had seen an aircraft attracting much attention. We weaved round other hot spots (as shown
when others passed over them) of Peronne, St-Quentin, Sedan and
Montmedy. In contrast to the lack of any such signs when flying
over Holland the number of 'V for Victory' signals that were aimed
at us was noticeable. One wondered at the contrast. We approached
the target from Saarlouis to the north-west and as we ran over the
marshalling yards at 7,000 feet we saw two Lancasters and a Stirling
below us, so we made a left turn and began our run once more. This
time all was clear and we saw a great flash on the ground by the
marshalling yards; seconds later the whole aircraft was lifted by

the shock waves from the blast. I was very glad we were at 7,000 feet. Two sets of searchlights and one heavy gun battery were still operative until silenced by two Lancasters firing from the front turret and a Wellington dropped a stick of 500lb bombs on flares laid by another on the gun site. As we turned away incendiaries ignited what appeared to be an oil tank and flame lit up the whole of Saarbrücken. Coming home over Brighton I could see the street where my wife and baby son were sleeping, unaware that I was so close to them.[18]

For the next Main Force raid, on Düsseldorf on 31 July/1 August, 630 aircraft,[19] for the first time including more than 100 Lancasters, were despatched. Again Bomber Command's training units made up the numbers. Sergeant Neville Hockaday continues:

We circumvented Eindhoven and weaved between Mönchengladbach and Krefeld until the Rhine once again made it easy to identify our target, which was already well alight by the time we got there, a column of smoke rising to about 4,000 feet. Many searchlights made it difficult to see the ground and we were aware that the night fighters were now using airborne radar. We bombed from 9,500 feet, Drew having a clear view of the target despite being held by the beams of a group of searchlights, which I eluded by diving away once the photograph of the bomb strike had been taken. As we approached Domburg Bruce saw a FW 190 turn to follow us but I gave him the slip by diving into cloud just below us and altering course 90° to starboard, towards the Hook of Holland – I hoped he would guess that I would turn to port, towards Knokke and Zeebrugge. We saw no more of him.

Bomber Command lost 29 aircraft that night but some extensive damage was inflicted and so ended the month of July and the 'moon period'.[20]

July had been an appalling month for the Wimpy crews at Binbrook and Grimsby. Seventeen aircraft were lost on the Ruhr, U-boat lairs and the north German ports. Four were lost on the raid on Hamburg on 26/27 July and it would have been five but for the bravery of an unnamed rear gunner. This Wellington was attacked by a night fighter over Mello; the navigator was killed and the pilot temporarily blinded by fragments from the cockpit shattered by cannon fire. The wireless operator believed that the aircraft was doomed and bailed out but the rear gunner took over the controls and flew the Wellington back to the English coast where the pilot managed to get the damaged bomber down. Other casualties that month included Wing Commander R C Collard DFC, Officer Commanding 12 Squadron, when he and his crew were shot down on the 25/26th. Collard and three of his crew survived and were taken prisoner. On the same night another 12 Squadron Wellington failed to return when

Squadron Leader P C 'Cheese' Lemon DSO DFC was shot down. On one of the first bomber raids of the war, on 18 December 1939, Lemon had flown a 37 Squadron Wellington on the disastrous raid on Wilhelmshaven. (His had been the sole surviving aircraft for the six Wimpys dispatched by the squadron when he put down at Feltwell.) Another 12 Squadron Wellington, which crashed just after take-off on 29/30 July, blew up. The remains of only one member of the crew were ever found.

On 15 August the first step in the creation of the Path Finder Force (PFF) to precede the main force and drop brilliant flares and incendiary bombs over the target, both to 'mark' the target and to provide a beacon for the main force of bombers, was taken when Bomber Command issued an instruction that a Path Finder Force was to be formed at Wyton. The new force, whose motto was 'We light the way', comprised 7 Squadron flying Stirlings at Oakington, 35 Squadron flying Halifaxes at Graveley, 83 Squadron flying Lancasters at Wyton, 156 Squadron flying Wellingtons at Warboys nearby and 109 Squadron flying Mosquitoes at Wyton. The force was commanded by Australian Group Captain (later Air Vice Marshal) Donald Bennett CBE DSO 'a good talker with more wit than humour; and yet essentially not a talker but a man of action'. 'Don' Bennett came from 'deep in the rich mud of the Darling Downs' of Queensland before the family moved to Brisbane. He had been a great civil pilot before the war. In 1938 he flew the *Mercury*, the upper component of the *Mayo* composite aircraft, from Dundee to South Africa and established a long-distance record for seaplanes. He joined the RAAF as a cadet in 1930 and was commissioned in the RAF in 1931. He took a flying boat pilot's course at Calshot in 1932, transferred to the RAAF Reserve in 1935 and the eve of war found him in command of the *Cabot*, the big flying boat which was to carry the mail from Southampton to New York. Soon after the Germans invaded Norway the *Cabot* and her sister flying boat *Caribou* were destroyed by the enemy in the Norwegian fjords. Bennett was among the founders of the Atlantic Ferry Service. He was re-commissioned in the RAFVR in 1941 and was called on for service on the active list. As captain of a bomber, Bennett, then a wing commander, was awarded the DSO for courage, initiative and devotion to duty when, after being shot down during an attack on the *Tirpitz*, in Trondheim Fjord, Norway on 17 April 1942. He and his second pilot, Sergeant N Walmsley, escaped to Sweden. It was soon after his return that Bennett became associated with the new Path Finder Force. 'There will be no living VCs in 8 Group' he announced. This would remain so for two years. The Path Finder men's only identification symbol – worn only when not flying – was a gilt eagle worn below the flap of the left breast pocket. After the PFF began operations, the rate of bombing rose from seventeen tons a minute to more than fifty tons a minute and the loss of personnel per ton of bombs was halved. The first operation in which the PFF technique was used was the attack on Flensburg,

Germany on the night of 18 August 1942 when 31 heavy bombers took part. Gradually refinements were made in PFF technique, particularly as the result of the improvement in radar methods.[21]

Arthur 'Johnnie' Johnson, a Wellington rear-gunner on 142 Squadron flew his first op on 16/17 August when 56 aircraft laid mines in the sea:

The Wimpy carried two of these cylindrical shaped mines with parachutes on each end to lower them gently in to the sea. The navigator had to be spot on and able to identify the selected target area visually (this was before any radar navigation aids) so the navigator, or observer as he was then known, had to know his gen on these trips. On this occasion we had to return to base with the mines as ordered as the target area was covered in very low cloud. We were always instructed that the mines must only be dropped at a height of only 800 feet. The hazards became obvious to me in later mining trips to the Friesian islands and the French ports of St-Nazaire, Lorient and La Rochelle. All these were important areas for enemy shipping activities and the dropping zones were usually in between islands and mainland, or narrow channels in large bays. During the run in therefore, we were normally subjected to crossfire from islands and mainland and flak ships that were always based in these waters. And of course, there was always the night fighter threat. After one of these trips, to Lorient, we got back to base and were informed that only half an hour after we left the target, it had been reported that the mines had sunk a large vessel. We all went to bed elated at this news. My second op was another mine-laying trip. There was a fair amount of haze and on the return journey the Skipper, Pilot Officer Ron Brooks, reported a problem with the port engine. We landed safely at base with no further incident.

My 3rd op was a trip to Frankfurt on 24/25 August.[22] The weather was perfect with a full moon. About 15 minutes from the target I spotted a Ju 88 flying on a steady course about 1,000 feet below, just above a bank of cloud. I reported this to the Skipper, who told us to keep an eye on him but after a few minutes he swung away and left us. We had just completed our bombing run over Frankfurt and began to weave our way out of the target area, when dead astern of us, approximately 400 yards, I watched another Wellington on its run in with bomb doors open. With the clear weather and moon I had a good view from my rear turret but I was not prepared for what was about to follow. I witnessed a huge explosion. Balls of fire, fragments and coloured lights were falling all over the sky behind me. After a short while I looked again for the Wimpy but it was gone. On this night I had seen my first enemy fighter and witnessed my first aircraft shot down. I was 19 years of age.[23]

Thirteen year old Hendrik Kleinsman and his family in the Dutch village of Bentelo in the province of Overijssel regularly watched the nightly procession of RAF Bomber Command aircraft roar overhead towards the German border. They were looking to the sky on the night of 27/28 August when a mixed force of 306 aircraft was detailed to bomb the German army headquarters and garrison at Kassel. One of the 15 Wellingtons on 142 Squadron at Waltham, five miles south of Grimsby, which was destined for Kassel was flown by Pilot Officer Alan Gill on 'B' Flight. Norman Child, the radio operator, recalls: 'At briefing we were told to expect the target to be heavily defended. We carried a mixed load of 500lb bombs and incendiaries. The Met report was good visibility over the target. Wind, light westerly.' At Bourn in Cambridgeshire Flight Sergeant Hugh Barton-Smith's Stirling crew on 15 Squadron – average age just 24 – sat through the briefing. One of the crew had been a milk-man, another was a chemist, two were former clerks, two had been farmers and one had joined the RAF from school. Two were fathers and one, Sergeant Leonard Moss, the 28-year-old air bomber from New Zealand, had only just discovered that his wife was pregnant with their child. Moss had trained in Canada and had arrived in Britain in July 1941. Within a month he met Josephine Hicken from Coventry and they fell in love. They were married in December and in July 1942 Josephine wrote to Moss's sister in New Zealand to tell her that she was pregnant. 'We are hoping hard it will be a boy' she wrote. 'I shall name him after Len, if he is,' she added. Moss had asked a fellow New Zealander, Robert Johnson, to take care of his young wife if he were killed.

Norman Child recalls:

We were routed in ten miles south of Münster. Flak ships were very active off the Dutch coast. There was no trouble so far. Visibility good. There was lots of flak up ahead. Somebody must have wandered off course over Münster. Good pinpoint. Approaching target and all hell let loose approximately ten miles ahead. Very heavy barrage – town ringed with guns and searchlights. Several kites had been hit and gone down … Running into target now – terrific smell of cordite – searchlights were blinding but dropped bombs on schedule at 8,500 feet. Weaved out of target area and for a few minutes every-thing was chaos. Set course for home. Same route as course in. Difficult to get a good pinpoint and aircraft ahead were running into heavy flak … there shouldn't have been any flak on this course. Checked the wind again. There had been a sudden terrific wind change round to the north and the whole force had been blown over the Ruhr Valley. Searchlights and flak were forcing us lower and lower and many aircraft were seen to go down. The flak was so bad and the searchlights so blinding, we decided to go right down full power to below a thousand feet. Front and rear turrets were firing at the searchlights and between them they accounted for five. We burst our way out of the Ruhr, knowing that we had been hit many times and climbed up to 8,000 feet again. We made for Overflakkee, an island off the Dutch coast just south of the Hook of Holland and an aiming point for a comparatively quiet exit from the Continent.

Near Bentelo at just after midnight the Kleinsman family watched thunderstruck as they saw a bomber crash in a fireball after it was attacked by a night fighter. It is believed that the German pilot was *Oberleutnant* Viktor Bauer of III./NJG1. Hendrik Kleinsman recalls, 'It was a giant ball of fire. The huge bomber hit the ground with such force that its cockpit, engines and four bombs were driven up to 15 metres into the sodden earth.' One of the crew bailed out before the crash at Delden, 5 kilometres west of Hengelo.

Thirty-one bombers, 21 of them Wellingtons, were lost and a Lancaster crashed at Waddington on return. Four of the missing Wimpys were on 12 Squadron at Binbrook. At Waltham, six Wellingtons were missing. Norman Child concludes:

Our aircraft looked a mess. Full of holes and big chunks off but miraculously, except for cuts and abrasions; none of the crew was hurt. The next day we were flown back to Waltham to discover, to our horror, that of the six aircraft from 'B' Flight, our crew were the only survivors. The Met report, or lack of one, could be held responsible for the debacle over the Ruhr Valley and the consequent loss of aircraft and crews force-landing all over the south of England, out of fuel.

For weeks after the crash Josephine Moss prayed that her husband had been taken prisoner and would return alive. 'They say there is very little hope of him being alive,' she wrote to her sister-in-law. 'But I cannot give up hope.' The stress put an intolerable strain on her pregnancy and her baby – a girl – was stillborn. Finally, the fate of the Stirling and Barton-Smith's crew became known. The rear gunner, 24-year-old Glen Smith, who had bailed out before the crash, was killed when his parachute failed to open. The others were believed to have been killed instantly in the crash. Two bodies were found and buried next to Glen Smith in Delden but they were never identified. When Robert Johnson learned of the crash he wrote to Josephine and the pair corresponded and slowly fell in love. They only married after the fate of the Stirling was known, and eventually had two children.[24]

In late August–early September 1942 Aircraftman First Class Jack Bennett, who served as flight mechanic and fitter on 214 Squadron at Stradishall, had the onerous duty of helping remove a dead gunner from a Stirling which landed at Newmarket Heath after getting shot up on a daylight raid on Sylt:

The kite was silhouetted against a sky that was breaking dawn when we arrived. It looked like a giant lizard on tall front legs. As we pulled closer to it we could see damage to the fuselage. The front turret was at 45° and there was a figure still inside. As there was no movement I assumed that the gunner was dead. The only way the gunner's body could be moved was by breaking the perspex of the gun turret. As this was 15 feet or so from the ground a trestle was required. I was told to stay with the kite whilst the rest moved off in search of some help. I felt very lonely with a bloody great kite and a dead man in the nose. I wondered if he was the guy I had seen lean over a landing wheel vomiting just before take-off. In the distance I could now hear the noise of vehicles and our Hillman Minx towing a mobile trestle with a 'Coles' crane following. They got closer and I was told, 'Get the fire axe out of the kite.' I entered the fuselage and peered at the partly turned turret with horror. After grabbing the axe I was told to smash the perspex. I got a closer look at the victim who was unrecognisable because of his flying helmet and intercom over his face. Blood spattered the perspex. Carefully I started to crack it but suddenly the axe was wrenched out of my hand by an orderly who shouted, 'You can't hurt the bugger now.' The mobile crane moved in and the crane driver was given the order, 'Take it up.' Within seconds shouts of 'He's coming in half,' echoed across the racecourse. In horror I could see half a body hanging on the crane and slowly being lowered to the ground. 'God almighty' I thought. 'Poor bugger.' The top half of the corpse was gently lowered. I felt quite sick and did not watch the rest of the operation but was jolted to my senses by Chiefy calling me to get aboard the Hillman truck and away we went back to Stradishall.

Twelve bombers failed to return from the 4/5 September raid on Bremen by 251 Wellingtons, Lancasters, Halifaxes and Stirlings.[25] For the first time the Path Finders split their aircraft into three forces. 'Illuminators' lit up the area with white flares, 'visual markers' dropped coloured flares if they had identified the aiming point and then 'backers up' dropped all-incendiary bomb loads on the flares. The weather was clear and the PFF plan worked well. Bremen reported heavy bombing and the Weser aircraft works and the Atlas shipyards were among the industrial buildings that were seriously hit.

Cloud and haze on the following night, 6/7 September, prevented concentrated bombing by the 207 bombers sent to hit Duisburg. Eight aircraft were lost, five of them Wellingtons. A Stirling and two Halifaxes also failed to return. One of the Halifaxes that was lost and which crashed

at Tegelen, four miles south-west of Venlo was flown by Squadron
Leader Clive 'Bix Sax' Saxelby on 103 Squadron. One of the tall New
Zealander's crew was killed. 'Bix Sax' and five others including Flight
Sergeant W J McLean and Flight Lieutenant L C Pipkin survived. Pipkin
was one of the few to evade from inside Germany. When a German
soldier tried to apprehend him Pipkin got into a fight and got the better
of him. He held the soldier's head under water in a ditch and left him
for dead. Later, Pipkin crossed the River Niers into Holland and on
11 September a Dutch guide took the evader across the Maas and across
the frontier with Belgium. Pipkin was soon back in England. Saxelby,
McLean and four others were taken into captivity.[26]

Sergeant (later Squadron Leader) Tom 'Ben' Bennett, a navigator on
49 Squadron at Scampton flew his sixth op this night. He could see the
Duisburg area burning ahead but the defences were strangely quiet.

> But then, as the bombing run began the blue stream of the master
> searchlight found and held our Lancaster. It was followed at once by
> other probing fingers of flight. We were held fast in a cone of search-
> lights. I crouched at my navigation table, throat dry and parched.
> Although I was wearing my flying helmet with its padded ear-
> pieces I could hear a sound like hail drumming on the sides of the
> fuselage. I knew without looking out that heavy shells were bursting
> all around us, pattering the aircraft with shrapnel. I felt the bitter bile
> rise in the back of my throat. My heart and pulses pounded under
> the mounting stress of the greatest fear I had ever experienced. The
> frantic gyrations of the aircraft were giving us a helter-skelter ride
> planned in hell! Time and again I felt myself leave my seat and the
> navigation instruments on my table rose with me as the Lancaster
> plunged earthwards in a sickening dive, only to find myself pinned
> down on the chart table, as now the aircraft clawed for altitude.
>
> These experiences added to my absolute terror until I felt that in
> some way I was detached from humanity and mankind, that no one
> in the whole universe had the slightest care for me. I felt so totally
> alone that I shivered as if being blasted by the lowest tempera-
> ture that could be measured. There was an emptiness within me
> that almost choked me with its volume. In a flashing, blasphemous
> moment I felt that I knew what had wrung the cry, 'Eli! Eli! Lama
> sabachthani?' from the soul of Christ as he hung upon the cross. I am
> not sure that I did not shout aloud with terror. Then a buoyant calm
> seemed to come to soothe away all my hysteria, all my unspeakable
> fear. It was almost as if someone had whispered a reminder to me
> that my wife, my mother, the great East End padre friend of my life –
> all these and others, were praying for my safety every night and that
> my faith required me to believe that their prayers would be heard
> in heaven. We were still behind in the full, awesome glare of the

searchlights but now I could sit calmly and wait the inevitability of what I felt must surely come. Watching the application of my friends in the cockpit I thought to myself, what a fine company to go with. I was still placidly resigned to what I regarded as the inevitable end of this nightmare. Without warning, inky blackness now replaced the blinding light in which we seemed to have lived for an eternity. The roar of our four Merlins was a deep-throated song of triumph in the lonely night sky. We had shaken free of that cone of death and now night, dear, dark, blessed night had lovingly embraced us in her protective, concealing cloak. Very soon we were heading home and safety and for touchdown at Scampton at 04.55 hours, a shaken but thankful 'sprog' crew.[27]

On 8/9 September 249 aircraft were dispatched to Frankfurt-on-Main. Norman Child, radio operator on Pilot Officer Alan Gill's crew on 'B' Flight on 142 Squadron at Waltham, recalls:

We carried one 4,000lb 'cookie'. Our route out took us via Overflakkee, south of Cologne, Koblenz and then due east to Frankfurt. The Met report said it would be probably hazy over the target but other-wise, good. Airborne at 20.20 hours. Set course for Overflakkee and climbed to 10,000 feet. Cloud thicker than expected over Holland and we fly in cloud up to the German border. Break in the cloud and we get a good pinpoint on the Maas. Steered well clear of Cologne but plenty of flak to port suggests that a number of aircraft have wandered off course in cloud and are over the city. Cloud now clearing and only 3/10ths cover. North of Mainz a night fighter attacked us and he scored a hit on our tail fin. 'Jock' Sloan, the rear gunner, gave him a burst and we weaved and dived our way to safety. Approaching the target we detected a Halifax just overhead with its bomb doors open. We took quick avoiding action and pre-pared for our own run in – very heavy defences and well-predicted flak – enormous flash in the sky and flaming debris falling – it looked as though two aircraft had collided.

We dropped our 'cookie' into the middle of a huge circle of explosions and fires and dived away into the night. Checked on the damage to tail but although it looked a ragged sight, it was still functioning satisfactorily. Steered course for home north of Koblenz and south of Cologne. We had a brief encounter with a flak ship off the Dutch coast and a few more holes punched into us. None of the crew was hurt. Message from base: 'Weather closed in – visibility very poor. Divert to Waterbeach.' Landed at Waterbeach. Duration of flight: 6 hours 55 minutes. Riggers inspected the tail unit and the damage was so severe they were amazed that the whole structure hadn't collapsed. The Wellington was a tough baby.

Even so, five Wellingtons and two Halifaxes were lost – four of them to night fighters. One was *T-Tommy*, the Wimpy flown by Flight Sergeant J C Heddon RNZAF on 142 Squadron whose navigator, Sergeant John Holmes, recalled:

> Crossing the city we were coned in searchlights and came under intense anti-aircraft fire. We were hit and the starboard engine lost power. We were unable to maintain course. We were hit again and found that we were losing fuel rapidly. We could not maintain altitude and it was obvious that we wouldn't make England and our base. We crossed out over the coast and took up ditching positions. The wireless operator sent out a distress signal on the Mayday wavelength and clamped down his key. Shortly thereafter, as we were still airborne, he went back to his seat and tapped out the SOS again. I reminded him to bring his Very pistol back with him. While climbing over the main spar he slipped and must have squeezed the trigger as a couple of stars shot past my face, burnt through the aircraft fabric and, in so doing, set fire to some leaflets which had blown back during the dropping operation. Between us, we beat out the flames and again took up our ditching positions.
>
> It was quite misty and while holding off just above the water, the starboard engine suddenly cut out; the wing dropped and struck the water and the poor old Wimpy broke her back. The lights went out and the IFF blew up in a blue flash. I was trapped, but eventually managed to struggle free and was washed out of the fracture in the middle of the fuselage. As I emerged, a couple of packages floated up beside me and I tucked them under each arm and pushed off on my back. In my hand was a Woolworth's torch which was switched on. I heard voices calling but I couldn't tell from which direction. The pilot, bomb aimer and wireless operator had got into the dinghy and guided by my torch, came alongside me. The wireless op seized me by the hair and the others hauled me into the dinghy. Apparently Sergeant Terence Bryce Treble, the South African rear gunner, had gone down with the tail.
>
> It was now 04.30 and quite dark. We baled water from the dinghy and made ourselves as comfortable as possible. At about 06.30 we heard the sound of an engine and saw a launch in the distance. Not knowing whether it was one of ours, or a German, we fired off a marine distress signal. We assumed the launch hadn't seen us or our signal, as it turned and disappeared from view. Five hours later we again heard and saw a launch. The bomb aimer tried to fire another distress signal, but the igniting tape broke so he used his thumb nail to ignite the flare and burnt the palm of his hand in so doing. The launch saw our signal and headed towards us. As it approached we saw the RAF roundels on the hull. The launch crew put out a

scramble net over the side and with assistance we climbed aboard. They told us that when we first saw them at 06.30, they were recalled due to a naval action taking place in the vicinity (about ten miles from the Channel Islands). When they got back to their base, their CO sent them out again immediately. They had plotted our position from our Mayday signal. We were given dry clothes, rum and hot coffee by the launch crew as we headed for the Needles on the Isle of Wight.[28]

Two nights' later training aircraft of 91, 92 and 93 Groups swelled the numbers in a 479-bomber raid on Düsseldorf. The Path Finders successfully marked the target using 'Pink Pansies' in converted 4,000lb bomb casings containing a red pyrotechnic, benzole, rubber and phosphorous, for the first time. All parts of Düsseldorf except the north of the city were hit as well as the neighbouring town of Neuss. As a result of the raid, 19,427 people were bombed out.[29] Thirty-three aircraft failed to return and the OTUs were hard hit.[30] Many training aircraft from various OTUs and Conversion Units were included in the force of 446 bombers which took off for Bremen on the night of 13/14 September. At East Moor, seven miles north of York, Sergeant Reginald Cantillon RAAF, a wireless operator on 158 Squadron was ordered at the last minute to replace the mid-upper gunner on Halifax *B-Baker* who was sick. The pilot – Sergeant F Caldwell – and his crew: two Englishmen, a Scot, an Irishman, a Canadian and an American, were on their first operation deep into Germany.

Almost 850 houses were destroyed and considerable damage was caused to industry, with the Lloyd Dynamo works being put out of action for two weeks and various parts of the Focke-Wulf factory for from two to eight days. Twenty-one aircraft failed to return.[31] Cantillon and the crew of *B-Baker* on 158 Squadron made it to the target and on the return had reached Holland when they were shot down to crash at Idaard. All of the crew survived and were taken into captivity.

When on the next night 202 aircraft attacked Wilhelmshaven the Path Finder marking was accurate and the city suffered its worst raid of the war to date. Two Wellingtons were the only aircraft that were lost.[32] This was the last raid by Hampdens and all four aircraft on 408 'Goose' Squadron RCAF returned safely.

Two nights' later 369 aircraft, including for the last time, Wellington and Whitley aircraft on OTUs, carried out a strong Bomber Command raid on the Krupp works at Essen. Squadron Leader Don Smith DFC, a regular officer who had flown 58 ops in the Middle East while commanding two Blenheim squadrons in Aden in 1940 and 1941, led a flight of 76 Squadron Halifaxes. He said:

We were over the Ruhr for about twenty minutes to make a reconnaissance report and we could feel the explosion of shells just beneath us and sometimes hear them. The defences were so strong and their area so vast that each of our aircraft must have been over it for at least fifteen minutes, especially if they had to search for their targets. That is a long time when guns and searchlights are trying to get you. If you are attacking a target on the outskirts of the Ruhr it is not so bad. It is rather like attacking Cologne, where there are about five hundred guns. But if it is right in the heart of the Ruhr, whichever way you go in you've got to get to the centre of a gun-defended area five times as big as that round Cologne. So to fly even within three or four miles of your target you will have to pass hundreds of guns.

Much of the bombing was scattered but effective, with 33 large fires and 80 'medium' fires being started. Much damage was caused to housing and eight industrial and six transport premises were struck by bombs. The Krupps Works were hit by 15 high explosive bombs and by a crashing bomber loaded with incendiaries. Many towns were hit, in particular, Bochum (with 50 fires), Wuppertal and Herne. Cochem, a small town on the Moselle, 90 miles south of Essen, received one bomb load which destroyed four houses and killed 15 people.[33] Forty-one bombers were lost, 21 of these to night fighters. *Oberleutnant* Reinhold Knacke, *Staffelkapitän*, 1./NJG1 claimed five victories to take his tally to 38. Eighteen of the 21 Wellingtons that were missing were on the OTUs. A Whitley V on 10 OTU at Abingdon flown by Warrant Officer L A D'eath RNZAF were last heard on w/t transmitting 'SOS' before they bailed out and were taken prisoner. The rest that were missing were nine Lancasters, five Stirlings and three Halifaxes Two of the missing Lancasters were on 9 Squadron at Waddington, the unit's first losses of this type since converting from the Wimpy. *T-Tommy* crashed near Düsseldorf with the loss of all on Sergeant Kenneth Beresford Hobbs' crew. *S-Sugar* and 31-year-old Pilot Officer Leslie James Musselwhite and crew were lost without trace. Musselwhite was on his first op as Skipper since being hospitalised with burns suffered on one of the April raids on Rostock when he had been the second pilot on Pilot Officer Taylor's Wellington crew, who were shot up by a night fighter that killed the rear gunner.

Musselwhite returned to crew status in June and he re-trained on the Lancaster. Essen was the first time that his crew had flown to Germany and it was their last. The Skipper left a wife, Doris Rosina, in Hampstead, London. His American rear gunner, 22-year-old Flight Sergeant Maurice Emanuel Buechler RCAF, was among the names added to the Runnymede Memorial for airmen with no known graves. (The memorial overlooks the place where King John signed Magna Carta in 1215, recognizing the rights and privileges of the barons, church and freemen.) Buechler, the son of a Hungarian-Jewish family from Newark, New Jersey, had joined the RCAF in September 1941, three months before Pearl Harbor, and he had trained as an aerial gunner before being shipped to Britain the following January for final training. The RCAF gave Maurice Buechler his air gunner's brevet posthumously on 27 September.

One of the missing Halifaxes was *E-Easy* on 405 Vancouver Squadron RCAF at Topcliffe flown by Flight Sergeant William Frederick Murray RCAF. *Easy* encountered mechanical problems shortly before reaching the target, losing the flame damper on one engine and suffering a malfunction of the oxygen system. All except one of the crew were Canadians. Sergeant Ronald Barnicoat RAFVR, the 22-year-old flight engineer was from Weymouth in Dorset. Murray came from Armstrong, British Columbia, while Sergeant Charles Paton, the 22-year-old navigator, was from Toronto, Ontario. Sergeant William Grant the bomb aimer was 27 and from Clifton Royal, New Brunswick. Flight Sergeant Joseph St. Louis, the mid-upper gunner, was 28 and from Renfrew, Ontario. Flight Sergeant Charles Kitson, the 20-year-old rear gunner, was from Austin, Manitoba.

The wireless operator was 24-year-old Pilot Officer Lorne Kropf. He had spent his early days in New Hamburg before he and his parents moved to Kitchener where he completed his studies at the K-W Technical School from which he graduated in 1934. After the death of his parents, he returned to New Hamburg and made his home with his aunt Mrs Elena Ritz in Fisher Street, Kitchener for two years, being employed as bread salesman for Miller's Bakery on the local route. He worked next at the Dominion Tyre factory at Kitchener where he was employed when he enlisted in the RCAF in June 1940. Due his excellence as a student, he was awarded his commission as Pilot Officer upon completion of his training at Macdonald. After a few weeks' furlough he arrived in England on Christmas Day 1941. He and the rest of the crew were on their fourth op, having taken part in Frankfurt, Bremen and Duisburg. The crew were mentioned in dispatches after a successful raid on Bremen. Kropf recalled:

> On our way back I was busy operating the wireless when a night fighter got on our tail and gave us a burst into the port wing. I could hear the bullets ripping into it. The plane immediately went out of control and started to spin. The Skipper Bill Murray ordered us to bail out. I heard the flight engineer ask him if it was really necessary. 'Yes' shouted the Skipper, 'the port wing's on fire'. The boys tried to get the escape hatch open but it was jammed. I figured we dropped about 10,000 feet in the next few seconds and then the gas tanks on the big plane exploded. I thought we had hit the ground and then I felt the wind rushing against me and I realised I was still falling. I pushed with my feet and hands and freed myself from the plane. Where I got out of the plane I don't know. It could have been the top, bottom or the side. I remember falling fast in the darkness of the night. I could see the flaming plane beneath me and away to one

side I saw another chute. I learned afterwards that it was the flight engineer. The others in the crew must have been killed instantly in the explosion. I landed in a field but I can't tell you in what country. About a mile away I could see the flames and smoke of the Halifax filling the sky. I don't know where the flight engineer landed but he evidently fell into enemy hands. For the life of me I can't remember pulling the rip cord, I guess the Gremlins did it for me. They tell me I am a member of the Caterpillar Club now, that having been my first jump. All I can tell you is that I landed safely with only a small scratch over my left eye. I was reported missing for six weeks.[34]

On the night of 19/20 September, 118 aircraft were dispatched to Saarbrücken and 68 Lancasters and 21 Stirlings went to Munich, or the 'Nazi shrine' where 'the aiming point, appropriately enough, was the beer cellar', as it was recorded in the station ORB (Operations Record Book) at Waddington.[35] At Saarbrücken the Path Finders had to mark two targets but ground haze caused difficulties and the bombing was scattered to the west of the target. Five aircraft failed to return and a Halifax II on 10 Squadron at Melbourne, 12 miles South-East of York, flew into a tree on high ground and was abandoned over Yorkshire. All the crew suffered injuries but otherwise they were none the worse after their ordeal. At Munich about 40 per cent of crews dropped bombs within three miles of the city centre and the remainder dropped them in the western, eastern and southern suburbs. Four bombers went missing in action and a Stirling on 149 Conversion Flight at Bourn was ditched off Ramsgate after an engine failure. Two of R-Robert's crew died and two were very badly injured when the Stirling broke into four sections. Sergeant I G Davies, the wireless operator, had fractured his spine and Sergeant L V Fossleitner volunteered to remain with him while Sergeant J Philip, the pilot, and Sergeant G K Reardon began swimming towards the Kent coast, towing Sergeant Fred King who was badly hurt, with them. After nearly four hours they were sighted by a fishing boat but King had not survived his ordeal. Meanwhile, an ASR launch had picked up Davies and Fossleitner but two other crew members were never found. Philip, Reardon and Fossleitner each received the BEM.

A-Apple on 9 Squadron flown by 28-year-old Flying Officer Lewis Boyd Haward from Surbiton was one of three Lancasters lost when it crashed at Gautling less than ten miles from Munich. Haward and five of his crew, including two Canadians and his WOp/AG, 32-year-old Pilot Officer Howard Houston Burton RCAF, an American from West Virginia, who was on his 19th operation, died in the aircraft. Sergeant M L Douglas the mid-upper gunner was the only survivor.

Four nights' later Lancasters of 5 Group bombed the Baltic coastal town of Wismar and the Dornier aircraft factory nearby. Many of the crews went down to under 2,000 feet but just four aircraft were lost. At

Flensburg only 16 of the 28 Halifaxes of 4 Group that were dispatched claimed to have bombed and five aircraft failed to return. Vegesack was visited by 24 Stirlings of 3 Group and just one, *A-Apple*, a Stirling I on 218 Squadron flown by Squadron Leader Cuthbert Raymond DFC, a New Zealander, was lost with all seven crew killed. *A-Apple* fell victim to a Bf 110 flown by *Unteroffizier* Karl-Georg Pfeiffer of 6./NJG2 at Wittmundhafen whose first victory this was since joining the *Gruppe* at Leeuwarden in late April.[36] Another eight Stirlings and 25 Wellingtons laid mines between Biscay and Denmark. Two Wellingtons failed to return.

A Bomber Command directive was now issued whereby crews stood down from night flying would be employed on daylight intruder missions to keep the German sirens wailing and disrupt industry by driving the workers into air raid shelters. The RAF crews' only protection was cloud cover and it was essential that there was sufficient cloud to hide in. A Wellington was no match for a German fighter and all aircraft captains had strict orders to return to base if the cloud cover broke up. On Monday 28 September three Wellingtons on 115 Squadron were detailed for a 'cloud cover' daylight bombing attack on Lingen on the Dortmund-Ems Canal. As the aircraft made their way east the cover thinned out rapidly to a scattering of isolated clouds. Sergeant Crimmin decided to turn back. Squadron Leader Sandes made a similar decision. Squadron Leader Robert James Sealer Parsons decided to press home the attack but eight kilometres south west of Urk, over the Zuider Zee, he was attacked by *Unteroffizier* Kurt Knespel of 10./JG1 in a FW 190. As Knespel's cannon shells tore through the fuselage Flight Sergeant John Austin Parker, the Canadian WOp/AG, was hit and died instantly. Flames from the ruptured wing tanks, fanned by the slipstream, spread rapidly. Parsons shouted over the intercom that he would try to ditch the bomber. Sergeant J M Golmour, the front-gunner, entered the cockpit from his turret and saw Flight Sergeant William Leonard Clough, the 31-year-old observer, with the cabin fire extinguisher in his hand vainly trying to subdue the raging furnace. The aircraft hit the sea and only the Canadian gunners, Sergeants Golmour and J J Stansell, emerged. They were both taken into captivity.[37]

As the October dawn began to break over the fields of England, Flying Officer George R Harsh RCAF, the 102 Squadron Gunnery Officer, with cold and trembling fingers, fumbled amidst the straps and buckles and flaps of his flying gear and extracted the flask of brandy from his hip pocket and took a long, gurgling belt of this time-tested restorative. Described as 'grey as a badger' and looking like a 'Kentucky colonel; a wild, wild man with a great spreading nose and a rambunctious soul', Harsh was an American born in Milwaukee and educated in North Carolina and at Oglethorpe University in Atlanta. Having found and circled over their home base at Pocklington, the crew spotted the operations officer standing at the end of the runway, signalling with his green Aldis lamp the call letters of the squadron and their aircraft: *O-Orange*. With the four magnificent Merlin Rolls-Royce engines straining against the lowered flaps, the crew settled in for the touch-down. Then, having taxied to the dispersal site the pilot shut off the engines and the sudden silence tore at their ear drums. One by one, they dropped out of the hatch and walked slowly over to the waiting lorry. Harsh wrote:

> The birds would just be starting their cheerful greetings to this new day and for some reason the sound always startled me, as though I thought those birds had no right to be any part of this crazy business. And yet I loved that sound, for I knew they were English birds and that once again I was on friendly soil. The same WAAF who had seen us off the night before and had watched unconcernedly as we each in turn had unbuttoned and peed on the port wheel for luck would be standing beside her lorry waiting for us with a big cheerful smile on her English-complexioned face. We had taxied out of the dispersal site and she had seen us off with that big smile and her arm held aloft and her fingers giving the Victory sign and this morning the smile was still there and so was her unvarying greeting: 'Morning, chaps. Have a nice trip?'
>
> And the reply would come from my polite British fellow crew members, as though we had just returned from a holiday cruise to the Caribbean. *'Veddy nice, thenk you.'*[38]

Life had started out with great expectations for George Harsh. He lost his father when he was twelve but at his death a half-million dollars was put in trust in young George's name. Then at age 17 Harsh shot a man in a hold-up, for kicks. He was sentenced to die in the electric chair, but at age 18 his sentence was commuted to life in prison and he spent the next twelve years on a Georgia chain gang. Harsh wielded a shovel for 14 hours a day; slept in a stinking cage; fought off the sexual attacks of other prisoners and learned how to survive a hell that would have killed most men. He was pardoned when he saved the life of another prisoner by performing an improvised appendectomy. Less than a year later Harsh had volunteered for flying service in the RCAF.

At 4 o'clock on the afternoon of 5 October, all air crew members at Pocklington were ordered over the tannoy system to report to the briefing room. The target for over 250 aircraft was Aachen, though George Harsh was not scheduled to fly that night. At take-off time he stood at the end of the runway, with the operations officer, enjoying this brief respite from what the American called 'this orgy of killing'. During the past two weeks 102 had taken more than its usual share of casualties. The operations officer with his Aldis lamp signalled the aircraft and got them airborne, one following right on the tail of the other. The third-from-last Halifax was standing poised, waiting for the 'go' flick of the light when suddenly the pilot signalled Harsh and the ops officer. In a dogtrot they hurried over to see what the trouble was. The pilot, Warrant Officer Frederick Arthur Schaw RNZAF, with a frantically jabbing finger was motioning them towards the rear turret. Schaw's was one of the green crews that had been sent to the squadron from the replacement depot. In fact this was the first combat operation for this crew. Running around to the rear turret and motioning with his hand because of the wash of the props and the tinny roar of the engines, Harsh got the gunner to understand that he wanted him to swing the turret around and open the door. 'What's the problem?' Harsh bellowed at him over the noise. The gunner, a huge farm boy from Yorkshire, held out his hand; and there, nestling in the great palm, were the remains of what had once been a finely adjusted gun-sight. *'It coom apart in me 'and!'* he shouted in his Yorkshire accent. It was as though a bear had got hold of a fine, jewelled Swiss watch.

Harsh continues:

'Get the bloody hell out of there!' I roared at him and as he extricated his lumbering bulk from the turret. I snatched off his parachute harness and buckled it on myself over my best uniform. That plane had to go on the mission and there had better be someone in the turret who could hit a target without the aid of a gun-sight. Perhaps I could do something with the help of the tracers.

As we got airborne and headed out across the Channel, the realization of how stupid I had just been crashed into my mind – and it was that parachute harness which acted as the catalyst. For some reason known only to himself the ploughboy had been wearing an unneeded sheepskin-lined leather flying jacket and the harness had been adjusted to all that bulk. There was now enough slack in the harness to hang a horse and it was all hanging down between my legs. If I had to bail out and the parachute opened, that slack would snap taut right into my crotch! With this sickening picture in mind I reached behind me for the adjusting buckles but in the cramped quarters I couldn't do anything with them, so I pulled the slack up around my chest and offered a small prayer. By now I was beginning to feel that I had used up all my luck, but maybe it would hold for one more time.

For an hour or more we droned along uneventfully. We had not run into any heavy concentrations of flak and miraculously no night fighters had challenged us. Intelligence had assured us the flak would be light. Suddenly a cold thought entered my mind: for the past half-hour I had not noticed any other bombers flying in our direction and this despite the fact we should have been right in the middle of the bomber stream. Slowly I swung the turret in its full arc – nothing out there but an occasional fleecy patch of white cloud, shimmering in the bright moonlight. And then I looked down at the ground 8,000 feet below us. Oh, no! But blinking my eyes wouldn't make it go away. The *Kölner Dom!* The majestic twin spires of the Cologne Cathedral were pointing into the sky at me. The bulk of the old Gothic edifice was bathed in moonlight and the moonlight was shimmering from the waters of the river as it made its un-mistakable bend around the church. There we were, right on top of Cologne ... alone.

The pilot must have instinctively sensed that something was wrong, for I heard a microphone click on and then his voice crackled in the earphones. 'Hullo navigator! Where are we?' For what seemed interminable seconds there was dead silence and then the well-bred, English-public-school accents of the navigator came over the inter-com. '*I'm fucked if I know old boy.*'

The groan of despair did not even have time to escape my lips before everything seemed to begin happening at once. The eerie purple light of the radio-controlled searchlight, the master search-light of the Cologne air defence system locked onto us and having seen this happen to other bombers I knew there would be no escaping it. No manoeuvring, no 'jinking', no diving nor turning nor any amount of speed would shake off that relentless finger. With the range signalled to them from this automatic light the entire search-light complex now locked onto us and we were 'coned', the most dreaded thing that could happen to any bomber crew. The sky around us and the aircraft itself were lighted up like Broadway on New Year's Eve and then it came. The German gunners had a sitting duck for a target and all they had to do was pour their fire up into the apex of that cone and there was no way for them to miss. In the bright, blinding light there was no flashing coming from the flak bursts now but suddenly our whole piece of illuminated sky filled with brown, oily puffs of smoke. Pieces of shrapnel began hitting us and it sounded like wet gravel being hurled against sheet metal. Then we started taking direct hits and the aircraft jumped and bucked and thrashed and pieces of it were being blown off and I could see them whipping past me. Then the fire started and I could smell it and see the long tongues of flame streaming out from the wings. The intercom was now dead and so was the hydraulic system that operated the turret but with the manual crank I quickly turned the turret around, opened the doors and was preparing to push myself backwards out into the sky when a burst of light, fine shrapnel sprinkled my whole back. It felt as though the points of a dozen white hot pokers had suddenly jabbed into me. My one prayer at that moment was that the flak had not cut the parachute harness draped over my back. The parachute harness! Oh, God ... get that slack out of your crotch! I dropped, clutching the slack around my midriff with my left hand and pulled the rip cord on my chest pack with my right. I was now conscious of the dead silence through which I was falling. Gone was the aircraft with its roaring engines and miraculously the flak had stopped. But one searchlight glued itself onto me and began following me downward. Then the chute opened and my fall was suddenly, jarringly halted and I bobbed upward like a yo-yo in the hand of some idiot giant. With a tearing, rending noise the slack snapped taut around my chest and I felt my whole rib cage cave in. Then I passed out.[39]

At Downham Market everyone on Flight Sergeant 'Bicky' Bickenson's Stirling crew on 218 Squadron had been keen to get going; none more so Jimmy Morris, the former engine mechanic and latterly, Fitter 2E, who had got his wish and was now aircrew. Until recently the Stirling bombers had always carried two pilots – first and second – but in the spring of 1942 the second pilot was replaced by a new crew member, a Flight Engineer. Morris had applied for the role and had been successful. He had spent about four weeks learning about fuel and systems, hydraulic components, pneumatic and electrical systems before passing a test paper. 'I fitted into my new crew OK. I guess I was like most of the flight engineers of that period, pushed in at the deep end as the rest of the crew had been together for six or seven weeks. I was the new bod.' He was also engaged to Pat, the love of his life.

Morris recalls:

Little did we know that the op was to be a complete disaster. To me, take-off with a full fuel and bomb load was always a difficult time. Once we got about 500 feet up I could relax a bit. The field at the end of our runway was ploughed up so much by bygone Stirlings that the farmer did not need to do it himself. We set course for target and when we were crossing the Channel, someone took a shot at us. I guess the Navy were a bit trigger happy. About 30 miles further on, we flew into an electric storm. It must have been the daddy of them all. The whole kite was lit up like a Xmas tree with water coming in from every hole and crack in the kite. At one stage, I turned round to speak to the WOp who was standing in the astrodome. Sandy Gandow didn't know it but I could see a great spark coming from his head and earthing to the kite. We had crossed to within sight of the Dutch coast when Jock Traynor the navigator and 'Bicky' discussed the situation.[40] They eventually decided we would have to turn back as we could not gain the height to get above the weather front. Besides that, it was impossible to navigate as the storm had made most of the navigation gear u/s. We landed back at Downham

Market to a rather cool reception. By this time 'Bicky' had risen from Flight Sergeant to Flying Officer but as a result of our abortive op (we didn't do missions; we left that to the Padre along with the Yanks) he was sent on a night flying course for a week. 'Bicky' was an old regular from the 1920s and 30s and had spent a lot of time at Felixstowe. He told me about his early days when LAC Shaw (Lawrence of Arabia) was the coxon on an ASR boat and shared a billet with 'Bicky'. Bit of an 'odd bod' was LAC Shaw. We, the crew, kicked our heels for a week and we all voted to carry on with 'Bicky' as Skipper because he was a good pilot and could not be held responsible for the weather that had put a halt to our first operation.

Aachen was hit with little Path Finder marking and bombing was scattered. A 214 Squadron Stirling taking off from Chedburgh near Bury St. Edmunds crashed almost at once and a 106 Squadron Lancaster caught fire on landing at Langar after an early return. Eight aircraft – five of them Halifaxes – were shot down over the continent. Q-Queenie on 103 Squadron flown by Warrant Officer Kenneth Fraser Edwards fought its way through a thunderstorm, but just as course was being set for home, a Bf 110 attacked and badly damaged the Halifax and set fire to both wings. The fires intensified and spread and when Edwards gave the order to bail out they were at quite a low level. He and two other members of the eight man crew died on the aircraft and four men were taken prisoner. Two of the missing 'Hallybags' were on 102 Squadron. One crashed at Stokkel with the loss of all seven crew. Warrant Officer Schaw was killed; all seven of his crew were taken into captivity. George Harsh spent two weeks in a hospital in Cologne before being incarcerated in *Stalag Luft III*, where he took charge of tunnel security in the 'X Organisation'.

'Home for Christmas' was the standard joke in prisoner of war camps but tunnelling went so smoothly at *Luft III* that Harsh said thoughtfully one morning, 'You know, this time it might really be home for Christmas for some of us' and for once nobody laughed.[41]

Bad weather caused the loss of many of eight more aircraft that crashed in England. A Wellington crashed near Princeton on Dartmoor killing the pilot and three of the crew. Another Wimpy that was abandoned and a Stirling both crashed in Kent. A Canadian Wellington on 405 'Vancouver' Squadron crashed at Wrotham killing five of the seven crewmembers, and two Wellingtons on 156 Squadron were abandoned over Huntingdonshire and Essex. All the crew on a 425 Squadron Wimpy, which crashed at Finchingfield in Essex, were killed. There were no survivors on a 218 Squadron Stirling at Downham Market, which crashed at Icklingham Marshes in Norfolk.

Flight Sergeant Gordon Mellor the navigator on Warrant Officer Edwards' crew evaded capture. He reached Paris and was passed along the escape lines to the Pyrenees where he crossed into Spain on 19 October with three other evaders. Mellor finally returned home from Gibraltar on 1 November.[42] Once back at Elsham Wolds 'no one spoke a word when they saw him appear', recalled navigator Sergeant Don Charlwood, 27 years old and from Melbourne, Australia. 'Mellor had long been considered dead and for some time his name had only been mentioned in a regretful sort of way. He glanced about the old haunts and then addressed them in a plaintive voice. "Has anyone seen my greatcoat?" he said. "I left it hanging here the night we went missing."'[43]

Charlwood had spent his early years in Frankston and attended Frankston High before working for more than seven years as a jackeroo, as young management trainees on a sheep or cattle station are known. He had been accepted for RAAF air crew in 1940, carrying out his initial training in Victoria and his air observer training in Canada under the Empire Training Scheme. Don Charlwood's great-grandfather and his sons had until 1850, been printers and booksellers in Norwich before transferring their business to Melbourne. Charlwood would discover that there was a village named Charlwood three miles from Horley and he would visit the local rector and his wife and identify the grave of his great-great grandfather, James Charlwood, who had been born in the reign of George III and died five years after Waterloo. Don Charlwood had become Sergeant Geoff Maddern's navigator at 27 OTU Lichfield where the 27-year-old west Australian pilot had wanted and had got an all-NCO crew. Maddern's and three other new crews – all sergeants – arrived on 103 Squadron at Elsham Wolds in September and soon they became known as the 'Twenty Men'. When Maddern's crew began flying ops Charlwood wrote in his diary: 'Tonight our orders are, "Bomb the centre of Bremen; make it uninhabitable for the workers." England! Cricket! Huh! Justifiable? I do not know; I only know that I shall kill women and children soon.' Charlwood later admitted that it was necessary to preserve the 'democratic way of life' but could not imagine Christ bidding men bomb little children. 'What things we mice have to answer for!' Maddern counselled Charlwood to keep his thoughts to himself for the sake of the morale of the crew. But his pilot had his own doubts about raids that were, he wrote in diary, close to the 'one thing we are supposed to be fighting against – barbarism'.

On 6/7 October the Path Finders succeeded in illuminating the Dummer See, a large lake north-east of Osnabrück, which was used as a run-in point when 237 aircraft were dispatched. The bombing was well concentrated. Six aircraft were lost. One of the two Halifaxes that failed to return was *E-Easy* on 103 Squadron at Elsham Wolds, which was flown by Sergeant James Porter, a soft-voiced Scot. *Oberleutnant* Georg 'Hermann' Greiner of IV./NJG1 is believed to have shot them down.[44] *Easy* crashed off Ameland with the loss of all the crew, including Flight Sergeant Benedict

'Ben' Hardesty, Porter's Canadian rear gunner. Twenty-four hours earlier he had said: 'I sure never wanted to come to 103 Squadron.' Potter was planning to marry at Christmas and had kept a photo of the girl above his bed. Their beds were soon occupied by strangers whose names no one knew and never were to know.[45]

No further Main Force ops were flown until the 13th/14th when the target for 288 aircraft was Kiel. Eight aircraft were lost. Entering the target areas at just below 11,000 feet and flying straight and level, they encountered moderate flak. Although now over Kiel a single-engined German night fighter positioned itself approximately 100 yards dead astern and level with Stirling *R-Robert* on 'B' Flight on 218 Squadron, then opened fire. The cannon tracer shells passed directly over the Stirling's starboard engines, missing by about three yards. The Stirling crew, despite helmets and engine noise, could still hear the phut-phut of the cannon firing. The Stirling pilot, Sergeant L T Richards, came on the intercom and said, 'Rear gunner, what was that?'

No reply.

The night fighter fired again, this time the shells going over the top of the starboard engines but missing by only one yard. Richards said, 'Rear gunner, there it is again!'

No reply.

Out of ammo, or disliking his own side's flak, the night fighter disappeared. The Stirling bomb aimer brought back a spot-on aiming point picture. The silent rear gunner from Canada was Romulus Helmer who, in civilian life before enlisting, was a lay preacher![46]

On 15/16 October, 289 aircraft went to Cologne. This time 18 aircraft failed to return. Two of these were Halifaxes on 103 Squadron at Elsham Wolds. Flight Lieutenant Kenneth Frederick John Winchester DFC and all except one of his crew on *A-Apple* were killed. With his ops cap battered full of character and his long experience etched on his face, Winchester was almost the idealized RAF type.[47] There were no survivors on Flight Lieutenant Graham Noel Parker's crew. Parker was a New Zealander serving in the RAF. The raid was not successful largely because winds were different from forecast and the Path Finders had difficulty in marking the target well enough to attract the Main Force away from a large decoy fire site, which received most of the bombs.[48]

After a favourable weather report, 94 Lancasters of Air Vice Marshal Alec Coryton's 5 Group took off on the afternoon of 17 October to the large Schneider factory at Le Creusot on the eastern side of the Massif Central. The factory, 200 miles south-east of Paris and more than 300 miles inside France, was adjacent to that area whose place names – Gevrey-Chambertin, Nuits-St-Georges, Beaune, Meursault, Mâcon – read like a melodious passage of a favourite wine list. But it was a long way, not far from the Swiss frontier; only Lancasters would have the necessary performance.[49] Le Creusot was regarded as the French equivalent to

Krupps and produced heavy guns, railway engines and, it was believed, tanks and armoured cars. A large workers' housing estate was situated at one end of the factory. Bomber Command had been given this as the highest priority target in France for a night attack but only in the most favourable of conditions. Air Marshal Sir Arthur Harris decided to attack by day, despite the failure of the Augsburg raid exactly six months earlier, when seven out of the twelve Lancasters dispatched were shot down. To maintain secrecy the code name Operation *Robinson* was chosen; a rather allusive name if the popular mispronunciation of Creusot is considered. Eighty-eight aircraft led by Wing Commander Leonard 'Slosher' Slee DFC, the 49 Squadron CO at Scampton, were to bomb the Schneider factory and the other six were to attack a nearby transformer station which supplied the factory with electricity.

Tom Bennett, navigator on Flight Sergeant Webster's crew recalls:

'Slosher' Slee sprang a surprise with a final announcement to hushed crews before they left the crew room. It had been decided that all eleven of 49 Squadron's aircraft would take off in formation! This was typical of the morale-boosting, almost 'spur-of-the-moment' innovations that 5 Group Squadrons introduced at Station level. I like to think that this inspiration originated from the alert and impish mind of Charlie Whitworth, truly an 'aircrews' Station Commander. The eleven Lancasters trundled and bounced their way across the grass airfield, to take up their appointed places, along the far north east boundary. They were hardly visible to the ground-crew, who had taken-up vantage points to observe this unique and historic take-off. At 12.08 hours the Squadron Commander's aircraft rolled forward, to be followed at precise intervals by the rest of the formation: We were airborne at 12.09 hours and were to hear next day the graphic accounts of the watching ground-crew as 'Webby' manoeuvred his aircraft adroitly between the dispersals and hangars!

'Slosher' flew at reduced speed until all aircraft had assumed the requisite vic-formations; with two of the NCO pilots tucked in behind the leading vie. Airspeed was then increased to normal cruising, heading for Upper Heyford. This Oxfordshire airfield was reached at precisely 12.45 hours, with 61 and 9 Squadrons positioned to join formation, while near Swindon a similar smooth procedure was followed by 97, 50 and 57, with 106, 44 and 207 completing the mass formation near Frome. I was to learn from Sergeant Mortimer, mid-upper gunner on Pilot Officer Ayres' crew on 49, that during the leg from Frome to Start Point, he had flown directly over his Somerset home. 'I looked down one side and could see the back-garden, whilst down the other I could see the front door! I was convinced that this was my last operation ... that I had been allowed to see my home for the last time!' So much for portents and premonitions!

Cloud-base was 1,000 feet on the leg to Start Point and 'Slosher' had dropped to 800 feet, with the formations behind him stepped down to 600 and 400 feet respectively. Between Start Point and the Lizard, we approached a small formation of tugs towing lighters, heading for Plymouth, escorted by what appeared to be an armed trawler. I was amused when the escort pugnaciously flashed the challenge letter of the period at the approaching 'air armada' ... it struck me that the combined slipstreams could have turned the whole lot over! Nevertheless, quite solemnly Gerry Fawke answered with the reply letter that Paul Fortin, our French-Canadian wireless operator, had readily to hand and the 'danger' was averted. South westwards from the Lizard and the whole loose formation dropped down to 300 feet. Some 400 miles of featureless sea legs lay ahead until we crossed the coast of France. I reverted to *Gee* navigation and was delighted with the strength and reception of the Southern Chain signals. Soon the w/vs and ground speeds were buttoned-up and confirmed.

There was the opportunity to have some sandwiches and beverage in the warm autumn sunshine that was now bathing the canopy from cloudless blue skies. I was able to ensure a supply of fruit drops on my table for the mouth – during land sequence ahead. I stood up and looked around ... no sign of any shipping ... so peaceful it was almost a time out of the war ... but what lay ahead?

At the turn at 0500W, I returned to the *Gee* set to check ... and re-check ... the forward ground-speed. Satisfied, I completed the preparation of my topographical maps. I switched off *Gee* and stood up behind the flight engineer when I knew we were in the lee of the Ile d'Yeu; with my maps ready I glanced out to port to confirm my assumption and was shaken to see the dim outline of a small boat two miles away, between us and the island. Was a transmitter already pouring forth some fateful warning? No time to worry, for here was the French coast! I shall *always* believe that if 5 Group had raised a pole on the west coast of France at the required crossing, Pilot Officer A S Grant, Slee's Australian navigator, would have guided Slee immaculately over it! The landfall was superb!

Airspeed climbed to 180 mph and unexpectedly 'Slosher' dropped his height to around 60 feet and we followed suit. The application required performing map-reading correctly at this height and speed was quite demanding but the days of training were paying off. There was no time to take much notice of the novelty of flying over France in daylight. One appreciated the quiet beauty of the sun-bathed landscape but clear non-operational details of that flight are just a kaleidoscope of memory ... rolling fields, rivers and streams ... I remember an open carriage pulled by two horses, jogging gently along a tow-path with what appeared to be an old lady and gent enjoying an afternoon spin. God knows how the horses reacted when the *en masse* thunder of those low-flying exultant Merlins hit them!

Across an internment camp, with an incredulous German-uniformed guard, too amazed to unsling his rifle! I felt that I would have no opportunity to man that Vickers gun by the exit door! Montrichard and the turn westwards to Sancerre ... No enemy reaction yet, in the air or from the ground but that was just a fleeting thought before the new track was embraced and the demands of map-reading met. As we approached Sancerre 'Slosher' pulled to port to allow the formation to come round over the town on course for Nevers. A river wound its way from Sancerre to Nevers, looking so peaceful in the warm sunshine ... but I did not notice if there was any boating or swimming activity. If there was, the majesty of this Lancaster formation must have left them deafened and speechless!

Just before Nevers, Slee again pulled wide, this time to starboard, and the formation came round to port, easily committed to this leg, the run-in to the targets. Green Very signals erupted from the lead aircraft to indicate the commencement of the climb to 6,000 feet and the assumption of the 'bombing arc'. The seven aircraft detailed to attack the transformers at Montchanin stayed low and moved to starboard of the climbing Lancasters. Two of these aircraft were drawn from 61 Squadron, three from 97 and the other two from 106.

We reached 6,000 feet and flew straight and level. I calculated the data for the automatic bombsight and passed it to Sergeant Erwin Osler our Canadian bomb-aimer. We always used this sight as a fixed sight. We found that trying to manipulate it in the automatic role often caused the bombs to fall early, if the wheel control on this bomb-sight was used clumsily. Then I noticed that 'Slosher's' aircraft was pumping out red Very signals agitatedly. I looked to starboard and saw that part of the arc formed by 9, 57 and 207 Squadrons was threatening to take over the run-in! I smiled inwardly, as I could imagine those bods saying 'Why should bloody 49 be the first in?' Slee abandoned the disciplinary attempt and poked his speed up to something approaching 195 mph. We followed suit, naturally, and I rapidly re-calculated the bomb-sight data from scratch, warning Oz to scrub all the current settings. Soon the sight was re-aligned. Gerry opened the bomb-doors and the bombing run was on. I looked out of the starboard blister. Opposition from the ground was negligible ... certainly nothing came our way. Gerry held the Lancaster level and steady at the indicated airspeed required. 'Bombs gone!' came confidently from the nose of the aircraft.

Dusk was gathering as I continued to survey the ground from the blister. Suddenly, my heart stopped in unbelieving horror, as black smoke and lurid flames belched from the thirty pound incendiaries as they burst amid a cluster of attractive French villas. I knew we were the first aircraft in with a part-load of HE and these bombs. It was the very first time that I had personally observed the impact of bombs we had dropped. I thought 'So much for the assurance that the incendiaries are timed to drop into the damage caused by the HE!' My feelings were a mix of anger and horror ... to think we had done this to French homes! Sickening!

But there were things to do ... I had set the course out on the pilot's repeater during the bombing run and Gerry was now coming round to starboard on to it, ensuring that he was well away from the bombers still approaching Le Creusot. The darkness had thickened considerably and Gerry decided to climb to 8,000 feet for the whole route home. On ETA we turned northwards for Bayeux and soon *Gee* was giving us its assurance and assistance.

We reached Bayeux without incident or interference and crossed to Worthing, to find the weather beginning to close in. Paul reported that Group was warning that weather at bases was deteriorating but Gerry decided to make for Scampton anyway, for diversion 'dromes could be so very uncomfortable and there was no place like home after an op like this! After crossing the English coast, 5 Group aircraft were required to contact base on W/T and ask for a 'turn to land'. On receipt of this figure, the pilot would adjust his ETA so that he would more-or-less go 'straight in' at Base, rather than be prey to possible enemy intruders. At the appropriate time, I asked Paul to get a 'turn to land'. After some interval, he came back on the intercom very puzzled. 'Everybody is getting "Q", which means wait,' he reported.[50] Eventually, Paul came up with the information sought and we duly arrived at Scampton to touch down at 21.57 hours.

All 49 Squadron aircraft landed safely at Scampton with Squadron Leader Couch last down at 22.24 hours, having lost an engine with a glycol leak at the south coast. It transpired afterwards that of the 94 aircraft that had originally set course on Operation *Robinson*, five had returned early and another had lost an engine just before the French coast and had abandoned, leaving a final attack total of 88 Lancasters. Of these, one was unable to open its bomb doors on the bombing run. Eighty Lancasters attacked the primary. The attack on the transformers was a great success but sadly the one aircraft lost went down on this target. Squadron Leader William Duncan Corr DFC of 61 Squadron was seen to hit a building during the attack and all except one of the crew perished. In the light conditions prevailing, the cause of the crash was not observed by the other six crews attacking this target.

Forty-one aircraft landed at their 'home' base in Lincolnshire but 45 'dropped-in' at 23 airfields south and south west of Lincolnshire, one as far west as Exeter. It is a fact that 'diversion offers' were sometimes welcomed by crews, as it occasionally gave them the opportunity for a 'gash' night at home!

Sergeant Ronald Wilson, pilot of the 207 Squadron aircraft that lost an engine and returned just before crossing the French coast had an interesting story to tell. Fifty miles west of Brest on the return, at a height of forty feet above the sea, his aircraft was attacked by three Arado Ar 196A-3 two-seater seaplanes. These aircraft were armed with two 20mm cannon and one 7.9mm machine gun, all forward-firing, plus a rear-mounted machine gun. The first Arado came in astern and opened fire at 300 yards. The rear gunner replied with four short bursts. The Arado flipped over on to its back, emitting black smoke and crashed into the sea. The second Arado attacked from the port beam. Wilson turned into this attack, with the mid-upper gunner firing two short bursts but this encounter proved indecisive. Arado No. 3 crossed from port to starboard of the Lancaster and attacked from the starboard beam, a bullet killing Sergeant Kenneth Chalmers the flight engineer. The front gunner gave a long burst, which struck the enemy aircraft. It plunged straight into the sea. The second Arado made a renewed attack from the port quarter. The mid-upper gunner gave two short bursts and the rear gunner managed a long sustained burst whilst it was within his compass. The enemy aircraft sheered-off towards the French coast, claimed heavily damaged. The Lancaster reached Langar, Nottinghamshire safely. This NCO crew received immediate awards of the DFM. It is ironic that they were the only crew to go missing on the night of 7/8 November 1942 during a raid on Genoa, one of the relaxing 'milk run' targets that were available to 5 Group crews during the support raids for the land offensive in North Africa.[51]

Tom Bennett continues:

Bombing results on Le Creusot were good but should have been better in the circumstances. The main section of the transformers at Montchanin was put out of commission by the low-level bombing and subsequent strafing by the six attacking Lancasters. This was one of the most vital points in the whole electric power system in France and was considered to be out of action for two years. Jim Davis' ploy worked. We obtained the only photograph with bombing. It showed our HE bursting on the locomotive machine shop. Charlie Whitworth was delighted but shared my reservations about the support timing for the incendiaries. He waived aside the graphs that the bombing leader produced to justify his calculations and sent a personal letter to 5 Group Headquarters, strongly recommending that immediate steps be taken to check the efficacy of the trials carried out with this weapon.

Keith 'Aspro' Astbury, 'Slosher' Slee's uncompromising Australian bomb aimer was having a mug of tea after debriefing when a young, eager news-hawk approached him. Apparently fit, military-aged Poms never cut much ice with 'Aspro'! 'Did the French civilians wave at you?' enquired the man invitingly. 'Aspro' looked at him speculatively. 'Mate, at the height and speed at which we were flying it was difficult to decide if they were waving or shaking their fists' he observed. The news-hawk disappeared in search of more amenable 'copy', leaving 'Aspro' grimly satisfied!

Sergeant N J Waddington RAAF, who was bomb aimer in a leading Lancaster, remembers that even over England the Lancasters flew so low to keep below German radar that the trailing aerial of his aircraft was taken off by a rock on the coast. Four aircraft were damaged by bird strikes and two men injured. *K-King* collected a bird in one engine over England; later three French partridges came bouncing through the bomb-aimer's perspex and another bird lodged in the camera. Going over France, the Lancasters hurdled telephone wires and houses, while people opened their doors and windows and waved. A horse with a plough burst its way helter-skelter through hedges and ditches while the plough-man stood and waved. Flying Officer Percy William 'Paddy' Rowling, *K-King*'s Australian navigator on 50 Squadron was exhilarated by it all:

I'd never seen so many bolting horses and oxen. Everything stampeded as we crossed France on the deck; some of the people stood and waved – others just stood and others, like one farmer, dived for cover or lay flat. This particular farmer had the quietest of horses and he was playing ostriches under his drag, head down and arse up, with the arse very much in sight.

Tom Bennett concludes:

In retrospect it is amazing how many of the aircrew engaged that day on the Le Creusot operation were to serve later on 617 Squadron. Guy Gibson, 'Hoppy' Hopgood, Dave Shannon (all of 106) and Les Knight with 'Spam' Spafford (50 Squadron) were all to form part of the original Squadron.[52] 'Aspro', Gerry Fawke and myself (49 Squadron) together with Drew Wyness (50 Squadron) and Trevor Muhl (207) were to serve later.[53] Sergeant L J King, a flight engineer badly injured in a bird strike over France in a 57 Squadron aircraft was to serve as Flying Officer King in Leonard Cheshire's crew in 1944. Ray Ellwood (97 Squadron), also a participant in the Augsburg raid, joined 617 in early 1944 and the same is probably true of other aircrew engaged on this memorable 1942 'daylight'!

The 5 Group crews claimed a successful attack on the Schneider factory but photographs taken later showed that much of the bombing had fallen short and had struck the workers' housing estate near the factory. Some bombs had fallen into the factory area but damage there was not extensive.[54] Flight Sergeant J E Taylor DFM, the pilot of *R-Robert* on 50 Squadron, arrived over the target to find the bomb doors would not open and had to carry his 4,000lb load back to Upper Heyford where he arrived dangerously low on fuel. The ten hour flight was, according to 'Paddy' Rowling 'a wizard trip and the whole world is talking about it today.'

The *Daily Express* claimed that the Lancasters had done a 'Grand National' over hedges to blast 'French Krupps'.

Notes

1. Sgts Frank Morton Griggs, Wildey, O'Hara, Flight Sergeant James Ian Cunningham Waddicar and Sgt Thomas Noel Castree Prosser the bomb aimer were awarded the DFM.
2. A Bf 110 of 6./NJG2 flown by *Leutnant* Hans-Georg Bötel, KIA 2/3 July 1942 with 3 victories.
3. N6082 was shot down at 02.04 hours and crashed in the Ijsselmeer near Wons, south of Harlingen. Collins was the only survivor.
4. June–October 1942, 75 Squadron RNZAF lost 35 Wellingtons and crews on ops, 10 of which FTR during the moon periods of July. Just 23 crewmembers survived being shot down to be taken prisoner, 2 escaped capture. The other 153 aircrew posted KIA or MIA.
5. *Gunner's Moon* by John Bushby (Futura 1974).
6. *Gunner's Moon* by John Bushby (Futura 1974).
7. See *The Bomber Command War Diaries: An Operational Reference Book 1939–1945*. Martin Middlebrook and Chris Everitt. (Midland 1985).
8. See *Chased By The Sun*.
9. See *Chased By The Sun*. F/O Robert Lorne Weatherall DFM was W/C Barron DSO* DFC DFM the Master Bomber's mid-upper gunner on Lancaster *C-Charlie* on 7 Squadron, which was lost in the target area on the raid on Le Mans on 19/20 May 1944. There were no survivors.
10. Listening stations in Britain would pick up the resulting continuous note. When the aerial touched the water the signal would stop. The listeners would have the DF loop fix of the position of the bomber when the signal vanished.
11. Clerides, a Greek Cypriot who had been educated at an English public school, recovering his senses and finding the a/c plunging to

earth immediately called up on the intercom. Not realizing he was no longer connected to the system and receiving no reply he assumed the others had bailed out. Scrambling back to the emergency hatch in the rear of the fuselage he bailed out. In the meantime Fereday had regained control and flattened out at 8,000ft. Without navigational instruments he was flying by the seat of his pants. The undercarriage and the open bomb bay were causing excessive drag. Clerides landed safely in the outskirts of a town and a crowd of civilians soon surrounded him. Mistaking his Greek features for those of a Jew the cry of '*Jude*' went up from someone in the mob. In a trice they were rifling his pockets, punching and kicking him. Luckily a detachment of the Luftwaffe arrived and rescued him. He was whisked off to hospital in Bremen where an immediate operation was carried out on his leg. After the war Clerides qualified as a barrister and eventually became President of the Creek Cypriots.

12. On Friday 21 August 1942 the body of Sgt Kelvin Shoesmith RAAF was recovered from Ho Bay in Denmark. Frank Skelley's body was washed ashore on the Dutch coast.

13. W1153 DY-H on 102 Squadron flown by P/O B V Hunter who was taken prisoner. Three of the crew were also captured, 3 were KIA.

14. 7.2% of the total force despatched – 15 Wellingtons, 8 Halifaxes, 2 Hampdens on 420 Squadron, 2 Lancasters and 4 Stirlings. 2 other a/c crashed on return.

15. See *Out of the Blue: The Role of Luck in Air Warfare 1917–1966* edited by Laddie Lucas (Hutchinson 1985). Dixon was the only survivor of the crew. Heinrich Dirks went to the Russian Front in an infantry regiment and was captured and became a PoW. His parents never heard from him again.

16. Bad weather over the stations of 1, 4 and 5 Groups prevented their participation. Ultimately only 256 aircraft – 165 of 3 Group and 91 OTU, comprising 161 Wellingtons, 71 Stirlings and 24 Whitleys took part. Sidwell, W/O W F Carter the flight engineer and Sgt A L Crockford, a new pilot on the Squadron who joined the crew late on to fly as 'second dickey' for experience, survived and were soon captured. F/L Whiteman, Sgt Albert Henry Charles Bates RAAF, a replacement for Sgt Paddy Leathem, the mid-upper gunner who had reported sick late on, Sgt Frank McIntyre RAAF the WOp/AG and Sgt John Boyle RAAF the navigator were KIA.

17. 16 Wellingtons and 9 Stirlings of 3 Group or 15.2% of those despatched FTR. A 10 OTU Whitley crashed into the sea and 4 Wellingtons on 16 and 22 OTUs also FTR. Only 68 crews reported bombing in the target area, their bombs scattering over a wide area, and relatively little damage was done to Hamburg.

18. Saarbrücken suffered severe damage and casualties in the centre and NW districts. 396 buildings destroyed and 324 seriously damaged.

155 people killed. Of the 291 aircraft despatched on 29/30 July, 9 aircraft – 3 Wellingtons, 2 Halifaxes, 2 Lancasters and 2 Stirlings – lost. Nightfighters claimed 7 of these losses.

19. 308 Wellingtons, 113 Lancasters, 70 Halifaxes, 61 Stirlings, 54 Hampdens and 24 Whitleys. 29 a/c FTR; 18 of which were shot down by *Himmelbett* night fighters.

20. 16 Wellingtons (11 of which were claimed destroyed by *Nachtjäger*), 5 Hampdens, 4 Halifaxes, 2 Lancasters and 2 Whitleys were lost. Sixteen of the missing aircraft were flown by OTU crews. More than 900 tons of bombs were dropped and 484 aircraft claimed successful attacks.

21. By the end of the war the PFF had flown over 50,000 sorties for the loss of 3,700 aircrew and 675 aircraft.

22. 226 aircraft were dispatched.

23. Of 16 bombers which FTR, 5 were Wellingtons, all of whom were shot down by night fighters.

24. Adapted from the story by Vanessa Allen 26/08/2006. Apart from Barton-Smith, Moss and Glen Smith the others who died were the navigator, F/Sgt Kenneth Wakefield; F E John Victor Robinson; WOp Sgt Peter Siegfried Sharman; mid-upper gunner, F/Sgt Edward Frederick Talbot.

25. *Oberleutnant* Ludwig Becker, *Unteroffizier* Karl Heinz Vinke, *Hauptmann* Helmut Lent and *Oberleutnant* zur Lippe-Weissenfeld of II./NJG2 at Leeuwarden claimed 7 bombers including 4 Wellingtons destroyed. Weissenfeld was killed in a flying accident on 12 March 1944. He had 51 night victories.

26. See *RAF Evaders: The Comprehensive Story of Thousands of Escapers and their Escape Lines, Western Europe, 1940–1945* by Oliver Clutton-Brock (Grub Street 2009). S/L Pipkin died in a shooting accident on 30 August 1944.

27. See *Out of the Blue: The Role of Luck in Air Warfare 1917–1966* edited by Laddie Lucas (Hutchinson 1985). Ben Bennett went on to serve on 617 Squadron at Woodhall Spa.

28. See *Bombers: The Aircrew Experience* by Philip Kaplan (Aurum Press 2000). WO J C Heddon and crew on 12 Squadron crashed at Lindstrup, Denmark on the operation on Kiel on 13/14 October 1942. He and his crew were taken into captivity.

29. *The Bomber Command War Diaries: An Operational Reference Book 1939–1945.* Martin Middlebrook and Chris Everitt. (Midland 1985).

30. At least 16 a/c, or almost half the losses this night were shot down by night fighters of NJG1 and NJG2.

31. 15 Wellingtons, 2 Lancasters, a Halifax, a Whitley and a Stirling.

32. *The Bomber Command War Diaries: An Operational Reference Book 1939–1945.* Martin Middlebrook and Chris Everitt. (Midland 1985).

33. *The Bomber Command War Diaries: An Operational Reference Book 1939–1945*. Martin Middlebrook and Chris Everitt. (Midland 1985).

34. Barnicoat and Lorne Kropf, who evaded the Germans and arrived, after an amazing journey, in England on 1 November 1942, were the only survivors. The Halifax crashed at Maubeuge, France. When Lorne was told by his friend F/O Lou Nault that the *Globe & Mail* had announced that he was to receive the DFC, he was amazed and said 'I feel I don't deserve it.' Lorne was also to say 'I only wish my buddies were still alive so that they would know about it.' Lorne Kropf returned to Canada and re-trained as a pilot before returning to England to join 410 'Cougar' Squadron. He was awarded his DFC at Buckingham Palace by King George V1 on Tuesday 10 October 1944. His navigator, F/O Alan B Sangster, attended the ceremony with him.

35. See Thorburn.

36. Pfeiffer had been banished to Wittmundhafen as a punishment for failing to lower the undercarriage of a new FW 190 when landing on his 1st or 2nd training flight. Four FW 190s had been allocated to NJG2 for day operations against Coastal Command aircraft that were becoming a nuisance to shipping and coastal targets in the Dutch coast area. *Major* Helmut Lent, the *Gruppenkommandeur* was so angry that he told Pfeiffer he did not want to see him again.

37. *Unteroffizier* Karl Knespel was shot down and killed in combat with four-engined bombers at Groningen on 28 July 1943.

38. *Lonesome Road* by George Harsh (Sphere Books London 1972)

39. *Lonesome Road* by George Harsh (Sphere Books London 1972)

40. Jock Traynor was KIA on 28/29 April 1943 when the Stirling flown by P/O Berridge was shot down on a *Gardening* sortie off Denmark. Traynor had stood in for a navigator that had gone sick. 218 Gold Coast Squadron Assoc Newsletter No. 50 March 2008.

41. *Lonesome Road* by George Harsh (Sphere Books London 1972). Fellow American 'Junior' Clark, a 'gangling, ginger-headed youngster in his twenties and a lieutenant colonel already' was chief of security and known as 'Big S'. At the beginning of March 1944, just before the 'Great Escape' took place, George Harsh and 18 other PoWs were ordered to pack and they were marched out of the gate at Sagan to a compound at Belaria five miles away. The move probably saved George Harsh's life and that of some of the others, including two of the tunnellers and Robert Stanford Tuck, who all worked in the escape organisation and would have been among those at the head of the queue when the 'Great Escape' took place on the night of 24 March. *The Great Escape* by Paul Brickhill (Faber and Faber).

42. See *RAF Evaders: The Comprehensive Story of Thousands of Escapers and their Escape Lines, Western Europe, 1940–1945* by Oliver Clutton-Brock (Grub Street 2009).

43. *No Moon Tonight* by Don Charlwood (Penguin 1988).
44. By the end of the war Greiner was Kommandeur IV./NJGI, had been awarded the Knight's Cross with Oak Leaves and had shot down 51 bombers.
45. See *No Moon Tonight* by Don Charlwood (Penguin 1988).
46. 218 Gold Coast Squadron Assoc Newsletter No. 31 November 2004.
47. See *No Moon Tonight* by Don Charlwood (Penguin 1988).
48. Middlebrook and Everitt.
49. *The Right of the Line: The Royal Air Force in the European War 1939–1945* by John Terraine (Hodder & Stoughton 1985).
50. The 'Q' mystery was solved soon after landing at Scampton. Slosher had been behind at the south coast. His WOp had heard aircraft beginning to call up for landing instructions and decided that the 'Wingco' should not be too far down the queue, so, off his own bat, he had been transmitting 'Q' to interrogating aircraft until he himself had been specifically asked to get a turn to land!
51. Lancaster I L7546 *G-George* and P/O Ronald Sydney Wilson DFM's crew were lost over France with no survivors.
52. F/O Frederick Michael 'Spam' Spafford DFC DFM RAAF, who was the bomb aimer on Guy Gibson's crew in the attack on the Möhne dam on 16/17 May 1943 and P/O Les Knight DSO RAAF, who also flew the Dams' raid, were both KIA on 15/16 September 1943 on the operation to Ladbergen. F/L John Vere 'Hoppy' Hopgood DFC* was KIA on the Dams raid on 16/17 May 1943.
53. S/L D R C 'Duke' Wyness DFC a six-footer, slim, 23, with blue eyes, a somewhat classical nose and really golden, curly hair, had a reputation as a 'press-on' type. *The Dam Busters* by Paul Brickhill (Evans Bros 1951). Wyness FTR from the operation by 617 Squadron on the Kembs Dam on the Rhine just north of Basle on 7 October 1944. He and three of his crew were shot in cold blood and three gunners who bailed out were never seen again. The Lancaster piloted by F/L C J G 'Kit' Howard was also lost with all the crew killed.
54. See *The Bomber Command War Diaries: An Operational Reference Book 1939–1945*. Martin Middlebrook and Chris Everitt. (Midland Publishing 1985). W/C Slee was awarded the DSO for his leadership of the formation and P/O A S Grant received an immediate DSO for his navigation on the raid. Later in the war he added a DFC and bar to his decorations.

CHAPTER 2

Italy Blitz

It almost seems a pity Keats and Shelley did not live to become airmen and fly with Bomber Command. They would have got a brand-new angle on nature – especially on the Italian side of the Alpine range. Poets however, like other mortals, are not always lucky. They might have been briefed for the attack on Genoa, the city where Columbus first saw the light of day …

Over the Alps – And Back, Bombers Fly East by Bruce Sanders

As a child John Anderson Hurst had been fascinated by aircraft and he would often cycle eight miles to an aero club to watch Tiger Moths flying from their grass field. His pocket money was spent on model aircraft kits and he spent many happy hours flying rubber powered models. He joined the Air Training Corps and when war was declared was eager to get into the RAF as aircrew. However he was employed making reticules for Browning gun sights and gate glasses for aerial cameras and was classed as Reserved Occupation. But so determined was he to fly that he constantly pestered the local RAF recruitment office and in October 1941 went before an aircrew selection board and was accepted for aircrew. At Cardington in Bedfordshire in December, he was kitted out and given the White Flash that trainee aircrew wore in their forage caps and he was very proud to wear it. A couple of days later he and other trainee aircrew were sent by train to Padgate near Warrington, a mill town with cobbled streets, where each morning they were woken by the mill girls as they noisily made their way to work wearing wooden clogs. Hurst recalls:

At Padgate we were given more kit. We also attended lectures about the RAF and were shouted at by NCOs. We only stayed for two days, but I still recall Padgate as the most depressing RAF station I was based at.

We were next sent by train to No. 3 Recruit Centre Blackpool. Five of us were billeted with an elderly couple in Albert Road, a grey road of terraced houses. Looking back I feel sorry for the couple and hundreds of others who had teenagers dumped on them and were paid a pittance; they certainly did not want us there. We had to do many of the daily chores: washing up, making the beds, peeling potatoes, etc but the lady of the house did the cooking. Much of the day was spent endlessly drilling on the promenade, in aircraft recognition classes, on the rifle range and being taught Morse by civilian instructors. Christmas in Blackpool was bleak. We were not wanted in the house but the local Salvation Army Hostel made us very welcome and we were well fed.

January 1942 was very snowy in Blackpool and the hundreds of RAF based there were kept busy on snow clearing. A vast length of the prom had to be cleared each morning before 'square bashing' could commence; the snow was often 6 inches deep. The Winter Gardens had been taken over by the RAF and we had pay parades there every fortnight and PT was done in the Palace Ballroom. We were allowed to go in groups to the Woolworth cafe beneath Blackpool Tower for tea and buns and on Sundays we could go free of charge to the Opera House to listen to *The Squadronaires* – a well known orchestra of the time – also variety acts, including the comedian, Max Wall. He was our drill sergeant and he would strut around with a pace stick under his arm, bellowing at us whilst we were drilling. Dinghy drill was held in the Derby Baths, where we had to swim around, inflate the dinghy and clamber in and paddle it around. It would have been somewhat different doing it for real in the North Sea on a cold dark winter's night, maybe with injured crew members aboard. I was a keen amateur boxer and when volunteers were called for I boxed for my Wing in the ring beneath the tower.

In March 1942 Hurst was posted to 103 Squadron at Elsham Wolds in Lincolnshire as a stop gap whilst awaiting gunnery training. New arrivals detrained at Barnetby Junction. These wayside stations were the first thing a new arrival saw and, if he survived, they were the last thing he saw as he departed.[1] He continues:

I got the feel of the atmosphere of an operational station and loved it. And I was fascinated and envious watching the Wimpys taking off on bombing raids. I had to earn my keep and I was detailed to work with the Adjustments Officer. This entailed collecting the kit of aircrew who had not returned from the previous nights, assorting it and returning personal items to their next of kin. There was just an admin flight lieutenant and me doing this and as there were heavy losses we were kept very busy. We had to vet personal letters and wallets and use our discretion as to what we returned to the next of kin, so as not to add to their grief. Seeing these nightly casualties did not put me off wanting to be aircrew.

On 22 June I was posted to the Aircrew Reception Centre at St John's Wood, billeted in what were private flats. We had our meals at Regents Park Zoo and did PT at Lords cricket ground. I found it interesting and enjoyable. All the NCOs were good types and seemed to respect us as future aircrew, but did have the attitude of 'rather you than me mate'. A week later I was posted to No. 2 Air Gunnery School at Dalcross several miles north of Inverness. The start of our training consisted of classroom work, learning about the Browning .303 machine gun that fired 1,150 rounds a minute. We had to be able to strip it down to its many parts and reassemble it in the dark. I spent hours learning about Bolton and Paul and Fraser Nash turrets and aircraft recognition was high on the agenda, as were fighter tactics. At last we were issued with flying kit and ready to fly in Boulton Paul Defiants for air-to-air firing. Airborne at last! The Defiant was a single engine aircraft, somewhat like a Hurricane with a mid upper gun turret housing two Brownings. The pilots were Polish and they were not content as 'bus driver pilots' flying trainees to and from the air firing range so they brought some excitement into their flying – mine too – when returning from the range, by lowering the undercarriage and attempting to spin the wheels on the wave tops, this was done in conjunction with another Defiant pilot that we would rendezvous with. We would fly at wave height and the pilots take it in turns to fly as near the wave tops as they could or dare. The whole time they would be laughing and chatting in Polish. Then when we reached the coast they would continue to fly at low level. And at the last second pull up and skim over the cliffs!

At the passing out parade Hurst and his fellow gunners were presented with an Air Gunner's Brevet and given their sergeant's stripes. Then they went on leave for seven days, having been told to report to RAF Harwell in Oxfordshire at the end of the leave. Harwell was where pilots, navigators, wireless operators, flight engineers, bomb aimers and air gunners crewed up.

There was nothing formal about this, it was up to individuals to crew with whoever they wished and no pressure was put on anyone. The choice each person made in joining a group of seven other newly trained air crew could be a major factor in relation to whether or not they survived operations. Yet one had no way of knowing how efficient others were at their job in an operational aircraft, or how they would cope with the many hazards of the job. It was an informal atmosphere and we were all chatting and drinking the coffee or tea provided. I eventually joined George Barker, a tall slim fair haired pilot, fresh from flying training school, who I felt I would be happy and confident to fly with. I certainly made the right choice. George assembled a complete crew that day and my name was changed! No longer was I to be John but Jimmy. The reason for this was because the pilot had already been joined by a navigator whose name was John and to have two Johns in a crew would cause confusion especially over the intercom. We flew many hours together. Sadly, two were shot down and killed when flying with other crews.

A couple of days later all the newly formed crews went by train to RAF Topcliffe in Yorkshire, which was a Heavy Bomber Conversion Unit. Here the crews flew together for the first time. Our aircraft were Halifax IIs. We did many circuits and bumps during the day and at night, so that our pilot could get used to flying the 22-ton aircraft. We flew cross countries – day and night – to various places in the UK so that the navigator could gain experience. On one flight we were lower than we should have been and found ourselves almost in the balloon barrage over Liverpool – we did have cable cutters on the wings but were not keen to test them! We did searchlight liaison flights over various cities, in which the search light crews were to pick us up and our task was to avoid them. They never did get us, unlike the German searchlights. Another activity was fighter liaison in which the Brownings in the turrets were replaced by camera guns. We would then be attacked by a Spitfire that also had a camera gun and we practiced our evasive action drill and the Spit pilot his attacking technique, all of which was recorded on 16mm film, which we were shown later. After about a month at Topcliffe crews were posted to various squadrons. Ours was one of several that went to 102 Squadron at Pocklington in 4 Group in the county of Yorkshire. A small farming community, it had three pubs, an old Anglican church and two rather ordinary hotels, which would serve you a very restricted wartime meal for five shillings. This was the top price allowed by the Government to any restaurant in wartime.

We were all keen to go on ops; little did we know that our crew was to be the only one to survive. The majority of my ops were over the Ruhr, hitting most of the main cities such as Essen, Munich, Cologne, Frankfurt, Manheim and Stuttgart. Then of course there was Berlin and three to Italy, as well as mine-laying around the Friesian Islands, so I had an exciting and eventful war and lived to tell the tale.[2] On one occasion we were on our way to Essen in very heavy flak, when there was a loud explosion in the aircraft and a rush of cold air and the Halifax bounced, around. The Skipper checked on the intercom that we were all OK and the flight engineer went to see what the damage was. A piece of shrapnel had detonated the photo flash, which exploded and destroyed its launching tube and blew a jagged hole in the starboard side of the fuselage just behind my turret. We measured it back at base and it was about

5 feet long by 3 feet high. This resulted in a gale blowing through the aircraft and made it very difficult for George to handle. Nevertheless we flew to the target – Krupps – and bombed it and set course for base. About half way home and still over enemy territory we lost an engine due to mechanical trouble. This reduced our airspeed even more and we lumbered home an hour later than the rest of the squadron. Being behind the main stream and flying low as we approached the English coast we attracted the attention of the Navy, who fired at us with pom-poms, despite us firing off the colours of the day. I could hear the pom-pom-pom of the guns above the sound of our three engines. When counting the hits on our plane, as we always did, we wondered how many were from enemy fire and how many from the Navy. It was surprising how much damage the Halibags could sustain and remain in the air. I would fly on 17 different Halifaxes during my tour (nine of which were shot down or crashed, some only a few days after they had got us home safely) and I wondered how many of them had the components that I had made.

In October 1942, Essen was the target for experimental daylight cloud cover raids by Wimpys, that other mainstay of RAF Bomber Command. Sergeant Bill Rae, a Wellington rear gunner in 142 Squadron at Waltham, Lincolnshire, recalls:

When on the morning of 22 October the operation was announced there was of course unusual excitement on the squadron. Wellingtons were once more being sent out on cloud cover sorties. When we got out to the dispersal point all the other crews were there along with the non-flying members waiting for us to taxi to the end of the runway. Probably the other crews were glad that we were to be the guinea pigs. Normally on a night trip the only people who would see us off would be the technical staff, i.e. the ground crew who serviced our aircraft. One aircraft from each of three 1 Group Squadrons was detailed and take off was at two hours intervals. Having experienced the efficiency of the German defences from the North Sea coast to the target and back we felt that we were being led like lambs to the slaughter. I know we all felt proud as one of the senior crews on the squadron to have been selected for this unique occasion, while at the same time wondering what was in store for us. 'Met' had promised cloud cover but it was very slight over the North Sea so I got a nice view of the Friesians for the first time. Cover did then thicken and we reached Essen to drop the cookie. Using our new *Gee* navigation the navigator was certain we were over Essen when we dropped our cookie bomb and I just cannot understand why we were not attacked. German radar could have tracked us for most of the trip, so why was there no reaction from flak or fighters? On part of the way back we were out of cloud cover but still no attack. I did see two aircraft but they were too far away to identify and did not seem to be interested in us. There was a marvellous reception awaiting us on our return and we were the heroes of the hour but having been keyed up to expect a life or death struggle, the whole thing was a bit of an anti-climax. It was a unique experience but not one we had any desire to repeat. Sending three Wellingtons to Essen may have had some effect but I doubt it.[3]

On 22/23 October 112 Lancasters of 5 Group and the Path Finders set out for the historic port city of Genoa to recommence the campaign against Hitler's *Axis* ally, timed to coincide with the opening of the Eighth Army offensive at El Alamein in Egypt. It was a perfectly clear moonlight night and the Path Finder marking was described as 'prompt and accurate'. This was the first heavy and really concentrated attack made on Genoa and 180 tons of bombs were dropped in the ideal conditions. Major Mullock MC, an anti-aircraft officer who had flown as special observer with Bomber Command on its raids on Lübeck, Rostock and the Renault works, went on the 1,500 mile round trip to Genoa. He watched the raid from the fall of the early bombs to the fading out of the resistance from the shore gunners and gave it as his opinion when he returned that the raid was the most concentrated made to that date. He saw only one stick of incendiaries miss the target area.

As we came down the other side of the Alps the valleys were shrouded in mist and we were afraid that Genoa might be obscured. But over the plain the weather cleared again. From thirty miles away I could see the light of the flares dropping over Genoa. As we got nearer it looked though the whole town was ablaze. There was a big oil fire, with flames spurting up into the air and clouds of black smoke on top of them – we circled round before making our bombing run and I counted thirteen big fires and innumerable little ones. Clouds of smoke were coming up. When we first came in there had been AA fire and a good deal of tracer. As the attack developed, the guns almost entirely stopped firing. I could see tracers coming from the sea; the ships in the bay were evidently firing.

It was the 46th operational flight for one DFC flight lieutenant and when he got back to base he enthusiastically announced that it was by far his most successful:

As we crossed the Channel on the way out we watched what was about the best sunset I have ever seen. We never saw land until we reached the Alps. The clouds above France were lit by the sunset glow. When the sun went down on our starboard side the full moon came up on our port and the clouds were still lit up. Up currents of air were driving the clouds away as we got to the Alps, mountain-tops soared above the clouds in the moonlight. The mountains were glistening white and almost purple in the shadows. We saw a wide glacier. As we passed the Alps the clouds were disappearing and the moon shone right down into the deep valleys. There was no mist or haze; we could see every river, lake and village.

We were early on Genoa, so we circled the Mediterranean. I think that we and one other bomber were the first to drop flares. They went down at the same time and showed up the harbour, lots of buildings and streets. At first I thought they were the shimmering white haze above Genoa but it was only the whiteness of the town, which has a great many white buildings. After the flares came our bombs. When I had seen them burst on the target we came down to just above the sea to watch the main attack. We never saw a bomb wasted. Oil-storage tanks blew up a sudden red glow and gave off great volumes of smoke. We did a slow climb over the sea and as we did so, we saw eight fires glowing in the target area. They were all well concentrated and five of them were very large indeed. We saw a searchlight trying to find us, though it was in the midst of a bunch of fires.[4]

No Lancasters were lost although one from 97 Squadron at Woodhall Spa crash-landed at North Luffenham after running low on fuel.

On 23 October more daylight cloud cover sorties were flown when 15 Wellingtons were sent to bomb Krefeld and 11 to Essen. Again there were no losses but Norman Child in 142 Squadron agrees with the same sentiments expressed by Bill Rae:

Our black-painted Wellingtons were quite unsuitable for this type of work and, to the crews, plain suicidal, but orders were orders. The order was to penetrate well into Germany, circle for a while and return. The Met report was two layers of cloud and 10/10ths at 6,000 feet with clear sky between the layers, 'these conditions extend-ing from the English coast to central Europe'. We were airborne at 12.40 hours. Climbed to 8,500 feet and flew in upper layer for approxi-mately one hour. When over the Dutch coast, the cloud started to thin and we ran into clear sky. Immediately, we dived for the thick lower layer and continued on course at 6,500 feet. It was noticeable that the cloud was beginning to thin and after three-quarters of an hour we suddenly ran out into clear sunshine, many miles short of the German border. We steep-turned back into cloud and headed home at full throttle, volubly cursing all the 'duff gen merchants' and what they could do with their forecasts. We came through unscathed amid light flak at the Dutch coast and flew low in thick cloud to avoid fighters. Duration of flight: 3 hours 30 minutes.

Only a few Wellington crews came through their operations unscathed and those who would complete their tour could be numbered on the fingers of one hand in most squadrons, as Sergeant pilot 'Tim' Timperley, who amazingly went on to complete 49 ops with 12 and later 166 Squadron, recalls:

We arrived at Waltham, just outside Grimsby on a cold, wet and dreary November afternoon. It was almost dark and we were shown into a crew room before we were told what time to report next day. We were hanging around waiting, so I started looking through the Authorisation Book, which is the authority to fly an aircraft for any purpose and is signed by the Flight Commander. I noticed that one could trace the names of pilots and their crews for maybe five or ten operations. Then sooner or later, it seemed that everybody failed to return. You just couldn't find a crew that went right through the book. Combined with the weather and the environment, it was one of the few times I had a real sense of gloom. I believed that I increased my chances of survival by sticking to the disciplined approach, doing the job properly, staying in the stream and if one encountered a fighter, sticking to the rules of combat. In training, in a Wellington, we were taught to accept instructions from the rear gunner, in the case of a beam or quarter attack. We had to turn into the fighter just fractionally before we thought he was going to open fire and because the pilot couldn't see behind him, he had to rely entirely on what he was being told. I only encountered three enemy fighters in the nearly fifty ops that I did and only two of those fired at me before I lost them. Of course, sheer luck played a large part in it. If an ack-ack shell had your name on it, then you were lost anyway. I always felt that if I stuck to the parts over which I had control, then that was the most I could do and I just kept my fingers crossed over the rest.[5]

The bombers returned to Genoa on the night of 23/24 October but conditions and the outcome could not have been more different. In all, 122 Halifaxes, Stirlings and Wellingtons[6] of 3 and 4 Groups and the Path Finders set out on what should have been a three-pronged attack on Genoa. The crews had to use oxygen all the way over the Alpine range and the navigators sent the aircraft low down. As one of them put it: 'We map read our way over the foothills to the Gulf of Genoa.' That night the *Regia Aeronautica* sent up night fighters to challenge the RAF bombers. Over the Lombardy plain shots were exchanged, but the Italian night fighter pilots had little heart for the work of close engaging the bombers. A squadron leader in a Halifax was surprised when a Cr.42 biplane suddenly swooped on him but the British gunners broke up two attempts to get in a vital burst on the part of the Italian pilot and then suddenly the biplane was falling away. A Stirling likewise met one of the biplanes and after dealing with it effectively encountered a Breda 88 and after that a Macchi 200. The bomber was hit in the tail-plane and fuselage and the rear turret's hydraulic apparatus was damaged. The gunner had to swivel himself round by hand, but he beat off the planes and saw his tracers biting into the Macchi. One of the Stirlings crashed into a mountain top over the Alps on the outward leg and exploded. The Alps peak at 16,000 feet and there was no chance of getting a loaded Stirling up to this height, so it was a case of picking their way around the mountain tops at about 12,000 feet. Two Halifaxes also failed to return from the raid. The target was almost completely cloud covered and it was later determined that Savona, 30 miles along the coast from Genoa, had been bombed.

Jimmy Morris on 218 Squadron recalled:

I guess that the chaps flying Lancs would regard such an op as a milk run, but it was a different matter in a Stirling as height was not one of its good points. We set off over the Channel and then France at a pretty low level. About half-way across France, I noticed that we were using a lot more fuel on the two starboard engines. I checked the controls and found that the mixture control was not working. There were just two mixture control levers, one for the two port engines and the other for the two starboard engines. Because the control for the two starboard engines had gone u/s the mixture had gone into full rich, which meant we were using more fuel than we should and we still had to climb over the Alps, down Italy, across the Po Valley and back again. We needed every drop of fuel we had. I told the Skipper about the problem which was caused by a break in the hydraulic pipeline to the Exactor unit. The only thing we could do was to carry on. So we started the climb over the Alps, levelling out at about 12,500 feet. We could still see the peaks of the Alps above us and as it was night, they just loomed up in front of us so we had to make our way between them. I think they topped about 16,000 feet. We were about half way across when the WOp, Sandy, said he could hear somebody sending out an SOS and he thought he could recognize the sender as being from 218 Squadron. A few minutes went by before there was an explosion in front of us and we saw the Alps spread out in full view as a kite hit one of the peaks. Fuel, bombs, the lot just rolled down the mountain and it was impossible for the crew to survive. I was really shaking. We carried on to the target and on to the Po Valley, keeping as low as we could to save fuel. At one stage I was looking out to starboard and saw an aircraft flying about 200 yards away, so I warned the gunners. It was a pre-war Italian fighter biplane. I think its pilot must have said to himself, 'they have eight guns against my two' so home he went.

We got to the target, dropped our load and set course for home, over the Alps again, flattening out as low as we could over France, to save fuel which was getting very low at this stage. Crossing the Channel, the engines were coughing and snorting. I drained the tanks one into the other. I talked to the Skipper and it was decided to make for Manston as it was just over the Channel. We landed OK and I reckoned we had about 100 gallons of fuel left, this being spread over the 14 tanks. It was another hour back to base so I guess we did the right thing to land at Manston. The staff at Manston must have wondered what had hit them that night. With daylight you could see about 30 four-engined aircraft scattered all over the place. We flew back to base the next day and I was told that my good mate Fred Hall and his crew were missing. You always hope they will turn up, but sadly they never did. I thought that the kite we saw explode over the Alps was Fred's but I learned many years later that they were shot down over the Channel about the same time as we were crossing it.' [*U-Uncle* flown by Pilot Officer Reginald Arthur Studd AFC crashed into the sea off Dieppe. There were no survivors from the eight-man crew].

Fuel shortages and engine failures caused some crews returning to England to put down where they could. A Stirling I had seven petrol tanks, 2,304 gallons in all, and on a long trip like this one, crews could not afford to waste any. *B-Beer*, a returning 149 Squadron Stirling piloted by Sergeant Adolph Antonio Siwak RCAF crashed out of fuel in Rye Street, Cliffe, five miles north of Rochester in Kent with the loss of all eight crew. A 214 Squadron Stirling also ran out of petrol and crashed at Chedburgh while trying to land. No serious injuries were reported. Two Halifaxes failed to return to Linton-on-Ouse. A Halifax II on 78 Squadron flown by Flight Lieutenant Harold Rhoden DFC was shot down over France with the loss of all eight crew. *C-Charlie*, a 76 Squadron Halifax flown by Flight Sergeant W C Richardson, crashed and caught fire trying to land on an unlit runway at Benson. The rear gunner was trapped for a while but he and the other crew members suffered no serious injuries. Two Halifax IIs on 102 Squadron failed to return to Pocklington when, during landing at Holme-on-Spalding Moor, 20 miles north-west of Hull, they were involved in a collision. *D-Dog*, Flight Sergeant J L Berry's aircraft, ran into *O-Orange* piloted by Wing Commander Sydney Bruce Bintley DSO DFC, whose aircraft had burst a tyre and was unable to clear the runway. Bintley and one of his crew were killed and two men were injured. Group Captain E J Corbally and three others were unhurt.

The next day, 24 October, 88 Lancasters of 5 Group were sent to attack Milan in daylight. This time a fighter escort of Spitfires accompanied the force across the Channel to the Normandy coast. The aircraft flew on independently over France close together and very low, hedgehopping in the manner in which the Augsburg and Le Creusot raids had been made possible and using partial cloud cover, to a rendezvous at Lake Annecy. The Alps were then crossed and at four minutes after 5 o'clock in the afternoon, the first Lancaster nosed down through the heavy clouds and unloaded. They came in rapidly, pinpointing their targets and wheeling round. Mixed in the general delivery of HEs and incendiaries were a goodly proportion of 4,000-pounders. Some of the Lancasters went down to fifty feet to bomb their targets. The raiders caught Milan by surprise and the bombing was accurate, with 135 tons of bombs being dropped in 18 minutes. Only when they were well on their homeward run did darkness come down and afford them any protection. Three Lancasters that failed to return were all presumed lost over the sea. A fourth Lancaster, piloted by Flight Lieutenant Dorian Dick Bonnett DFC on 49 Squadron at Scampton, crashed on approach to Ford airfield in Sussex. Bonnett and five crew members died and two men were injured; one of whom died six days later.

When the crews landed it was to hear news that at the very moment they had touched down more bombs were scheduled to be dropped on the targets they had left. Seventy-one Stirlings, Halifaxes and Wellingtons of 1 and 3 Groups and the Path Finders[7] were continuing the Milan blitz by night. A 218 Squadron Stirling developed an uncontrollable engine after taking off from Downham Market and crashed SSW of Ipswich with the loss of seven of the crew.

Storms *en route* dispersed the bombers and some of the aircraft flew over Switzerland, as Norman Child recalls:

We climbed to 9,000 feet over France. Clear starlit night. Fighter reported on starboard bow cruising at same speed so we throttle back and descend to 15,000 feet to clear Swiss Alps – extremely cold. Good pinpoint on Lake Geneva to port and mountain range looming ahead. Mont Blanc identified quite easily in clear night air and set new course for target. Box barrage over target, which quietens down when bombing commences (unlike German targets) and we bomb through comparatively little opposition. Many fires started and large explosions seen. Bombed at 12,000 feet; turned on course for base and climbed back to 15,500 feet. At course change at Haute Savoie we noticed the port engine was leaking oil badly and beginning to overheat. The port engine was throttled right back and we started a very slow descent across France to keep up a reasonable airspeed. Everyone was keyed up and anxious. We reached the French coast at 3,000 feet and pinpointed St-Valéry. Everything was quiet and we stole out to sea untouched. The port engine temperature was now so high we decided on a forced landing at West Malling. They cleared us for emergency landing and when we taxied to a halt the port engine died. The fitters found a shell splinter had damaged an oil-feed line and the engine was starved of oil. Across France we had the choice of feathering the prop and probably a forced landing there, or pressing on and risking the engine catching fire. We made the right choice – just. Duration of flight: 7 hours 50 minutes.

Bill Anderson in the Path Finder Force recalls:

I was lucky enough to have been invited to take a ride on this trip over the Alps. The mountains were very lovely. We flew past Mont Blanc and the waning moon shone on the snow-covered slopes which outlined the cliffs of sheer black rock. It seemed awful to be passing by such beauty with such murderous intent and a Lancaster flying below looked wicked against the white snow. The sense of guilt was not appeased by the target, for the defences were hopeless. Searchlights waved frantically about like the legs of a vast over-turned and helpless beetle and guns were firing wildly and to no purpose. Precisely on the minute which had been chosen fifteen hours before in England, the middle of the target was remorselessly lit up by the flares and then pounded with bombs. The flares that Pathfinders carried in those early days did sometimes cause fires in aircraft if they got hit. But that was the least of their drawbacks. Imagine yourself setting out with a string of flares that you are determined to drop on the exact aiming point. You arrive over the place where you think the target must lie and everything below is pitch-black. Then the snag appears. You mustn't drop your flares unless you have seen the aiming point. And you won't see the aiming point until you've dropped your flares! This problem was solved by attacking in two waves. First of all, special aircraft would drop long sticks of flares over the target area to light up that part of the Third Reich and shine on the lakes and rivers round about. This would enable a second wave to come in and guided by the light from those first long sticks of flares, to drop their own candles across the aiming point itself. This system worked perfectly on Milan but this type of attack was not so successful against the industrial cities of Germany. For they were often covered in smoke and haze so that the flares did little more than create a glare through which the crews would peer, vainly trying to see the aiming point.[8]

Only 39 aircraft claimed to have bombed Milan. Four Wellingtons and two Halifaxes on 103 Squadron failed to return. *U-Uncle* crashed in France with the loss of all the crew. *D-Donald*, flown by Squadron Leader Sidney Horace Fox DFM, was brought down by bombs dropped from another aircraft over the target. A week earlier he had told crews that the squadron would soon convert to Lancasters. Narrow eyed and panther-footed, he had commanded his crews' immediate respect: DFMs were not given for nothing and not many sergeants became squadron leaders.

'Dizzy' Spiller had not made squadron leader but he was now a warrant officer with the DFM. Famed for his casualness and for the bare minimum of navigational instruments he carried with him on ops, he was nevertheless one of the best navigators on the squadron.[9] Their pilot dead, Flight Sergeant 'Lofty' Maddocks and 'Dizzy' Spiller were the only crew members able to parachute from the aircraft. Spiller evaded capture and he arrived back in England many months later, distressed to find that there were only two crews left on the squadron who knew him. Maddocks was taken into captivity.

Bomber Command returned to Italy on the night of 6/7 November. It was a dark night and a large number of flares had to be dropped by the Path Finders to light up the port of Genoa for the 72 Lancasters of 5 Group. Flak was heavier than before, especially from the dock area, and most bombs fell in residential areas. Flying Officer 'Paddy' Rowling on 50 Squadron wrote: 'The Alps in the moonlight were really wonderful but gave one the impression of great groping fingers reaching up to drag you down amongst them. They are the most precipitous mountains I have ever seen with sheer drops of a couple of thousand feet or more in some cases; some of them even seemed to be leaning out.'

Three Lancasters of 83 Squadron failed to return to Wyton. One was believed to have crashed in the Mediterranean and none of the crew survived. A second was lost without trace and a third, which attempted to land at Mildenhall on the return, overshot the runway. While going around again the Lancaster stalled off a steep turn and crashed near the airfield, bursting into flames on impact and killing all seven crew.[10]

The next night, when some aircraft on 50 Squadron were among the force of 175 Lancasters, Halifaxes and Stirlings and a few Wellingtons that were briefed to bomb Genoa again, 'Paddy' Rowling and the rest of the crew were not down to fly and he wrote that he was 'very envious of the boys ... It should be a wizard trip.' Genoa received its heaviest raid of the war. When the port outer engine on a 10 Squadron Halifax failed not long after take-off from Melbourne, the pilot turned for home, jettisoning the bomb load into the sea off Skegness. Flight Sergeant L J Hampton reached base but on landing the undercarriage collapsed and the Halifax caught fire. No serious injuries were reported. Weather conditions over the target were very favourable for bombing but all the way to the Alps rain and cloud brought visibility to only a few feet, while icing and sudden electrical storms gave the pilots some cause for anxiety.

'It was as if we were flying in the slipstream of another aircraft,' was the description given by a pilot later. One front gunner reported that as his plane penetrated cloud, ice came crackling through the turret ventilators in handfuls, while up-currents threw the bombers about. The night was bitterly cold and a thick hoar frost coated the pilots' windscreens, each watching the luminous altimeter needle as they climbed above the clouds. Over the Alps snow was falling steadily. Ice flew in large chunks from the whirling airscrews, rattling against the windscreen like hail.'

One of the RAF's Public Relations officers flew in a Stirling that night. He kept a very detailed log of the raid, noting times and his own personal reactions to the conditions of the flight. At 19.30 hours he recorded:

St. Elmo's fire round the propellers. Now again in the astrodome I can see the circles of flame round the propeller and the front-gunner reports blue darts – on his gun-barrel and flame trickling around the metal of the turret. This lasted about ten minutes. We are climbing for the Alps and cat flight engineer switches on oxygen. The smell and feel of the mask are strange at first and rather like an anæsthetist's apparatus.

At 20.14 hours the RAF guest was becoming a little more accustomed to the journey and the cloud-top scenery. He jotted down:

I am lying flat over the bottom blister. Though there is no moon, the Alps come into view – surfaces of a grade of purplish-white peppered with black. The captain suggests that if I come forward again I shall soon see Genoa. I take several deep breaths of oxygen and then plug out to struggle forward. Though the Stirling is a huge aircraft, it seems that nothing could be big enough for me, a novice, to move gracefully in. As I climb towards the nose my dangling intercom winds itself around everything, from the automatic pilot to the flight engineer's neck. Just visible in his macabre red light, the captain looks up, grins and shouts, 'How are you feeling?'

'Fine,' I say.

'Liar,' says he. 'Don't worry. It's always the same on your first trip.' While talking, I have to stop half-way and plug in for oxygen and intercom. 'If we are worried,' says the captain, 'Think what those poor silly Eyeties must be feeling. Look over there. That's Genoa. No future being in Genoa on a night like this.'

That particular Stirling was the leader of the raid. It was the first plane to approach the target and the searchlights wavered as they came on and the ack-ack fire was desultory and uncertain, though some red fire-balls were thrown up with the light flak.

At 21.05 hours the RAF officer put this down:

Now it becomes frightening. There appears to be no way through the wall of searchlights and flak. The front gunner goes down into the bomb-aimer's hatch and the captain starts violent jinking. From the astrodome I can see the glow of our exhausts and the great hump of the outer engines rising up and descending again against the vivid light of the flashes and the beams. As we wind our way along the giant humps on either side continue to rise.

Fifteen minutes later: 'Bomb-doors open!' comes through the intercom and then, 'OK, bomb-doors open.' I lift my oxygen mask and bite into a small English Newton apple. For some reason it gives me great pleasure to munch an English apple over Genoa. As we get over the searchlights I am less scared. Down below, the gun flashes reveal the blocks of building. Searchlights wander across our propellers, edge and wingtips, flick the tail and fantastic, as it seems, never catch us. But the flak comes nearer and the red fire-balls closer as the captain levels out for the bombing run and calls to the bomb aimer, 'OK. Remember the precise target.' We are dear steady for a mighty long twenty seconds before the bomb aimer reports, 'Bombs gone.'

The job then is to get home. At 01.36 hours the next morning the RAF visiting officer sees the lights of the flare path spring up on the runway of the home base and his Stirling, which led the raid (*V-Victor*) gets the instruction from below, 'You can land now.'[11]

A Lancaster on 207 Squadron at Langar and a 76 Squadron Halifax, which was abandoned by the crew near Chaumont, were missing over France. All members of the Lancaster crew died; the crew of the Halifax were taken into captivity. One man died later. A Wellington on 156 Squadron at Warboys flown by Pilot Officer David Chell, who as a flight sergeant had flown the Thousand Bomber Raid as captain of a 22 OTU crew, was lost without trace. Two other Halifaxes on 78 Squadron failed to return. Flight Lieutenant 'Paddy' Dowse DFC lost an engine while outbound but the crew decided to continue to the target and the bomber was then ditched off Valencia, Spain. After being rescued the crew were interned but all were later released and they returned home via Gibraltar in February 1943. The other 78 Squadron Halifax, out of fuel, ditched in the North Sea 65 miles off Newcastle. *M-Mother*, a 158 Squadron Halifax, which ran low on fuel while returning to Rufforth was ditched in the River Humber. Three crew were killed and two were injured. A Halifax on 10 Squadron crashed on landing back at Melbourne. Returning to Waddington two Lancasters on 9 Squadron were destroyed and all fourteen crew members killed when one collided with the other in the circuit.

Stirling *N-Nan* on 218 Squadron flown by Sergeant L T Richards, whose Canadian rear gunner had not fired at their attacker on Kiel on 13/14 October, were severely tested once again. After take-off from Downham Market Pilot Officer H A Winfield, the navigator, the only officer on the crew, set a course for Dungeness, St-Julien and on to Genoa but he had left his maps at Downham. South of Amiens slight icing occurred and Richards, remembering very severe icing conditions in clear air over the Alps on a previous operation, which actually caused a stall, reduced height from 8,000 feet to 4,500 feet. This meant two rich-mixture climbs were necessary to clear the Alpine range. Over the Alps whilst on No. 5 tank the starboard outer engine cut out due to lack of petrol, although the gauge was registering 30 gallons. Changing to No. 6 tank the engine picked up again. At 11,000 feet the conscientious bomb aimer insisted upon a third run over the target to drop his five 1,000lb bombs accurately across the aiming point. Crossing the French coast on return the flight engineer turned on the wing interbalance cocks. Richards, who was on his 8th op, attempted to land at Oakington but was refused permission and was diverted to Bourn. In the circuit and in the pitch black of the night, Richards put out one-third flap at 1,150 feet and prepared to land. Suddenly and simultaneously all four engines stopped. Richards said, 'Sorry boys, bail out!' The bomb aimer politely questioned this action considering the height was below 1,500 feet and the Stirling was on an extremely steep glide path. N-Nan crashed into one of Chivers' fields at Red Brick Farm near Bourne, Cambridgeshire. The well known fighter pilot, Sailor Malan, had once crashed in the same field. Romulus Helmer, the Canadian rear gunner, and Richards were the only members of the crew to suffer injury. Richards was thrown 50 yards clear of the crash and suffered a severe headache and a few days' memory loss.[12]

Genoa was bombed again on the night of 13/14 November by 67 Lancasters of 5 Group and nine Stirlings of the Path Finder Force. Among the individual targets attacked was the Ansaldo works, to the west of the port, which constructed naval armaments and marine engines. There was a bright half-moon and visibility was good. Objects below were picked out with comparative ease and one Halifax observer who had been told to look out for a statue of Mussolini in a new square had little difficulty in pin-pointing it. The pilot of another Halifax was fascinated by a fire, which he saw start at the end of a row of warehouses on a small peninsula extending into the inner harbour. The fire ran like liquid along the entire row. He also saw a stick of bombs straddle the western docks, where a large liner was berthed. Night fighters were met going out and on the way back, and over France one German machine was sent down in flames. The entire British bombing force, for the second time, returned without losing a bomber during a raid on Genoa. Some days later a message was received in England from a man who had stood on a hill above Genoa and viewed the stricken port:

The burned and destroyed areas in Genoa are so large and many that it is useless to attempt to give details of the damage. Seen from a height, one has the impression that half of the town has been destroyed and in the port almost everything seems to be destroyed, burned, or damaged. Among the few exceptions in the port area are the silos where the grain for Switzerland was stored. Lack of small craft in the port, as a result of a large number having been sunk or severely damaged, is causing difficulties to the port authorities.

On the night of 18/19 November, 77 aircraft were set to attack Turin. At Bourn, seven miles west of Cambridge, a XV Squadron Stirling crashed on take-off when the pilot lost control in conditions of a very severe cross wind. The crash totally blocked the runway and prevented the four waiting Stirlings from taking part in the operation.

The pilot of one of the Halifaxes said:

It was even brighter than Genoa. All the streets and bridges across the river stood out clearly. There were thick clouds all the way across France and right up to the Alps but on the Italian side the weather was perfectly clear. We stayed around the city for about half an hour and I saw fires increasing very rapidly. There was plenty of flak at the beginning of the attack but it all died down towards the end. I did not see a single searchlight.

When the RAF bombers left, smoke from the blitzed Fiat Works and other industrial targets, was drifting in a wide stream of mourning north-wards across the town.

Wing Commander Basil Vernon Robinson DSO DFC, the 35 Squadron CO, was captain of a Halifax, which unloaded flares and bombs over Turin. Shortly afterwards, however, fire began spurting from the bomb bay. An extremely powerful flare, one designed to light up practically an entire city, had got hitched and ignited. The fire swept across the Halifax in gusts, spread to the port wing and it was not long before the whole aircraft was filled with smoke and noxious fumes. There was an explosion, which staggered the aircraft, and the bomb doors were quickly opened but the blazing flare did not drop through. The fire continued to take stronger hold on the aircraft, which was now racing back towards the Alps, barely a thousand feet above ground level. Robinson tried every-thing he knew to retain height but slowly the aircraft sank. It looked as though nothing could prevent the Halifax smashing into the granite sides of the Alpine peaks. There was only one thing to do and the captain did it. He ordered the crew to bail out. They did so. He saw the last man go down and was preparing to follow, when inexplicably the fire went out. One moment flames were shooting up from the bomb bay, the next they were not. Robinson thought fast and took a chance. He stayed with his crewless aircraft. He got it over the white-tipped peaks and continued the flight towards home knowing that he had no flight engineer if any-thing went wrong mechanically, no navigator to plot a course for him past the heavily defended areas of France and no gunners to fight off any night fighters. He crash-landed at Colerne at 01.50 hours.[13]

Pilot Officer John A Martin DFC was a Stirling flight engineer who flew on ops on Turin. He recalls:

One night Mac McDonald, the Skipper said he could see the TIs (Target Indicators) going down 'now'. We were over Milan and not Turin! We went around again. We were the only aircraft there at this time; the others had been and gone. We got an aiming point and dropped our bomb load and returned to base. Another night we were briefed that we were going to have to climb over the Alps again and do a low level bombing on the Fiat Works and then climb back up to get back over the Alps again. When we were on our way over I admired Mount Blanc above our level of flight. It was a beautiful night; there was snow on the mountain. The journey time for raids on Turin was about 8 or 9 hours which was very close to the limit for a Stirling. Part of my duties was the balancing the seven fuel tanks in each main plane. Your main tanks were 2 and 4. They held 250 and 300 gallons of fuel. On the trailing edge you also had fuel tanks. If you were caught by a fighter you couldn't use the trailing edge tanks as the fuel wouldn't run from them to the engines so you had to change to tanks 2 and 4 during combat. During the flight over the target you also went onto tanks 2 and 4 so that you could get out of the target area as quickly as possible. This meant that you were juggling all the time with the tanks so that you finished with fuel in tanks 2 and 4. During the flight I kept a watch on the oil pressures and temperatures and advised the pilot what engine settings to use so that we could save as much fuel as possible.

Bomber Command went back to Turin on the night of 20/21 November with a force of 232 aircraft – the largest raid to Italy during this period. Italian targets were not considered worthy of a bomb symbol painted on the nose of a bomber; being represented instead by ice-cream cones.

Ray Corbett, an 18-year-old ex-Halton apprentice, was the Halifax flight engineer on Sergeant Roger Coverly's crew on 78 Squadron at Linton-on-Ouse:

The Squadron was equipped with the early edition Mark II Series I Halifax, nose and upper turrets and all and powered by four Merlins. DT574 was quite new and about to double its previous flying time on this trip. We knew the way having just been to the same city on the 18th. However, although long in duration, these trips were considered to be reasonably safe, particularly when the target defences would start to collapse as soon as the first stick of numbs dropped. Occasionally someone would see a night fighter aerobatting in the vicinity and it was rumoured that one enterprising crew had actually chased one trying to get in a shot! On this particular night the weather was beautiful under a brilliant moon but it was extremely cold at altitude. It was always interesting and for that matter encouraging, to experience the reaction of the Swiss defences as we pinpointed a corner of Lake Geneva on the way out. Their searchlights would spring up and their AA guns would start firing but there would never be any bursts anywhere near us. In fact the searchlights would wave backwards and forwards along our track as if they were pointing the way to the target! Surely the Swiss were maintaining their neutral status, or were they? Certainly it was encouraging, especially when several members of Bomber Command aircrew had made unscheduled visits to Switzerland and had experienced the wonderful hospitality of the Swiss!

German night fighters were posted far to the south inland from the French coast to attack a force of Bomber Command invaders should it return. At Holme-on-Spalding Moor 101 Squadron was flying Lancasters for the first time since converting from the Wellington and they had a number of encounters with German pilots. Their wing commander's aircraft was attacked three times. First, Wing Commander D A Reddick had to fight it out with a Ju 88 on the French side of the Alps. By diving, the wing commander got below the Junkers and the mid-upper gunner got in a burst that sent the German airman winging away. It was shortly afterwards that a twin-engined Me 110 rushed in, with cannon blazing. The Lancaster replied, with fire too hot for the Messerschmitt pilot. He also disappeared. Later, on the way back, the Lancaster was approached by another Ju 88 but by rolling off into a patch of cloud an encounter was avoided.

Wing Commander George Holden DFC, commanding a Halifax squadron, that night was over Turin when the first flares sailed down. He had the task of remaining over the target area to make a special report. He stooged around for more than half an hour by which time a good many fires were blazing furiously and there was one enormous fire pouring from a large warehouse. A column of smoke rose to 8,000 feet and one hovering Lancaster, seeking its own special target, flew right through the black cloud.[14]

This was another successful attack. Three aircraft – a Halifax, a Wellington and a Stirling – were lost. Squadron Leader John Searby, a Lancaster flight commander on 106 Squadron at Syerston, six miles North-West of Newark, Nottinghamshire, witnessed the demise of one of these aircraft as they re-crossed the Alps.

On the way home I overtook a Stirling [sic] flying a little below me. This was in the region of the highest peaks ... Apparently unharmed he was making steady progress and, no doubt looking forward to his bacon and eggs. As I came level he commenced a slow turn, dropping the nose until he was below the mountain top. In the bright moon light I saw him make a feeble alteration of course which brought him clear of the shining peak but the nose was dropping even further until he plunged into a deep ravine to strike with a burst of flame followed immediately by a large explosion, which lit up the icy walls – an enormous torrent of red light and then nothing more. It was a remarkable occurrence because no parachutes were seen – no one attempted to get out though there was time. I wondered: oxygen starvation? Perhaps flak damage? Possibly ... Amid the heat and flurry of a big raid one saw bombers destroyed from time to time but this was almost outside one's consciousness – one willed it to be so because there wasn't time for reflection and every ounce of effort and concentration went into the task of getting the bombs on target. This was different; in a peaceful setting, his job done, he went without fuss or bother to certain death.[15]

Although Searby remembers it as a Stirling, the only one lost on the raid was a XV Squadron aircraft flown by Squadron Leader M Wyatt DFC who lost an engine near the Alps while outbound. The crew carried on and bombed the target and then set course for Spain where the Stirling was force-landed at Playa de Aro (Gerona). Following a brief period of internment the crew was taken to Gibraltar, from where they returned home by ship, arriving on 26 January 1943.[16] Two other Stirlings on 214 Squadron returning to Chedburgh were also lost when one crashed at its home base and the other, low on fuel, was abandoned over Suffolk. A Wellington was abandoned east of Paris due to engine failure. Another Wimpy overshot and crashed while trying to make an emergency landing at Manston in Kent, killing four of the crew and injuring a fifth. It would appear that the aircraft Searby saw crash was a Halifax on 76 Squadron flown by Sergeant Bruce Alexander Wisely RNZAF, which crashed at Bardonecchia close to the frontier with France, about 75 kilometres west of Turin.[17] All the crew perished.

Sergeant Roger Coverly's crew on 78 Squadron had an eventful return, as Ray Corbett recalls:

The old 'Halibag' was under climbing power throughout most of the outbound leg in order to clear the Alps, which were a wonderful sight close up in the moonlight but not too close! Our troubles commenced during the let down about two thirds of the way back over France when the starboard outer started to overheat after losing its oil pressure. This was not too bad; we were pointing in the right direction and did not have too far to go. We easily feathered it but when the port inner exhibited the same symptoms we feathered that as well and anyone who has flown Halifaxes knows that on two engines it's time to get serious. Our Welsh WOp, who had been unaware of recent events, pulled back the curtain over his little porthole and looked out. Suddenly the silence on the intercom was broken by his inimitable accent announcing 'Roger, the port inner's stopped!'

All was not over. As our rate of descent increased the throttle altitude control on the port outer failed and the engine began to surge up and down in power. There was no question about feathering this engine if we wished to reach the UK without taking a bath in the Channel. We were not completely sure of our position except that we did know that those waves that we could easily see were part of the Channel. We eventually staggered across the south coast at a very low height and coming down.

Normally I do not believe in miracles but one occurred at that moment. There to our left were the lights of a runway approach funnel with the runway lights beyond. There we were, beautifully aligned with the runway at the right height! My function at this stage was to rapid fire the Very pistol in case there were other aircraft in the circuit. Later we found out that there were 16 Polish Wellingtons returning from a trip to St-Nazaire. We did not see one of them!

We contacted the runway with some emphasis so that several incendiaries that had frozen in their containers now broke loose, burst open the wing bomb bay doors and spread their light in a neat line down the centre of the runway. We did not know what airfield this was so Roger swung off on to the grass area off the runway, shut down and we all jumped down on to *Terra Firma* in a somewhat hysterical state. But all was not over. After a while as calm started to return, I remembered my duties and climbed back in to bleed off the hydraulic systems by opening the bomb doors. As I did so there were shouts and flashes of light from outside and I departed quickly. Once outside I found the rest of the crew joyously kicking burning incendiaries away from the area underneath, apparently previously frozen in their containers but which had not broken like the others now illuminating the runway for our Polish friends! Some transport arrived and we then found out that we had arrived at RAF Tangmere. The aeroplane obviously was not going to be going anywhere soon so we were given railway vouchers and sent on our way back to Linton. As it happened, London was on our route and somehow we just had to make a night stop; suffice it to say that a particularly good time was had by all![18]

Bomber Command returned to the bombing of a German target 48 hours later, on Sunday 22 November, a clear, crisp day; cold but invigorating.

The destination for 222 aircraft was Stuttgart but the route was planned to make the Germans think that Italy again was the target and the flight would be down through France, until south of Paris the force would swing east and hopefully, 'catch Jerry with his pants down'. It was however the full moon period and normally fighter attacks higher up in full moonlight could be expected. At Wyton, where 83 Squadron had moved to in August, the CO, Wing Commander M D Crichton-Biggie laughed and said to Bill Williams' crew, whose faithful L-London had been taken by a new crew on the 6/7 November raid on Genoa and was one of three squadron aircraft that did not return: 'Guess this just isn't your night!' They remembered his words for a long time. They missed R5673, 'as one does a household pet'. Williams, who had recently been commissioned and awarded the DFM, was taking Lancaster ED311 K-King. As usual the cockney Skipper wore his famous five feet long, multi-coloured scarf around his neck. Equally, John Bushby had put on his left flying-boot before the right and he and Lambert the mid-upper gunner bid each other a solemn good-night before they climbed into their turrets before take-off. For a long time Bushby had thought that it was his own superstition until once Lambert revealed in a chance remark that he attached to it the same importance and for the same reason.

A thin layer of cloud and some ground haze concealed the target area and the Path Finders were unable to identify Stuttgart city centre.

Bill Anderson recalls:

This was the raid where the reflection of the haze was particularly dazzling. I was flying with a most amazing crew. They were famous as pretty determined 'dicers', a dicer being one who dices (with death). And that night they certainly lived up to their reputation. This was not a true Pathfinder crew and the Skipper [Squadron Leader Brian Grimston DFC] was not a typical Pathfinder pilot. The Honourable 'Grimmy', captain of a Wellington; so tall that you felt he ought to wear oxygen when he was standing up, was more the sort we needed. Before each trip he would calculate the exact angle of the moon for each part of the journey and then if he saw it reflected on a lake, he would work out how far away the lake was and in what direction! (I hoped to be allowed to fly with him as a regular crew member but it was banned, so I found him another navigator, 'Alfred'. Over Kiel one night a direct hit blew them up so that they were all killed.[19] I felt pretty bad about this).

We took off – in spite of the fact that one engine wasn't functioning quite properly and set course, only to find out after a few minutes that we were heading in the opposite direction! This sounds an impossible mistake to make but it could happen, for the compass pointer was double-ended! Realizing we might be late, we turned and batted off to the target, cutting all the corners; luckily, we were not molested and arrived on time but unfortunately we could not see the ground. Long strings of flares were shining down on to the haze below and the glare was dazzling. The Skipper, only too grateful for the chance to have some fun, promptly dived below the flares. It was rather beautiful with the lights of tracer shells and the houses standing out like toys with their very red roofs, white sides and olive green grass. As we pulled out, we passed over a little train industriously puffing away to the north as if quite unconcerned with the whole fantastic business of war. We came back low and we got lost. Mist covered the ground and we could see nothing. However, we managed at last to pick up our position just in time to avoid flying over some pretty lively enemy defences. It wasn't a stroke of genius or even a snappy piece of work with the stars. Just that we happened to see something sticking up out of the mist below, the one landmark in all Europe that we could not have mistaken, the top of the dear old Eiffel Tower.[20]

At Stuttgart heavy bombing developed to the south-west and south, and the outlying residential districts of Vaihingen, Rohr, Mohringen and Pliengen, all about five miles from the centre, were hit. Two of the bombers attacked the centre of Stuttgart at low level and dropped bombs on to the main railway station, which caused severe damage to the wooden platforms and some trains in the station.[21] Ten aircraft, five of them Lancasters, failed to return. Sergeant Jack Glyn Ashton on 57 Squadron was shot down over Belgium by *Oberleutnant* Ludwig 'Luk' Meister of I./NJG4 with the loss of all the crew. All three Wellingtons that were lost over France were also shot down by night fighters of NJG4; by *Hauptmann* Wilhelm Herget, *Hauptmann* Heinrich Wohlers and *Oberleutnant* Hans-Karl Kamp. Herget, nicknamed *Der Kleine* or 'the small one' because of his stature, had destroyed twelve aircraft in May–September 1940 before becoming a night fighter pilot in 1941. He became one of the leading *Nachtjagd Experten*, finishing the war with 73 victories.[22] The two Halifaxes that did not return were shot down by flak over France.

K-King had left Wyton's runway and two parallel canals that ran from the Wash almost to Huntingdon behind and the four big Rolls-Royce Merlins roared as the Lancaster swept out over the sea. Wyton was a nice station with good pubs in the area of St. Ives and Huntingdon, and Cambridge was within striking distance. The university city was the Mecca for all aircrew within a reasonable radius. Every 'night out' was a virtual reunion with chums. Tonight there would be no time to get to the pubs when they got back. But would there be other nights?

K-King made the turning point exactly on time and had swung east to start the long climb up to target height. Over Stuttgart there was more cloud than expected and they flew around for some time, weaving and dodging the flak bursts until the point where they let go with their load of flares: 'Then the long descent back across the rolling hills of Schwaba and over the Rhine back into France and again a repeat of that wild, exhilarating moonlit ride over rooftops and valleys.' As they reached the Normandy coast at the cliff edge a single searchlight shot up and was hurriedly extinguished as Lambert and Bushby loosed off a few rounds at it together. Then it happened. One single, solitary burst of light flak, not more than half a dozen rounds and coming from directly underneath, probably fired from a flak ship, got them. Williams was forced to ditch in the sea, which he did in a superb piece of flying. Everyone except Tommy Armstrong made it into the dinghy. 'Tommy! Where is Tommy?' They began calling his name. Only John Bushby heard him answer with a clear cry, which showed that he must have been at the ultimate moment in a man's life: a moment when the instinctive, despairing cry of a little boy afraid in the dark comes to his lips and when once again he is a child afraid and lonely and cries the same thing in his last moment as in his first.

'Mother!'

'That was all. Just once from somewhere out in front of the sinking Lancaster ... Somewhere Tommy, no longer worried, was sinking down to peace.'

'Guess that's it' muttered Dick Williams, half of his moustache singed off, the other half as luxuriant as ever.

As the French coast came perceptibly nearer the survivors fell silent. Then they heard it, the soft chugging of a boat engine. It grew louder and then a small spotlight gleamed on their dinghy. A rifle was pointed at them.

'*Englander? Kanadien?* The German with the rifle waved it around their circle.

'*Englander*', said someone.

Another German looked down into the dinghy. Then he said something John Bushby was to hear over and over again for the next three years. And always it was said with that half-envious wistfulness.

'*Ach, vell*', in halting English. '*For you the war is over.*'[23]

Winter conditions didn't just affect flying operations, as Jimmy Morris on 218 Squadron recalls:

By now the winter was setting in and the lack of fuel for the heating stove became a problem. So on my next leave, I asked my dad if he could get me an axe, which he did. It was a four-inch felling axe and I put it to good use right through the winter. I can honestly say that Downham Market where 218 Squadron were based was the worst camp I was ever on for accommodation. The station was still being built when we got there and they were still working on it when I left about 11 months later. It was always a sea of mud in winter and summer. In the winter the Nissen hut I shared with another chap, not my crew, was not just damp it was wet. If you were away on an op, you came back to a cold miserable billet. One particular op sticks in my mind. We were briefed to go to Berlin on 3 March 43, the kite was an old bitch and we could hardly get 12,000 feet out of it. We got a good photo of the aiming point and the bomb aimer, Steve, was pleased with the results but it was a long hard op and, like all ops, it is nice to get back and get some sleep. But it was not so for me on that occasion. There was no fuel for the stove which had been out for two days and when I went to get into my bed, the bedding was wet. So, I ended up on the top bed with my flying gear on and my greatcoat on top of me. Such was life at Downham. The aircrew mess was a bit Spartan, the washing facility was a lean-to with about six galvanised washbowls and to get washed and shaved with your back to the elements was not a bit like the Ritzes that the officer types had. But for all the downsides, station morale was good and the chaps and girls got on with their allotted jobs and made the best of it.

Notes

1. *No Moon Tonight* by Don Charlwood (Penguin 1988).
2. 102 Squadron would have the second highest losses in Bomber Command.
3. 22 Wellingtons made cloud-cover daylight raids on Essen, the Ruhr and the Dortmund-Ems Canal at Lingen again. 13 a/c bombed estimated positions through cloud. One Wellington came down low and machine-gunned a train near Lingen, setting some of the carriages alight. No a/c losses.
4. *Bombers Fly East* by Bruce Sanders. (Herbert Jenkins Ltd 1943).
5. *Letters from a Bomber Pilot* by David Hodgson (Thames Methuen London 1985)
6. 53 Halifaxes, 51 Stirlings and 18 Wellingtons.
7. 25 Halifaxes, 23 Stirlings and 23 Wellingtons.
8. *Pathfinders* by W/C Bill Anderson OBE DFC AFC (Jarrolds London 1946)
9. See *No Moon Tonight* by Don Charlwood (Penguin 1988). Spiller later served on 617 'Dam Busters' Squadron.
10. A fourth Lancaster and three Stirlings were lost from 65 aircraft dispatched on *Gardening* operations to lay mines from Lorient to the Frisians.
11. *Over the Alps – And Back, Bombers Fly East* by Bruce Sanders.
12. 218 Gold Coast Squadron Assoc Newsletter No. 33, March 2005.
13. Another Halifax II, in 158 Squadron piloted by Sgt S M Benford RCAF, an American, which was hit by flak near Paris on the homeward

flight was finally abandoned 11 miles SSE of Grantham in Lincoln-shire. All the crew were safe and soon after Benford transferred to the USAAF. G/C Robinson DSO DFC* AFC was killed when his Halifax was shot down during the raid on Berlin on the night of 23/24 August 1943.

14. S/L George Holden DSO DFC* MiD, now commanding 617 Dam Busters Squadron, was killed on the night of 15/16 September on the raid on the Dortmund-Ems Canal at Ladbergen.

15. *The Everlasting Arms*, John Searby, ed. Martin Middlebrook (William Kimber 1988).

16. *RAF Bomber Command Losses of the Second World War, Vol. 3 1942* by W R Chorley (Midland 1994).

17. *RAF Bomber Command Losses of the Second World War, Vol. 3 1942* by W R Chorley (Midland 1994).

18. DT574 crash-landed at Linton on return from a Gardening trip on 8/9 December 1942.

19. S/L The Honourable Brian Grimston DFC and crew on 156 Squadron at Warboys were killed when their Lancaster crashed in the target area on 4/5 April 1943.

20. *Pathfinders* by W/C Bill Anderson OBE DFC AFC (Jarrolds London 1946).

21. *The Bomber Command War Diaries: An Operational Reference Book 1939–1945.* Martin Middlebrook & Chris Everitt (Midland 1985).

22. Wohlers was KIA on 15 March 1944 in a crash near Echterdingen airfield. He had 29 night victories and was a *Ritterkreuzträger.* See *Nachtjagd: The Night Fighter versus Bomber War over the Third Reich 1939–45* by Theo Boiten (Crowood 1997).

23. *Gunner's Moon* by John Bushby (Futura 1974).

CHAPTER 3

Through the Storm

We shall bomb Germany by day as well as night in ever-increasing measure, casting upon them month by month a heavier discharge of bombs and making the German people taste and gulp each month a sharper dose of the miseries they have showered upon mankind.

Winston S Churchill, 22 June 1941

Mary Giddings was looking forward to afternoon tea with 'Ron', her 26-year-old dark haired, good looking and unassuming pilot from New South Wales. They always met at Tilley's pantry at the top of Mill Street in the picturesque little town of Mildenhall, 19 miles north-east of Cambridge. In the window was a sign that said, 'Luncheons, teas and light refreshments: everything home-made.' It was where their romance had started after they had first met on the RAF station, known locally as Beck Row. Tilley's offered a quiet haven away from the station dances and raucous parties 'during black-out' at the 'Bird in the Hand' across from the main gate. If 'Ron' was likely to be flying on operations he would tell Mary and when he returned he would either telephone her immediately or a telephonist friend of hers would let her know that all the Stirlings on 149 Squadron were back. Ron was a flight sergeant with his own crew. When he had been told that he would be transferred to PFF less one or two of his crew who were not quite up to scratch, he said that he would prefer to stick with his crew and remain on 149. Mary was a corporal in the WAAF and a nurse in the hospital at the airfield. Their lifestyles could not have been more different. She was from Wiltshire and at age 19 had trained as a nurse before being posted to Mildenhall. Lean and tough, Rawdon Hume Middleton had worked as a 'jackeroo' before the war at the Wee Wang Sheep Stations at Yarrabandai near Bogan Gate where his father was manager. He had attended Dubbo High until part way through his fifth year. In 1938 he went to Sydney for a few weeks and he had taken flying lessons at Mascot. Descended from an 1820 immigrant, the Reverend G A Middleton, a Cambridge graduate,

79

Ron was earnest and a steady type of pupil and he entered Bradfield Park with a record as a sportsman, a higher level of education than most Australians and a demonstrated commitment to and knowledge of flying.[1] When, in April 1942, 149 Squadron moved a few miles north to RAF Lakenheath in Breckland on the edge of Thetford Forest, Mary and her companionable Aussie pilot would hop on their bicycles and they would meet and talk, not about flying or the war but of their contrasting backgrounds and what they might do when the war was over. Middleton knew all he needed to know about Mary and they agreed to announce their engagement at the end of 1942.

Middleton had not always been buoyant and companionable. He had been introspective and even melancholic. But that had all changed on the night of 6/7 April 1942 when he was second pilot of a Stirling on the raid on Essen. Over the target they were caught in the searchlights and then repeatedly attacked by a night fighter, which ripped pieces out of the starboard wing and set an engine on fire. The crippled Stirling made it back to Lakenheath only to break up completely when the undercarriage collapsed on landing. The incident seemed to have had an astonishing effect on Middleton. It roused him out of his melancholy and galvanised him into a buoyant, companionable mood, which never left him.[2] Bomb aimer Flight Lieutenant Huia Russell DFC, who flew several ops as Air Observer on Middleton's crew, recalled that on one occasion they 'stooged' around the 'drome for two hours trying to wind down the undercarriage without success and finally they were instructed to fly to Newmarket and belly-land on the famous horse racing course. On making a circuit the starboard engine started backfiring and then failed completely as they were about to land. The ground controller instructed Middleton to put the Stirling down in a corner of the airfield as he did not want the Rowley Mile obstructed for night flying. They nipped in just over the perimeter hedge and touched down perfectly. As they came to a halt, earth came in through the bomb aimer's position. The main damage was bent airscrews. Middleton said later that they flew the first aircraft to pass the winning post at Newmarket!

On the night of 28/29 November, seven of 149 Squadron's Stirlings were among the 47 that set off for the Fiat Works at Turin, along with 117 Lancasters, 45 Halifaxes and 19 Wellingtons. Three of the Stirlings that took off from Lakenheath were forced to turn back through fuel and icing troubles. Middleton, who was on his 29th op, carried on to the target where he took *H-Harry* down for a low level attack, knowing that as he did so it would further deplete their already low fuel state. They would have to land at an airfield in southern England on return. Flak was intense and they were hit, but Middleton, unable to get his bombs on target, went around for a second try. It was two or three minutes before they identified the Fiat Works, levelled out at 2,000 feet and started their bombing run.

'Turin received a packet last night,' Wing Commander Guy Gibson DFC*, CO of 106 Squadron, gave as his opinion when he returned.[3] Gibson, who was to earn the VC later for his brilliant attack on the Möhne dam with his Lancasters, and Flight Lieutenant 'Bill' Whamond, dropped the first 8,000lb bombs on Italy. Pilot Officer F G Healy had also set out carrying an 8,000lb bomb but as the Lancaster's undercarriage would not retract its bomb had to be jettisoned into the sea. A great amount of high explosives and 100,000 incendiaries were dropped on the city's targets by 228 Lancasters, Stirlings, Halifaxes and Wellingtons. The 'packet' made up three wide areas blazing from end to end.

H-Harry, a veteran Stirling on XV Squadron, was making its 66th operational attack when it glided down to attack a large factory in Turin from a height of 2,000 feet. The pilot had to spiral down over his target, which meant passing over it about a dozen times. At 4,000 feet light ack-ack opened up on it. The Stirling pilot recalled:

> We fought a kind of duel with them. We could see most of the details of the works. The long sheds looked to me just as if a small boy had carefully drawn his fingers along some sand. After bombing it looked as if the same boy had smashed his fist into the lot. Our stick of bombs dropped diagonally across the works. We were thrown up by the force of the blast and my rear-gunner reported that from his turret he could see stretches of the roof being held up among showers of burning material.[4]

Huge fires raged in the locality of the royal arsenal, the flames shot with bright reds and yellows and vivid greens. The way back was strewn with night fighters. One Lancaster crew sighted as many as 23 over northern France and had a running fight with eight, sending one FW 190 down in flames.[5]

At Mildenhall, Mary Giddings waited anxiously for the telephone call from Ron Middleton to say that he had returned from the operation. The senior MO then told her that Ron was missing. Two Stirlings and a Wellington had failed to return from the raid on Turin. One of the missing was a 149 Squadron aircraft. It was *H-Harry*. A few days later Mary was given details of his Stirling crashing in the English Channel. She was told to stay on duty at the hospital. The bodies of the front-gunner, Sergeant John Mackie, a Scot from Clackmannanshire who was on his 31st op, and 18-year-old Sergeant James Ernest Jeffery, the six foot four flight engineer, formerly a Halton apprentice who was from Dorset, had been recovered. Middleton was apparently unable to leave the aircraft: his body was recovered from the sea. Gradually the details became known. *H-Harry* had experienced great difficulty in climbing to 12,000 feet to cross the Alps and this ate up fuel fast. The night was so dark that the mountain peaks were almost invisible. His fuel barely sufficient for the return journey, Middleton had to decide whether to go on or turn back. Flares were sighted ahead but he pressed on and even dived to 2,000 feet to identify the target, despite the difficulty of regaining height. Three flights were made over Turin at this low altitude before the target was identified and the aircraft came under fire from AA guns. A large piece was shot out of the port main plane and then a shell burst in the cockpit, shattering the windscreen and wounding both first and second pilots. A piece of shell splinter struck Middleton's face, destroying his right eye and he was probably wounded also in the body and legs. The second pilot, Flight Sergeant Leslie Hyder, an ex-Glasgow student, on his fifth operation, was wounded in the head and both legs. The wireless operator, Pilot Officer Norman Skinner, 31 years old and a former journalist from Scarborough, was wounded in one leg. Middleton became unconscious and the aircraft dived to 800 feet before the second pilot regained control and took the aircraft up to 1,500 feet where the bombs were released. Flak was still coming up and the aircraft was hit many times. The three gunners replied continuously until the rear turret was put out of action. Middleton had now recovered consciousness. Getting clear of the target, he ordered the second pilot back to receive first aid. Before this was completed the second pilot insisted on returning to the cockpit as the captain could see very little and could speak only with great difficulty and pain.

Course was set for base, facing an Alpine crossing and a homeward flight in a damaged aircraft with insufficient fuel. Abandoning the aircraft or landing in northern France was discussed but Middleton decided to try to reach the English coast so that his crew could parachute to safety. Because of his wounds and diminishing strength he knew that by then he would have little or no chance of saving himself. Four hours later the French coast was reached and there the aircraft, flying at 6,000 feet, was once more hit by AA fire. Middleton, still at the controls, mustered sufficient strength to take evasive action. After the Stirling crossed the Channel, five minutes' fuel was left. Middleton ordered the crew to jump while he flew parallel with the coast for a few miles, after which he intended to head out to sea. The aircraft crashed into the sea soon afterward.

Flight Sergeant Rawdon Hume Middleton RAAF was posthumously awarded the Victoria Cross, the first of two such awards made for actions on raids to Italy, and Australia's second air VC in the Second World War.[6] On 5 February 1943 the RAF gave Middleton a warrior's burial. In the tiny airfield chapel at Mildenhall four sergeants from the Australian's squadron maintained an hour's vigil with bowed heads and reversed rifles, guarding a flag-draped coffin bearing Middleton's forage cap and side arms. The mourners included Mary Giddings and Canadians, New Zealanders, Americans and others who had been his friends. The pall bearers were members of his squadron. Middleton was buried with full military honours in the Military Cemetery in the churchyard of St. John's Church in Beck Row. He was buried in the rank of Pilot Officer, although news of his commission had not reached him before his death.[7] After the funeral Mary Giddings arranged for a flower holder to be attached to Middleton's headstone. Later she married a RAF wireless operator on 622 Squadron at Mildenhall.

On 29/30 November 1942, 29 Stirlings and seven Lancasters of 3 Group and the Path Finder Force were dispatched to Turin with the Fiat Works again the target. Weather conditions were poor and only 18 aircraft – 14 Path Finders and four Stirlings of 3 Group – are known to have reached the target and bombed. Two Stirlings were lost.

On the night of 2/3 December when 112 aircraft were dispatched to Frankfurt, a Master Bomber – Wing Commander Sidney Patrick 'Pat' Daniels DSO DFC*, Commanding Officer of 35 PFF Squadron at Graveley – was used for the first time, as Bill Anderson recalls:

The idea was almost entirely morale-raising. We did not even call ourselves 'Master Bombers' but a far more genteel name, 'Master of Ceremonies'. Pat, who had already about sixty visits to the Reich by night, had built up a reputation for having an uncanny ability to find the target. In these difficult times, before the magic 'box' had come into service and on nights when mist covered the ground, he would fly out over Germany, cruise around for a little while and then come home admitting ruefully that he had been hopelessly lost. The photographic types would then develop the picture he had taken with his flares and to the surprise of everyone; and no one seemed more amazed than Pat himself, there would be the aiming point, slap-bang in the middle. There were two secrets of Pat's success. The first, which one only learnt about by flying with him, was his uncanny sense of direction. I am quite sure that if you put Pat in the middle of the ante-room in the mess, blindfolded him and spun him round twenty times, he would still know exactly in which direction was the bar. His second great asset and he spoke much more freely about this, was his navigator, a silent Australian flight sergeant, a most exact craftsman, reliable and utterly calm. I am sorry to say that when Pat was taken off operations shortly after this trip, his crew flew with another Skipper and went missing at once.

Just as the first Pathfinder trip to Flensburg was disappointing, so was this first Master Bomber trip to Frankfurt. And for the same reason: weather. We went out a little early full of hope and flew about amongst the searchlights. Luckily the Hun did not shoot at us at first, probably because they did not want to give the position away, but they did chase us with searchlights. And peer at the ground though we did, we could see nothing, for it was covered with that old enemy, Rhine Valley mist. The first flares went down rather to the south of where we were flying and the defences promptly started up. Almost immediately afterwards, a couple of long sticks of flares lit up below us, and lying down in the nose peering at the ground wearing my best bombing spectacles, I thought I caught a glimpse of the river than runs into Frankfurt from the east. Yet I could not be certain, for I was looking for this very landmark and when you look desperately for something at night, you are liable to imagine you can see it. So we asked for more flares up north where we were flying but meanwhile the bombing had started to the south. We were not certain enough to try to switch it farther north. So we flew round dropping odd flares ourselves in the hope of spotting something but the searchlights would catch us and then we could see nothing.

The attack finished [most of the bombing fell in country areas south-west of Frankfurt] and we flew home baffled and disappointed. Our photo did not come out: a searchlight spoilt it. But Pat must have been somewhere over the right place, for the other boys' pictures were too far to the south. But we had learnt some useful lessons. It was obvious now that until the flare droppers were equipped so that they could guarantee that some of the flares at least would light up the aiming point, the Master Bomber could do little on his own. So the scheme was shelved for a while to be revised later by Pathfinders when the necessary equipment had been fitted to the flare-droppers and developed further for special purposes by determined dicers such as Group Captain Cheshire vc DSO DFC.[8]

Six aircraft – three of them Halifaxes on 102 Squadron at Pocklington – were lost. The one piloted by Sergeant H A E Chapman was shot down at 13,000 feet by 21-year-old *Leutnant* Heinz-Martin 'Hannibal' Hadeball of 8./NJG4 near Laumersheim for his eighth victory.[9] The Halifax crashed on the slope of a vineyard near the town cemetery. Both gunners lay dead, the others were taken into captivity. A Stirling on 75 Squadron at Newmarket, a Lancaster on 103 Squadron at Elsham Wolds and a 115 Squadron Wellington at East Wretham were the other aircraft lost. Everyone on board the Lancaster and the Wimpy were killed. A Stirling on 218 Squadron crashed on its return to Downham Market without injury to the crew.

On the night of 8/9 December, when the RAF paid the first of three more visits that month to Turin, fires were raised by incendiaries and more 8,000-pounders dropped by the force of 133 aircraft of 5 Group. The target was marked well by the Path Finder Force and bombing was very accurate. Residential and industrial areas were both extensively damaged. One Lancaster was lost. When 227 aircraft of Bomber Command returned the following night the inferno had not completely subsided. 'Jimmy'

Hurst, the Halifax tail gunner on George Barker's crew on 102 Squadron at Pocklington, flew on the raid:

It was not unusual for the air temperature to be –20°C and ice would build up on the wings of the aircraft, often adding weight and making the plane difficult to fly and sometimes causing it to crash. Returning through the Alps from Turin, my oxygen tube froze solid, cutting off my supply of oxygen. The crew became aware of this, because I had switched on my intercom and was singing into my mike! (This was due to me being starved of oxygen which has a similar affect to drinking too much alcohol.) The Skipper sent the flight engineer to my turret to see what the problem was. On finding my oxygen tube solid with ice, he went back into the fuselage and returned with a flask of hot coffee, he removed my mask and poured coffee into it and this quickly thawed the ice in the tube, enabling me to breathe the oxygen vital to survival at 18,000 feet. I was so starved of oxygen that I was hardly aware of what was happening; the quick thinking of the engineer surely saved my life – another of my nine lives gone!

The raid was described as 'disappointing' with the Path Finders unable to mark as well as on the previous night, and the smoke from the old fires partially obscured the target area. A Wellington and a Lancaster failed to return and two Lancasters crashed in England. *K-King* on 57 Squadron at Scampton piloted by Flight Sergeant Gordon Howard Ramey crashed at Roughton Moor. The Canadian pilot and all his crew were killed. The other Lancaster crashed at Swinderby without injury to the crew.

On 11/12 December the 82 Turin-bound bombers flew though a thick curtain of snow. One Lancaster bomb-aimer reported: 'Only a small part of the glass of my compartment was clear of ice and through it I searched for a gap in the clouds. Ice had formed all over the aircraft and snow fell as we approached the Alps. When I went into the front turret after bombing I found several inches of snow behind the gunner's seat.'

Another Lancaster captain reported:

Shortly after crossing the Channel we ran into thick cloud. The further we went the worse it got. Then we struck an electrical storm. Vivid streaks of bluish light darted along the glass in front of my cabin and there were bright sparks between the barrels of the guns. At first we thought they were flashes of flak. The windows began to ice up and then we ran into driving snow. Very quickly the fronts of my windows and of the gun-turrets were covered with ice and snow, which also interfered with the smooth running of the engines. We began to lose height. Three of my engines cut out for short periods and for about ten seconds only one engine was working. The flight engineer got the engines running again but I had to decide not to risk crossing the Alps. The weather was equally bad coming back.

More than half of the force turned back before attempting to cross the Alps and only 28 crews claimed to have bombed Turin. Three Halifaxes and a Stirling failed to return.

Because of bad weather no major night raids to Italy or the greater *Reich* were possible and minor operations to small German towns and mine-laying trips like the one by 68 aircraft to Texel, Heligoland and the Friesians on 14/15 December, were flown. By the end of 1942 the *U-boat* menace was threatening Britain's Atlantic sea lanes and the *Gardening* or aerial magnetic mine-laying campaign off the coastlines of the *Third Reich* was intensified and would last until the start of the Battle of the Ruhr in March 1943. Twenty-one-year-old Australian Sergeant (later Flying Officer) Colin 'Col' Moir, flew 25 trips on Wellingtons with 420 'Snowy Owl' Squadron RCAF and then five on 432 'Leaside' Squadron RCAF, from 30 May 1942 to 21 June 1943, as rear gunner on the crew of Canadian Sergeant (later Pilot Officer) Jim Thomson. Moir recalls:

An important target group were the *U-boat* bases located at St-Nazaire, Lorient, Hamburg, Wilhelmshaven and Kiel. These places were consistently harassed and heavily bombed. Special Intelligence officers at briefings impressed on us crews that the Battle of the Atlantic could be lost, or the war prolonged if supplies, personnel and trained reinforcements could not reach England. In comparison to the Ruhr Valley, these coastal targets were not heavily defended and in some ways jokingly referred to as a 'Cake Run' or a 'Piece of Cake'. We did our best but we were only of a nuisance value. The pens were protected by very thick reinforced concrete, which was hard to penetrate.

When the day dawned, the weather had to be shocking and the then powers that be decided that 'Ropey' Thomson's crew needed a work out with a mining operation with one or two unlucky crews to keep them company, but only in the briefing room, a Nissen hut – rarely did you see another aircraft in the air, when flying on this type of operation. The Nissen hut would have been more crowded for a maximum effort. During briefing, the Wing Commander would state the target: 'Sea lane here off Borkum Island, or Heligoland Bight, etc. Drop Zone of the mine exactly here', marking it on the map. The navigator was briefed carefully as to the exact details, as timing was essential. I had to study the islands carefully. They were quite flat. I had to memorise details, coves, inlets and bays, especially when the target was Borkum.

On our way in, the English navigator Bill Shakespeare located the correct island by his reckoning. The aircraft then descended through the 10/10ths weather to make visual identification. We were usually met with a hail of light flak. Enemy flak ships or gun emplacements only fired when your aircraft was in sight as you came out of the fog, cloud, rain or snow squalls. They knew you were alone and obviously they did not want to reveal their position. The Wellington bomber was very low and slow and the tracer shells and bullets were a brief but spectacular sight. Each time you went round or approached, the shooting became more intense. They knew you meant business. I never fired back. Luckily they mostly missed. My important job was to read the ground accurately and ignore the fireworks. The correct cove identified, I notified our Canadian pilot Jim Thomson, 'Yes. That's it.' The mine was then primed by the bomb aimer or navigator. From the identified spot, a correct height of 500 feet was given, a course set, time in minutes and seconds given to follow the correct path – don't descend below 300 feet etc, keep straight and level with bomb doors open. The pilot decided which height to keep on according to the prevailing conditions. The minutes and seconds were counted off – and we didn't deviate. The 2,000lb mine was dropped on an attached parachute, which opened. It then descended quickly into the sea right where we had been briefed it had to go. Naturally we did not stay around and set course for Middleton St. George, six miles East of Darlington.

Our fourth and most eventful mining operation – in *A-Apple* – took place on the night of 14 December. Our *Gardening* target lay in the Heligoland Bight, briefing went as usual. When the target was due, I identified a flashing light off a headland jutting out into the sea. You could not miss it as the weather was clear and you could see for miles. Our run was made once and the course set, the mine primed, then all hell broke loose. The flak was murderous and when you can smell it, it's bloody close.

'BANG'.

On the intercom our pilot said, 'Starboard engine gone. Hell, I can't hold it; you can bail out.'

I said: 'No bloody way Ropey. You can fly it on one engine. The water's too bloody cold and I like Yorkshire better.'

'Mine jettisoned. Get out of the bloody turret and hurry up here and help me.'

That's just what I did. There was no alternative. I passed Jock McCaffer (WOp/AG) and Bill Shakespeare, whose job it was to shut down the petrol lines to starboard and then later alter the petrol cocks to transfer fuel to the port engine. The forward part of the aircraft was full of activity. Tragically, we lost a young Canadian bomb aimer on his first – and last – operation. He must have panicked and jumped through an open hatch and perished. Luckily Jim Thomson and I were very fit and strong and flew the lopsided old Wimpy back over the English coast and belly-landed on a fighter aerodrome. We arrived back at Middleton St. George by train a very sorry lot. No one had noticed our new crew member leave and that was our story at debriefing.

Pilot Officer Kemble Wood RAAF played a few games of billiards and snooker and then went to see *Beyond the Blue Horizon* starring Dorothy Lamour, finishing with a bath before deciding to retire to the mess. The 17th of December was a stand down for all except 104 crews of the Main Force, and Kemble Wood made the most of it. His first sight of the Irish coast on 13 August seemed to have started a new era for the Sydneysider 'by suddenly clicking him from a spirit of holiday to a known nearness of war'. At 4 OCU Stranraer, curving round the sheltered inlet, of Loch Ryan, he had inherited a 'headless crew' (one that had lost its pilot).[10] By December Sydney and his wife Ethel seemed even further away. A corporal brought him the news that a telegram had arrived from Australia saying: DAUGHTER BORN. BOTH WELL. Although Kemble Wood was expecting it, the news had 'rocked' him for a bit so he left the mess and went to bed to enter it in his diary.

In bright moonlight and without cloud cover 27 Lancaster crews of 5 Group were en route to raid eight small German towns, and sixteen Stirlings and six Wellingtons of 3 Group were detailed to attack the Opel Works at Fallersleben. Another 50 aircraft were to lay mines from Denmark to southern Biscay and five OTU crews were being dispatched on sorties to France to find their feet. Five Stirlings on 75 New Zealand Squadron, led by Wing Commander Victor Mitchell DFC, a 27-year-old Scot, took off from Newmarket for the Opel Works. The New Zealand squadron, which had only recently re-equipped with Stirlings after having flown Wellingtons since April 1940, suffered disastrously. Mitchell and his crew were lost without trace and all fourteen men on the two other crews were killed. A fourth Stirling flown by Flight Sergeant K J Dunmall was shot down by a combination of flak and fighters and crashed in the Westeinder Plas in Holland. All seven crew were soon taken prisoner.[11] Two Stirlings on 218 Squadron at Downham Market and two Wellingtons on 115 Squadron at East Wretham also failed to return. One Lancaster, which went to lay mines in the 'Broccoli' region of the Great Belt was shot down by a night fighter. *N-Nuts* on 101 Squadron at Holme-on-Spalding Moor was shot down by anti-aircraft fire while returning to base; the Lancaster crashing at Grangemouth between Middlesbrough and Redcar in Yorkshire with the loss of all the crew.

At Waddington three Lancasters on 44 Squadron were shot down on the operation to Nienburg, *D-Dog* on 9 Squadron went missing in action

Having been recalled from the USA where he was head of the RAF Delegation, Air Marshal Sir Arthur T Harris, seen here with his opposite number, General Ira C Eaker, Chief of VIIIth Bomber Command, became Commander-in-Chief of RAF Bomber Command on 22 February 1942. Harris was directed by Marshal of the RAF, Sir Charles Portal, Chief of the Air Staff to break the German spirit by the use of night area rather than precision bombing and the targets would be civilian, not just military. The famous 'area bombing' directive, which had gained support from the Air Ministry and Prime Minister Winston Churchill, had been sent to Bomber Command on 14 February, eight days before Harris assumed command. (*IWM*)

On 28 July 1942 Group Captain the Duke of Kent (seen here inspecting members on 419 Squadron RCAF) and the Honourable Vincent Massey, Governor-General of Canada, visited RAF Mildenhall to watch 419 Squadron leave for Hamburg that night. News was later received that X3488 carrying Wing Commander John 'Moose' Fulton DSO DFC AFC, the squadron CO, had been shot down off the Friesians. The duke, who was killed in a Sunderland flying boat a month after this photograph was taken, had visited Mildenhall on 25 June 1941 to inspect 149 Squadron. (*IWM*)

On 27/28 June 1942, 144 aircraft of Bomber Command visited Bremen just two nights after the third 'Thousand Bomber' raid. Nine bombers FTR. Stirling I N3751/BU-P on 214 Squadron flown by Sergeant Frank Morton Griggs RAAF was damaged by flak and hit repeatedly by enemy fighters during which Sergeant Horace Arthur William Sewell the rear gunner was killed. Griggs successfully made a wheels-up landing at Stradishall. (*IWM*)

Avro Lancaster production line. (*Avro*)

Stirling I N6082 QJ-Q on 149 Squadron at Lakenheath piloted by Squadron Leader George William Alexander, which was shot down on the Bremen raid on 29/30 June 1942 and crashed at Wons in Holland. All the crew were killed. (*IWM*)

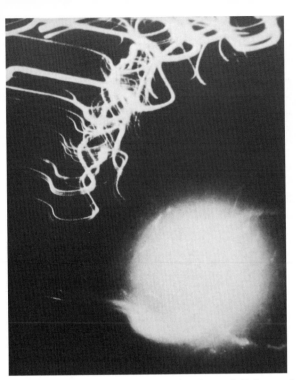

(*Left*) A 'cookie' explodes at Karlsruhe on 2/3 September 1942.
(*Right*) Sergeant Ronald McCauley RAAF, 27-years old, a WOp/AG on 12 Squadron at Binbrook, armed for a snowball fight. Later promoted to Flight Sergeant, McCauley was KIA on the night of 8/9 September 1942 when Wellington III Z8644 PH-A flown by Pilot Officer Charles Henry Doyle Moseley RAAF was lost on the operation to Frankfurt. *A-Apple* crashed at Nackenheim on the east bank of the Rhine 11km south of Mainz. All five crew died and they were laid to rest in Rheinberg War Cemetery. (*AWM*)

Wellington destroyed by fire on the raid on Bremen on the night of 13/14 September 1942 when twenty-one aircraft were lost, fifteen of them Wellingtons.

Stirling I N3725/HA-D *Mamprusi* on 218 (Gold Coast) Squadron being bombed up at Downham Market in June 1942. On its 31st operational sortie on 14/15 September 1942, N3725 lost the starboard outer over Wilhelmshaven and Pilot Officer J C Frankcombe nursed the aircraft back to Norfolk to the vicinity of home base, only to have the remaining engine on the starboard wing cut out. The Stirling immediately did a wing-over and crashed near Stoke Ferry. Only the wireless operator and the mid-upper gunner survived, badly injured. (*IWM*)

American aircraft production representatives visit the English Electric factory at Preston in the autumn of 1942 where they saw Halifax II DT567. This aircraft and Pilot Officer Alan Lionel Holmes' crew were lost on a mine-laying sortie while operating on 51 Squadron (as MH-F) at Snaith on 7/8 March 1943. (*IWM*)

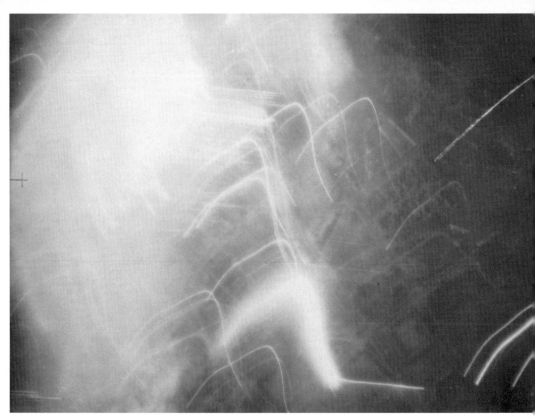

Raid on Turin, 20/21 November 1942. (*IWM*)

Major engine work on Halifax II BB194/ZA-E on 10 Squadron at Melbourne, Yorkshire in December 1942. This aircraft was later operated by 1658 HCU where on 3 February 1943, it overshot when landing and was burnt out. The pilot, Sergeant J N Willoughby, suffered a fractured skull and two of his crew were also injured. (*IWM*)

light Sergeant Rawdon Hume Middleton
RAAF who was KIA on the night of
28/29 November 1942 returning from the FIAT
works at Turin. He was awarded a
posthumous Victoria Cross. (*IWM*)

Hamburg fire raid. (*IWM*)

A Lancaster silhouetted against the searchlights, bursting flak and exploding bombs over the blazing inferno of Hamburg on the night of 30/31 January 1943. (*IWM*)

German fire crew at work dousing the flames after a raid by RAF Bomber Command.

Flak.

Window.

Distraught German civilians after a raid.

German fire crews.

Short Stirling I R9257 *C-Colander* on 7 Squadron at RAF Oakington, which Wing Commander Thomas Gilbert 'Hamish' Mahaddie DSO DFC AFC MC (Czech) flew back from Cologne on 1 February 1943 with 174 cannon shell holes, courtesy of a Ju88 night fighter. Mahaddie and this crew were due to attend an investiture at Buckingham Palace to receive a total of 11 decorations but on their first trip without their skipper, on 11/12 March 1943, the crew were all lost in action on the operation to Stuttgart with Squadron Leader Michael Edward Thwaites DFC. R9257 was later operated by 214 Squadron at Chedburgh and crashed on takeoff on the operation on Turin on the night of 12/13 August 1943.

Wing Commander 'Hamish' Mahaddie at the investiture at Buckingham Palace early in 1943.

Dead German civilians following a raid.

Tommy's crew, skippered by Flying Officer John Fergus Greenan RCAF (centre), in front of Lancaster I W4201, which was usually flown by Wing Commander Frederick Campbell Hopcroft (CO of 57 Squadron, September 1942–July 1943; note his pennant painted below the cockpit). W4201 and Flying Officer W E Jeavons' crew crashed on return to base at the end of a *Gardening* operation on the night of 13/14 March 1943. John Greenan and his crew were KIA on 1/2 March 1943 returning from Berlin, when *T-Tommy* crashed near Riseholme.

T-Tommy's mid-upper gunner, Sergeant Frank Cyril Edward 'Dusty' Miller, a 33-year-old former pi
salesman, in the Frazer-Nash FN 50 turret at Scampton. 'Dusty' Miller was KIA on Greenan's crew
on 1/2 March 1943. These photographs were part of a sequence taken in February 1943 for an Air
Ministry picture story entitled *T for Tommy Makes a Sortie*, which portrayed the events surrounding
single Lancaster bomber and its crew during a typical operation. (*IWM*)

Back at Scampton, *T for Tommy*'s bomb aimer, Sergeant Herbert Henry 'Bert' Turkentine, a 29-year-
old former blacksmith from southeast London (left) and the Canadian navigator, Sergeant Frederic
Warren 'Muse' Music (21) are given cups of tea by a WAAF. Turkentine and Music were KIA on
1/2 March 1943. (*IWM*)

Squadron pose for the press at Syerston early in 1943 (note the censored white area behind).

(*Left*) A WAAF wireless operator guiding a returning Lancaster at Scampton in February 1943. The Women's Auxiliary Air Force had been formed in June 1939 to release men from certain ground trades for duties elsewhere. By 1944 nearly a quarter of all ground staff on RAF bomber stations were WAAFs. (*IWM*)

(*Right*) Munich after a raid on the *Alstadt* or old town by RAF Bomber Command. On the left the new town hall is on fire; in the background are the flaming tower of the old town hall and the Holy Ghost church. This photo was taken by a tower warden inside the Church of Our Lady. On 9/10 March 1943 Munich was devastated by bombs from over 360 bombers, which destroyed over 290 buildings and badly damaged over 2,700 more, including many public buildings, the cathedral and four churches, as well as fourteen 'cultural buildings'.

Krupp Works at Essen in March 1943.

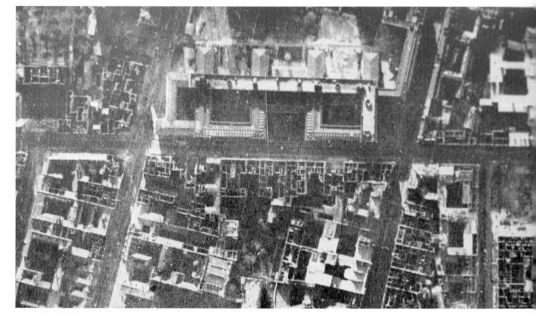

German flak gunner.

Wing Commander Gerry B Warner (third from left), the 78 Squadron CO at Linton-on-Ouse, with his crew and with Halifax II W7930/EY-W behind, March 1943. W7930 FTR with Flight Sergeant Ernest Arthur Tipler's crew on 22/23 June on the operation to Mülheim. All the crew were killed.

View of Essen on the night of 3/4 April 1943 from Lancaster *V-Victor* on 83 Squadron at Wyton, whose pilot, Flight Sergeant Glen Alexander McNicol RCAF, was commissioned but lost in action just two weeks later, on the night of 16/17 April when the target was Pilzen. All the members of his crew survived and were taken into captivity.

On 20/21 April 1943, Stirling III BF476/LS-P was one of fifteen 15 Squadron aircraft that set off from Mildenhall bound for Rostock, each with a 1,000lb HE and 270 4lb and 40 30lb incendiaries. When one of the engines failed Flight Lieutenant C P Lyons RNZAF made a successful crash landing near Vejle in North Jutland where the crew set fire to the aircraft before they were captured. (*IWM*)

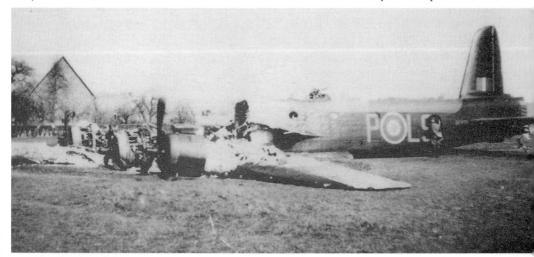

on the raid on Diepholz and *S-Sugar* piloted by Sergeant J Wilson RCAF went down at Berkhausen between Varel and Rastede on the operation to Cloppenburg. The Canadian pilot and five of his crew survived and they were taken into captivity but Sergeant William Harvey Penn RCAF, the American mid-upper gunner who was from Tulsa, Oklahoma, was killed. Two Lancasters on 97 Squadron at Woodhall Spa failed to return from the raid on Neustadt. Two Lancasters on 50 Squadron at Skellingthorpe were lost on the operation to Soltau. One was piloted by Flight Lieutenant John Charles Atkinson DFM, whose crew included the navigator, Flying Officer 'Paddy' Rowling and Pilot Officer Charlie Walker, one of the air gunners.

Six weeks' earlier Rowling had shared a room at the Strand Palace in London and lunched at 'The Boomerang Club' – motto: 'I go out to return' with Mrs. Tennant, a hostess. This favourite haunt of Aussie airmen, just north of the Strand on the Aldwych curve leading into Kingsway was opened early in 1942. The Club took up two floors of Australia House and served all Australian services and ranks. Men registered at the reception centre (entrance off Melbourne Place), scanned the Club for friends and consulted the notice boards – one for the men to attach notes for mates and the other listing entertainment. The Club helped men find accommodation, sold drinks, snacks and meals and provided a place to write letters, read Australian newspapers, gather around the piano, have a haircut and play billiards and yarn. The Boomerang Club attracted and disturbed aircrew, they wanted to catch up with news and comrades but so often they learnt of the deaths of another three or four of their old course from Narrandera or Parkes or Calgary. The Strand was central to many of the places the Australians had to or wanted to visit. In December 1941 the Overseas Headquarters of the RAAF opened in Kodak House at 63 Kingsway just off the Strand, which the Australians made their own.[12] Canadians had the 'Beaver Club' in Trafalgar Square. The conviviality of wartime London was unimaginable. People who had not seen each other before five minutes ago became comrades. Romantic attachments were formed on the spot, sometimes with no more than a searching look. Complete strangers drank out of the same bottle with no thought of disease. Virtuous girls quickly availed themselves of the chance of dinner and dancing and a one-night stand with boys who would be dead within the week. Australians, Canadians and Yanks prowled the city together, denigrating their English cousins and declaring their undying friendship. Language was no barrier. The bottle was the universal language bestowing upon Pole, Norwegian, Free French and Yank alike perfect understanding and instant communication.

After London 'Paddy' Rowling visited Twickenham to see his English girlfriend Sandra and he stayed the night. Next day, they ran into 'Charlie' Walker who was on 48-hours' leave from his gunnery course. Walker had toured England in 1930 and again in 1938 with the Australian cricket team as a wicket keeper, though he was not selected for any of the Test Matches. He and Rowling and Sandra went to see Lupino Lane in the show, '20 to 1'. 'Charlie' knew Lupino and they chatted with the comedian back stage after the show. He even gave them an open invitation to make use of his theatre any time they wanted to see a show. They would never get the chance. Rowling and Walker, two fellow Aussies and the rest of Atkinson's crew were lost without trace on the operation to Soltau.

One of the final big raids on Germany in December 1942 was the one on the night of the 20th/21st when over 230 aircraft took off for an attack on the docks at Duisburg-Ruhrort.[13] At the Lancaster and Halifax, Wellington and Stirling stations preparations for take-off went ahead as normal. Flight Sergeant T G O'Shaughnessy, the navigator on *S-Sugar*, a Halifax aircraft on 35 Squadron at Graveley flown by Flight Sergeant 'Ron' Wilkes, a bomber captain of exceptional ability, recalls: 'The tail wheel of the plane had just been christened; a dark figure drummed on a fin; other strange figures performed a slow war-dance in time with the drumming. The dance finished, they climbed aboard. Engines roared into life, the ground crew stood back and *S-Sugar* rallied slowly forward from the dispersal point.'

Two Lancasters collided shortly after take-off from Waddington with the loss of all fourteen crew members, and *Q-Queenie*, a 158 Squadron Halifax crashed three miles from Rufforth, killing three crew. The pilot and three other crew members were injured. Twenty miles from Duisburg crews could see the Rhine gleaming in the frosty moonlight. The customary haze lay in patches along the valleys but they could pick out quite easily the course of the Ruhr itself and crews found that the target area was clear. One Lancaster pilot observed far below him the vapour trails spread by other aircraft going low to make their bombing runs. It was a concentrated attack in the new style that had developed from the thousand-bomber experiments. Huge explosions were seen and large fires spread and much damage was claimed by the returning bomber crews.

O'Shaughnessy continues:

Seventeen thousand feet. Below on that morning of 20 December the grey Rhine snaked across a black countryside. A little ahead lay the target, the fat fingers of the docks of Duisburg, pointing eastward. On the ground, red splashes of fire marked exploding bombs and the flashes of ack-ack guns. Incendiary bombs, like diamond necklaces, were strung across the target. A dull, red glow covered part of the town and a dense smoke-haze drifted slowly across the area. The flak rose slowly in multi-coloured lights into the dark sky, to burst in star-like points of light. Searchlights probed the air and flak-happy German night fighters pursued the bombers even into their own murderous barrage. In rapid succession came three flak bursts right under our tail.

'For Christ's sake weave!' screamed Flight Sergeant Mick Bradford, the Australian tail gunner. A vicious crack came on the starboard side; shrapnel rattled on the fuselage and a piece ripped through above my head, cutting cables and smashing the radar equipment.

'You're losing the starboard outer,' said Sergeant Tom Brown, the flight engineer.

Uneasily I watched the propeller come to a stop and stand, black and awesome, silhouetted against the sky. The barrage had not abated but we were no longer a focal point.

'Nearly there,' said Pilot Officer Ron Wheatley the Australian bomb aimer. 'Bomb doors open.'

'Bomb doors open' replied Ron Wilkes. I noted in the log 'Height 7,500 feet; air-speed 175 knots: compass 200°; time 20.03 hours.'

Suddenly the German gunners found our range. Flak burst along our port side. 'Port-inner on fire!' yelled Tom. 'Where are the ruddy fire-extinguisher buttons?' shouted the pilot.

Across the hubbub cut the bomb-aimer's voice: 'Straight and level now.' The crew became silent; smoke streamed from the port-inner; sweat ran down the pilot's face; the bomb-aimer steadily took his aim. 'Bombs gone!' exclaimed Ron Wheatley; then: 'Wait for the photo-flash.' Thirty more seconds of straight and level flight. 'OK! Weave like hell now!'

The aircraft turned east away from the worst of the flak. The fire in the port-inner seemed to be extinguished. For a brief moment we rested and took stock: two engines gone, one turret out of action, radar gear smashed – a fat chance we had of getting home.

'This is not the way home,' I remarked. 'Turn and fly west.'

'Not through that ruddy flak again,' said the rear-gunner, with vehemence. The pilot turned and flew south. 'The Rhine's a hell of a big place,' I said. 'You must fly west.' And I gave him the course.

We crossed the Dutch border at about 10,000 feet; losing height rapidly. The pilot ordered that everything possible must be jettisoned to lighten the aircraft. Ammunition boxes went first, leaving only a short length of belt on the track and then flares, signals and the Elsan toilet. Someone suggested the parachutes as well but got a very rude answer. Another looked at the oxygen bottles without success. The bomb-sight, although heavy, was secret and so was retained.

Flight Sergeant Frank Hay, the wireless-operator, began tapping out 'SOS' and reported our plight to base. At 5,000 feet things looked serious. Our plan had been to fly as far west as possible and ditch on the North Sea but as things were now going we should land well inside Holland. The pilot asked me what I thought. 'Bail out soon,' I said.

'Right, at 4,000 feet I'll give the order.' he replied. I watched the needle of the altimeter creep lower and lower with sinking heart. At 4,000 feet came the order: 'Abandon aircraft!'

'What the hell!' cried Frank; 'You blighters have all had some coffee. Wait while I drink mine.'

We waited. And as we waited the needle of the altimeter, still wavering, showed a slower rate of descent. 'We must go at 2,000 feet' I said. 'We shall be all right but the pilot won't have much chance.' (He was encumbered by a heavy seat 'chute.)

'Pull your finger Ron' said Freddy Vincent, the mid-upper.

'We're holding height!' I interrupted. At 2,000 feet our descent had ceased. The crew were jubilant; we stood a chance after all. Quickly we went about our tasks. At all costs we had to avoid flying over a heavily-defended area such as a big town. We were not much worried about fighters; we were well south of our proper course and hoped they would all be busy in the main bomber stream. After a short while I noticed some grey, winding lines on the ground. I called the bomb-aimer forward and he pinpointed our position as over the island of Walcheren, off the Dutch coast. About the same time the wireless-operator obtained a 'pin' giving the same position. We set course for the nearest 'drome – Martlesham.

Twelve minutes later the pilot remarked, in conversational tones: 'Enemy fighter dead ahead.' My heart missed a beat. Had he seen us? 'He is circling round,' continued the pilot; 'he *has* seen us all right.' My heart sank. Below us glided the cold North Sea. It was beating up for a gale. What were our chances? If we were hit we should probably catch fire and if we tried to ditch we should probably burn like a torch on the water. We could bail out, to float thirty miles off the Dutch coast in icy cold water in half a gale. How could we fight back? Two engines gone, one turret out of action; the tail turret desperately short of ammunition.

'We'd had it!

'He's coming in,' said Tom. 'Ready to turn port.'

'I see him!' cried the rear-gunner, his voice tense with excitement.

With agonizing slowness the port wing dipped and the Halifax lumbered round. I thanked God I was not the rear-gunner, I should have been frozen with fear. The fighter fired and missed and Mick's guns hammered in reply, while Freddy, in a gesture of defiance, sprayed an ineffective burst into the sky. The second time our enemy attacked from the starboard side. Again he missed but Mick did not.

'You've got him!' screamed Tom. 'I saw the trace going in him.' The fighter attacked a third time, again from the port. His shots were very wide but Mick's aim was deadly. 'My God!' cried Tom. 'See those flashes on his belly as you hit him?'

'Yes,' replied Mick 'and he's going down.'

We watched the German diving steeply; smoke pouring from his machine until he disappeared into the sea.

The remainder of the crossing was made in utter silence except for the purr of the engines. We wondered how long they could stand the belting they were getting. When we saw Martlesham's beacon flashing dead ahead my task was finished.

'Get her down quick' said Tom the engineer. 'The starboard outer is losing oil.'

'OK. I'll do my best.' In a few minutes we landed and I noted the time. 22.26 hours, in the log. A fire-tender and an ambulance raced alongside of us. Willing hands tried to help Mick from his turret. 'Hey, lay off' he cried indignantly. 'I'm OK.'

And honestly although he was, so keen were the rescue-squad to do a good job, that I had half a feeling that they were just a little disappointed.[14]

Twelve bombers that had flown to the target were missing, mostly shot down by night fighters or flak. One of the three Halifaxes lost was flown by Warrant Officer James Albert Hunter RCAF of 78 Squadron, who reached the Norfolk coast when both port engines failed and he ditched into the sea about 30 miles off Great Yarmouth. The Canadian Skipper and four of his crew perished. The two survivors, who were injured, were not rescued until five hours later. The two other Halifaxes that failed to return were on 76 Squadron at Linton-on-Ouse. *D-Dog* piloted by Flying Officer Douglas Anderson, who came from Rio de Janeiro, Brazil, was shot down by *Oberleutnant* Viktor Bauer of III./NJG1. There were no survivors from either Halifax. There were no survivors either from the six Lancasters that were shot down. Two of the three Wellingtons that were lost were from 156 Squadron at Warboys. A third Wimpy, on 425 'Alouette' Squadron RCAF, was shot down over Holland by *Hauptmann* Werner Streib of I./NJG1. Flight Sergeant L F Causley and one of his crew were the only survivors.

Meanwhile, 75 Squadron, which returned to Newmarket Heath without any losses, counted its blessings. When news of the disastrous operation to Fallersleben had reached the New Zealand High Commission in London, Mr. Jordan, High Commissioner for New Zealand, and Air Commodore A de T. Nevill, Officer Commanding New Zealand Air Headquarters in the United Kingdom, made plans to visit the Squadron. They arrived at Newmarket on the afternoon of 21 December just in time to see Squadron Leader G M Allcock's shattered Stirling return from Duisburg. The pilot from Auckland was among the later bomber crews that encountered night fighters as they approached the target. Silhouetted against the glow of flares and searchlights the Stirling was a tempting target and it was attacked by a Ju 88, but Allcock's rear-gunner was alive to the swooping danger and got in the first burst. He saw the pieces ripped off the Junkers as his bullets found the enemy. But the Ju 88 hit the Stirling fore and aft with cannon and machine gun fire. The starboard elevator and the fin were holed and made useless and hits just behind the inner port engine set the dinghy storage blazing, while a starboard fuel tank was ruptured and petrol flooded the fuselage. A cannon shell smashed through the window of the rear-turret and exploded on impact and for a while the gunner was blinded. The second pilot took a splinter in the knee and the flight engineer was folded up in his seat, suffering agonies. His face had been badly scorched by a shell, which had burst inside the aircraft. The wireless operator's radio set had been badly knocked about by another shell and he tried to mend it with a hand bound in a blood-soaked rag. The mid-upper gunner had been biding his time and as the night fighter lifted a trifle he fired and the Ju 88 turned slowly over and went down. Allcock then set about finding the target, made his bombing run and he turned back, with the fire in the dinghy storage still burning. Reluctantly he gave the order to prepare to bail out but while the fire in the dinghy storage continued to burn, it did not spread. They reached Holland and the Dutch coast and headed across the North Sea. Allcock crossed the English coast with the fire still crackling and reached Newmarket, only to discover, as he made his landing circuit, that his undercarriage was jammed. He made a risky belly-landing well clear of the runway, so that it would not be blocked for the other aircraft of the squadron when they came in.

The final Main Force operation in 1942 was the attack by over 130 aircraft of 1 and 5 Groups and the Path Finders on Munich, which took place on the night of 21/22 December. The force was mainly made up of 119 Lancasters, of which one, a 61 Squadron aircraft, crashed shortly after take-off from Syerston. Most of the bombs fell in open country although 110 aircraft claimed to have bombed the city. Three of the nine Stirlings dispatched by 7 Squadron at Oakington and a Wellington on 156 Squadron whose all-Canadian crew was killed, as well as eight Lancasters, failed to return. Two of the missing Lancasters were on 106 Squadron at Syerston. Sergeant John Derek Brinkhurst and crew were attacked over Belgium by a night fighter and the pilot ordered the crew to bail out. When he was told that the forward escape hatch had jammed, Brinkhurst left the controls and went down into the nose and freed the hatch. He then returned to his cockpit to hold the doomed Lancaster steady while his crew bailed out. Brinkhurst and two of the crew died in the aircraft but four men got out and were taken prisoner after landing by parachute. On his release from captivity, Flight Sergeant J A Shepherd RNZAF was able to relate the story of his pilot's gallantry and Brinkhurst was posthumously awarded a DFM. The other Lancaster was piloted by Flight Lieutenant Grimwood C Cooke DFC DFM, who had joined up with his twin-brother

Harold, a Whitley V air gunner on 10 OTU, who had been killed on the Thousand Bomber raid on Bremen on the night of 25/26 June 1942. Harold's all-sergeant crew, which was captained by Norman Maxwell Oulster RCAF, was shot down in the vicinity of Lingen-Ems, where they were first buried. Later they were re-interred in the Reichswald Forest War Cemetery. Grimwood Cooke's Lancaster crashed not far from Verdun in France at Beaufort-en-Argonne where he and four of his crew were laid to rest in the churchyard. The only survivor was taken prisoner. A fifth member of the crew who also died has no known grave.[15]

At Elsham Wolds, home to 103 Squadron, no word was received from the Lancaster flown by Flight Lieutenant John Colin McIntosh Rose DFC RAAF or from *S-Sugar*, that of another Australian, Sergeant 'Col' Bayliss. *S-Sugar* had been so badly crippled by a night fighter that the captain ordered 'abandon aircraft'. Bayliss was struggling to hold it steady for the crew to bail out when it exploded. He was thrown clear but the others perished.

At their home in Melbourne, Australia, Mrs Robb awaited Christmas greetings from her son Ian, a sergeant air gunner on 'Col' Bayliss' crew. Ian Robb went to Mannheim on the 6th of December, laid mines off Denmark on the 9th and wrote his last letter home on the 17th. He signed it 'Love from Ian, the airman.' The RAF withheld the terrible news of his death on the 21/22 December operation to Munich until the Yuletide was over and then they cabled his mother. She expected the telegram that arrived on Boxing Day to be Christmas greetings from her son.

In July 1942 three newly qualified RAF navigators at 33 ANS (Air Navigation School) set out from Mount Hope in Canada in their serge uniforms and white armbands on a couple of weeks' leave to hitch-hike to Niagara, Buffalo, Schenectady and New York City. It was so easy. The Americans had not long been in the war and they were unusual people. The hospitality of everyone they met was overwhelming. Pilot Officer Jack Furner [16], who had passed out as a navigator, remembers that they met up with a bunch of young girls in Buffalo. The girls took the RAF navigators to one of their homes for a transatlantic party. One of their fathers was a senior Buffalo policeman and another worked in the Fire Department. On leaving Buffalo to head further east into New York State, the Fire Department drove Furner and his two companions to the city limits and the accompanying Police car stopped the first suitable vehicle going to Schenectady. Service, indeed! Schenectady, the home of the General Electric Company, was remarkable (then) for orange street lamps. Furner had never seen the like before. In New York, after half a dozen more generous and inquisitive responders to their thumbs, they were put up at the YMCA and saw everything and did everything they could in the time. Particularly memorable for its welcome and camaraderie was Jack Dempsey's Bar on Broadway: New Yorkers queued up to buy them

drinks. The whole trip was magic. But it had to come to an end and they
hitched back up to Canada. Packing kit bags, they were soon on a train
which took them the reverse way back to New Brunswick, since Moncton
had the honour of being the focal point both into and out of the Canadian
Training organisation. Furner had been one of 'a bunch' called up in early
1941. He was 19. They were instructed to report to the Recruiting Office
in Southend High Street, where they were allowed to state a preference.
He volunteered for the RAF, for aircrew and, specifically, for navigator.
It seemed to him that personality and mathematical inclination made
navigator a more sensible choice than pilot: less of the gung-ho, more of
the steady as she goes. The powers that be must have agreed: Furner
attended at Air Crew Reception Centre (ACRC) in the hallowed grounds
of the MCC at Lords, where the RAF was receiving and dispatching
tens of thousands of aspiring aircrew, in May 1941 – as an Aircraftman
second class (AC2) – with navigator training ahead of him.

I put on the rough serge uniform for the first time and kept essential
belongings (knife, fork, spoon, razor comb and lather brush, we
sang) in a kitbag. I was billeted in what would have been in headier
days in peacetime a very prestigious and luxurious apartment building facing Regents Park – Viceroy Court. The bombing of London
was still going on sporadically, particularly around the middle of
June when Hitler decided to scrap another piece of paper and turn
east to invade the vast territories of the USSR. One night during
a raid I saw a marvellous Eisenstein film called *Alexander Nevsky*,
which drew a remarkable parallel between 1941 and the invasion of
the Teutonic Knights 600 years before; the background music of
Prokofiev made a lasting impression on me.

The training pipeline was a long one. It was to be nearly two years
before I was fully trained to enter a front line Squadron in Bomber
Command. It has to be said that the Empire Aircrew Training
Scheme, as it was known, was one of the organisational wonders of
World War II. Hundreds of thousands of young men from the UK,
from the Empire and from European escapers, filtered through a
training plan set up on hundreds of airfields in the USA, in Canada,
in South Africa and in Rhodesia as well as the UK itself to feed all
the operational Commands of the rapidly expanding Royal Air
Force – Bomber, Fighter, Coastal, Transport – with pilots, navigators,
signallers, engineers and gunners.

Having performed a bit of smartening-up drill in the back streets
of NW8, some of us went from the ACRC to RAF North Luffenham,
attached to an operational station, to view the RAF at work and to
learn some basic subjects such as Air Force Law and other administrative matters under the tutelage of Education Officers. It was there
that 'Stand by yer beds!' became a familiar call as we assembled a

neat pile of three 'biscuits' and sheets on the bed frame for inspection. It was there also that I first met an officer who was much later to become well-known to me and a legend in the RAF: he was North Luffenham's Station Commander and he came round to our little hut one day to encourage us in our studies – it was a very young (29!) Group Captain 'Gus' Walker. He had both his arms then.[17] North Luffenham was equipped with Hampdens and I managed to take a local flight in the perspex nose of one of them – my first experience in the air – exhilarating!

Next we were off to Eastbourne for EANS (Elementary Air Navigation School) – no flying, lots of navigation theory, living in a guest house. By spring 1942, since the United States had been hurtled into the war by Pearl Harbor a few months earlier, a US troop-ship had become an allied ship; and on one of them I found myself bound for New York, travelling very slowly in massive convoy. It took two weeks; enjoying rich American food with lashings of cake and ice-cream; swinging wildly on US rating hammocks; and squatting on long lines of 'heads' with the effluent flushing in great torrents beneath our twelve-holers. From New York City – no time to stop and look – we were put on a special train all the way up north through New England to Moncton, New Brunswick, in Canada. I can't remember how long the journey took but it must have gone into a second day. On arrival at midnight, we marched (trudged might be a more accurate word) with our kit bags through a swirling blizzard to a very well heated Canadian barrack block. The following day another train took us south-westwards along the Saint Lawrence River through Montreal and Toronto to Hamilton, Ontario, where we disembarked and were driven up an escarpment called Mount Hope. Here on top of the 'Mount' was 33 Air Navigation School, which was to be our home for the next six months. Mount Hope was an exhilarating experience. Of course there were many hours of classroom lectures, on maps and charts, physics, instruments, signals, meteorology, reconnaissance, aircraft recognition, as well as the basic elements of navigation but these were complemented by practical work in the air, flying through a Canadian summer; a total of 38 flights in the twin-engined Anson. The flying represented the most significant part of our training so far. It was our first opportunity to put theory into practice. My log book records a gradual assumption of greater responsibility: Map-reading; Wind Velocity by Track and Ground speed; Ground speed, Course and ETA (Estimated Time of Arrival); Airplot, Course and ETA; Climbing on Track; Reconnaissance; Drift finding; DR (Dead Reckoning) positions, snap course, recce; Square search exercise; Position lines; Target to be reached two hours after setting course; Operational simulation at 10,000 feet, evasive action, certain landfall. I suppose the most telling phrase in this list is Dead Reckoning (DR).

On 31 July 1942 I was passed out of Course 47 as a Pilot Officer in the General Duties Branch (that is, the flying Branch), wearing an 'O' for observer wing and a white band round sergeant's stripes on the left arm because Hamilton had no officers' uniforms. In order to put the result of the Mount Hope course into telegraphese, I sent a cable home reading, amongst other things: Top of Course. I had meant the three words to be factual but at home, the second and third words, all appearing in upper case, were misconstrued and thus taken to confirm my usual conceit.

After equipping ourselves properly as Pilot Officers in Eaton's Department store in Moncton, we returned to the UK in style by a one-class ship from Halifax to Liverpool and eventually made our way to Bournemouth for another short period of waiting – waiting for the next stage in the pipeline along with raw aircrew from all parts of the world. It was here that the decision was made as to disposal – which Command, Bomber, Coastal, etc. For me and for most trainees at that time, it was Bomber and I was told to report to 2 OTU (Operational Training Unit) at RAF Westcott. We grouped ourselves into crews for training on Wellingtons. My Skipper was a tall laconic New Zealander named John Verrall and like the rest of the crew, in his early 20s: dedicated and reliable. The rest of the crew hailed from Scotland, Wales, Yorkshire and New Zealand: Sergeants McDonald, Beswarick, Boyd, Shankland and Wilkes. Up to this point, relationships with one's colleagues were transient: through London NW8, Luffenham, Eastbourne, Moncton, Hamilton and Moncton again, then Bournemouth, I had made many friends at each place but we never saw one another again. Now, for the first time we were a crew of seven who were to be together for a tour of Bomber operations, who were to rely on each other for the safe completion of that tour and who were thus dependent on each other for our lives.

We are in late 1942. The news was good in North Africa but nowhere else. Severe losses of shipping tonnage were being reported every month as the U-boats found their targets on the Atlantic: the Russians were withdrawing hundreds of miles to team up with General Winter; the vast area of the Far East had been overrun and the USAAF had not yet got into its stride in the UK. The only punishment to be inflicted on Germany itself was from night raids by Bomber Command which were gradually becoming more effective under the leadership of 'Butch' Harris. Westcott was one of his 100-plus airfields. Our flying at Westcott – 20 Wellington sorties – was vitally important for two reasons: firstly, to accustom ourselves to Bomber Command procedures in all their aspects; and secondly, after the unnaturally good weather conditions and lighted towns in

Canada to get used to the much worse weather conditions and the black-out in the UK and across Europe. The good news navigationally was the addition to the navigational set up of *Gee*, an electronic aid based on master and slave stations on the ground, giving rise to measurements of time differences and thus a lattice of hyperbolic lines, two of which would give a 'fix'. The navigator would align blips on a CRT and read off co-ordinates, which would relate to the lines on a pre-printed chart. Near the ground stations, the lines would cross at a marked angle and accuracy was good; at increasing distances, for instance into Germany, the lines crossed at a small angle and accuracy fell off. Euphoria over this new black box was to be short-lived: we discovered later that, along with any electronic device, it was jammable.

By the time we were crewed I had been promoted to Flying Officer (nothing special – time promotion). John Verrall was (initially) a sergeant and was commissioned during his time later on the Squadron. Sergeant or no, he was the Skipper. Army visitors – and we had them from time to time – could never understand this. A lieutenant calling a sergeant 'Skipper'! Unheard of; definitely infra dig. In the RAF in the air, it worked. We all had our separate jobs in the air, our separate responsibilities and we worked as a team, pilot (Skipper), navigator, bomb aimer, engineer, signaller and two gunners, mid-upper and tail. Woe betide those crews who couldn't work together. Nothing worse than an argument in the air, between the pilot and the nav' say. It got the rest of the crew unsettled and nervous. My relationship with John Verrall was excellent. He was a very good pilot, steady, reliable, cautious and yet decisive. I did my best to match him in navigational expertise.

The next stage – no, we haven't reached our operational Squadron yet – was for our crew to be posted to 1651 HCU (Heavy Conversion Unit) at Waterbeach, because of the need for all of us to become accustomed to the Stirling itself, the first of the four-engined bombers. Nine sorties were sufficient to declare us ready at last for the front line. Whilst at Waterbeach we spotted a Stirling one day that looked different. It was pregnant with a huge curved bulge under the forward part of the fuselage. Ah, somebody said, you can see the ground at night with that thing. We were mystified. In a few months we would know more.

In early 1943, as it had been since the London *Blitz*, RAF Bomber Command and certain Groups of the USAAF constituted the only offensive action against Germany; and so it was to be until 6 June 1944. There were six Heavy Bomber Groups established in Bomber Command. Nos 1, 3, 4, 5, 6 (Canadian) and 8 (Path Finder Force). No. 2 Group consisted of medium bomber squadrons, principally Blenheims, Mosquitoes and Venturas. AM Sir Arthur Harris had been

Commander-in-Chief since February 1942 and would continue to be so until the end of the war, following directives from Air Ministry based on policies of the War Cabinet. Four-engined aircraft were joining the Heavy Bomber Groups in increasing numbers – principally Halifaxes and Lancasters. The Stirlings, the earliest of the four-engined, were all in 3 Group in East Anglia. John Verrall and his crew were posted to the strength on 214 Squadron at Chedburgh in March 1943; 22 months after I had joined the queue of recruits at Lords. I used to say. 'Verrally, thou shalt operate'. Our tour on the Squadron was to last only five months. A word about the Stirling: we called it the Queen of the Skies. On the ground, with tail wheel and not nose wheel, the cockpit was an awesome couple of storey's high. It was a beauty to fly at low level and it looked magnificent. But its height performance was abysmal. It was a struggle to reach 14,000 feet. In consequence we had the uncomfortable feeling that the Halifaxes and the Lancasters – up at 20,000 feet – were always dropping their loads through us – not nice. The problem with the Stirling was the wingspan. Had it been designed a few feet wider the height performance would have improved but hangar width demanded that wingspan should be less than 100 feet and so that is how Short Brothers built them. We were ready for war.

So too was Sergeant Charles Cawthorne. He had joined the RAF as a Boy Apprentice and volunteered for aircrew duties as a flight engineer. At age 18 he became part of Australian Warrant Officer Warren 'Pluto' Wilson's newly formed Lancaster crew at 1660 Heavy Conversion Unit (HCD) Swinderby. Wilson was said to have won so much gambling his way across the oceans, to face worse odds in the air in England, that he was known as the 'filthy plutocrat'.[18] The crew were posted to 467 Squadron RAAF at Bottesford near the hamlet of Normanton, just north of Bottesford village. The main gate and the station sick quarters were in Nottinghamshire and the guardroom, technical site and billets were in Lincolnshire, while the main runway and bomb dump were in Leicestershire. Nearby the spire of the 13th Century church of St Mary the Virgin soars 210 feet above the stunning countryside of the Vale of Belvoir. Said to be the tallest village spire in Leicestershire, it was both a landmark and a hazard for the 467 Squadron crews.

Cawthorne recalled:

The Station Commander was a very experienced bomber pilot, Wing Commander Cosme Gomm DFC, and the Squadron Commander was Squadron Leader David Green. Both men were keen to show the rest of 5 Group what an Aussie squadron could do and to this end were keen to build one of the highest totals of operational sorties within the Group.[19] The Squadron flew their first operational *Gardening* sorties on 2/3 January 1943. These were quickly followed by an *Oboe* trial bombing operation against Essen in the Ruhr valley.[20] Our crew's first operational sortie was on 2 April when we bombed the strongly defended *U-boat* pens at St-Nazaire. As we approached the target, Harry Crumplin, the navigator, was persuaded to come forward into the cockpit to see the target area ahead all lit up with searchlights, TIs [Target Indicators] and the irregular flashes from exploding bombs and flak. He took one look, muttered 'Bloody Hell' and quickly disappeared behind the black curtain around his crew position. In complete contrast to this experience, less than 24 hours after facing the flak of St-Nazaire, I accompanied our wireless operator, David Booth, to his wedding in Manchester. Our tour of operations progressed very satisfactorily and we soon found ourselves involved in what was referred to in the newspapers as, 'The Battle of the Ruhr'. Despite Bomber Command sustaining heavy casualties during this period, our crew remained relatively unscathed but nevertheless we were alarmed to find that every time we went on leave, another crew become a squadron casualty whilst using our aircraft.[21]

By early 1943 Kammhuber's *Himmelbett* defences had been completed and the *Lichtenstein* AI-equipped[22] *Nachtjagd* aircraft were now capable of exacting a toll of up to six per cent bomber casualties on any deep penetration raid into the *Reich*. Thus, Bomber Command losses rose rapidly during the first few months of 1943, although in early January operations were of necessity, on a limited scale, normally restricted to the *U-boat* bases on the Atlantic coast.

At a minute past midnight on 1 January 1943, 6 Group RCAF officially ceased to take orders from 4 Group HQ at Heslington Hall on the outskirts of York. The Canadian Group had been in temporary accommodation at Linton-on-Ouse before moving in December to Allerton Park, a 75-room Victorian mansion near Knaresborough, which had been requisitioned from Lord Mowbray, premier baron of England. At 'Castle Dismal' as it was known, Air Vice Marshal George Eric Brookes, one of Harris' 'Bomber Barons' and a Canadian nationalist yet still proud of his Yorkshire upbringing, took control of six airfields in the North Riding with six of the Wellington squadrons and two of the Halifax squadrons.[23] The topographical features of the Vale of York were such that airfields had to be constructed close together and landing circuits overlapped. Smog from the industrial areas at Leeds and Bradford in the south and Middlesbrough in the north would often mix with low cloud and reduce visibility for much of the time, and for two days weather kept the aircraft grounded. Then on the night of 3/4 January when three Path Finder Mosquitoes carried out a 5 Group *Oboe*-marking experimental raid on Essen, six Wellingtons on 427 'Lion' Squadron RCAF took off from Croft to lay mines in the shipping channels of the Frisian Islands. All six Wimpys, including one with several flak holes in the wing, returned safely.

Three of the 19 Lancasters of 5 Group were shot down on Essen. *U-Uncle* on 207 Squadron, piloted by 21-year-old Flight Sergeant 'Barry' Chaster of Duncan, Vancouver Island, was attacked repeatedly by *Oberleutnant* Manfred Meurer of I./NJG1 flying a Bf 110. In the first attack the *Experte* set the starboard engine petrol tank on fire and flames also spread through the main batteries aft of the main spar, causing the intercom to fail. Chaster gave the order to bail out by word of mouth. Twice more Meurer attacked, raking the length of the Lancaster's fuselage with cannon fire. Ken Pugh the 30-year-old wireless operator, Bill Moger the flight engineer, Ivan Lineker the 21-year-old mid-upper gunner and Wally Harris the 21-year-old rear gunner were killed. Sergeant Gordon K Marwood, the 22-year-old navigator from Barking, Middlesex, and 20-year-old Sergeant John Banfield, the newly qualified bomb aimer who had been an apprentice printer before joining up, bailed out. Marwood hit the tail unit and suffered deep cuts in his left leg. He and Banfield were soon captured and they were hospitalized in the Queen Wilhelmina *Luftwaffe* hospital in Amsterdam for four weeks. Chaster successfully evaded capture and with the help of the *Comète* escape line was back in the UK within three months. East of Arnhem, *A-Apple* on 9 Squadron flown by 31-year-old Flight Lieutenant Douglas Herbert Scott Lonsdale DFC was shot down by *Unteroffizier* Christian Költringer for his first victory. South of Maastricht *Hauptmann* Reinhold Knacke shot down *V-Victor* on 61 Squadron piloted by Flight Sergeant Raymond Harry Bird. There were no survivors on either crew. Next day Lonsdale's wife Patricia received the Air Ministry telegram at their home in Westham, Sussex to say that he was missing.[24]

On the night of 13/14 January, 66 Lancasters and three *Oboe* Mosquitoes were dispatched to Essen. Two of the Lancasters were *L-London* and *B-Beer* on 103 Squadron at Elsham Wolds, high above the flat fenlands of Lincolnshire and bounded by the Humber Estuary and the Weir Dyke to the north. The Battle Order for the night showed that Sergeant Geoff Maddern's crew would be giving up *B-Beer*, their regular Lancaster, to Sergeant Bertram Edwin Atwood RCAF and his crew on 12 Squadron, who arrived from Binbrook for one night at Elsham. Maddern considered Lancasters 'the most beautiful kites imaginable to fly, very light and responsive to the controls'. And they could climb 'like a bat out of hell'. The main trouble he found was to keep the speed down. 'They were quite easy to land – you feel them down like Tiger Moth' he once said. Even though he had experienced trouble with *B*'s port engine the night before, having to fly *L-London* was unthinkable. When the squadron was equipped with Halifax Is his crew had been caught in a raid on Hull in '*L*' and Maddern's crew had survived another 'shaky-do' in Lancaster *L-London* over Denmark. The pilot protested to the wing commander who changed the order so that Atwood's crew took *L-London* while Maddern's crew would fly *B-Beer*.

At 17.00 hours Maddern's crew lined up for take-off in their familiar *B-Beer*, carrying a 4,000lb bomb plus ten cans of incendiaries. On take-off Maddern noticed an unusually big swing to port and he corrected it as best he could, hauling the Lancaster off the runway at 120mph. The rear gunner called up to say that bags of smoke were pouring from the port inner. A moment later the engine caught fire. Doug Richards the engineer feathered it immediately. They weren't a hundred feet off the deck and indicated airspeed was less than 120. Maddern levelled out and built up speed for the climb out.[25]

Don Charlwood continues:

Fortunately, our aerodrome was fairly high and it happened that take-off was over a valley. In Brigg, the fire brigade saw our trouble and quickly turned out to shadow us. By a superb piece of flying and close cooperation from the flight engineer, our pilot nursed *B* to a safe altitude. The fire brigade were astonished to see us vanish into the North Sea. A con rod that had passed through the sump of our port inner engine was found on the runway. Some hours after our safe return we learned that the crew of strangers in *L-London* had failed to return from the operation. At first we expressed feelings of guilt over their fate but then it struck us that if they had taken *B* without knowledge of its faults, their fate would almost certainly have been the same. And *B*'s bomb load might well have exploded on one of those Lincolnshire villages we knew so well.[26]

Three other Lancasters were also lost on the raid. Two of the *Oboe* Mosquitoes had to return without marking and the sky markers of the third aircraft failed to ignite above the cloud. German aircraft also appeared to have dropped decoy flares to distract the Lancasters.

The night following, Bomber Command carried out the first of eight area attacks on Lorient on the French Atlantic coast. Some 122 aircraft were dispatched, including 63 Halifaxes, 33 Wellingtons and 20 Stirlings. It was also 6 Group's first bombing operation, and the Canadians were detailed to send 35 Wellingtons and 19 Halifaxes, but as some stations were fogged-in, only nine of the Wimpys and eight Halifaxes were to get airborne. The Path Finder marking of the target, the *U-boat* base, was accurate but later bombing by the Main Force was described as 'wild'. Two Wellingtons were lost. Over 150 heavy bombers returned to Lorient the following night and bombing was more accurate this time, with at least 800 buildings destroyed.

On the night of 16/17 January Sir Arthur Harris sent 190 Lancasters and 11 Halifaxes[27] on their way to Berlin – the first attack on the German capital in 14 months – with the words, 'Tonight you are going to the Big

City. You will have the opportunity to light a fire in the belly of the enemy that will burn his black heart out.'

Sergeant pilot Robert Raymond, an American volunteer who originally served in an American Ambulance Unit in France in 1940, before travelling via Spain and Portugal to England, wrote:

We all knew that sooner or later during this winter we should go there. Any raid on that city has tremendous propaganda value and is good for morale. Nevertheless, although it was not entirely un-expected and everyone wanted to have it on a line in his Log Book, I felt rather weak in the knees when I walked into the Briefing Room and saw that name on the big board. Price, my wireless operator, said, 'I'd rather go to Essen than Berlin and I hate Essen as a target.'

We took off about dusk and never saw the ground after leaving Base until we were over Berlin, which fortunately was in a clear area. Just heavy flak and lots of it over the target; no tracers from light guns, which only reach up to about 8,000 feet, no balloons, no search-lights or night fighters, etc. They knew what height we were and put up a box barrage all around us. We were straight and level for two minutes for the bombing run and every second seemed like a year. The whole of northern Europe is covered with snow and the moon being nearly full, the ground detail was clearly visible. The only colourful parts of the target were half a dozen flares and the great glowing mushrooms from our four thousand pounders. We carried one 4,000lb bomb and nearly a thousand incendiaries and got a fairly good photo of our results. Since Carter has been AWOL [Absent Without Leave] for three weeks, we took another rear gunner. It was his first Operational flight and he was so excited before, during and after the trip that he wasn't worth much. Much of our report on the trip depends on his accurate observations over the target where he has a better view than anyone else. Before take-off he looked up into the bomb bay and asked if that big cylindrical object was a spare petrol tank. It was the 4,000lb 'cookie' [blockbuster bomb] and he had never seen one before.

Cloud over base when we returned was less than 1,000 feet and I did a short cross-country flight until most of the others had landed. I don't like being stacked up on a circuit in cloud at 500 feet intervals with a dozen other tired pilots.

This raid saw the first use of varicoloured markers, or Target Indicators (TIs), dropped on the aiming point by selected crews. The operation, however, was a disappointment. Thick cloud *en route* and haze over the target caused problems and the bombing was scattered. The Berlin flak had proved light and ineffective and it was assumed that the greater altitude of the attacking force had surprised the German gunners. Only one Lancaster was lost.

Harris repeated the raid on the 'Big City' the following night when the weather was better. Robert Raymond wrote:

Had eight hours sleep and all crews that had serviceable planes were briefed for Berlin again. Over the North Sea climbed up through layers of cloud tinted with the red glow of the setting sun. In the clear air between them it looked like some of those dreamy cloud-land shots in *Lost Horizon*. Just a space without a horizon except for the banded cloud of soft greys, mauve, purple and grey blues and with 'George' flying I had plenty of time to think – odd thoughts as mine always are – how scared I had been in a nearby town two nights ago when sitting in a cafe during an Air Raid Alert. Several enemy planes bombed from low level and one bomb demolished the building across the street. The blast effect even from that small effort was considerable and made me appreciate what we were doing to the enemy targets with our forces and weight-carrying capacity. Verily it is better to send than to receive in this racket. Then I thought about the message from the Chief of Bomber Command which had been addressed to us tonight and read out at Briefing, 'Go to it, Chaps and show them the red rose of Lancaster in full bloom.' Someone behind a desk had given an order to a great organization and here we were a few hours later, one of the pawns in the game, sitting up over the North Sea with the temperature at minus 30° Centigrade, wondering if we would ever see England again.

Vapour condensation trails were plainly visible in the clear moon-light above cloud, showing that many other planes were a few minutes ahead on the same track. They are always a curious phenomenon and form at the trailing edge of your wings, due to the decrease in pressure there. Out over the sea we pay no attention to them, but over enemy territory they always result in attacks by night fighters. Conditions over the target were about the same as the previous night, except the visibility was even better. Several members of the crew heard shrapnel from spent bursts bounce off our fuselage and the rear gunner saw five members of a crew bail out and go down on their white silk umbrellas. We passed quite close to them. Flak was more accurate than the previous night and several times I saw the black smoke puffs indicating shell bursts right in front of us as we were leaving the target area.

Collected some ice on the return trip, but I have no fear of that now, having studied diligently and knowing why, when and how it occurs. It is only necessary to be able to recognise the type of cloud, the frontal weather conditions and have an accurate thermo-meter to avoid its cumulative effects. Each time I climbed to lower temperatures or descended to clearer areas and we went through it confidently although I have reason to believe that it accounted for some that are missing.

Impossible to land at base and we were diverted nearly 200 miles, by which time we were running on the fumes that came from the last drops of petrol that Griffiths was squeezing out of the tanks.

Came back to base today and found many missing and the rest scattered over England in various ways. More and more I find that knowledge is a more valued asset than courage. Each member of the Crew is still learning. Griffiths has found the best speeds to fly and rates of climb for most economical fuel consumption. We keep our own charts and are improving steadily.

Two consecutive nights to Berlin leaves me with but one thought when I have finished this letter. To sleep for at least 12 hours. And my stomach reminds me that I haven't seen an egg for nearly a month and our food is very poor.

The routes taken by the 170 Lancasters and 17 Halifaxes to and from Berlin were the same as those followed on the previous night and German night fighters were able to find the bomber stream.[28] Broadcaster Richard Dimbleby reported on the raid for the BBC, flying with Wing Commander Guy Gibson DSO DFC*, the CO of 106 Squadron at Syerston in a 9 hour 15 minute round trip. It was Gibson's 67th op.[29] Next morning British listeners tuning in to the BBC Home Service heard Dimbleby's broadcast on their wireless sets. They also listened intently to the number of losses. Nineteen Lancasters and three Halifaxes did not return.

Four of the dozen Lancasters dispatched by 9 Squadron at Bardney, ten miles east of Lincoln, failed to return. Sergeant A G Carswell RCAF crashed about 25 miles from Magdeburg. He and four of his crew were taken prisoner. Nothing was heard and no trace found of 23-year-old Sergeant John George Bruce Chilvers' Lancaster, all of whose crew were killed. Likewise, no trace was found of 24-year-old Pilot Officer Trevor Gibson, an experienced Aussie from New South Wales who once flew through the Alps on three engines rather than over and who flew his way out of an attack by three Bf 109s at Aachen in October. Flying Officer Eric William Mitchell Jacombs his 27-year-old second dickey from Auckland, New Zealand was among the dead. There was no happy ending either for Flying Officer Anderson Storey, a 6ft 4 inches tall American from one of the oldest and best New England families, or his crew. Before the war 'Andy' Storey who came from Jamaica Plain, Massachusetts, had holidayed in England and he had become something of an Anglophile, flying his first op, as a second dickey, on 3 June 1942. The Berlin operation was his 30th and last of his tour. The Lancaster flown by 22-year-old Sergeant Arthur Hobbs, which carried Flight Sergeant Frank Goheen Nelson, a 24-year-old American pilot, from Wilkinsburg, Pennsylvania, as his second dickey, did return to Bardney, whence Frank Nelson was reunited with his own crew, but it had been no picnic. Another American pilot to die this night was Pilot Officer James Woolford RCAF who was from Charleston, Illinois. He and his Lancaster crew on 61 Squadron at Syerston were killed.

Bardney airfield was a sprawling layout of drab Nissen huts with a few larger buildings of the same ugly but functional construction. Two miles away the village of the same name had only 1,000 population and no fewer than seven pubs! Lincolnshire was dotted with wartime airfields like Bardney, built hurriedly on farmland for the duration, but some airmen were lucky to be billeted at permanent stations with cut-stone manor houses for billets and messing. In January 49 Squadron gave all this up when it moved from Scampton to Fiskerton about 8 miles away. By this time Roy Thomas had become romantically involved with Aircraftwoman Betty Ragg, a pretty young girl who used to drive Guy Gibson around the station at Scampton and who now drove the bomb loads out to the aircraft; a rather dangerous job, as Roy recalls:

One day Betty had delivered a bomb load to one of the aircraft. The armourers managed to let one of the bombs fall off one of the bomb hooks in the Lancaster. Panic for ground staff, they all disappeared into adjoining fields and woods. I had a telephone call to attend the bomb immediately. I got Betty with her tractor to drive me to the bomb under the Lancaster *N-Nuts*. I asked her to leave while I defused the bomb but she refused and between us we managed to get the bomb onto a bomb trolley and took it away for disposal. At this point the ground staff appeared out of the woodwork just like the Pied Piper of Hamelin and carried on as if nothing had happened.[30]

Notes

1. See *Chased By The Sun*.
2. *Strike Hard, Strike Sure* by Ralph Barker (Pen & Sword Military Classics 2003)
3. The award of the DSO was made to Gibson in November 1942 and a bar would follow in March 1943.
4. Stirling N3669 *H-Harry*, a veteran of 67 raids, served with Nos 7 and XV Squadrons and was put on display outside St. Paul's Cathedral during February 1943 as part of London's contribution to 'Wings For Victory' Week.
5. *Bombers Fly East* by Bruce Sanders. (Herbert Jenkins Ltd 1943). According to research by Steve Smith writing in a 218 Gold Coast Squadron Assoc newsletter: 'Records suggest that N3721 flew the

highest number of Stirling sorties. Initially delivered on 23 February 1942 to 218 Squadron, it was transferred to 1653 Conversion Unit on 1 November 1943 and on 4th was belly landed. Quickly repaired, it remained active until struck off charge as obsolete on 1 May1944. Its operational career began on 26 March 1942. As HA-C it set off for Essen, first of its 61 sorties. Its first mining sortie came on 22 April. After 12 sorties it was overhauled returning, as HA-S to attack Bremen on 6 June. Between then and the 29th it flew seven sorties: four to Bremen, three mining. It then came off operations, returning to battle on 23 September as HA-P for the Vegesack raid. Thus identified, it flew 29 bombing and eight mining sorties. Its only visit to Berlin was on 1 March 1942. It once crossed the Alps, to Turin's Fiat works on 28 November 1942. On 13 May 1943 it returned to operations as HA-J. Nine mining sorties were flown before its final operation against Hamburg on 25 July 1943. An incendiary bomb struck the tail unit, ending its front line career.'

6. The rest of Middleton's crew comprised mid-upper gunner F/S Douglas Cameron, an ex-gamekeeper, and Sgt Harold W Gough, rear gunner, an ex-garage mechanic from Scarborough who was on his 33rd op, and P/O George R Royde, navigator. Middleton was the only Australian on the crew. F/S Leslie A Hyder and Sgts Cameron and Gough were awarded the DFM. F/O Cameron later joined 635 Squadron and he was shot down on 4 August 1944 when he was flying with Acting S/L Ian Willoughby Bazalgette DFC RAFVR. Cameron survived and evaded capture. Bazalgette, known within his family as 'Will' to distinguish him from his father Ian, had his early education at Toronto Balmy Beach School. His family returned to England in 1927 and he grew up in New Malden, suffering from poor health and diagnosed with tuberculosis as a teenager. He underwent lengthy treatment at the Royal Sea-Bathing Hospital in Margate. Bazalgette was awarded a posthumous VC for his actions on 4 August 1944. He told four of his crew to bail out but remained aboard his crippled Lancaster and tried to save the lives of two of his badly wounded crew by belly-landing the bomber in a field. But within seconds there was a massive explosion and all three men died.

7. Middleton's medal is now on display in the Australian War memorial in Canberra. The RAF Mildenhall Officer's Club was renamed in his honour – Middleton Hall – in 2002.

8. *Pathfinders* by W/C Bill Anderson OBE DFC AFC (Jarrolds London 1946).

9. Hadeball's final tally was 33 night kills and he was awarded the *Ritterkreuz* in July 1944. He survived the war.

10. Kemble Wood's crew would join 405 'Vancouver' Squadron RCAF, which was formed in 4 Group on 23 April 1941 and flew Wellingtons and Halifaxes until posted to Coastal Command in October 1942.

The Squadron returned to Bomber Command in March 1943 and operated in 6 Group RCAF.

11. P/O Eric E 'Bill' Williams, the bomb aimer, was sent to Stalag Luft III at Sagan where on 29 October 1943 he was one of the three men in the famous 'Wooden Horse' escape from the East Compound. Williams, Lieutenant Michael Codner, a Royal Artillery officer captured in the Western Desert and F/L Oliver L S Philpot DFC, a Coastal Command Beaufort navigator who was shot down on 11 December 1941, all made 'home runs'. Each received the award of the Military Cross. *Footprints On The Sands of Time; RAF Bomber Command PoWs in Germany 1939–45* by Oliver Clutton-Brock (Grub Street 2003).

12. *Chased By The Sun; The Australians in Bomber Command in WWII* by Hank Nelson (ABC Books 2002).

13. This same night the first *Oboe*-aimed bombs were dropped by six Mosquitoes on a power-station in Holland.

14. Adapted from *Bomb Raid on Duisburg* by T G O'Shaughnessy in *70 True Stories of the Second World War*, (Odhams Press).

15. See *RAF Bomber Command Losses of the Second World War*, Vol. 3 1942 by W R Chorley (Midland 1994).

16. Later AVM D J Furner CBE DFC AFC.

17. On the night of 8/9 December 1942 133 bombers and Path Finders including 108 Lancasters were ready to be dispatched. While bombing-up at Syerston incendiary bombs fell from the racks of a 61 Squadron Lancaster, exploded and set fire to the aircraft, and the inhabitants of Newark and district were able to hear for themselves the explosion of a 4,000lb bomb. G/C Clive 'Gus' Walker, the Station Commander went out to the bomber on a fire tender and the Lancaster blew up killing two men and taking the Group Captain's arm off. 'Gus', who had played rugby for Yorkshire, Barbarians and England, returned and post war became AVM Sir Gus Walker CBE DFC AFC.

18. *Chased By The Sun; The Australians in Bomber Command in WWII* by Hank Nelson (ABC Books 2002)

19. W/C Cosme Lockwood Gomm DSO DFC who was born in 10913 in Curitiba, an industrial town in Panama State, Brazil, was killed on 15/16 August 1943 on the operation to Milan, on his 24th sortie of his second tour of operations, his first tour having been on 77 Squadron. He had also flown Beaufighters on operations on 604 Squadron. Gomm's parents, who lived at Sao Paulo in Brazil, were notified of his death.

20. *Oboe* was the most accurate form of high-level blind bombing used in WWII and it took its name from a radar pulse, which sounded like a musical instrument. The radar pulses operated on the range from 2 ground stations ('Cat' & 'Mouse') in England to the target. The signal was heard by both pilot and navigator and used to track the aircraft over the target, If inside the correct line, dots were heard,

if outside the line, dashes, a steady note indicated the target was on track. Only the navigator heard this signal. When the release signal, which consisted of 5 dots and a 2-second dash was heard, the navigator released the markers or bombs.

21. *Thundering Through The Clear Air: No. 61 (Lincoln Imp) Squadron At War* by Derek Brammer. (Toucann Books, 1997)

22. Airborne Interception (AI)

23. 420 'Snowy Owl', 424 'Tiger', 425 'Alouette', 426 'Thunderbird', 427 'Lion' and 428 'Ghost' Squadrons and 408 'Goose' and 419 'Moose' Squadrons respectively. 429 'Bison' Squadron, a Wellington unit detached to 4 Group, joined 6 Group at the beginning of April. That same month 405 'Vancouver' Squadron at Leeming, which was equipped with Halifaxes and which had only just returned to Bomber Command in March after serving in Coastal Command, departed for 8 PFF Group. 432 'Leaside' Squadron was brought into being at Skipton-on-Swale on 1 May. That same month Nos 420, 424 and 425 Squadrons were sent to the Mediterranean theatre.

24. Knacke was KIA on 3/4 February 1943.

25. *See Out of the Blue: The Role of Luck in Air Warfare 1917–1966* edited by Laddie Lucas (Hutchinson 1985)

26. *No Moon Tonight* by Don Charlwood (Penguin 1988)

27. The Stirlings were withdrawn from an original plan so only the higher-flying heavies would participate. Most of the force was from 5 Group. So far this was the largest number of Lancasters on one raid.

28. Nineteen Lancasters and three Halifaxes were lost on the night of 17/18 January. On both raids the Path Finders were unable to mark the centre of Berlin and bombing was inaccurate. (The experiments with the Lancaster/Halifax force using TIs against the 'Big City' now ceased until H_2S became available).

29. The award of the DSO had been made in November 1942 and a bar would follow in March 1943.

30. Betty and Roy married in 1944 at Great Glen Church. That same year he received a MID for bomb disposal after one of 49 Squadron's Lancasters had crashed at Colerne airfield with bombs on board.

CHAPTER 4

'Juggling with Jesus' –
'Gambling with God'

You can only live once
It's a matter of months,
And it doesn't take long to die.

Song of 100 Squadron, RAF

It was very dark and cold and still on 20 January when Don Charlwood, back from leave, arrived at Barnetby Junction, the nearest railway station to Elsham Wolds. From third-class compartments smelling of dusty seats and stale cigarette smoke, heavy-booted workmen with coarse remarks in thick Lincolnshire accents stepped off the LNER train and boarded lorries for work on the aerodromes at Kirmington, Grimsby or half a dozen others. From two of the compartments, the closed windows misted by their breaths, 20 heavily-clad Land Army Girls detrained for the beet fields on the Wolds. Like most of the aerodrome villages, Barnetby had been lifted from obscurity by the war and gave the impression that after the RAF had passed by it would lapse into obscurity again. When he was setting out on leave, or going for an evening off camp, Charlwood would see the station as a gateway to the gaiety of London or Lincoln. It would beckon him with its promise of escape to places where time did not exist. But when he returned he would see the same station darkly, as a gateway to fear and tension. He walked up the hill to the Barnetby crossroads, past the 'WAAF-ery' and past the last farm. Charlwood's first question when he reached the gate at Elsham Wolds was to enquire how many had the squadron lost in the last six days.

'No-one' said the guard, muffled to his chin and heavily gloved. 'All back safe – even from Berlin.'

Charlwood went immediately to Sergeant Keith Webber's room, feeling relieved and light-hearted. The barracks smelled of last night's fire, of dirty clothes and unwashed bodies. RAF gunners were asleep in shirts

111

that appeared welded to their bodies by the dirt of weeks. Webber, older than most of them, tall and a little stooped, was the 30-year-old navigator and one of three fellow Australians on the crew of Sergeant 'Ted' Laing RAAF. Laing had been a teacher and his and Maddern's crews were close friends. They had arrived on the Squadron at the same time as Syd Cook's and Col Bayliss's crews; twenty sergeants in all. But of the 'Twenty Men' only eight were destined to depart from Barnetby station a few months later.

Bayliss had gone down in France on the operation to Munich on 21/22 December 1942. His aircraft had been so crippled by a night fighter that he ordered 'abandon aircraft'. Bayliss was struggling to hold it steady for the crew to bail out when it exploded over Vavincourt. He was thrown clear; the others perished.

On arrival at Elsham Wolds 20-year-old 'Syd' Cook had told Charlwood that death was the only thing they had left to fear. 'Syd' Cook rose in rank from sergeant to a squadron leader of the Path Finders on 156 Squadron at Warboys and awards of the DFC and DFM. He and his crew were KIA on the operation on Frankfurt on 4/5 October 1943 on the eve of his 22nd birthday. He had flown over fifty operations.

Charlwood entered Webber's room:

Keith sat on his bed packing a canvas bag in preparation for leave. A well stoked fire glowed in the stove behind him. He looked up, smiling. 'Welcome back! How was the leave?'

'Perfect – until they broadcast the losses on Berlin. What was it like?'

Keith cleared some clothes from his bed and motioned me to sit down. I thought at that moment how old and tired he looked. I believe operational life was harder for him than for any man among us. Although he never complained and was a careful and exact navigator, I sometimes felt that he had seen into his own future and had realized that, whatever his ability, he was faced with impossible odds. Lately he had been unable to eat many of the mess meals and had become more stooped and greyer about the temples. But he remained the soul of courtesy.

'It wasn't as bad as we expected,' he said. 'A tremendous concentration of searchlights but we've seen worse flak. I think it must have been a fighter night and we were lucky enough not to strike any.'

Later, at the crew room door Charlwood met Webber, dressed to go on leave. 'I thought you'd be down at the station' said Charlwood: 'He shook his head. "Our leave is scrubbed. We're going on ops." ... He smiled wryly. "The squadron is short of a crew. Roly Newitt force-landed after Berlin and hasn't been able to get back ..."[1]

In Lincolnshire on the morning of 21 January it was overcast but calm and the visibility clear. Ops were 'on'. Seventy-nine Lancasters and three Mosquitoes were going to Essen and 70 aircraft were to drop mines off the Frisians. Don Charlwood saw Keith Webber at the navigator's briefing, stooped intently over his chart.

> As he glanced up I was surprised to see that his disappointment had vanished. There was more youthfulness about him than I had seen since we had left Canada, as though a conflict within him had suddenly been resolved ... They sat in front of us at main brief-ing: Ted Laing, plump and happy-looking, his complexion always glowing, as though he had emerged from a shower; Keith, stooped, serious and intent; Tony Willis, rosy-cheeked and black-haired. Again and again my eyes were drawn to them, to Keith's greying temples and to Ted Laing's fresh complexion. Ted in particular looked so vibrant that my forebodings were hideous by contrast. We did not speak again to them until the time came to drive to the 'planes. They were sitting in a small van, Ted Laing and Keith nearest the back. We exchanged the usual words with them and then they were gone.[2]

At Essen the force encountered 10/10ths cloud and bombs were dropped on estimated positions. Four Wellingtons and two Halifaxes were lost on the mining operation and four Lancasters failed to return from the raid on Essen. Two of them were from 103 Squadron at Elsham Wolds. No word was received from *A-Apple* flown by Flight Sergeant Edgar Heaton Burgess or *F-Freddie* piloted by 'Ted' Laing. He had been shot down by *Feldwebel* Theodor Kleinhenz of III./NJG1 at Twente and had crashed at Enschede in Holland with four blazing fuel tanks fluttering down behind the burning fuselage. There were no survivors from either crew. Kleinhenz, who received the Iron Cross, 2nd Class the next day, was killed in an air battle near Bucharest on 5 April 1944.

The next Main Force raids were on Lorient and Düsseldorf on 23/24 January when just over 200 bomber sorties were flown. A Stirling was lost on the raid on Lorient, where successful bombing was claimed, and two Lancasters failed to return from the operation on Düsseldorf, where some bombs fell in the south of the city. One of the Lancasters was *C-Charlie* of 460 Squadron RAAF at Breighton, flown by Squadron Leader Richard Osborn DFC the 'A' Flight commander. The route to the target began with a climb to 20,000 feet from Breighton and course was set for Mablethorpe and across the North Sea to Holland. At ETA the target was cloud covered and no *Oboe*-placed markers were seen. The bombs, there-fore, were dropped blind on ETA and heading set for home. Estimating a coast-out at Noordwijk a diversion signal was received to proceed to Bradwell Bay, but instead of coasting out over Noordwijk *C-Charlie* was attacked over the Ijsselmeer, about 50 miles to the north east by *Ober-leutnant* Wolfgang Küthe and *Unteroffizier* Helmut Bonk of IV./NJG1 in a Bf 110F night fighter. Küthe approached *von hinten unten* (from behind and below) and raked the Lancaster with cannon fire. Osborn was hit in his left upper arm by a shell and a deafening roar filled the cockpit. The intercom was put out of action and the TR equipment[3] was knocked out, while the fuel tank between the two starboard engines was soon ablaze and a sheet of flame stretched back towards the tail-plane. Badly wounded and with the aircraft on fire, Osborn made the decision to turn back and force-land in Holland.

Küthe closed in and delivered a second attack, which ruptured the hydraulic system and killed the rear gunner, Pilot Officer Stuartson Charles Methven RAAF. Executing a 270° turn to port, Osborn put the Lancaster into a rapid descent. By now he had no reference to his flight instruments but, by the light of the flames, sensed the ground coming up rapidly, and levelled off. Unable to lower the undercarriage or lower the flaps he cut the throttles. The Lancaster ploughed through a dyke and moments later slithered to a halt near Stavoren and the de Boer farm just west of the village of Warns. Rapidly evacuating the aircraft through the various upper surface hatches, five of the crew gathered on the soft turf, the wounded mid-upper gunner helped by the wireless operator. *C-Charlie* was now burning fiercely from the cockpit area to the tail. Of the bomb aimer, Sergeant John Vincent Conlon RAAF, there was no sign. Presently Harmen de Boer, his son Meindert and his daughter Maria appeared and ushered the five into their farmhouse, bearing the mortally injured rear gunner on a tarpaulin sheet, and began to tend the crew. Any hopes of escape for the others were dashed by the swift arrival of a party of German soldiers from the *Eisbar* sector control station at Sondel. Dr. Tromp Visser was summoned to tend to the wounded and then an ambulance arrived and the two were driven off with the doctor to St. Bonifacius hospital in Leeuwarden. Conlon's body was found with unopened parachute the next day, 500 metres east of what remained of the Lancaster. A fire extinguisher bottle, which Martje de Vries-Jagersma, pregnant with her first child, 'liberated' from the wreckage, was adapted with a screw-top to use as a hot water bottle for her new baby's cot and later for her nine siblings! Following spells in hospital (osteomeyelities having set in) and in PoW camps, Richard Osborn was repatriated in a prisoner exchange in September 1944.[4]

Nearly 160 aircraft returned to Lorient on 26/27 January 1943 when two Wellingtons and a Lancaster were lost. The following night Düsseldorf was attacked again when *Oboe* Mosquitoes carried out 'ground marking' for the first time. Bombing was well concentrated on the southern part of the city. Three Halifaxes and three Lancasters were lost. A return to Lorient was detailed on the 29th/30th when 75 Wellingtons and

41 Halifaxes of 1, 4 and 6 Groups were dispatched. Crews encountered thick cloud and icing, and with no pathfinder marking the bombing was well scattered. Two Halifaxes and two Wellingtons failed to return.[5] On Saturday 30 January, 19 Wellingtons of 4 Group and 17 Bostons went to various places in Germany and Holland, and only two Wellingtons and one Boston found targets to bomb. Four of the Wellingtons failed to return. Pilot Officer Don Bateman, pilot of one of the eight Wellington crews on 466 Squadron RAAF dispatched to Emden was scathing:

> This operation was set up at very short notice and did not appear to be co-ordinated. A hurried briefing gave no mention of the primary target. My bomb aimer could not be located in time and a spare man had to be drafted in. I did not relish flying over Germany in daylight at this stage of the war. British bombers were heavily outgunned by cannon firing German fighters and were easily out-manoeuvred but I believe the majority of pilots when briefed to fly in daylight to Emden were more concerned about the weather conditions at take off, which were the worst I had experienced up to that time. Aircraft took off as soon as they were ready into heavy rain, low cloud and a strong gusty wind. The met forecast was accurate except for being two hours out in the timing of the dispersal of low cloud over Holland and Germany. I did not see any Boston aircraft. I spotted a Wellington approaching the Dutch coast but did not attempt to formate on it, as we were about to enter a layer of cloud. The height flown varied between 1,500 and 2,500 feet; given the forecast weather conditions my main concern being to fly within the densest cloud layer. I did not anticipate any fighter attacks whilst flying in cloud. We were told at briefing that the German fighters were likely to be grounded by the weather.
>
> We had been told to expect barrage balloons protecting the target, the bomb bursts were both felt and heard, though no results were observed, the bombs being fused with several seconds delay. Reaching longitude 6' 30' east on the return flight we emerged into clear skies and unlimited visibility. I was tempted to turn on a northerly course and get out to sea as quickly as possible but there being no ground fire or fighters to be seen. I decided to continue on my westerly course and to get down low. I may well have passed within a mile or so of Leeuwarden airfield but my main occupation was scanning the skies for fighters. Crossing the North Sea we ran into the cold front that had been over base at take-off. Visibility under the low cloud was poor so I climbed to 4,000 metres to avoid the possibility of icing and was glad to break cloud just clearing the Yorkshire coast.[6]

At Waddington that Saturday night Frank Nelson's tour was cut short when his aircraft was one of five that returned early from Hamburg with bad icing and mechanical trouble. He was diverted to Leeming but flew into the Hambleton Hills at Hawnby. All the crew, who were on only their second op together, were killed. Flight Sergeant Jack Findlay Thomas, a 26-year-old Australian pilot from Wollongong, New South Wales and his crew who were on their fifth op, failed to return when they were shot down near Vechta.[7]

All told, 148 heavies, 135 of them Lancasters, went to Hamburg on the night of 30/31 January. They carried out the first H_2S attack of the war, with Path Finder Stirlings and Halifaxes using the new device to mark the target. Its use was not successful even though Hamburg, close to a coastline and on a prominent river, was the optimum target for using H_2S. The bombers reached Hamburg in extremely unfavourable weather that led to large amounts of ice forming on their wings. Despite the violent whirl blasts they dropped thousands of incendiary bombs on a 9-mile-long stretch of the port district. In addition, HE bombs dropped in a 30-minute period were aimed at oil refineries, shipyards, warehouses, fuel depots and various industrial plants. Bombing however was scattered over a wide area and most of the 315 tons of bombs that were released probably fell in the River Elbe or the surrounding marshes. Even if the raid was not a technological success, the *Daily Express* account painted a different picture to its readers:

> In half an hour on Saturday night Bomber Command made one of its heaviest attacks this year – on the *U-boat* building centre of Hamburg. Four-ton bombs were dropped, so were two-tonners, so were tens of thousands of incendiaries. And most of the bombs fell in the new 'thunderbolt' fashion in less than 15 minutes. So it was that our crews, many miles on their way home, could see the glow of the enormous fires they had caused. Over the target the sky was clear and the pilots could see the Aussen-Alster and Binnen-Alster lakes pointing the way to the great docks a mile or so away across the Elbe river. Several pilots reported that they saw the four-tonners burst among buildings and that the target area became completely obscured by incendiaries. Hamburg has the reputation of being one of the most heavily defended cities in Germany but on Saturday night the flak was only moderate and there were no reports of night fighters. The dock area extends for nine miles along the Elbe. It was Hamburg's 94th raid; the last one was in November. The RAF on Saturday also bombed objectives in Western Germany and from the night's raids five planes [all of them Lancasters] did not return.

In February, attacks were made on German cities, on French seaports on the Atlantic coast, and once more against Italy. The night of 2/3 February when 161 aircraft went to Cologne, was cloudy, and a further experiment was made using a four-engined bombing force with various forms of

Path Finder techniques. Markers were dropped by two *Oboe* Mosquitoes and H₂S heavy marker aircraft. Damage was caused right across the city. Five aircraft failed to return.[8]

The 7 Squadron Stirling that Squadron Leader Thomas Gilbert 'Hamish' Mahaddie, an incorrigible Scot from Leith, was flying from Oakington, 'went out as *'C-Charlie* and came back *'C'* Colander with cannon shells peppering its fuselage'. Mahaddie had started his RAF life as a non-commissioned metal rigger at the age of 17. In 1933 he was posted to RAF Hinaidi near Baghdad in Iraq. A year later he was accepted for aircrew training and earned his wings in Egypt, flying Avro 504Ns. Posted to 55 Squadron for two years, he bought a horse called 'Hamish' but his fellow aircrew claimed that there was no real difference in appearance between the horse and its owner and Mahaddie acquired the nickname 'Hamish' for the rest of his life. Returning to England in 1937, he was serving as a Sergeant pilot on 77 Squadron in 4 Group, flying Whitleys at Driffield in Yorkshire when war began. During the Dunkirk evacuation he flew 23 operations against the advancing Germans and received his commission, before being sent to instruct on Whitleys at Kinloss. He had received the Air Force Cross, which he referred to as an 'Avoiding Flak Cross' and had begun a second tour of operations in August 1942 on Stirlings on 7 Squadron.

Shells passed on either side of Mahaddie's seat on *C-Charlie* and the instruments were 'a mess' but he was only 'pinked' through his parachute by an armour-piercing round, which left a stain on his pants 'no bigger than the size of a sixpence'. The mid-upper gunner, bomb aimer, and Eddy Edwards the wireless operator, who had three fingers shot off while he was *Windowing*, were injured. All the compasses and navigational equipment were destroyed with the exception of the astrocompass. Flight Lieutenant Fred Thompson DFC, whose father Walter was Winston Churchill's personal bodyguard, was able to provide navigation bearings that would get them back to Oakington as long as the aircraft continued to fly. The ailerons had been severed simultaneously with the burst of cannon shells, and without any warning Mahaddie began a violent diving turn to starboard. After reaching an 'alarming' attitude, with no apparent ability to counteract it, he realized that effective lateral control had gone. As they were diving under full power, Mahaddie made to grab the throttles. Providentially he caught hold of the two port throttles and this had the immediate effect of bringing the Stirling's wings level. He could then trim the aircraft out of the dive to regain the 10,000 feet they had now lost. Flight Sergeant Charles 'Jock' Stewart, the flight engineer, crawled into the root of the wing to try to establish where the aileron cables had been cut but almost at once he had to be brought back to tend to Edwards.

By 'a cunning and crafty use' of the throttles Mahaddie got the Stirling back on course and Jock Stewart managed to rejoin the two severed ends of the aileron cable with, as Bob Pointer, the rear gunner, recalls, 'pieces of wire he had conjured up from somewhere that enabled the Skipper to gain partial control and set course for home.' But their troubles were not yet over. Halfway back to the coast they were stalked by a Ju 88 night fighter, which concentrated its guns on the Stirling's fuselage instead of the petrol tanks in the wings. The bomber survived, in no small measure because of Mahaddie's limited evasion tactics. In doing so, it destroyed Stewart's 'handiwork' and Mahaddie once again had to 'juggle' with the engines to maintain control. A count the next morning revealed that Hamish had suffered '174 cannon shells up my kilt'. Mahaddie reflected that maybe the experience followed the ancient Scots maxim; 'The de'il looks after his ain!'[9]

The devil also looked after Squadron Leader Edward Gerard Gilmore DFC RCAF who took his 405 'Vancouver' Squadron Halifax to Cologne this same night. He described events afterwards:

> We had just dropped our bombs when one of the crew reported that fighters were following us. I swerved but while we were still trying to get away we were caught in a cone of searchlights. Flak blew off the starboard inner propeller and the astrodome, punched holes in the fuselage, wings and aileron and threw the aircraft over on its back. All the engines stopped together and we whirled into a dive. The aircraft fell from 18,000 feet to 4,000 feet and I gave the order to bail out. The navigator almost got clear but I called him back just in time. The rear-gunner told me over the intercom that he was hacking his way out of the jammed turret. In the twisting, turning, rolling dive a parachute broke loose and after smashing the master compass, got jammed between the control column and the instrument panel. Suddenly all the landing lights went on. We were 4,000 feet above the target, lit up for the gunners to see us.

Any bookmaker would have offered a thousand to one against that Halifax getting home. Falling straight on to the Rhineland city, lit up by its own landing-lights, it could seem only a matter of seconds before it either crashed or was blown to fragments. But a thousand to one chance is not too slender for an RAF bomber crew to take. Gilmore continued:

> Only two of my engines were working properly at this stage, [Apparently they had started up during that headlong spiralling spin earthwards] and we had lost so much height that it was no good trying to take evasive action. Besides, some of the bomb-doors were open and the Halifax was very difficult to manoeuvre. The only thing I could do was to fly straight and level. Somehow we got out of the searchlights without being badly hit again. The third engine had now picked up. We thought that our troubles were now over but when

we got over the enemy coast we were caught by searchlights again. By good luck we escaped. Navigation was just about as difficult as it could be. We had lost the master compass and we had to find our way back to base on the bomb-aimer's compass. It was quite a trip.

Very much it was quite a trip. The lame duck was all but plucked bare.[10]

The night following it was Hamburg when 263 aircraft braved icing conditions over the North Sea. The Path Finders failed to mark the target effectively and bombing was scattered. Sixteen aircraft, including eight Stirlings, were lost. On 4/5 February when a total of 188 aircraft were sent to Turin, the 156 aircraft that reached the target caused serious and widespread damage. Three Lancasters, including one that crashed in Morocco with the loss of all seven crew, failed to return. Four Path Finder Lancasters were sent to attack the port of La Spezia with new 'proximity fused' 4,000lb bombs, which exploded between 200 and 600 feet above the ground to widen the effects of the blast. Three of the PFF Lancasters dropped their bombs successfully and all returned safely. An all incendiary raid on Lorient by 128 aircraft caused large fires. One Wellington failed to return.

For the next two nights Stirlings, Wellingtons and Halifaxes carried out *Gardening* sorties in the Frisian Islands and between St-Nazaire and Texel. A Stirling, which ditched two miles off Cromer, and another Stirling, were lost on the first night of mine-laying operations. Three Wellingtons failed to return on the second night when 52 Wimpys and 20 Halifaxes were dispatched, and a 466 Squadron Wimpy crashed at Leconfield on the return. Lorient was attacked again on 7/8 February when just over 320 aircraft were dispatched. The Path Finder marking plan worked well and the two Main Force waves carried out a devastating attack. Seven aircraft were lost. Before the next big raid, on Wilhelmshaven on the 11th/12th, mine-laying took place over two successive nights in the Baltic and between Brest and Texel. Six Lancasters laid mines without loss, while the 21 Wimpys dispatched also returned with no losses. When the raid on Wilhelmshaven went ahead 177 aircraft were dispatched, but cloud completely covered the city. The Path Finders were forced to carry out sky-marking by parachute flares using H_2S but it was carried out with great accuracy and bombing was remarkably successful. Three Lancasters failed to return and a Halifax on 102 Squadron at Pocklington crashed north of Dalton, killing the pilot and six of his crew.

The raid by 466 aircraft on Lorient on 13/14 February was the heaviest attack on this port by Bomber Command during the whole war, and more than 1,000 tons of bombs were dropped for the first time. Three Wellingtons were shot down, two of them crashing in the target area. Three Lancasters were lost returning to England. *P-Peter* on 12 Squadron crashed returning to Wickenby and all the crew were killed. *G-George* on 49 Squadron returning to Fiskerton crashed in the sea off Plymouth.

All the crew perished. *Q-Queenie* on 207 Squadron crashed returning to Langar. The pilot was injured. Lancaster *Q-Queenie* on 50 Squadron at Skellingthorpe crashed in the sea with the loss of all seven crew. A Halifax on 158 Squadron at Rufforth and a Wellington on 166 Squadron at Kirmington were involved in a collision over Langport in Somerset. Everyone on board the Halifax was killed. The Wimpy was crash-landed with one crew member dead. *B-Baker*, a Halifax on 35 Squadron, and a Stirling on 75 Squadron at Newmarket that was abandoned near Plouay, also failed to return. The Halifax was piloted by Pilot Officer 'Tommy' Thomas RCAF and had taken off from Graveley at 18.20 to mark the target. Just after the TIs had been released *B-Baker* was hit by flak and the port inner engine caught fire. Thomas tried to put the flames out by diving the aircraft sharply but it was in vain. Near Carhaix in Brittany he ordered his crew to abandon the bomber. Flying Officer Bill Freeman, the Canadian tail gunner, was fatally injured when his parachute became entangled and he died shortly after midnight; Sergeant D C Young the flight engineer was taken prisoner. Thomas succeeded in reaching Switzerland on the night of 12/13 March and there he remained for the next 18 months. He returned to the Allied lines, leaving behind his wife, whom he had married on 2 November, and a young son, Peter, born on 28 August 1944. Three other sergeants on the crew evaded capture in France with the help of the Underground.

In Bronxville, New York at 10.18pm on 16 February, the parents of *B-Baker's* navigator, Flying Officer Carter DFC* RCAF, received a telegram informing them that their son was missing in action. On 22 March the *New York Daily News* noted briefly that he had been reported missing. That same day another newspaper telephoned Mr. Carter telling him that they had learned that his son had been killed. Gordon Henry Francis Carter was an Englishman born in Paris and living in Bronxville, New York, when he enlisted in the RCAF as soon as he became 18 in June 1941. Contrary to reports, he was very much alive and safely in the hands of the Resistance. He had bailed out 'in the nick of time' and jumped into the dark void his 'guts cramped with fear'. He was wearing civilian clothes under his battle dress when he was shot down and he could speak fluent French. He even went to the town hall in Ploermel, claimed to have lost all his possessions during the raid on Lorient and left with a replacement identity card in the name of Georges Charleroi, food and tobacco ration cards, clothing and shoe coupon books.[11] Carter has been described as 'tall, sleepy-looking, very dark, very handsome and very reserved'. During his time in northwest France he met and fell in love with Mademoiselle Janine Jouanjean 'an attractive blonde'. Early in April, Carter left for England with sixteen Frenchmen in a sardine smack, which safely reached Cornwall. Back at Graveley he talked at length about his new girlfriend who he described as his fiancée. Flight Sergeant Napoleon Barry RCAF, the mid upper gunner, and Sergeants' R Martin and Eddie

Turenne were meanwhile passed along the escape lines to Spain and they too reached England safely.

On 14/15 February, 243 Halifaxes, Wellingtons and Stirlings were sent to bomb Cologne, and just over 140 Lancasters of 1, 5 and 8 Groups visited Milan. At Cologne 218 crews claimed to have bombed the target but the real total was only about 50, whose bombs hit mostly in the western district. Nine aircraft failed to return. Two Lancasters were lost on the raid on Milan where fires could be seen 100 miles away on the return flight. One of the Lancasters crashed in France. The other missing Lancaster was *P-Peter* on 103 Squadron, flown by Squadron Leader Walter Harry Powdrell, a New Zealander serving in the RAF. He had succeeded Squadron Leader Fox whose aircraft had also been downed by bombs over Milan the previous October. Powdrell gave the order to abandon *P-Peter* over the target area after the aircraft was hit by a stream of incendiaries from another Lancaster. Sergeant John Duffield the flight engineer recalled:

> We were just turning off to clear away. All of a sudden I heard this awful battering noise. I don't know what he thought he was bombing because we were a minute clear of the target so he wasn't bombing that. All the engines stopped. I heard the pilot say 'We've had it. You'd better jump.' I was very lucky that I had my parachute with me. So I made my way to the rear door. But I couldn't open it. The aircraft started to twist and I put my back against the bomb compartment on the fuselage floor and braced myself there. The aircraft was spinning like mad by this time. I was just stuck there with the force of the spin. Suddenly the spinning stopped I made my way to the rear door and leapt out. My harness was loose and the jerk of the opening parachute ripped into my groin. The pain was something to be believed, agonizing.

Duffield landed heavily, limped to a farm nearby and was soon apprehended by Italian soldiers. Powdrell and three of the crew died in the Lancaster.

One of the pilots who flew the trip to Milan was John Verran. The New Zealander was now on his second tour and flying Lancasters on 9 Squadron at Waddington. As they neared Milan Verran's crew could see anti-aircraft fire and searchlights, and they knew it would soon be their turn. John Moutray DFM the WOp/AG recalls:

> Jimmy Geach the bomb aimer was in charge as he called out directions on the intercom to Jim Verran. His calm voice was saying 'Left – left ... Right a bit ... Steady ...' as we started the most dangerous part of any bombing raid – the straight and level bombing run, which had

to be held for another twenty seconds or so after the bombs had gone, waiting for the photoflash to go off. At that point my job was to stand on the step ahead of the main spar and put my head up into the astro hatch to assist the gunners in keeping a look out for fighters. For some inexplicable reason, I did something I had never done before; I looked directly above and got the shock of my life. In the glow from the searchlights and target I saw another Lancaster 30 feet above us on exactly the same heading and, like us, his bomb doors were open! The 4,000lb bomb looked enormous and I knew it could be released at any second. I yelled into my microphone, 'Hard-a-port!' Somewhere I had read that it was a natural reaction of pilots to go to port; anyway our crew was well-trained and Jim stood ED495 on its wing tip and we got an unusually good view of Milan! We went round again to do another bombing run.

Visibility was good and bombing was concentrated. Fires could be seen from 100 miles away on the return flight.[12]
· A 101 Squadron Lancaster crew captained by Sergeant Ivan Henry Hazard that had bombed and were on the home run was attacked by a Fiat Cr.42CN *Caccia Notturna* (night fighter).[13] The Lancaster caught fire amidships almost immediately, one engine stopped dead and two of the petrol tanks were holed. Sergeant Leslie Airey, the rear-gunner, was wounded in the leg but he sat at his gun-button, waiting until the attacker was a bare 50 yards away, then he gave it a burst, which put its engine on fire. Flight Sergeant George P Dove DFM, the mid-upper gunner, who had flown on Whitleys earlier in the war, likewise remaining at his guns waited while the flames lapped his turret and at the right moment, gave the fighter another burst, which sent it whirling down out of control, the flames from its engine spreading over fuselage and tail. Meanwhile the fire in the Lancaster was pronounced out of control and the captain reluctantly gave the order to prepare to abandon the aircraft.[14] However, the rear-gunner with his injured leg could not make a parachute descent so Hazard decided to make a crash-landing. But before he could find a spot to land, the navigator, Sergeant Bill Williams, and Pilot Officer Fred Gates, the wireless operator from Cheam in Surrey, got the flames under control. The mid-upper gunner, though burned badly about the face himself, hauled the rear gunner out of his turret. Again Hazard revised his plan, determined to try and make it home on three engines. He got up to 15,000 feet, staggered over the Alps, and with his tanks practically drained dry[15] eventually landed at Tangmere. Hazard and Dove were awarded the Conspicuous Gallantry Medal. The wireless operator received the DSO.[16]
   On 16/17 February 377 aircraft returned to Lorient and 363 aircraft dropped mainly incendiary loads in clear visibility. *F-Freddie* on 103 Squadron, flown by Sergeant John Charles Harley Young RAAF, crashed

in the target area with the loss of all seven crew. Young was a particularly coarse but good-natured Australian, known to everyone as 'Bull'. He was built like a bull; he had the voice of a bull and the instincts of a bull. When ops were scrubbed and an extra bus was put on for Scunthorpe it would be drinking and no popsies that night. Just before the operation 'Bull' had confided in fellow Australian Don Charlwood, a navigator who was not flying that night, that if anything happened to him would he get his personal belongings home to his mother? Charlwood said that the target was supposed to be 'easy' but Young cut him short and said, 'I know all about that, son but I've got an idea.' Young's Lancaster was the only one lost when it crashed in the target area. All Young's crew, including fellow Australian, Sergeant Andy Stubbs, short and dark and permanently cheerful, died with him. 'About his neatness and the friendly cock of his head' there was something that reminded Charlwood strongly of a bird. Charlwood refused to believe that the operation would claim 'Bull' Young but it did, and before he had time to arrange for his belongings to be sent home the men of the Committee of Adjustment arrived and removed them. Charlwood wished that he had risen earlier and he believed that he had let 'Bull' down.[17]

Over 190 aircraft went to Wilhelmshaven on 18/19 February. The Path Finders claimed accurate marking in clear visibility but most of the bombs were dropped in open country west of the target. Four Lancasters were lost. Despite the dreadful weather conditions on 19/20 February, three experienced German night fighter crews were given permission to take off from Leeuwarden to try and intercept the returning Wilhelmshaven force. Twelve bombers, including five Stirlings, failed to return. *Oberleutnant* Hans-Joachim Jabs destroyed three Stirlings of XV Squadron in 44 minutes over the North Sea, operating in *Himmelbett* box *Schlei* at Schiermonnikoog Island, to take his score to 29 victories. *Leutnant* Wolfgang Küthe destroyed a fourth Stirling over the North Sea. *Oberleutnant* Paul Gildner and *Unteroffizier* Heinz Huhn in a Dornier 217 night fighter shot down two Lancasters and a Stirling which they misidentified as a 'Boeing'. Four days later, on 24/25 February, Gildner was killed when his Bf 110G-4 crashed on final approach to Gilze-Rijen following an engine fire. His score stood at 44 victories. Huhn bailed out at low level and survived. Küthe was killed on 14 April 1943 in a flying accident at Leeuwarden airfield. He had eight victories.[18]

During the 1943 strategic night bombing offensive the life expectancy of a bomber crew was between eight and 11 operations, whereas each crew member had to complete 30 'trips' before being sent on 'rest' at an Operational Training Unit. Flying Officer Harry Barker, a Stirling bomb aimer on 218 'Gold Coast' Squadron, May 1943–July 1944, adds:

We all knew that in 1943 the average 'life' of a crew was ten operations so you can imagine that everyone was a bit jumpy at their 13th! If you really begin to analyse it the options open to us were limited. We had to consider the following: 1. We had all volunteered to do the job. 2. We all wanted to hit back at the enemy, who were attacking London, Coventry and Liverpool etc. 3. The camaraderie was so strong on the Squadron that no one would seriously consider letting his friends down. 4. There was a keen determination to achieve 30 ops and complete the tour. 5. The alternative was refusal – followed by a court-martial and the awful consequences. 6. The reward on returning from an op was a breakfast of bacon and eggs, a luxury only available to successful aircrews. When you take this lot into account, together with the youthful confidence that 'only other crews get shot down', you may understand how we felt about the incredible risks we were taking. It is similar to the attitude of cigarette smokers who are all convinced that it is only other people who get lung cancer!

In general the morale of aircrews was good. It was easier for the young unmarried and unattached men to cope than it was for those with wives, children or steady girlfriends. One could cope with the prospect of death if this did not result in the misery and hardships for others. This inevitably caused some differences in attitude to the war and the way we behaved under fighting conditions. I am not saying that the men with family commitments were any less dedicated to the job but I believe they were under much greater strain than many of the rest of us. We did tend to 'let ourselves go' when off duty. We drank a great deal of beer and used any excuse for a party commonly described as a 'piss up' either in the mess or at a local pub. We got to know the locals who were always friendly and understanding. Some shared their Sunday dinners with us and of course there were the girls. Life on the Squadron was a mixture of fun, laughter, friendships, excitement and hell, just around the corner. In the Officers Mess we had a very good standard of living. The food was very good. Sleeping quarters were comfortable and we had either a batwoman or batman to look after us, cleaning shoes, brass buttons etc and pressing uniforms and making beds. I usually had a cup of tea brought to me in bed every morning! I was one of the few who survived and it seems dreadful to admit that I enjoyed the life on the Squadron. The only way I can admit this is in the belief that my friends who were lost also shared the good side of this time of battle for survival. That is how we saw it. The tragedy was that so many did not survive.

Flight Lieutenant Stanley Freestone, a Wellington pilot on 142 Squadron in 1942 and Stirlings on 199 Squadron in 1943 recalls:

As an operational heavy bomber I felt the Wellington was a better aircraft than the Stirling. The Wellington could cruise fully laden around 15,000 feet and with its fabric covered geodetic airframe construction could take a great amount of damage. Of course the Stirling could carry a greater bomb load but its weakness was the inability to cruise laden much above 12–13,000 feet. A further weakness was a lack of performance on only three engines. However the Stirling had a strong airframe and violent manoeuvres to escape from searchlight cones and fighters bore it in good stead. It was the best of the four heavy bombers for a tight radius turn.[19]

The most undying vivid memories I had were seeing a huge area – the target – covered in flame and explosions. Above the immediate target area the Germans maintained a 'box barrage' of heavy anti-aircraft fire. This was constant and fire only diverted when searchlights had captured an aircraft in a cone of intense light. Aircraft would be caught in these beams such as an octopus holds its prey with tentacles. The aircraft would twist and dive to extricate itself but would immediately receive a concentrated volume of fire. Sometimes a still fully laden bomber received a direct hit – then a huge ball of fire would explode as bomb load, hundreds of gallons of petrol, oxygen bottles and the huge photo flash bomb we all carried by which we photographed our target sighting, exploded. A terrifying cascade of brilliant colours would follow this explosion, as the whole inferno fell to earth. A very quick death for some but many airmen fell to earth without a chance to operate their parachutes. Often a bursting shell was so close one could hear the explosion above the din of the engines and through the helmet and earphones all crewmembers wore. One also heard the metal shrapnel as it tore through the aircraft. This made a rather strange tinkling bell-like sound. In the brilliant light over the targets both from enemy searchlights and ground fires and explosions one could see the hundreds of balls of smoke left after exploding anti aircraft fire.

By March 1943 Josef Goebbels, the *Nazi* propaganda chief, was deeply troubled:

Reports from the Rhineland indicate that in some cities people are gradually getting rather weak at the knees. That is understandable. For months the working population has had to go into air raid shelters night after night and when they come out again they see part of their city going up in flame and smoke. The enervating thing about it is that we are not in a position to reply in kind ... Our war in the east has lost us air supremacy in essential sections of Europe and we are completely at the mercy of the English [*sic*].

March came in with a roar, when on the 1st, RAF bomber crews were briefed for Berlin. Air Marshal Sir Arthur Harris was to say later: 'We

can wreck Berlin from end to end if the USAAF will come in on it.'
Just over 300 aircraft of Bomber Command were despatched but the Path
Finders experienced difficulty in producing concentrated marking because
individual parts of the extensive built up area of the 'Big City' could not
be distinguished on the H₂S screens. Though the attack was spread over
100 square miles, because larger numbers of aircraft were now being
employed and because those aircraft were now carrying a greater average
bomb load, the proportion of the force which did hit Berlin caused more
damage than any previous raid to this target. Much damage was caused
in the south and west of Berlin, 22 acres of workshops were burnt out
at the railway repair works at Tempelhof and 20 factories were badly
damaged and 875 buildings were destroyed.[20]

Squadron Leader Geoff Rothwell, now a Flight Commander on
75 Squadron RNZAF at Newmarket, took part in the Berlin raid:

> Because my crew had no operational experience we started my
> second tour with two mining sorties off the Friesian Islands on
> 26 and 27 February. We carried six mines and dropped them north
> of Terschelling on the first operation. The fifth mine exploded on
> contact. The second operation was to the north of Ameland. We
> were shadowed by a fighter, which did not open fire. After a one-
> night rest from operations we were briefed on 1 March for an attack
> on the German capital. It was the heaviest weight of bombs to be
> dropped on Berlin and fires were still seen 200 miles from the target.
> On the return journey we strayed off course and were engaged
> by intense heavy flak over Osnabrück and fought off five attacks by
> German night fighters, one of which was claimed as destroyed by the
> front-gunner. The aircraft had numerous holes from the flak, which
> also shattered the windscreen. My impression after the first raid over
> Germany in just over two years was that there had been enormous
> changes in tactics, technology and the ferocity of the bombing. It was
> obvious that there had been tremendous developments in attack and
> defence by both sides.[21]

When *J-Johnny* returned at about 02.30 hours Flight Lieutenant Jim
Verran on 9 Squadron, who had been awarded the DFC on 23 April 1941,
'had nothing to complain about'. They were using *Gee* lattice lines to aid
their navigation and the New Zealander broke cloud near Waddington
at 800 feet, but the visibility was poor. When Lancasters left from the airfield, rear gunners could watch the light on the central tower of Lincoln
Cathedral and when the light was sharp the weather was usually clear.
The light was a welcome sight for crews returning. It not only told them
that they had survived but also that they did not have to worry about a
final hazard.[22] But there was a final hazard and it was about to happen to
Verran, as he recalls:

We were in the circuit; I could see the flare path and was talking to the control tower. It was my turn to land and as I looked up there was another Lancaster [captained by a Canadian, Flying Officer John Fergus Greenan on 57 Squadron] breaking cloud and heading straight towards me. At that height I had no wish to put the nose down so tried to climb over the other aircraft but did not manage it. The next thing I knew he hit me almost head on. I don't think he saw me and still often wonder what he was doing there. He was from Scampton and using his *Gee* lattice lines should have been nowhere near us. We came down [at Heighington, three miles ESE of Lincoln] and he flew on hitting a high tension pylon [at Riseholme near Scampton] with no survivors. I remember when the aircraft hit us saying to myself: 'well that's your bloody lot; you won't get out of this'.

Verran was knocked out in the air when the fuselage section aft of the mid-upper gun turret was torn away causing the control column to snap back, striking him in the face and breaking his lower jaw. He had been thrown clear when the remaining part of the aircraft struck the ground, propelling him through the cockpit canopy. He suffered a broken left femur, his right arm was paralyzed and he had lacerations of the head and face around both eyes. 'I came to in a ploughed field. Bits of the aircraft were burning around me and ammunition was exploding. An ambulance arrived and I was carted off to hospital.'

Pilot Officer 'Jimmy' Geach the bomb aimer, Sergeant Ted Smithson the flight engineer and Sergeant Ken Matthews the tail gunner were killed on impact. Sergeant Ken Chalk the mid-upper gunner was able to climb out of his turret uninjured. Frank Johnston, the Australian navigator, survived, though his brain had been partially detached from his skull. John Moutray the Canadian WOp/AG walked out of the torn fuselage with minor injuries. Moutray, an artist, who was raised on a small cattle ranch at 4,100 feet in the interior of British Columbia and had joined the RAF in 1938, had previously flown on 51 Squadron and he had received the DFM in October 1940. Moutray would complete 65 operations on Bomber Command. Amazingly, Jim Verran, who after a few days in the RAF hospital at Rauceby developed a high temperature and pain around his right lung, would, in time recover from his injuries and return to operational flying.

Nineteen aircraft had failed to return from Berlin. Two of the Lancasters that were lost were on 103 Squadron at Elsham Wolds. There were no survivors on the crews of Flight Sergeant Bill Austin DFM or Flight Lieutenant G W Stanhope. Austin and his crew, who had flown five ops in seven nights, were on the 29th operation of their tour. Don Charlwood remembered Austin as a 'likeable fellow, plump, rather pale with straight, black hair that often fell across his forehead. He had brown eyes and the casual manner that often accompanies them. Somehow his battle dress looked slightly big for him. Perhaps it was the way he walked. 'Never curse a scrub' Austin had always said. 'It might have been the op you were to go missing on.'[23]

103 Squadron lost another Lancaster and all its crew on the night of the 3/4 March when the visibility was clear over Hamburg, which was under attack by the Main Force.[24]

Next day, Flying Officer Nebojsa Kujundzic, a Yugoslavian pilot, took *B-Beer* off from Elsham Wolds on a cross-country flight. South of Peterborough the starboard inner engine caught fire. The engine was feathered and the fire extinguished but the Yugoslav unfeathered the engine. It burst into flames again but as there was now no extinguisher, the fire spread rapidly and burnt off the wing at its root. Six of the crew bailed out but Kujundzic went down with the aircraft and was killed.

Losses prompted some crews to take a philosophical view of their lives and their chances of survival. Pilot Officer Errol Crapp RAAF, navigator on the crew of Flight Lieutenant Richard Alexander Curle on 100 Squadron at Waltham just outside Grimsby was from New South Wales, where his father, the Reverend Arthur Frank Crapp, had a parish at Singleton. In a diary entry to 'Dad and family' he once wrote: 'Now I realise there is not much between life and death in this racket and we have to face the fact that Jerry might get us any minute on these excursions. So without being morbid, I want to say that if he does get us please don't grieve. Our troubles are over; and don't feel bitter because hundreds of families have made bigger sacrifices.' Erroll knew he was on borrowed time. While at 27 OTU Lichfield in 1942, eight Wimpys had been lost due to operational commitments; Richard Curle's crew were the sole survivors. In September, just a month after first flying on a Wellington, they had gone on a raid to Bremen and then three days later flew to Essen where their Wimpy was hit by flak, which destroyed the port aileron. The navigator left his table to help his English pilot control the battered Wimpy, which despite severe handling problems and lack of air speed managed to regain the south coast of England before the crew bailed out near Andover in Hampshire. They went to their operating squadron qualified to wear the caterpillar badge.[25]

On the night of 3/4 March, Errol and several of his friends had gone into Grimsby for an evening at the theatre. In his diary later that night Errol Crapp wrote about the 'tawdry' show they had seen at the Tivoli: 'Wasn't worth sixpence. We will probably operate tomorrow.' He was right. It would be the Squadron's first operational sorties since reforming so no one knew what to expect. In the event the 4th/5th was a quiet night with no Main Force activity, and 100 Squadron's Lancasters were to lay mines off the enemy coast. One of these was *S-Sugar*; the other was *D-Dog*, which would be flown by Richard Curle. They and 25 other aircraft were to lay mines in areas as far south as Bayonne and as far north as Gdynia. The only other aircraft that were operating this night were 16 OTU aircraft, which were to drop leaflets. A 28 OTU Wimpy crew at Wymeswold that had the unenviable task of *Nickeling* was hit by flak and abandoned by three of the crew off the Dutch port of Vlissingen. Their pilot was killed and the rear gunner was lost in the sea and was never seen again. Lancaster *S-Sugar* on 100 Squadron crashed at Langar airfield ten miles south of Nottingham while trying to land on the return. Six of the crew died and one was injured. *D-Dog* was presumed to have crashed in the target area. Flight Lieutenant Richard Curle's body was recovered but Pilot Officer Errol Crapp and the five other crew members were lost without trace. Their names were added to the lists at Runnymede of ever-increasing numbers of RAF and Dominion aircrew with no known graves.

In RAF parlance 'Missing' at least gave loved ones a glimmer of hope. 'Missing, believed killed' did not. In aircrew circles 'missing' were those who had 'gone for a Burton' (a beer) or more commonly 'gone for a shit'; 'bought it' or had 'got the chop'; never 'killed'. Difficult targets were 'the arse-hole of death'. Sergeant Angus Robb, a Wellington rear gunner on 431 'Iroquois' Squadron RCAF at Burn, south-west of Selby, recalls. 'Very seldom did we, amongst ourselves, say we were on "operations". It was either "dicing with death", "juggling with Jesus" or "gambling with God", reduced in most cases to "dicing", "juggling" or "gambling". I suppose you could say that the night of 5/6 March "was the night that changed my life".'

This night has gone into history as the starting point of the Battle of the Ruhr. Essen, the most important and the most difficult target in the Ruhr-Westphalia region to find, was the destination for 442 aircraft whose targets included the vast Krupp concern, the mining section of the United Steelworks of the Rheinische Coal Syndicate, the Rheinische Steelworks and many other great firms. Two thirds of the bomb tonnage was incendiary. One third of the HE bombs, which included 150 of the huge 4,000-pounders, were fused for long delay. Eight *Oboe* Mosquito marker aircraft on 109 Squadron were designated to mark the target, the first of which was to drop blind a salvo of red TIs at 21.00 hours. The first Mosquito was to be followed two minutes later by a Path Finder who would reinforce the red markers with green. A second Mosquito, again using *Oboe*, was to re-mark the target one minute later, with a third seven minutes after that. In between the Mosquitoes, the Path Finders would reinforce the reds with greens at one or two minute intervals. The pattern was to continue throughout the 40 minutes in which the Main Force was concentrated. Yellow TIs would be dropped 15 miles from the target to act as a lead-in point. Only if there were no reds visible were the Main Force to bomb the 'greens'.

For most of the way out the route was cloudy. Fifty-six aircraft (including three Mosquitoes) turned back early because of technical problems and other causes. Wellington *Z-Zebra* on 429 'Bison' Squadron RCAF crashed on take-off at East Moor. Two other Wellingtons, *J-Jig* on 196 Squadron and *L-Love* on 466 Squadron RAAF, collided over the North Sea after takeoff from Leconfield. Both Wimpys were damaged but one held on and reached the target and both returned safely. Angus Robb's Wimpy took off at 18.15 hours and for the first hour or so they flew 'happily' over the North Sea with, it seemed.

> No one but us in the sky. It was strange, flying on night operations; the sky, for most of the time, seemed completely empty, although you knew for a fact that there were hundreds of your compatriots all over the place. It was when we reached the coast of Holland things started to happen. Searchlights were much in evidence, and flak, although not close, was very active. It was as we approached the Ruhr Valley for the first time that I realized I had made a mistake in volunteering for aircrew and should have accepted their offer of being a member of an air-sea rescue launch. I have never been so frightened in my life and in fact I would better describe it as terror-stricken! There was no way, in my opinion, that any aircraft could fly into that amount of flak and come out the other side and that was without taking into account the German night fighters that were patrolling the skies just looking for me! It really is impossible, for anyone who was not there, to fully comprehend the sheer weight of metal that was thrown into the sky over those German cities. What with that and the fiery red glow, intermixed with explosions of all colours, from the ground, it was a scene from Dante's *Inferno* brought into reality. There was also the spectacle of bombers exploding in a shower of red-hot debris when they received a direct hit from a flak shell, or had come off worst from an encounter with a German night fighter. It was a terrifying experience. If there had been some way I could have got out of ever flying on operations again, without losing face or being graded LMF; in other words a coward, after that second trip I would have taken it.[26]

Fifteen miles from the target the weather cleared, although pilots reported that natural valley mists were still seeping in from the river. These and industrial haze did not affect the outcome of the raid. The five *Oboe* Mosquitoes marked the centre of Essen perfectly, right up to the last greens, 38 minutes after zero hour, and the Path Finder 'backers up' arrived in good order and dropped their Green TIs blind on the target. Squadron Leader Geoff Rothwell, who now commanded a Flight on 218 (Gold Coast) Squadron at Downham Market, recalls:

> The success of their target-marking techniques was most obvious from photographic reconnaissance after bombing attacks. From the

point of view of the bomber crews, operations were made considerably simpler as Path Finder markers were dropped at turning points so making adjustments to course possible without the necessity to obtain fixes and position-pinpoints continually. The responsibility for identifying target aiming-points had lifted from the shoulders of the bomber crews as TI markers were dropped by the Path Finders making the work of the crews easier.

Although the actual bombing operations were more effective through the employment of new techniques, there was an added danger from the technological advancement of the German defences. It was a terrifying sight to approach a target such as Essen and know that one had to run the gauntlet of searchlights, flak and night fighters to reach the target. The display of these defences could be seen from a great distance and there is little doubt that they had an effect on morale when the Ruhr Valley targets were attacked repeatedly in 1943. Strangely, although searchlights were not lethal in themselves, like flak, they were feared far more, probably because of the psychological effect of being exposed, since a night bomber hoped the darkness would be a protection.

Some 367 aircraft were thought to have reached the target and 345 crews claimed to have hit it. The Main Force bombed in three waves which took forty minutes to complete. In the first wave were 94 Halifaxes, three of which were lost. A Halifax pilot reported: 'While I was over the target bombers were being caught and held in the searchlights and were twisting and diving to escape from the beams. Flak was being fired up the cones of the searchlights and bursting near the bombers. I saw three of our aircraft coned like this and hit.'

The raid had been in progress no more than seven minutes when fires obtained a firm grip of the target and there was a 'tremendous' explosion after which, 'the whole target area seemed covered with fire and smoke'.

In the second wave were 131 Wellingtons and 52 Stirlings. A Wellington pilot when he got back described how, despite his best efforts, the 'Ruhr searchlights held him in their beams for five minutes. We were hit time and again and when we landed our Wellington looked like the top of a pepper pot. The extraordinary thing is that none of my crew got a scratch.' Four Wimpys and three Stirlings were lost. In the third and final wave were 157 Lancasters, four of which failed to return. In all, 14 aircraft failed to return and 38 were damaged.

A Halifax crew on 51 Squadron at Snaith got their bomber home after it was badly mauled by a Ju 88 night fighter over Essen. The rear-gunner was wounded in the left leg, the flight engineer took a bullet through the chest, the navigator was hit by shell splinters in the back and one leg and the mid-upper gunner and the bomb-aimer were both wounded in the feet. The pilot, Flying Officer R D Johnstone of Glasgow, reported:

I had no idea that the bomb-aimer had been wounded. He said nothing about it until we landed but went about with the wireless operator giving first aid to the others. The wireless operator gave me great help. He told me how our fuel consumption was going and gave me the engine temperature; in fact he took over the flight engineer's job. His wireless set was smashed and we were completely out of touch with home, so he went to and fro bandaging the wounded men and giving them coffee. In spite of his wounds, the navigator was able to give me an approximate course and we reached an aerodrome in the South of England.

While the flight engineer may not be able to fly again, the rest of us hope to crew up once more. We were all trained together and have made twelve trips in company.[27]

They did fly together again but on 13/14 May, Flight Lieutenant Johnstone's crew did not return from the operation on Bochum.[28]

A week later photo reconnaissance revealed that an area larger than 160 acres was laid waste, as well as 450 acres extensively damaged, by fire. Of the Krupps' plant alone, 53 separate large workshops were affected by the bombing. Thirteen of the main buildings in the works were completely demolished or virtually put out of action. Three coalmines, a saw mill, an iron foundry and a screw works also suffered severely. The plants of the Goldschmidt Company, smelters and makers of sulphuric acid and of the Machinenbau Union, were partly gutted. The power station, gasworks and the municipal tram depot suffered a like fate, as did the goods yard of the Segerth suburban station. Seven hundred houses, blocks of flats, offices and small business premises in or near the centre of the town were destroyed and 2,000 more rendered uninhabitable. A number of hutted camps housing slave workers were almost entirely destroyed. The public buildings which suffered very extensive damage, mostly from fire, included the Town Hall, the Exchange, the town baths, four buildings of the Post Office, an enclosed market, nine churches, five schools and a theatre. Nearly a thousand tons of high explosive dropped by the RAF had caused the havoc. 'Essen,' said the special Air Ministry announcement on 12 March, 'is now the second most blitzed town in Germany. Only in Cologne is there a greater area of devastation.'

On 8/9 March, 335 bombers went to Nuremburg but haze prevented accurate visual identification of the target area and both marking and bombing spread over more than ten miles along the line of the raid. More than half of the bombs fell outside the city boundaries. Even so, more than 600 buildings were destroyed and 1,400 others, including the M.A.N. and Siemens factories, were damaged. Squadron Leader Ray Glass DFC, pilot of a 214 Squadron Stirling recalls: 'On the way we were coned by one of the concentrations and again over the target, returning with 27 holes in the aircraft.' Eight aircraft – four of them Stirlings – failed to return. A fifth Stirling crash-landed near Sudbury. One of the missing Stirlings was *V-Victor*, a 7 Squadron Path Finder aircraft at Oakington piloted by Sergeant Lionel Louis Victor Toupin RCAF, who after running low on fuel, ordered the crew to abandon when he thought that they were over France. The Canadian left the aircraft flying on automatic pilot and six crew men bailed out but they were over the Channel and all drowned east of Dungeness. Sergeant Derek Richard Spanton, the mid-upper gunner, did not receive the call to bail out and remained aboard. He parachuted to safety over Kent before the Stirling crashed into the Thames Estuary. Sergeant Spanton went on to fly a further twelve operations but his aircraft was one of three Stirlings on 7 Squadron that failed to return on the night of 24/25 June 1943 on the operation to Wuppertal. He and the rest of Squadron Leader John Ronald Savage RAAF's crew were lost without trace.

Sergeant 'Jimmy' Hurst on 102 Squadron recalls:

Searchlights caused problems on many ops. One would light our Halifax as it swept the sky but on 9/10 March when on our way to Munich we were locked onto by a blue beam. These were radar-controlled from the ground and referred to as master searchlights. Immediately it illuminated us several other searchlights locked onto us and George Barker our Skipper took violent evasive action. He seldom flew straight and level. I was never airsick but invariably when a new member joined the crew they were sick on their first trips with George. To be aboard when he corkscrewed – descending 2,000 feet weaving as we went, then up again – with a bomb load on, was something to experience but it worked and on several occasions enabled us to escape when coned by a group of searchlights. How he could see his instruments I do not know, as so intense was the light from the beams that I was completely blinded. We seemed to be held for ages but it was maybe a couple of minutes before we were out of the beam. So violent had our evasive action been that the gyro in the compass toppled and we had to abort our op and return to base. The engineer thought that at one stage the Skipper had rolled the Halifax onto its back. We still had our full bomb load aboard during these manoeuvres and back at base we landed with them aboard. I can't recall just why we did not jettison them. We were lucky that night, as usually when a plane is caught by a master beam, fighters come in and shoot it down whilst the crew is disorientated.[29]

'Three hard ops in a row' was how Jimmy Morris on 218 Squadron at Downham Market described the raids on Berlin, Nuremburg and Munich. He now had a new crew. Just after Christmas 1942 he had developed sinus trouble and ended up about three ops short of the rest of 'Bicky' Bickenson's crew:

> As they had had a few rough ops, the Boss decided to make 'Bicky', who was now a flight lieutenant with the DFC, and the rest of the crew 'ops completed'. But the CO had another crew for me and that was Sergeant Richardson who had been let down by some of his crew and I was to be his replacement flight engineer. When I first spoke to Dick Richardson I think he was a bit taken aback, me coming from Liverpool. I was considered lowbrow. Dick was a bank clerk from London and that was a big step above a lowly Scouser flight engineer from Liverpool. The rear gunner, Mac Clark and Dick hit it off OK but the rest of the crew were just that – the crew which consisted of me, Tom Harvey WOp, Bill Pidgeon the mid-upper, Max Clark rear gunner, Bill Hieles bomb aimer and Bruce Hissok navigator. Bill Pidgeon was the sole survivor of a horrific crash at Waterbeach at the beginning of 1943. He was the rear gunner in a Stirling which was taxiing out to the runway and he could see another Stirling taxiing towards a different runway. He rotated his turret and suddenly realised that the other Stirling was actually taking off. Before Bill could alert the Skipper, both kites collided at the intersection of the two runways. I think Bill was the sole survivor of the crash. His turret became separated from the fuselage and rolled down the runway with Bill in it. Apart from a few cuts and scratches, Bill got out of the turret but the rest of the crew perished in the resulting fire.
>
> The Skipper was a good pilot and we all got on very well with each other. I remember coming back from one op, when it had become daylight, I found the mid-upper gunner lying across his guns. I thought Bill had been hit and went to investigate. Bill was unconscious but not from a Jerry bullet. We had been using some Very light flares and Tom, the WOp, had disposed of the used ones through the hole in the fuselage where the gun fitted. These had gone through the Perspex of the turret, hit Bill on the head and knocked him out. If Bill had been in the American Air Force, he would have been awarded a purple heart for wounds in action. I think the best we could do for him was a cup of coffee.

On 11/12 March, the fourth night of attacks in the Battle of the Ruhr, Stuttgart was the target for 314 Lancasters, 109 Halifaxes and 53 Stirlings. The attack was not a success as the marking was inaccurate, perhaps in part because of the reported first use by the Germans of dummy Target Indicators. The main weight of the attack fell to the south-west of the city, although some suburb areas were hit. Eleven aircraft failed to return. One of the three Stirlings lost was *A-Apple*, piloted by Squadron Leader

Michael Edward Thwaites DFC on 7 Squadron, which came down at Minaucourt in the Marne. The crew comprised of most of those who had flown with 'Hamish' Mahaddie on the operation to Cologne on 2/3 February. Downing Street was informed that Flight Lieutenant 'Fred' Thompson DFC*, Winston Churchill's bodyguard's son, was missing in action. Sir Arthur Harris wrote a personal letter to Mr. Thompson saying that he thought that there was good reason to hope that his son might have survived and was a prisoner. However, it was soon learned that Thwaites, Thompson, 'Jock' Stewart and the rest were dead.

A fourth Stirling crashed on return to Lakenheath after an engine failed, and it swung off the runway, coming to a stop when the undercarriage collapsed. No injuries were reported. Six of the missing aircraft were Halifaxes: four of them on 405 'Vancouver' Squadron RCAF at Topcliffe, south-west of Thirsk, who were flying their first operation in Bomber Command. *E-Easy* was flown by Pilot Officer B C Dennison RCAF, who was on his 21st operation, and his all-Canadian crew. In the early hours of 12 March they were picked out by a German fighter. At 01.00 they saw a red flare, which the crew decided was a fighter flare. The wireless operator advised Dennison to start weaving as he had picked up a German conversation on the *Tinsel* frequency he was searching. Dennison began weaving and the bomb aimer reported a searchlight astern of the aircraft. Five minutes later cannon tracer hit the aircraft and fire broke out between the starboard inner and the fuselage. Obviously the Halifax was doomed and the Canadian pilot ordered the crew to bail out. One of five of the crew to evade capture, Dennison recalled:

> When my turn came to leave, the Halifax was diving fast and I was pressed up against the Perspex canopy so I could not manoeuvre to get down onto the floor. I held on to the control column and managed to get my feet onto the dash. The elevators still seemed to be working as I was suddenly thrown to the floor and then I managed to crawl to the exit. I was hampered by either my oxygen tube or my intercom lead, which I had been unable to disconnect owing to my parachute having been put on over them. After getting through the hatch I was unable to get away from the aircraft and accordingly I pulled the ripcord and was jerked away when the aircraft was at a height of 5,000 to 6,000 feet. I sustained two broken ribs while in the aircraft.

Of the three crew that did not manage to escape, two were killed and one was taken prisoner. Dennison and his navigator, Flight Sergeant G L Spencer RCAF, were taken to Paris but they escaped to England in July and August.

'Happy Valley was brighter and merrier than ever,' one pilot proclaimed when on 12/13 March the Main Force attack again fell on Essen.[30]

'They seemed determined that we shouldn't get through,' another said. 'As we approached the town I saw three huge cones with at least fifty searchlights in each.' The captain of a Stirling reported: 'When we arrived the whole of the target was lit up by fires. Suddenly there was a huge explosion below us; a great sheet of flame shot up to about a thousand feet. Despite the thick cloud of smoke rising from the target we could see the glow of the flames when we crossed the Dutch coast on our way home.' That cloud of smoke, it was estimated, reached a height of 15,000 feet – three miles! Another Stirling crew went strafing searchlights on their own:

> When we arrived over the target, explosions were going on almost continuously. By comparison, the tiny pinpoint flashes of the ack-ack guns seemed almost absurdly small. Against the background of one of the fires I could see a tall chimney stack. Immediately after we had bombed the searchlights caught us and then the shells hit us fair and square. It burst inside the fuselage, just beneath the mid-upper turret. We were all blown out of our seats but none of us were hurt. Then tracer came up all round us. We were still in the search-light and I put the nose down and only flattened out when we were 200 feet above ground. We got clear and nothing more happened until we got to the Dutch coast. Then we were again coned by searchlights and again peppered by flak. I told the front gunner to shoot at the searchlights. I made straight for them and he put two of them out. The rear-gunner disposed of a third. Then the fourth searchlight came on but it turned away from us as we went for it. We were almost suffocated by fumes from our own guns and from the shell that burst inside the fuselage.

The centre of the bombing was right across the plant, with later bombing drifting back to the north-western outskirts. The next day at 3 o'clock in the afternoon large fires were still burning in the centre of the giant Krupps works just west of the city centre, and photographic reconnaissance photos taken later revealed that the factory received 30 per cent more damage than on the earlier successful raid of 5/6 March. The Secretary of State for Air, Sir Archibald Sinclair, sent the following appreciative message to Sir Arthur Harris: 'Your cunningly planned and brilliantly executed attack on Krupps has destroyed no small part of Germany's biggest war factory. Congratulations to you and all under your command on this achievement in the teeth of Germany's strongest defences.'[31]

World observers were vastly impressed by the performance of steadily increased bombing made by the men in Sir Arthur Harris's command. The *New York Times* found it appropriate to comment in a leader:

Germany is apparently reaching the point where she cannot cope, materially or physically, with the effects of bombing. Her enemies did not wait to pummel her cities until the population was strained by years of war and the armies were scraping the bottom of the barrel for men and material. They waited because they were unable to hit sooner. But if Allied strategy had been dictated not by necessity but by a plan to reserve its full striking power until German force was spent, the results would be very much like what they are now.

The next major raids would not take place until late in the month, when almost 360 aircraft set off for St-Nazaire, and four nights' later when over 450 aircraft would attack Duisburg. In the meantime, small numbers of Wellington and Lancaster crews made themselves useful sowing their 'vegetables' on *Gardening* sorties to 'regions' that stretched from the French Atlantic coast to as far as the Kattegat. Each 'region' had codenames like 'Spinach', 'Geraniums', 'Tangerines', 'Sweet Pea' and 'Silverthorne'. On the night after the raid on Essen over 50 Wellingtons and 17 Lancasters were dispatched to waters off St-Nazaire and in the 'Spinach' area off Gdynia in the Baltic. A Polish Wimpy and another crewed almost entirely by Canadians were lost without trace, and a Lancaster on 57 Squadron, which was badly shot about by a night fighter, crashed at Scampton on return. Sergeant Arthur Hobbs on 9 Squadron landed back at Waddington after ten hours in the air, his effort proving fruitless in the sea fog at 'Spinach', such that he dropped his mines in another region. Unfortunately, there was no word from *G-George* flown by 21-year-old Flight Sergeant Howard Clark Lewis, who despite the 'RCAF' flashes on the top of each arm was, like many of his countrymen, a 'Yank in Canadian clothing'. Originally from Ann Arbor, Michigan, Lewis, who had entered pilot training in Canada in 1942, had flown his first operation as 'second dickey' on one of the Wilhelmshaven trips a month earlier with Flight Lieutenant Jim Verran. A second trip as 'second dickey' followed and by early March he had flown a further half dozen ops. He would get no more. Lewis and his crew were lost without trace.[32]

On the night of 29/30 March, 329 aircraft of Bomber Command raided Berlin. The force was made up of 162 Lancasters, 103 Halifaxes and 64 Stirlings.

Twenty-five-year-old Pilot Officer Alfred Ernest Fisher and his crew of Lancaster *Z-Zebra* on 57 Squadron probably felt a rush of excitement and trepidation in equal measure, as this was their first bombing operation. Fisher took off from Scampton at eleven minutes before 10pm and headed for the rendezvous point for the flight to Berlin. Crews found that the weather conditions over the North Sea were appalling; with spring thunderstorms and very severe icing that ultimately forced 95 aircraft to return early. Laden with their heavy bomb loads, many of the remaining bombers found it impossible to climb through the overcast.

The icing conditions continued *en route* but the forecasted winds proved to be inaccurate and this had a profound effect on the overall success of the operation. Route-marker flares that were supposed to be dropped over the datum point of Muggelsee (the largest of several lakes south-east of Berlin) fell too far south and the winds caused the main force of aircraft to either arrive late or bomb well short of the markers. Some aircraft captains did not even attempt to reach the datum point for their briefed run into the target and this resulted in most bombs falling in open country six miles south-east of Berlin. The long trip home now faced them. Over Holland, the German night fighters were waiting to pounce. Early in the morning of 30 March *Leutnant* Werner Rapp and *Unteroffizier* Johan Ortmann, his *Bordschütze*, found Fisher's Lancaster and fired. None of the crew was able to bail out as *Z-Zebra* fell to the ground near the Van Wick home at Waverveen, south-east of Amsterdam. Their neighbour, Jan Treur, was in his barn feeding his cows when he heard the Lancaster scream overhead and slam into the soft earth behind the barn, 6 hours and 22 minutes after it had lifted off from Scampton. It was one of 21 aircraft – 11 Lancasters, seven Halifaxes and three Stirlings – that never returned from the raid on Berlin. As dawn broke, the scene that greeted the farmers was horrific. There was little left of the Lancaster that was recognizable. The grim task of retrieving the remains of the crew began.[33]

Eleven Lancasters on the Berlin raid failed to return. The Lancaster piloted by 26-year-old Flying Officer George F Mabee RCAF on 49 Squadron at Fiskerton was shot down by *Leutnant* Hans Krause and his crew of I./NJG3 at Wünstorf near Hannover. *K-King*, a second Lancaster on the squadron, flown by Flight Sergeant D W Fyffe, was shot down by *Hauptmann* Herbert Lütje and crashed at Nieuw Heeten. Fyffe and three men survived and were taken prisoner. *Leutnant* August Geiger of III./ NJG1 claimed five bombers, including *E-Edward* on 460 Squadron at Breighton, flown by Flight Sergeant David Harold Victor Charlick RAAF, which crashed at Lievelde with no survivors. *Unteroffizier* Christian Költringer of III./NJG1 attacked *S-Sugar* piloted by Flight Lieutenant Kenneth Hugh Grenfell RAAF on the same squadron. It was his third and final victory. The German crew were killed by return fire before the Lancaster went down in flames at Kloosterharr. Grenfell and all his crew, including the 28-year-old navigator, Flying Officer Stephen Falcon Scott McCullagh of Mosman, NSW, a clerk with AMP Society in Sydney before enlisting in March 1941, were killed.

While the Berlin raid was in progress 149 *Oboe*-guided Wellingtons formed a diversionary force aimed at the small town of Bochum, a few miles east of Essen. Twelve Wellingtons on 166 Squadron were dispatched from Kirmington, an airfield that had opened in October 1942 on the

Grimsby to Scunthorpe road. Crews could go to the pub without leaving the station, as the 'Marrowbone & Cleaver' or the 'Chopper' as it was known to all bomber crews, was across the road from the sick quarters, but it was not used often. Brigg was just down the road; plus at Scunthorpe there was the 'Oswald', the 'Bluebell' and the 'Crosby' or one could see a floor show and get drunk at the 'Berkley' on the outskirts of the blacked out town. It was generally accepted that aircrew NCOs used the 'Bluebell'. It would not have been out of place in a Western. It had a large, open saloon bar with a sawdust-covered floor and a raised wooden platform in the corner on which a man in bowler hat played piano non-stop. It only needed busty, silk-stockinged girls to complete the illusion but the ladies provided did their best and this made up in humour what it lacked in propriety.[34]

Weather conditions were bad at take-off time and *V-Victor* abandoned the operation, leaving eleven crews to continue to the target. Sergeant pilot 'Tim' Timperley, whose 22nd birthday this was, piloted one of them.

Once we had left the main bomber stream, maybe forty or fifty miles on towards Bochum, I remember thinking that it was unusually quiet. There were no searchlights, no anti-aircraft gunfire, no fighters, not even any sign of the other bombers. Of course, one would not expect to see much of them anyway, except over the target against the searchlights and fires but nevertheless one usually had some feeling, some clue that they were close by. On this raid I felt this great sense of loneliness, even at one stage to the extent of thinking that perhaps we had made some navigational error, or our timing was wrong but when we finally saw the Path Finder flares hanging over the target, I knew we had found the right place. There was some flak over the target as we made our approach and I remember thinking that this 'firework display' was Herman Goering's birthday present to me. We dropped our bombs and as we turned out of the target area, I realised we had made a mistake and were heading in the wrong direction. I don't remember quite why this was; perhaps the navigator had given me the wrong course. I really don't know, but one thing I was sure about was that it was essential that we rejoined the bomber stream for the return journey. It was much too dangerous to fly on your own; you were too likely to be spotted on German radar and easily picked off by a ground directed night fighter. The only way to get back on the right course was to fly in over the target once again and take the correct course out. In spite of the protestations of my crew I took the aircraft over the target once again. It was self-protection rather than pedantry. All this time I did not see any other aircraft. I still had this impression of an almost eerie sense of loneliness. It was very unusual. It may have been that the stream was more spread out than normal because this was the first time that we had been to Bochum. Precise navigation at night was still very difficult. We arrived back at Kirmington a few hours later. It had been a very quiet trip.

Timperley's Wellington landed at 00.57 hours, the third aircraft to return to Kirmington. At 01.15 hours Flight Sergeant M L Dewing's Wellington III was the last of the Wellingtons to get back. The weather over the target area had been good and 166 Squadron's Wimpys dropped 44 500lb GP bombs and over 1,700 4lb and 30lb incendiaries. *H-Harry* and *L-Leather* were missing, nothing having been heard after taking off from base. *H-Harry*, Sergeant James R A 'Bob' Hodgson's Wellington, had been on its way to Bochum when it was shot down near Arnhem by a Bf 110 flown by *Oberstleutnant* Werner Streib, *Kommodore*, NJG1 at Venlo.[35] All the crew were killed. Hodgson was at 22 the oldest of seven brothers and four sisters.

Sergeant Owen Eastwood Collins RNZAF and the crew of *L-London* were lost on the way back and went in to the sea just after crossing the Dutch coast. A third Wellington in 166 Squadron was attacked by a Bf 109 and damaged. In all, 21 Berlin raiders and 12 Wellingtons of the Bochum force failed to return. 'Tim' Timperley concludes:

> There was a great difference between people not turning up in a crew room and seeing, as people must have done in ground warfare, their immediate companions lying there either dead, or terribly mutilated. In aviation, if you saw somebody being shot down, you didn't see individual bodies; you weren't close enough. Very occasionally you did see people abandoning their aircraft and their parachutes opening up but it was always far away. You didn't let your imagination run riot. People just weren't there the next day.[36]

The same situation pervaded life in war-torn Berlin and the devastated towns and cities in Germany. *Das Reich* carried the following descriptive article in April 1943:

> It was like the aftermath of a battle. Afterward we talked about how quietly we had sat there together while the signals of death went whistling past our ears. [The air raid] lasted barely one hour but it seemed an eternity. Each second wrought more devastation on the city. There was fire all around us. Fire was racing along the street. Red tongues leaped at the sky. The flames chased up and down the road on the wings of the noisy wind. With a monotonous lamenting sound, staircases, curtains, furniture, fabric, paper and leather collapsed into the blazing blast furnace and turned into ashes. Glass splintered and flew into the street and an endless train of sparks travelled over the sky. People incapable of saving what had fallen

prey to devastation in the last hour, ran searchingly under the spark-strewn arch of the sky, scarcely knowing who they were or what had happened. At the same time high clear sirens signalled the approach of the fire brigades, one after another. They sent high jets of water hissing out of the hoses while timbers broke and trees bent down in the growing conflagration. As I walked along, a soldier with an amputated arm walked beside me. I felt that there was nothing separating us even though we did not know each other. This night's battle had turned us into soldiers too.

The sun shone next day. We bathed our eyes, which were burning from the smoke and sulphur. We saw with amazement that every-thing that had interested us the day before – a new film, a hat we wanted to have – no longer had the remotest importance. We had given up so much that night: the amenities of a large progressive city, its movie-houses, opera, theatre, cafes, the beautiful fashion houses – but we had also given up our claims, our demands, our desires. Suddenly so many things had ceased to mean anything to us: a trip, a fight, a plan. Many of the wall remains were inscribed with big chalk letters written by survivors, saying: 'We are all alive and we're living at No. 28 W-Street. Wherever you looked you saw the grim, resolutely determined faces of people fetching their belong-ings out of the cellars in baskets and boxes and sheltering them in a place of fragile safety. Already you could buy flowers in the stalls again, blooming bizarrely in the face of the ruins: Italian mimosas and tulips with soft dark red cups. Enquiries multiplied as relatives and friends sent telegrams and urgent phone calls to find out how we were. The post office was the assembly point for thousands of people sending out their good and bad news. The hands and heads of many people were wrapped in bandages.

We are fighting for our lives. We have no other weapons than our hearts but they are bright and sharp. So our lives, delayed now and then by painful shocks, are seeking a familiar trail that yet is narrower than before. The opera house is used to distribute food to the homeless. Varicoloured buses from many different cities are stitching the torn traffic network together again. Sometimes a bird sings behind our window; the screaming siren may drown out his little song in the next moment. Every night we are ready to ward off the barbarous enemy with the naked blade of our hearts.

On 1 April *G-George*, a lone Lancaster on 103 Squadron flown by Squadron Leader Charles O'Donoghue, set off from Elsham Wolds to make a dawn attack on the town of Emmerich, just over the Dutch border. O'Donoghue had previously flown a lone operation to Leer, near Emden on 20 March when the Main Force was grounded for a few days by equinoctial gales across Britain. The newspapers announced that night that a lone Lancaster had bombed a town not far inside the German coast. O'Donoghue, who was new to the squadron, was a permanent RAF man who had operated in India by daylight. His crew once remarked that he disliked night operations strongly. At 9 o'clock the tannoy at Elsham Wolds called all crews to the briefing room. A listening post in England had heard a Lancaster calling for help. It had been hit by *Oberfeldwebel* Fritz Timm of 3./JG1 at 07.22 hours as it crossed the enemy coast, homeward bound. 1 Group believed that O'Donoghue may have ditched in the North Sea and crews were ordered to search an area east of The Wash. The search proved fruitless. When the crews returned it was to hear that the German radio had claimed a single heavy bomber shot down. All members of the crew they said had been killed. *G-George* had crashed at Hulshorst in Gelderland. There were no survivors. Timm himself was later killed on 28 May 1944 in his Bf 109G-6 'Yellow 3' during combat with P-51 Mustangs of the USAAF.

Essen was the target for 348 aircraft on 3/4 April when the Path Finders prepared a plan both for sky-marking and ground-marking the target because the weather forecast looked ominous for the operation. When the bombers arrived at Essen they found no cloud over the target and the two types of marking confused the Main Force aircraft. Bombing was accurately delivered, however, and there was widespread damage in the centre and in the western half of the city. Fourteen Halifaxes and nine Lancasters failed to return. When Goebbels and his cohorts visited the city on 10 April they had to go to their hotel on foot because driving was quite impossible in many parts of Essen. The city's building experts told him that they estimated it would take twelve years to repair the damage.

Twenty-four hours later 577 bombers were dispatched to Kiel, the largest 'non-1,000' bombing force of the war so far. The Path Finders encountered thick cloud and strong winds over the target so that accurate marking became very difficult. Decoy fire sites may also have drawn off some of the bombing. Twelve aircraft failed to return. The 9 Squadron crew of *W-William*, better known as *Cutty Sark* and captained by Sergeant (later Flying Officer) Jimmy McCubbin, survived an attack by a single engined fighter, believed to be a Bf 109, shortly after bombing the target.

A year earlier, on 29 October 1942, McCubbin's crew had survived a ditching in the Bay of Biscay in their Whitley during an anti-submarine sweep while flying operations with Coastal Command. They had been forced to ditch 40 miles off the Scillies after the starboard engine had failed and the propeller had refused to feather and windmilled until the engine caught fire. All the crew managed to clamber into their dinghy. At dawn on 31 October the 19-year-old spare pilot died. They were finally rescued by HMS *Cutty Sark*, a navy frigate bound for Devonport. The crew found out that Cutty Sark is Scottish for 'short skirt' so when they had joined 9 Squadron they had a young lady wearing one painted on the nose of their Lancaster.

Leaving Kiel the Bf 109 was seen 200 feet below and directly astern at 100 yards by Sergeant Charles 'Arse-end Charlie' Stewart the rear gunner, while McCubbin carried out continuous weaving at 21,000 feet. Stewart warned his Skipper, who carried out a diving turn to starboard while the rear gunner fired two three-second bursts at the enemy fighter, the second of which was seen to hit. The enemy pilot immediately dived away and disappeared. Stewart was badly wounded in the legs and was hospitalised.[37]

Not for the first time there would be weeping in the 'WAAF-ery'.

Notes

1. See *No Moon Tonight* by Don Charlwood (Penguin 1988). Newitt was a tall, blond Canadian who would survive two tours at Elsham Wolds.
2. See *No Moon Tonight* by Don Charlwood (Penguin 1988)
3. The T1154/R1155 transmitter/receiver, which was the standard radio set in use by Bomber Command.
4. Adapted from the *Bomber Command Assoc Newsletter*, No. 28 February 1995. Wolfgang Küthe was killed in a flying accident on 14 April 1943 at Leeuwarden airfield. He had eight victories.
5. Middlebrook and Everitt.
6. P/O Mackeldon aborted the operation and 5 crews returned. Nine aircraft, including 3 Wellingtons, were lost to night fighters, and two were claimed by *Ritterkreuzträger* Paul Gildner, who after the death in combat of Reinhold Knacke on 3/4 February had been given command of 1./NJG1 at Gilze-Rijen airfield. Gildner, a Silesian by birth, had volunteered for the *Wehrmacht* in 1934 as an infantry officer but had transferred to the *Luftwaffe* and became a *Zerstörer* pilot, joining *Nachtjagd* in July 1940. As the third *Nachtjagd* pilot Gildner had been awarded the *Ritterkreuz* on 9 July 1941 after his 14th *Abschuss*. His score stood at 38 *Abschüsse*, 2 in the Battle of France and 36 at night. At Leeuwarden on 26 February 30-year-old *Hauptmann* Ludwig Becker, *Staffelkapitän* 12./NJG1, a great night fighting tactician with 44 night victories, waited to fly his very first daylight sortie. Shortly before taking off from Leeuwarden 1135 hours in a formation of 12 Bf 110s of IV./JGI led by *Hauptmann* Hans-Joachim Jabs, in pursuit of the American daylight raiders Becker was informed of the award of the *Eichenlaub* (Oak Leaves) to his *Ritterkreuz* (Knight's Cross), which had been bestowed on him on 1 July 1942 after his 25th night victory for his leading role in the development of the night fighter arm. They intercepted the B-17s and B-24s, returning with claims for two shot down, but Becker's Bf 110 was lost without a trace.

Completely at ease and master in the night battle against the British bombing offensive the 'Night Fighting Professor' and his *Funker* Josef Staub fell victim to the gunners of B-17s or B-24s of the 1st and 2nd Bomb Wings. Losses to *Experten* like this was not good for German morale, which was under pressure due to the intensifying air war over Europe.

7. See *Bombers First And Last* by Gordon Thorburn (Robson Books, 2006).

8. Stirling R9264, a Path Finder aircraft on 7 Squadron, which was shot down by a night fighter and crashed near Rotterdam, was examined by the Germans who retrieved the H_2S set from the bomber. This was only the second night that this new device was used. The set was damaged but Telefunken in Berlin were able to reassemble it. This gave the enemy an early indication of the operational use of H_2S and eventually led to the development of a radar device known as *Naxos*, which would enable night fighters to home on to a bomber emitting H_2S signals. On the 1 March 1943 raid on Berlin, some bombs hit the Telefunken works and the H_2S set was completely destroyed, but a Halifax of 35 Squadron with an almost intact H_2S set, was shot down by *Leutnant* August Geiger of III./NJG1 and crashed in Holland on this night, and the Germans were able to resume their research into H_2S immediately. *The Bomber Command War Diaries* by Martin Middlebrook and Chris Everitt (Midland 1985).

9. *Out of the Blue: The Role of Luck in Air Warfare 1917–1966* edited by Laddie Lucas (Hutchinson 1985). Hamish Mahaddie joined the Pathfinders in October 1942 and by 3 December he had completed his 50th operation. Mahaddie completed his operational tour on the Pathfinders in March 1943 and, at the age of 32, was promoted to Group Captain and assigned to 8 (PFF) Group Headquarters as 'Group Training Inspector'. In the six months following 15 August 1942 the manning of the Path Finders suffered alarmingly because groups (other than 4 Group) were not earmarking good crews for the Path Finders and some even used PFF as a 'dumping place' for crews. All this had to change and it did. Mahaddie became Don Bennett's 'horse thief' and took care of PFF's own manning. Mahaddie ended the war as a 34-year-old Group Captain with the DSO, DFC and two AFCs.

10. Adapted from *Bombers Fly East*. S/L Gilmore was KIA 4/5 May 1943 when he and his crew FTR from the operation on Kiel.

11. *Bomber Crew* by John Sweetman. (Abacus 2004)

12. *Out of the Blue: The Role of Luck in Air Warfare 1917–1966* edited by Laddie Lucas (Hutchinson 1985)

13. A night fighter version of the CR.42 *Falco* biplane fighter-bomber with exhaust flame dampers, radio and small underwing searchlights.

14. P/O Moffatt, the bomb aimer, bailed out.

15. After leaving his position to help with the fires, Sgt James Fortune Bain, the engineer, returned to find the starboard tank holed and leaking. He turned on the balance cocks and manipulated the petrol system throughout the return flight with the greatest skill and on landing only 15 gallons of petrol were found still in the port inner tank. *In Action With the Enemy; The Holders of the Conspicuous Gallantry Medal (Flying)* by Alan W. Cooper. (William Kimber 1986).

16. Sgts Bain, Airey and Williams were all recommended on 16 February for awards of the Conspicuous Gallantry Medal (CGM), P/O Gates the DSO, while Hazard and Dove were recommended for the Victoria Cross. These two latter recommendations went as far as AVM Edward Rice the AOC of 1 Group who approved them but upon reaching the C-in-C, were changed, on 11 March to immediate awards of the CGM. All five CGMs and the DSO to Gates were gazetted on 23 March. On returning after special leave Hazard was assigned a new Lancaster and on 20 March he took it up for an air test. He made a low pass over Hornsea beach but on pulling up at the end of his run, the tail wheel struck a concrete pill box on the beach. The impact caused the Lancaster to break up. All ten men including Hazard, Bain and Williams, were killed instantly. *In Action With the Enemy; The Holders of the Conspicuous Gallantry Medal (Flying)* by Alan W Cooper. (William Kimber 1986). P/O Gates DSO died when the Lancaster in which he was flying, crashed when returning from Dortmund on 5 May 1943.

17. See *No Moon Tonight* by Don Charlwood (Penguin 1988)

18. See *Nachtjagd: The Night Fighter versus Bomber War over the Third Reich 1939–45* by Theo Boiten (Crowood 1997).

19. In March, 115 Squadron began converting from the Wellington to become the first Lancaster unit in 3 Group, which had on strength six Stirling squadrons, all of which were gradually converted to the Lancaster. The Lancaster (and Halifax) crews could fly up to 10,000ft higher than Stirling, which was slower and had to be routed independently to lessen the risk of being hit by bombs dropped by the other two types of aircraft.

20. Some bombs hit the Telefunken works at which an H_2S set taken from a Stirling shot down near Rotterdam was being reassembled. The set was completely destroyed in the bombing but a Halifax of 35 Squadron with an almost intact H_2S set crashed in Holland on this night and the Germans were able to resume their research into H_2S immediately. *The Bomber Command War Diaries* by Martin Middlebrook and Chris Everitt (Midland 1985).

21. After completing nine operations on 75 Squadron on 24 June 1943 (his 55th operation overall) Rothwell was posted to an OTU. He had flown just over 115 operational hours on his second tour. He recalls. 'I must admit to being relieved when my tour ended. It had been stressful;

Berlin was the target on three occasions; Hamburg, Nuremburg, Munich, Frankfurt, Kiel and Stuttgart once and the Ruhr Valley six times. And I had come close to disaster on a number of occasions through enemy action and fuel shortage. On one occasion we hit a high tension electric pylon in Luxembourg whilst en route to Stuttgart when new tactics were being tried, which required the Stirlings to fly at low level until nearing the target. There were very few cases of nervous breakdowns when crewmembers had to be taken off operations; in fact those who completed tours and were given jobs on instructional units very often applied to return for a further tour of operational duty. Most applications were returned to the applicants marked 'not recommended' because there was a need for operational-experienced instructors on Operational Training Units.'

22. *Chased By The Sun: The Australians in Bomber Command in WWII* by Hank Nelson (ABC Books 2002)

23. *No Moon Tonight* by Don Charlwood (Penguin 1988). Main Force crews were then stood down for one night and the only activity was by 60 aircraft on minelaying operations in coastal areas between Texel and the River Gironde. Three aircraft failed to return.

24. Some 417 aircraft, including 14 H_2S equipped Path Finders, were dispatched but of the 344 crews who had confidently reported bombing, only 17 had actually hit the city. Six Path Finders suffered radar failures including one PFF aircraft whose crew decided to 'press on regardless'. But the radar operator still managed to pick out distinctive features such as the Alster Lake in the centre of the city and the point where the Elbe narrowed at Hamburg. However, the tide was out and revealed extensive mud-banks, which on H_2S screens looked like a river narrowing several miles downstream of the city. It was not the Alster Lake that the H_2S operator had seen; it was the Wedel Lake, 13 miles downstream. The marker flares went down over the small town of Wedel where most of the bombing was concentrated although in Hamburg a proportion of the bombing force did hit the city and the fire brigade had to extinguish 100 fires. Ten aircraft failed to return and a Stirling was lost on *Gardening* operations off the Frisians.

25. The Irvin Parachute Company of Hertfordshire provided a certificate and a gold caterpillar pin for those men saved by an Irvin parachute. The caterpillar was the silkworm and these men were saved by silk. Leslie Irvin was the honorary secretary of the club. The GQ Parachute Company of Woking also gave a badge for those in the GQ Club.

26. *Night Airwar: Personal recollections of the conflict over Europe, 1939–45* by Theo Boiten (Crowood 1999). During August 1944–April 1945 W/O Angus Robb completed a second tour of ops as air gunner in the Path Finders on 405 'Vancouver' Squadron RCAF. RAF aircrew considered unfit for flying were labelled 'LMF' ('Lack of Moral Fibre'). Flight

Lieutenant John Price recalled. 'Morale and discipline were every-thing. If you refused to go on a particularly dangerous operation, or cracked up on an operation, all aircrew (NCOs) were stripped of their rank and became an ordinary airman and whatever RAF Station you were posted to you had to produce your flying log book with the dreaded words stamped in black letters "Lack of Moral Fibre". Naturally, through the Orderly room, word spread throughout your new Station, "He's a coward" – it must have been hell on earth for some of these once brave aircrew whose nerves were stretched to breaking point. Thereafter they peeled potatoes in the kitchen or were forced to perform menial tasks.' LMF cases remained a very low percentage of total numbers of Bomber Command. Throughout the war, 4,059 cases were considered – 746 officers and 3,313 NCOs. The 'charges' against most were dismissed and only 2,726 (389 officers, 2,337 NCOs) were actually classified as LMF; a total less than 0.4% of all the aircrews of Bomber Command. The NCO's total was higher because there were more of them than officers.

27. Adapted from *Bombers Fly East*.
28. Halifax II DT526 MH-V crashed at Grevel. Johnstone and four crew members were taken prisoner. Two of the crew were killed.
29. Eight of the 264 aircraft of Bomber Command were lost on the Munich raid.
30. 457 aircraft – 158 Wellingtons, 156 Lancasters, 91 Halifaxes, 42 Stirlings and ten Mosquitoes – were despatched. 23 aircraft – eight Lancasters, seven Halifaxes, six Wellingtons and two Stirlings were lost.
31. *Bombers Fly East* by Bruce Sanders. (Herbert Jenkins Ltd 1943)
32. See Thorburn.
33. The remains of Alf Fisher and Sgt's Frank Bandeen (flight engineer, 21), Harry Richardson (navigator, 22), Don Simmons (mid-upper gunner, 21), Roy Taylor (air bomber), Jack Westerdale (WOp/AG) and Alick Deane (rear gunner) were put in three wooden coffins, which were placed in the back of a horse-drawn cart and Mr. Van Wick drove them to the Waverveen church for burial, escorted by several German soldiers marching behind. Following the funeral ceremony, the crew was buried in the church cemetery accompanied by a gun salute from the German soldiers. They joined 191 airmen that had died on that miserable night. After the war, they were moved to the war cemetery in Bergen op Zoom. I am grateful to Bob Van Wick and Andy Bird for sending me this story.
34. P/O Peter Beechey writing in *Not Just Another Milk Run; The Mailly-le-Camp Bomber Raid* by Molly Burkett & Geoff Gilbert (Barny Books 2004).
35. *Letters from a Bomber Pilot* by David Hodgson (Thames Methuen London 1985). On 19/20 July 1940 Streib had been the first German pilot to shoot down a RAF bomber at night. He claimed 68 victories

before he was promoted to *Inspector of Nachtjagd* in 1944. He was awarded the Knight's Cross on 6 October 1940 and he later received Oak Leaves and Swords.

36. *Letters from a Bomber Pilot* by David Hodgson (Thames Methuen London 1985)

37. McCubbin would fly 20 of ED654 *Cutty Sark*'s 62 operations before the Lancaster was lost on the operation to Stuttgart on 20/21 February 1944 with P/O William Chambers' crew. LL853 *Cutty Sark II*, which was later lost on 25 June 1944, was its replacement. McCubbin was flying *Cutty Sark* on the night of 10/11 August 1943 on the operation to Nürnberg when they were attacked again, this time by a Ju 88. Charles Stewart was injured and Sgt Percy 'Dicky' Lynham, the 24-year-old mid-upper gunner, was killed, probably in the initial burst of fire from the night fighter. Sgt Ken Pagnell the bomb aimer/front gunner managed to get in several good bursts which brought sparks from the attacker, which dived and disappeared below. See *Bombers First And Last* by Gordon Thorburn (Robson Books, 2006).

CHAPTER 5

Whoever It Happens To, It Won't Be Me

Indiscriminate attacks on civilian populations as such will never form part of our policy.

John Slessor, Director of Plans at the Air Ministry,
7 September 1939

Sergeant Edwin Thomas, a wireless operator-air gunner, sat down to write another letter to his mother. He had arrived on 78 Squadron at Linton-on-Ouse at the end of March and had flown his first op on the night of 2/3 April, when over 100 Halifaxes and Lancasters bombed Lorient and St-Nazaire. Three days later Bomber Command was relieved of its obligation to bomb these ports. In Germany, Grand Admiral Karl Dönitz informed the Central Planning Office of the *Reich* that 'the towns of St-Nazaire and Lorient have been rubbed out as main submarine bases. No dog or cat is left ... Nothing but the submarine shelters remain.' For Thomas the operation had come two and a half years after he had joined up. He had written to his mother telling her she was not to worry now that he was on ops because the squadron 'has a fine reputation and loses few kites.' His Halifax on this first op had been piloted by Sergeant Bill Illingworth. They had arrived over the target nine minutes ahead of the bombing time so they had to circle until they could bomb. In his letter he added 'The flak was said to have been light by the veterans but there was sufficient to keep us weaving and turning.'

On 7 April there was a cocktail party at the house of Linton's popular station commander, 37-year-old Group Captain John Rene Whitley AFC. The son of a civil engineer, he had spent his early childhood in Chile where his father was in charge of building what was then the highest railway line in the world. After his mother's death he was brought up in France by his grandparents. He learned to speak fluent French, and this and the knowledge he gained would stand him in good stead much later.

149

Joining the RAF before the war, Whitley was a wing commander by May 1940 and he was given command of 149 Squadron at Mildenhall, but in November he was promoted to Operations Officer at Bomber Command headquarters. He had taken command of Linton-on-Ouse on 25 May 1941. Pam Finch, one of the WAAF Intelligence Officers, was accompanied to the party by Flight Lieutenant Edward George 'Morty' Mortensen, an educated Cockney pilot on 78 Squadron who had trained in Canada and who, with a macabre sense of humour, usually stated in the mess before an op that 'The condemned men ate a hearty breakfast.' Morty's close friend was Flight Lieutenant Ron Read DFC – and the pair were some-times referred to as the 'Terrible Twins'. Read, who flew a tour as a pilot on 78 Squadron, recalls that Morty's father was a Dane who had come to London as a young man in the tailoring business. He had drifted to the East End of London to set up his own business. He must have done well, as Morty went to Highgate public school. Dark, saturnine, with a long, serious face, which denied his satirical sense of humour, 'Morty' was a mixed-up person. Strongly anti-Semitic, a bit of a snob without any reason to be, much of his attitude was a pose, acquired from a conflict between his public schooling and his residence in a predominantly poor Jewish community. Apart from those idiosyncrasies, which were soon laughed at or ignored, Morty was a wryly-humorous person who became a lot more likable on closer acquaintance.[1] He confided to Pam Finch that he was awed by the honour of 'Groupie's' hospitality: 'now I'm sure to get the chop!'[2] Pam had a sympathetic understanding of the way air-crew felt. At debriefing she usually accepted the crews' brief statements without probing too much for detailed expansion. The life expectancy of a wartime pilot was forty flying hours and that did not do a lot for the confidence, but most everyone got on with the job. One never thought that one day he could be the one who did not return. It always happened to someone else.

On 8 April, Edwin Thomas put pen to paper once more, telling his mother about a possible twelve days' leave in four or five weeks' time. 'This will suit our purposed admirably because Pat, the rear gunner, will be 21 in May and is going to have a GRAND PARTY.' He added that he had never had so much time to spare and in the afternoons he would 'buzz' off to York with the crew.

At Betty's subterranean wood-panelled bar opposite the 13th century St. Helens church cakes would be served at the entrance on the corner of cobbled Davygate. In the evenings crews scratched their names on the mirrors lining the walls. Later they would hit the dance halls. Thomas asked his mother to send a pair of shoes from home as soon as she could because he did not want to be deprived of his favourite enjoyment. He promised to reward her kindness by saving some more sweets and a tin of orange juice.

His mother had received a letter her son had written from 15 OTU at Harwell just before Christmas, asking if she remembered him mentioning 'Wee' Baxter, his old friend from Blackpool'. He had been killed in a night crash. Only the week before they were talking about prangs and he said: 'I shall be all right; I have a good pilot. They say only the good die young ...'

Nineteen bombers were lost on the Duisburg raid of 8/9 April from a force of 392 aircraft, only one of which was shot down by a night fighter. Another eight Lancasters failed to return from a force of 104 Lancasters and five Mosquitoes that went to Duisburg again the following night. Thick cloud again caused a scattered attack and bombs fell over a wide area of the Ruhr. On the night of the 10th/11th a force of 502 Lancasters, Halifaxes, Stirlings and 144 Wellingtons took off for a raid on Frankfurt. At Linton, 21 Halifaxes of 76 and 78 Squadrons were detailed for the operation. 'Groupie' Whitley wanted to get an updated view of the problems of his crews but normally station commanders were not allowed to go on ops – it was considered that they were privy to too many secrets – but he had managed to get 4 Group's permission to go on the raid. He shaved off his moustache, bundled up a set of civilian clothes that he had always carried with him on operations and went on *V-Victor*[3] with Flight Lieutenant Arthur Horace Hull, one of 76 Squadron's more experienced pilots.

Sergeant H J 'Jack' Adams and his crew, who had recently joined 78 Squadron, on 28 March, were another of the crews that went. Their Halifax, *F-Freddie*, had been christened *F-Firkin* by the crew. Sergeant 'Stan' Reed, one of the air gunners, recalls:

F-Firkin was a fairly new kite and hadn't done too many operations. It was a Mark II Series 1 (Special) of which, the nose and mid-upper gun turrets had been removed to help improve the rather poor operational performance, leaving only the rear turret for defence. The mid-upper gunner now manned a ventral position when on operations, looking downwards through a small Perspex blister fitted to the floor of the aircraft just aft of the rear door. Not a well sought after position as it entailed lying flat out on the floor for hours with one's head in the perspex blister. This position had been brought in to reduce the heavy losses caused by the deadly attacks from below, which were so favoured by Jerry night fighters. Alas, the position was not armed until later with a .5 calibre Browning machine gun. An intercom point, oxygen outlet together with a signal light and switch were installed alongside the blister but no form of heating was provided and a cold, draughty and noisy position it was indeed.

On the night in question our take off time was 23.34 hours. It was a very dark night with no moon and 10/10ths cloud cover. After leaving base we did not see another aircraft, although on several occasions we became aware of their unseen presence as we flew through their slipstreams. I flew from Yorkshire to the south coast sitting up front alongside our Skipper on the second pilot's seat, whilst Sergeant Joe Enwright our mid-upper gunner manned the rear turret until it was time for me to take over; somewhere over the English Channel. I very much enjoyed riding up front in the utter dark of the night, watching avidly all that went on about me with great interest. It was all so different to my normal lonely vigil in the rear turret. I studied Jack at the controls, clad in his leather Irvin flying jacket and helmet with his face half hidden behind his oxygen mask, in the dim red glow from the instruments on the panels before him. Being at the very heart of this huge powerful bomber made me feel privileged to be aboard. An enormous and deafening constant roar from the four big Rolls-Royce Merlins dominated everything up front. I was conscious of Sergeant 'Nobby' Clarke, our flight engineer, behind me, busy as always at his engineer's panel. Flying Officer Phil Hyden, navigator, Sergeant Cliff Price, wireless operator and Sergeant 'Stan' Hurrell, bomb aimer, were at their respective stations on the lower deck of the Halifax, beneath and in front of me.

My job during this part of the outward flight was to maintain a constant lookout for other aircraft in case one should come just a little too close for comfort. Flying blind on the aircraft's instruments alone in a night bomber stream with no radar could, to put it mildly, be disconcerting at times. Hopefully all the bombers were not at the same height, even though we were all flying in the same direction or at least, should be doing so. Imagine if you can a corridor of air space one hundred miles long, ten or more miles wide and about a mile and a half high with the lowest strata being at least at 12,000 feet. In this corridor in the sky were at least 500–600 bombers all heavily laden with petrol and a large bomb load and all were heading in the same direction in the pitch darkness. Each wave kept to a specified height. The poor old Stirlings with their rather poor maximum operational ceiling were always at the lowest level. Behind and above them at 15,000–16,000 feet would come the Wellingtons and then the Halifaxes at about 18,000 feet, with the Lancasters bringing up the rear in the last wave at 20,000 feet or more. With all these unseen heavy aircraft around us collisions in mid air were known to occur but officially the percentage was less than half of one per cent of the total force. It had to be for morale purposes did it not? Many more aircraft were lost through enemy action!

Having left the English coast we were soon well out over the Channel. I prepared to go aft and take up my normal station in the rear turret for the remainder of the operation. I gathered up my parachute pack and the rest of my gear, including a big thermos flask of hot coffee. Then I discovered that my microphone in my face mask

fusillade of 20mm cannon shells and 7.9mm bullets from a Luftwaffe night fighter was
responsible for this damage to Stirling III BF517/AA-O on 75 Squadron on the night of 26/27 April
1943. The rear gunner, Sergeant Brian Arthur Rogers, was mortally wounded and two other crew
members suffered minor wounds. The pilot, Pilot Officer P J Buck, managed to evade further attacks
when the Stirling was intercepted 30 miles north of the target, Duisburg, but had difficulty in
maintaining altitude. Other crew members jettisoned all movable equipment on the flight home, a
crash-landing being made at Newmarket without further injury to the airmen.

Lancaster III ED413 DX-M on 57 Squadron in the early hours of 15 June 1943, which returned from Oberhausen with Sergeant Reginald Frank Haynes dead in his rear turret. ED413 later served on 630 and 207 Squadrons and finally, 1651 CU.

At Pocklington on 19 June 1943 Halifax II DT743/DY-O with Sergeant T H Dargavel at the controls begins its take-off run as airmen watch, give the thumbs up and wave the bomber off with a good luck wish. None of the twenty-three Halifaxes on 102 Squadron bound for Le Creusot that night was lost.

A Halifax crew on 51 Squadron at Snaith, Yorkshire hand in their parachutes to a WAAF in the parachute store after returning from an operation to the Ruhr, probably the raid on Wuppertal on the night of 29/30 May 1943. (IWM)

Lancaster I R5740 KM-O on 44 Squadron, which went MIA with Pilot Officer Derek Mindon Sharp and his crew on the operation on Gelsenkirchen on 25/26 June 1943. All the crew were killed.

Halifax II HR837 ND-F *F-Freddie* on 158 Squadron that Flight Sergeant D Cameron and his crew landed back at Lissett, Yorkshire after attacking Cologne on the night of 28/29 June 1943, with a hole in the fuselage measuring 5 feet by 4 feet after a bomb had passed right through without exploding. HR837 was repaired and operated on 1656 HCU before it was SOC on 11 January 1945. *(IWM)*

ancaster III ED657 PO-Z on 467 Squadron RAAF, part of the shuttle force that bombed riedrichshafen, at Blida in June 1943. This aircraft crashed at Nunhem on the costly raid on Duisburg on 21/22 May 1944. Flying Officer Robert Maxwell Harris RAAF and all the crew were illed.

urin, 12/13 July 1943 photographed by a 97 Squadron Lancaster flown by Flight Sergeant Baker.

Group Captain Percy Pickard DSO* DFC (left); Squadron Leader Bill Blessing DSO DFC RAAF (centre) and Group Captain Geoffrey Leonard Cheshire DSO* DFC (right) at an investiture at Buckingham Palace, 28 July 1943. Pickard, who had commanded Wellington and Whitley squadrons early in the war, was the pilot in the popular 1941 documentary *Target for Tonight* which featured the crew of Wellington *F for Freddie*, 149 Squadron's P2517. When commanding 51 Squadron at Dishforth, Pickard flew one of the Whitleys that dropped paratroops in a daring raid to capture a radar installation on the French coast at Bruneval. He was killed leading the Mosquito raid on Amiens Prison on 18 February 1944. Blessing was awarded the DSO for the Mosquito raid on the Zeiss optical works at Jena on 27 May 1943. Leonard Cheshire, a former 76 Squadron CO, who later commanded 617 Squadron, completed four operational tours and was awarded the Victoria Cross for outstanding and sustained courage and leadership.

A Polish aircrew member killed on one of the raids on Hamburg in July–August 1943.

Group Captain John Searby (centre), 83 Squadron at Wyton, was Master of Ceremonies at Peenemünde on 17/18 August 1943. Left is Squadron Leader Richard John Manton (who was KIA on 20/21 October 1943 on the raid on Leipzig) and right is Squadron Leader Shaw. In the background is Lancaster B.III EB114 Q².

Flares going down at Peenemünde on 17/18 August 1943.

Lancaster III ED611 KM-J on 44 (Rhodesia) Squadron captained by Pilot Officer D H Aldridge had a lucky escape on the night of 17/18 August 1943 on the raid on Peenemünde when the aircraft was attacked by a night fighter which raked the starboard side and damaged the outer engine, right undercarriage assembly and the turret hydraulics. Aldridge however, successfully got the bomber down safely at Dunholme Lodge with a burst right tyre. ED611 was repaired and joined 463 Squadron RAAF at Waddington in February 1944 where it was named *Uncle Joe*, painted with a likeness of Stalin and had operations denoted by stars. ED611 flew 115 ops. (*IWM*)

Tail section minus gun turret of a Lancaster III, probably JA916 OF-L on 97 Squadron piloted by Wing Commander Kenneth Holstead 'Bobby' Burns DFC, which broke up over Berlin on 31 August 1943. JA916 exploded and crashed in the target area. Burns lost a hand and he and four crew were taken prisoner. Two men were killed. (*IWM*)

Halifax II JN909 on 102 Squadron which crashed near Sinningen on the night of 31 August/
1 September 1943. The pilot, Sergeant Edward Thomas Samuel Rowbottom, and four of his crew
were killed. One initially evaded capture but was later taken prisoner.

On 16/17 September 1943 eight Lancasters on 617 Squadron and four on 619 Squadron set out to
bomb the Anthéor viaduct near Cannes on the coastal railway line leading to Italy. The Lancaster
crews found the viaduct in the moonlight without trouble but their bombs missed the target.
American bombers finally destroyed the viaduct.

Crews on 76 Squadron at Holme-on-Spalding Moor get ready to board their transport out to their waiting Halifaxes for the operation on Kassel on the night of 22/23 October 1943. (*IWM*)

Halifax V DK270 NA-U on 428 'Ghost' Squadron RCAF at Middleton St George, which crashed at Framlingham (Parham), a USAAF airfield in Suffolk, returning from the raid on Hanover on the night of 27/28 September 1943. Sergeant R Wilson the pilot and one crewmember were injured. Four others died and only one man was uninjured. (*USAF*)

Lancaster III LM326 EM-Z *Z-Zebra* on
207 Squadron, which was shot down by
Hauptmann Friedrich Karl 'Nose' Müller, a
Wilde Sau pilot of *Stab* JG 300 on 18/19 October
1943 on the raid on Hanover. All seven of Flight
Sergeant Geoff Taylor RAAF's crew were taken
prisoner. (*Frau Katherine Holterhoff Grote*)

Hauptmann Friedrich Karl 'Nose' Müller, a pre-war
Lufthansa airline captain and a *Wilde Sau* pilot of
Stab JG 300 who shot down Lancaster III LM326
EM-Z *Z-Zebra* on 207 Squadron on 18/19 October
1943 for his 19th *Abschuss*. (*Fritz Krause*)

(*Left*) A WAAF member cleaning sparking plugs at RAF Syerston in 1943. (*IWM*)

(*Right*) Bill Reid VC who flew the operation to Düsseldorf on 3/4 November 1943. On 31 July 1944 Reid became a PoW when his Lancaster was brought down over France by a 1,000lb bomb dropped by an aircraft overhead during the bombing of both ends of a railway tunnel at Rilly-La-Montage, which was being used as a flying-bomb store. (*Bill Reid Collection*)

The Salle Strasse area of Hanover ablaze on the night of 18/19 October 1943. (*IWM*)

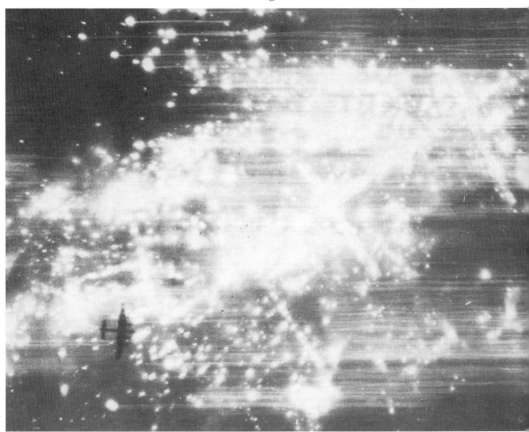

Halifax B.Mk.V Series I (Special) on a Canadian squadron in 6 Group undergoing engine repairs after landing in emergency at a USAAF base. (*USAF*)

Bombing up Halifax B.Mk.II *Q-Queenie* on 405 Squadron RCAF.

(*Left*) Halifax silhouetted over Leipzig on the night of 3/4 December 1943.

(*Right*) On the night of 8/9 December 1943, 133 bombers and Path Finders, including 108 Lancasters were ready to be dispatched to Turin. While bombing-up at Syerston incendiary bombs fell from the racks of a 61 Squadron Lancaster, exploded and set fire to the aircraft. Group Captain 'Gus' Walker, the Station Commander (left in the picture, with Sir Arthur Harris, right) went out to the bomber or a fire tender just as the Lancaster's 4,000lb bomb exploded, killing two men and blowing the Group Captain's arm off. 'Gus', who had played rugby for Yorkshire, Barbarians and England eventually returned to duty and post war became Air Marshal Sir 'Gus' Walker.

Squadron Leader Hugh Everitt DSO DFC who completed two tours, the second on 50 Squadron.

Briefing at Wickenby for the raid on Berlin on the night of 16/17 December 1943.

Halifax *S-Sugar* at a snow-bound airfield in the winter of 1943–44.

Lancaster VN-M on 50 Squadron at Skellingthorpe.

A Lancaster on 463 Squadron RAAF at Waddington. This Australian squadron had formed in November 1943 with Lancasters, from 'C' Flight on 467 Squadron and it was the last Aussie unit to be raised in Bomber Command.

had gone unserviceable and no one could hear what I was saying. No amount of banging would clear the fault, although I could hear perfectly well through my flying helmet earphones. We didn't have a spare headset on board and I made a mental note to remind Cliff Price to draw a spare set from stores come the morrow. Jack decided that Joe Enwright would now remain in the rear turret for the rest of the trip whilst I would take the ventral position in his place. It was essential that the rear gunner was able to communicate with the pilot. Joe was our sole means of defence. Even if the intercom system became unserviceable, communication was still possible between crew members and their pilot by means of small lights fitted at all crew positions. Any trouble would be flashed immediately to the pilot using the appropriate letter in Morse code like 'F for Fighter'! The pilot would then take immediate avoiding action by frantically weaving and corkscrewing the aircraft until hopefully clear of danger.

I settled down in the blister position aft, laying on some none-too-clean canvas engine covers, which were stowed in the aircraft adjacent to the ventral blister position. I had done one operation with my head in the perspex blister, which did not suit me at all but I could only try to make the best of the situation. After all it was my mike that had gone U/S wasn't it? I always felt very much at home behind four Browning machine guns in the rear turret with a little armour plate beneath my seat. Now I felt rather naked and very vulnerable lying flat out on the thin metal floor. I flashed Jack up on my signal light to let him know that I was in place and received a reassuring acknowledgement in return before settling down to gaze upon the awful nothingness below. We were flying around the 18,000 feet mark. Normally, with a full petrol and bomb load on board we couldn't get the old Mark II Halifaxes, even with all their recent modifications, much higher than this. I could see nothing below, just total blackness. It was damn cold too with no heating available. I could hear the rest of the crew going about their duties with Jack quietly in command and not saying much. Phil our navigator was trying to work wonders from his *Gee* set, which was being 'bent' by 'Jerry'. Phil was telling Jack that the set was practically U/S and he would have to rely on his D/R plot from now on.[4] Stan Hurrell in his bomb aimer's position was busying himself looking out for PFF flares and markers, which should be showing up soon as we approached our next turning point, a little to the north of Dieppe. Cliff Price was conscientiously searching his allotted wave bands hoping to pick up Jerry night fighter controllers nattering to their airborne charges so that he could give them a blasting from a microphone positioned alongside one of our Merlin engines and thus interrupt their broadcasts with some beautiful aero engine noise. Nobby Clarke was checking his petrol tank gauges and effecting changeovers from one tank to another to maintain our centre of gravity in flight as petrol was used. We used an awful amount of petrol per hour when airborne. Joe Enwright in the tail obtained permission from Jack to test his guns. I then heard the familiar rattle as Joe fired off a short test burst from the four .303 Brownings. That very morning he and I had harmonised those guns down to one hundred yards.

Jack warned us that we were approaching the French coast just north of Dieppe per Phil Hyden's calculations. It was always a gut tightening occasion and put everybody on their mettle. Jack then commenced a gentle weave (a winding course on a general heading of intended flight with variations of height) to distract enemy night fighters and predicted radar controlled flak. I could see no flak near us. No one mentioned seeing any close to us up front either. Stan Hurrell counted the yellow PFF flares aloud. We were heading towards Metz in eastern France where there was to be another change of course on PFF markers. Jack warned us that we were now in the Jerry night fighter belt. Nothing keeps you on your toes than the prospect of being caught by a Jerry night fighter. It concentrated the mind wonderfully.

However, all was going well. *F-Firkin's* four aero engines were all roaring on. All was quiet up front with just the occasional word from Phil warning Jack of a slight alteration of course. The golden rule was that no one spoke on the intercom over enemy territory unless one had to. Jack however did speak individually to us from time to time with quiet words of encouragement which always went down well. All was completely black below. It must have been 10/10ths cloud cover all over northern Europe. We duly turned onto our new heading over Metz amid a sprinkling of yellow PFF markers but other than that I saw nothing of the French city beneath me at all. We flew on, weaving more vigorously now with everybody on the *'qui vive'* maintaining a close vigil of the black sky all about us.

Suddenly from out of the utter nothingness below and a little astern, came several blinding lines of very bright green lights. Tracer and lots of it! *'CHRIST!'* I cried out loud. A bloody night fighter had caught us from below. The lines of tracer tore into us at a terrible speed. Our 'Hally' was raked from tail to nose in just one long savage burst, which could not have lasted for more than three seconds. The noise was considerable and above the roar of the engines too. It was as if a giant was tearing up sheets of corrugated iron by hand and doing it very fast indeed. It was 20mm cannon fire that was hitting us and some of the cannon shells were exploding on impact in bright little splashes of light. How I was not hit I just do not know, for the tracer appeared to go all around me lying there on the engine covers on the floor of the Hally, as if frozen stiff. I was just 2° from being absolutely petrified. Faintly, over the intercom I heard that someone up front had been hit. Fire must have broken out immediately from amidships where the main petrol tanks and our bomb load, mainly incendiary bombs in metal containers, were, and flames streamed back underneath the aircraft.

I saw nothing of the Jerry night fighter that had caught us. He obviously knew his profession very well, creeping up quite unseen, entirely on his airborne radar no doubt and then hitting us plumb amidships just where he could do the most damage. And all in the one short burst too. He must have then stood off and watched our demise. I was told after my capture that a Bf 110 night fighter had shot us down and that we were one of 20 bombers brought down that night.[5] Cliff had been hit in the leg. I could now hear over the intercom and Nobby was saying that he had badly burnt hands. Fortunately, no one else appeared to have been hit in the attack, which was miraculous considering what had gone by me and struck up front. There was some shouting and a bit of a flap but no real panic. I heard nothing from Joe in the rear turret but that wasn't unusual as Joe never did say much nor had I heard his guns firing. He couldn't have seen the fighter either. I gathered quickly that we were now well alight and that it was impossible to control the fire, let alone put it out. All this had happened within seconds although it appeared to last for an age. In fact less than 20 seconds only were to pass from the moment of attack to the time Jack and the last to leave our doomed Halifax bailed out. Time certainly seemed to stand still. I still couldn't believe that it was all happening to us. It was all so unreal. Was this a nightmare? I kept telling myself that this is what befell other crews; it just couldn't happen to us. I came back to reality rather abruptly when I heard Jack on intercom say very calmly, 'This is it chaps. Better get out quickly. We've had it.'

Phil then shouted something about Switzerland but by then I had pulled my intercom plug out and was making my way to the rear door on the port side of the Halifax, having grabbed my parachute pack. I opened the door inwards up to the roof of the aircraft and saw fully for the first time the whole mass of flames tearing past underneath me. '*CHRIST*' I said. It was damn noisy too. We had really had it all right. I had to get out fast before the kite exploded. I paused looking down into all that blackness I was about to jump into. Beyond the tearing flames I saw two bodies flash by so I knew that at least two members of the crew had managed to get out OK and wondered which two it might be. I sat down on the floor with my legs out of the doorway and prepared myself to abandon the 'Hally'. I must have been sucked out or drawn out by the roaring rushing slipstream tearing past and in the mere seconds of receiving Jack's 'bail out' call I found myself out in the cold night air with the huge tail of the Halifax shooting past over my head. She was certainly well on fire amidships and diving away obviously out of control.

Was I the last one out, I wondered?[6]

Complete cloud cover in the target area again led to failure. At Linton-on-Ouse there was no sign of *V-Victor* and Flight Lieutenant Hull's crew. Ron Read was OC Flying for 78 Squadron that night. He remembered the 'long weary wait as it became apparent that Hull was not coming back.'

'The Group Captain was missing. A little shiver ran through us in the control tower; if they could get "Groupie" Whitley we felt that they could get anybody.'[7]

Max Chivers was just 19 years old when he joined the RAF in 1940. After basic training his first posting was to RAF Rochford near Southend. While on ground duties at this fighter station, he applied for aircrew duty and was accepted for pilot training. In November 1941 he crossed the Atlantic to the USA and was taught to fly at No. 2 Basic Flying Training School in California. After graduating as a pilot from the basic flying course he returned to the UK and flew Wellingtons at an Operational Training Unit (OTU), where he crewed up with a navigator, bomb aimer, wireless operator and rear gunner. Later, in January 1943 at a Lancaster Heavy Conversion Unit (RCU), a flight engineer and mid-upper gunner was added to his crew. After intensive crew training and accumulating the necessary number of flying hours on Lancasters, the Chivers crew was posted to 61 Squadron at Syerston. By the start of April 1943 the crew had successfully completed ten bombing operations by attacking various industrial targets in Germany and *U-boat* base installations in France.

On the night of 13/14 April, 208 Lancasters and three Halifaxes were briefed to attack the San Vim arsenal: the shipyards and the submarine base at La Spezia in Italy. This operation was regarded as a maximum range target and therefore the balance between fuel and bomb load was critical if the crews were to return safely to England. They would have to fly 700 miles on an outward journey to La Spezia. Chivers' crew took off in Lancaster *S-Sugar* at dusk from Syerston and headed south on the first leg of the 900 mile long trip over France, to the target on the northeast coast of Italy. Shortly after flying over the enemy coast of France at 20,000 feet, *S-Sugar* was attacked by two German night fighters. Both gunners opened fire on the attackers, and following instructions from the rear gunner, Chivers lost the enemy fighters by diving the aircraft in a wild corkscrew manoeuvre. As soon as he had the aircraft under control and climbing again Chivers called over the intercom for a new course from his navigator but he received no reply. After a short interval the wireless operator, Danny Shea, reported that the navigator was unwell and in his opinion would not be taking part in the rest of the operation.

Under these circumstances Chivers could have aborted the operation and returned to base but as they were half way to the target he decided to press on. By using his route map plus a visual fix from the bomb aimer a new course was set for La Spezia. Two hours later as the aircraft was approaching the target area, Chalky White, the mid-upper gunner, reported seeing another night fighter on the starboard side, and after giving it a long burst of fire from his twin Brownings, the fighter dived away and was not seen again. After five and a half eventful hours they arrived in the target area. Most of the other 200 main force Lancasters had already blitzed the area leaving behind many large fires and a huge column of smoke rising from the docks and oil depot. After assessing the situation from 8,000 feet Chivers turned his Lancaster onto its bombing run and ran a gauntlet of defensive fire from both harbour and naval ship flak before the bomb aimer released the bomb load. On clearing the target area over the Mediterranean, a north-westerly course was set for home.

Flying Officer Victor Albert Wilson on 57 Squadron, the captain of the last Lancaster to leave the port, saw the dockyards burning furiously:

I could see below me the interiors of the buildings looking quite black but with the walls white-hot. And there were wide areas as red as the inside of a furnace. There was not much flak and the searchlights waved hopelessly like grass in the wind. In fact the only dangerous moment we had was when we were over the Alps. I was looking at the white caps of the mountains and the dark valleys when suddenly everything seemed to blur. I looked at my instrument panel and I could see only a luminous haze. I realized that I was passing out and made a quick check of the oxygen supply. Somehow or other we had developed a bad leak and there was no oxygen left. Clouds then came between us and the ground. I asked the navigator if it was safe to lower. In a rather weak voice he said he didn't think it was. But by that time there was nothing else to do, as I knew I should become unconscious at any moment, so I put nose down and hoped for the best. We lost 5,000 and then found we were just clear of the mountains and over France. We began to feel less 'muggy' and came home the rest of the way in good spirits.[8]

Chivers and his crew had meanwhile taken a heading which took them over the Rhône valley in the south of France and then in a westerly direction to exit the enemy coast south of the Cherbourg peninsula. Four hours after leaving the target area, the flight engineer reported a serious loss of fuel, possibly due to flak damage. Chivers realised they were in a desperate situation. They had already been in the air for almost ten hours and he was uncertain of their true position along the return route. He decided to carry on, however, in the hope of reaching an airfield on the south coast of England for an emergency landing, rather than abandoning the aircraft over enemy territory. An hour later, flying over the sea in a north westerly direction and almost out of fuel Chivers ordered his crew to take up their ditching positions and sent out a Mayday call, giving their approximate position. As dawn was breaking the pilot turned the aircraft into wind before putting QR-S skilfully down on the Atlantic swell. The impact broke the aircraft's back near the mid-upper turret but it kept afloat long enough for the crew to escape. The crew, although badly shaken were otherwise unhurt and soon clambered out of the emergency ditching exit above the aircraft's main spar and onto the port wing. After releasing the dinghy from its storage position, they all scrambled aboard with their emergency rations. Unfortunately, in his haste to get out, the navigator left the emergency portable radio inside the sinking aircraft. So began a distressing and unhappy time for all the crew. They had come down half way between Cherbourg in France and the Isles of Scilly. Without the radio they would have to wait and hope the air sea rescue organisation could find them. However, their chances of being picked up by friendly shipping in this area were slim because they were too far away from the coastal shipping lanes along the southern coast of England. Nonetheless, as the weather remained good and the sea calm, they had a good chance of surviving a long exposure to the elements. For two days the despondent crew drifted in the small open dinghy and saw no ships or aircraft to raise their hopes of rescue. Suddenly, during the morning of the third day they heard the sound of an aircraft and fired off some red distress flares. This attracted the attention of a Whitley of Coastal Command, which was returning to its base from a *U-boat* patrol of the Bay of Biscay. Moments later the Whitley flew low over the now elated and waving crew of QR-S. Fortunately their luck held and the weather remained good throughout the day. Late in the afternoon, much to the crew's relief, they saw a Royal Navy air sea rescue launch heading towards them. Once aboard they were given a great reception by the sailors, several tots of rum, dry clothes and then quickly taken to the naval base on the Isles of Scilly. After recovering from their harrowing ordeal the Chivers crew, apart from the navigator who was suffering from operational fatigue, returned to RAF Syerston to continue their tour of operations.[9]

Flying Officer Alan James Johnson RAAF and crew on 460 Squadron RAAF also endured a harrowing return flight. One of his gunners was Flying Officer Clifford Timothy O'Riordan, who in civilian life was a leading member of the Sydney Bar, a King's Counsel. His younger crew members thought he was over 40 but officially his birthdate was 12 May 1909, and at age 33 he was a little old for air crew. Having been rejected for training as a pilot, he had qualified as an air gunner, and after briefly serving on 103 Squadron, had joined 460 in late 1942 as a spare gunner affiliated to no particular crew. O'Riordan recalled in his diary the events of 13/14 April thus:

Big do on and we're operating. 2,250 gals petrol and ammunition cut down to a minimum. Much speculation as to the target. Austria? Czechoslovakia? New navigator in crew and did x-country in afternoon to try him out. Dropped in at Elsham and saw Blue Freeman whom I'm defending at Court Martial, since Tom McNiel has gone. Seems to have an outside chance. Briefing at six. Target Spezia, Italy. They think there are battleships there. Uneventful trip out. The Alps looked like a travel poster. We were bang on course and the first aircraft at the target. The town lights were on and we could see cars and buses going up and down in the streets. Stooged across and had a look. Height 7,000. No ships. Made a second run. Some of the town blacked out. Made a third run and dropped in on the docks. Caught in searchlights and lots of light flak. Climbed into cloud. Extraordinary effect of reflections in cloud, with coloured flak and own aircraft silhouetted a dozen times. Soon out of trouble and heading for home. After an hour or so Camp asked if we had crossed the Alps. No one had seen them. Later we passed over lighted towns which hastily blacked out. Hopelessly lost and the navigator couldn't take an astro shot. Later we came over the sea and kept stooging along. Airborne for eight hours and lost. Mitch, the WOp, finally got a QDM and we set course due south of Southampton. After a while land appeared and we lost height to find where we were. Flak came up to welcome us and we were over Lorient. For good measure our navigator took us over Brest and a convoy. They all had a poop at us. Diverted to Harwell. Bright sunlight and down to 1,000 feet, feeling secure, when we went straight through the Yeovil balloons. Finally made it, but well overdue, 11 hours 5 minutes in the air. Found we had set course wrongly from target and went bang across Spain and up the Bay of Biscay. Shaky do. Got to Breighton at 4 pm and left for London at 5. Caught midnight train.

Squadron Leader Geoff Rothwell recalls:

Wednesday the 14th April was a beautiful spring day. The aircrews filed into the briefing room and soon produced a stifling fug from the tobacco smoke of numerous cigarettes and pipes being puffed. My crew was recovering from celebrating their Skipper's 23rd birthday the previous night. The small, teetotal navigator from Wellington sympathized with the suffering wireless operator, Whistle, his friend from Hawera, who had entertained the patrons of the Red Lion the night before by performing a solo haka in the middle of the saloon bar. I was almost a foot taller than Jackie, the navigator, and I often wondered how the little chap avoided becoming waterlogged by all the lemonade he drank. Protocol demanded that the diminutive officer kept the kitty, into which they had all put in five bob, as he was the only one of the party likely to be in a trustworthy condition by the end of the evening. It also required him to drink pint for pint with the crew, whose capacity for beer was legendary. The arrival of the briefing party focused their attention on the stage on which the Station Commander stood. He rolled up the screen which covered the map of Europe hanging on the wall. It was dotted with coloured pins showing the enemy's defence concentrations. Coloured wool showed the route to the target. Everyone's attention was on the point where the wool finished and eyes were strained to read the name of the target – Stuttgart. A long trip but not, as exacting as 'Happy Valley', particularly Duisburg and Essen, which had been the targets recently. The very thought of having to fight through lanes of flak and searchlights to reach a Ruhr target made the stomach sink and Stuttgart was a welcome change.

'We are trying new tactics tonight', said the Wing Commander, 'Total effort will fly to this point on the coast of Belgium at 10,000 feet.' He indicated on the map with a pointer. He went on to explain that the new plan was designed to confuse the German radar and involved splitting the main force into three, the Lancasters climbing to 20,000 feet, the Halifaxes and Wellingtons remaining at 10,000 feet and the Stirlings dropping to ground level and climbing to bombing height just before reaching the target. As there was a full moon there was no problem for the Stirlings flying low. It was certainly an innovative idea and a buzz of excited discussion began after the briefing ended. All pilots loved low flying and, although there was an element of danger in carrying out the manoeuvre over enemy territory, most were looking forward to the experience.

That night Stuttgart was the destination for 462 Wellingtons, Halifaxes, Lancasters and Stirlings. One of the Halifax IIs on 35 Squadron was *N-Nuts*, which was being flown by Pilot Officer Ron Wilkes who had received an immediate DFM, gazetted 15 January 1943 for his outstanding airmanship during the operation to Duisburg on 20/21 December 1942. *N-Nuts* took off from Graveley at 2128 hours. The low-flying Stirling flown by Geoff Rothwell sped across the Luxemburg countryside with air gunner Wal, in the front turret, letting rip with the twin Browning machine guns at anything that moved:

The briefing officer had authorized such action on the grounds that anything moving on the roads after curfew must be enemy operated. I was enjoying the exhilarating experience of low flying. The navigator stood beside me map-reading and directing me so we avoided townships where there might be a danger of running into light flak. A goods train was puffing up a gradient when a stream of tracer hit the engine and burst the boiler. The escaping steam prevented the engine driver from seeing the four-engined aircraft but explosions from the trucks behind the engine indicated that something was attacking the ammunition train. My attention was momentarily distracted by the fascinating firework display. Disaster struck within the next second as a huge electricity pylon loomed up ahead in the path of the aircraft. Instinctively, I hauled hard back on the control column and, for a fleeting moment, it appeared that we had cleared the obstacle. However, a dreadful graunching noise told a different story. As metal bit into metal at 150 mph the air was filled with vivid blue and white flashes as the live wires shorted. The aircraft shuddered as it approached the stall but, with throttles rammed forward against the stops, the Hercules engines delivered maximum power for the propellers and, gradually the Stirling climbed away from the scene. The drama was not over, however, for the bomb aimer announced over the intercom that the incendiary bomb load was on fire. I immediately operated the bomb door switch and pulled the jettison toggle so that the blazing incendiaries dropped into the paddock beside the transformer station. The aircraft was flying more or less normally except for the port inner engine running roughly. I asked for a damage report from the flight engineer and learned there was a gaping tear which ran down from the rear of the bombing panel into the bomb bays, otherwise we seemed to have come through the ordeal practically unscathed.

At the target the Path Finders claimed to have marked it accurately but only a few bombs fell in the centre of Stuttgart. The main bombing area developed to the north-east, along the line of approach of the bombing force. This was caused by 'creep-back', a feature of large raids, which occurred when Main Force crews and some Path Finder backers-up failed to press through to the centre of the marking area but bombed or re-marked the earliest markers that were visible. On this night the creep-back extended over the suburbs of Bad Canstatt, an industrial area with large railway-repair works where damage was caused. The neighbouring districts of Münster and Mülhausen were also hit, and the majority of the 393 buildings that were destroyed and the 942 severely damaged were in these northern areas.

Twenty-four bombers failed to return.[10] One of them was N-Nuts, which was shot down from 18,000 feet by a night fighter. Wilkes, Ron Wheatley his Australian bomb aimer, and Flight Sergeants Frank Hay the wireless-operator and 'Mick' Bradford the Australian rear gunner, were killed. They were laid to rest at Rheinberg War Cemetery. Flight Sergeant T G O'Shaughnessy, the navigator, Sergeant Tom Brown, the flight engineer and Freddy Vincent the mid-upper bailed out and were taken prisoner. It took the total of Halifaxes lost to four. *W-William*, a Halifax on 76 Squadron piloted by Sergeant J Carrie was very badly shot about over France by two night fighters, one of which was claimed destroyed by the Canadian rear gunner. On regaining the south coast, Carrie crash-landed wheels down but without flaps at Manston. Sergeant Michael Frederick Weir, the critically injured air bomber was rushed to hospital but he died from his wounds on 15 April. Nine of the missing aircraft were Wellingtons – three of them on 431 'Iroquois' Squadron RCAF, one of which was abandoned near Baden in Switzerland. The crew were interned and repatriated on 29 June. Seven Stirlings, including three on 7 Squadron at Oakington, failed to return and a 214 Squadron Stirling was wrecked on return to Chedburgh. *H-Harry*, a Lancaster III on 106 Squadron at Syerston, piloted by Flight Lieutenant L C J Brodrick, crashed southwest of Moreiul in France on the way home. Brodrick and two of his crew survived and were taken prisoner. (Brodrick finished up in *Stalag Luft III* where he became the 52nd man out of the tunnel in the Great Escape by 76 officers on 24 March 1944. Re-captured, he spent 21 days in solitary). Five others, including Lieutenant G Muttrie RNVR attached from HMS *Daedalus*, and Squadron Leader Jerrard Latimer DFC were killed. Latimer, who had changed his name by deed poll from Jeffries, had flown Hurricanes on 310 Czechoslovakia Squadron in the Battle of Britain, and on 15 September 1940 he had destroyed a He 111 and was one of three pilots who shared in the destruction of the so-called Victoria Station Dornier, part of which hit the forecourt of the railway station. Other wreckage fell on a building in Vauxhall Bridge Road.[11]

At Downham Market there was an anxious wait for Geoff Rothwell's crew. After hitting the pylon he decided to fly back to base at 5,000 feet, assuming the German night fighters would be operating above 10,000 feet where the main force of bombers would be flying:

Without any warning the rear gunner came on the intercom. 'Cork-screw port, corkscrew port, go.' I immediately wrenched the wheel anti-clockwise and pushed the control column forward. The aircraft dived steeply and the smell of cordite wafted down the fuselage as the rear gunner opened fire with his four guns. Tracer from the enemy aircraft passed harmlessly over the Stirling.

'Two Junkers 88s above us on the starboard beam, Ginge.'

'OK, Jock, I've got 'em' came from the mid-upper gunner.

The sound of firing from the turret just behind him caused me to ask directions. Ginge advised that the two aircraft had broken away to starboard. There was a short discussion and the crew decided the night fighters were returning to base for rearming and refuelling after engaging the main force. There could be no other explanation for their failure to press home their attack on a solitary bomber flying in bright moonlight. The remainder of the flight was incident-free and the concern now was how much structural damage had been done in the collision with the pylon. When Flying Control learned of the predicament the short runway was substituted in order to keep the main runway open in the event of a crash landing. Not exactly a confidence-building decision, I thought, but understandable in the circumstances. I tested the flaps which worked satisfactorily, circled the airfield, lowered the undercarriage and made an approach. I ordered the crew to brace themselves as I levelled off and closed the throttles. The flight engineer cut the power to all engines and stood by with a hand fire extinguisher for use in an emergency. A fire tender was following us down the runway but, fortunately, was not required. The Stirling settled down and ended its run well before the airfield boundary. A relieved crew climbed out and were astounded when we viewed the damage. There was a great, jagged gash from the rear of the bomb aimer's Perspex panel extending six feet or more into the bomb doors, a section of which was buckled and hanging loose. The pitot head fairing had been bent back so that it lay parallel to the fuselage; the port inner propeller showed extensive scarring and the tip of one of the blades was bent back. The most spectacular damage was a rip down the port side of the fuselage from the bomb bay to the entrance hatch near the tail. It looked as though a pair of giant shears had opened up the side of the aircraft. Also, the bomb bays showed scorch marks from the fire when the incendiaries ignited. Next day Wing Commander Don Saville DSO DFC the chunky Australian Squadron Commander who was noted for his puns was heard describing the incident as 'a revolting experience with a shocking conclusion'. This brought howls and groans of protest in the Mess.[12]

On 16/17 April the AG Farben Industrie on the banks of the Rhine at Mannheim-Ludwigshafen, which sit on opposite banks of the Rhine in southern Germany, was effectively marked by the Path Finders. Bombing by 271 Wellingtons, Stirlings and Halifaxes was reasonably concentrated causing extensive damage, but clear conditions made it ideal for the single-engined fighters. Twenty-four aircraft failed to return, one Wimpy was abandoned over Surrey and two other aircraft crashed on return. Sergeant Geoffrey Hall, navigator on Flight Sergeant Steve Tomyn's crew on 427 'Lion' Squadron RCAF at Croft, was on his first operation:

We took off at dusk and headed south-east, climbing on course. My last glimpse of England was the fading grey arm of Flamborough Head. We passed through the French coastal barrage uneventfully and soon after that the *Gee* set became useless, the Germans jamming it with waving streamers of 'grass'. From then on the navigation was dead reckoning only. Bill Ostaficiuk the rear gunner startled us once by giving a night fighter false alarm and firing his guns at the planet Jupiter. Then it was a tedious but suspenseful journey. We saw flak going up in streams in the moonlit haze many miles to starboard and I identified it as Saarbrücken. Soon after we were approaching the target and the first Pathfinder marker flares were going down. Because of inexperience we made a mess of our first bombing run and went round and tried again. The bombs went but we were held in a powerful blue searchlight. I heard Bill shouting over the intercom, 'Get weaving, Skipper, for Christ's sake.'

There was a dull thump like someone hitting a wall with his fist and the port engine stopped dead. The Wimpy lurched, hung in the sky for a moment and then dropped like a stone. She went down so fast that I left my seat and remained suspended in mid air for a few seconds. Also floating near my nose were my dividers, ruler and pencil. Through my headphones I could hear the crew shouting at Steve and above all Ostaficiuk screaming, 'We gotta get out. She's going down.' Then the aircraft must have righted itself because I suddenly hit the floor violently and immediately was very sick. I heard Steve asking me for a course to steer and collecting my charts together gave him a direction pointing to the nearest part of France.

By this time the starboard engine was making a noise like an old lawnmower and we were not doing much more than gliding west. It was obvious that we would never make the French border. However we had bombed from 21,000 feet and despite our momentary loss of altitude during the stall we were still at a considerable height. While Steve held the Wimpy in a steep glide, Albert Johnson and Tony Symons the WOp/AG worked frantically at the balance cocks which changed our fuel tanks over. They wondered whether the engines were starved of petrol by fuel lines being cut. But it was useless, and presently Steve, probably thinking he couldn't hold the Wimpy much longer, gave us the order to bail out. I clipped my chute on the two harness rings on my chest, pressed a button to blow up the still secret *Gee* set and made my way forward to the front escape hatch. Only an hour or two ago I had entered the hatch so confidently at the beginning of my career with Bomber Command and the Navigation Officer saying, 'Good luck, see you at breakfast.' No chance of that now.

Ostaficiuk swung his turret and dropped out backwards. Tony and Albert went out of the front hatch and I paused a moment on the brink, looking down. The moonlight picked out a great river in the black landscape. Steve was still in his seat, holding the plane steady. He jerked his thumb down and the next moment I was gone. The black shape of the aircraft was silhouetted for a second against the silver backcloth of the clouds then it too disappeared. I pulled the ripcord and was momentarily horrified by the sound of tearing stitches as the heavy leather straps broke away to be stopped by the steel bands on the shoulders. Unaware of the principle, I believed that the chute had torn itself away from me. But no, after a tremendous jerk on the shoulders, I was floating gently peacefully down and saying over and over again, 'Oh, my poor mother, my poor Jo' and thinking about them receiving a 'missing' telegram in the morning. I still could not see the kind of terrain in which I was going to land but over on the right a fire was burning fiercely where the bomber had crashed and I could hear crisp popping as thousands of rounds of ammunition exploded. Then the ground came up swiftly, soft, ploughed earth, but even so I bit my tongue with the impact. Undulating countryside; no noise but a faint, pervasive scent that was new to me: Magnolias? It was easy to bury the parachute in the soft earth. I then ripped off the button from the shoulder of my battledress and unscrewed the escape compass. The tiny, luminous needle flickered to the north and I began to walk west towards the big river I had seen in the moonlight, towards France. Overhead a very lonely sound as bombers from some other raid droned home.

I was dressed in blue battledress tunic and trousers, a white air-crew issue roll-neck-collar pullover and brown suede leather flying boots with rubber soles. On my battledress tunic was a whistle to summon other members of the crew if down in the drink, and three lucky charms – a Land Army brooch my girl had given me and two tiny toy dogs from my future mother-in-law. In my pocket was a slim box called an escape kit, which contained essentials for this kind of emergency. I was in enemy country with no clear idea of exactly where I had landed but I knew that I was hundreds of miles from England.

Geoffrey Hall landed safely, was captured and spent the rest of the war in German prisoner of war camps, as did the other members of the crew except Steve Tomyn, who was killed.

In a separate operation, 327 aircraft – 197 Lancasters and 130 Halifaxes – were detailed to bomb the important Skoda armaments factory at Pilzen in Czechoslovakia. The Air Ministry bulletin said that the two raids were very concentrated and successful. It went on to quote two reports, one from a bomber pilot who took part in the operation on the AG Farben Industrie and another from one who flew on the raid on Pilzen. The first report was fairly accurate:

Our unit admittedly was quite a bit smaller than the one that bombed the Skoda works but we used the heaviest bombers in the RAF. The targets of the operations were machine and electrical plants, as well as a factory that manufactured diesel engines for submarines.

Several squadrons succeeded in flying underneath the flak and dropping 2- and 4-ton bombs fitted with time fuses from an altitude of 150 to 500 feet directly into the plant installations. There was considerable ground and air defence. We could only watch as several of our heavy bombers crashed into the sea of houses while flying directly over Mannheim and Ludwigshafen. As we flew away we counted more than 30 large conflagration and numerous smaller fires.

The bomber pilot's report of the raid on the Skoda plant went as follows:

The 1,500-mile flight over enemy territory was all the more dangerous because the sky was almost cloudless and the bright moonlight put the German night fighters into the ideal position to attack. All the crews knew perfectly well that many of them might be making their last flight. To our amazement the outbound flight went off without any obstacle; some dogfights took place only on the return flight. But over the Skoda plant itself we were greeted by numerous night fighters and extremely strong flak fire. The Skoda plant, which covered 325 acres, lay clearly visible to us in the bright moonlight. Nevertheless our pathfinder aircraft dropped hundreds of magnesium signal flares which lit up the individual targets – the steel works, the machine sheds and the blast furnaces and forges as well as the assembly shops – as bright as day. Meanwhile the other bomber wings had arrived and now the bombardment began to devastating effect. Many of the new model 2- and 4-ton bombs went off inside the plant causing multiple explosions. After only a few minutes, whole rows of factory buildings collapsed and 25 minutes after the attack began, nothing could be seen of the Skoda plant but a single gigantic sea of flame. Finally a special unit of Lancaster and Halifax bombers carried out low-level precision raids and destroyed five more industrial installations that had gone unscathed at first. We all had the impression that all hell had broken out underneath us.

In fact the Path Finders mistook a large lunatic asylum near Dobrany, seven miles away, for the Skoda Works, and though 249 crews claimed to have attacked the target only six had got their bombs within three miles of it. Unfortunately it was a night of bright moonlight and the fighters got into the bomber stream early. From then on it was a fight for survival, with mainly luck deciding who was caught. Thirty-seven aircraft failed to return, with one of the missing Lancasters ditching in the sea off the French coast on the way home. Five of the crew were rescued. A Halifax crash landed at Lewes: all the crew were injured. Three of the Lancasters that were lost were on 460 Squadron at Breighton, which took the Australian unit's losses to eleven crews in just sixteen days. Three more Lancasters were lost on 467 Squadron at Bottesford.

Four of the Halifaxes that were lost were on 408 'Goose' Squadron RCAF at Leeming, which had dispatched 12 aircraft. Halifax *T-Tommy* on 102 Squadron, flown by Squadron Leader Wally Lashbrook DFM, who had just begun his second tour and was on his 36th operation, did not make it back either. Lashbrook and one other member of his crew, Flight Sergeant D C Knight, had joined the RAF as apprentices at Halton on 15 January 1929. After bombing the target Lashbrook flew into the Mannheim region at 9,000 feet and experienced very severe icing. After he climbed to 14,000 feet the ice began to evaporate, then as the height of the cloud tops became lower, he reduced height to 9,000 feet. In the Ardennes region an aircraft was seen going down in flames on the starboard side; tracer was seen and it was assumed to be a fighter attack. About three minutes later a Lancaster was seen going down in flames on the port side. Lashbrook told Sergeant L Neill, the mid-upper gunner, to keep a sharp lookout, and almost immediately bullets hit the aircraft. The fighter, a Bf 110 flown by *Oberleutnant* Rudolf 'Rudi' Altendorf of 2./NJG4, was not seen but was apparently attacking from astern and below. Flying Officer Graham George Williams GM, the 22-year-old rear-gunner, was killed and Neill was wounded. Lashbrook put the Halifax into a steep dive to port and at once saw there was a very fierce fire between the port inner engine and the fuselage. After losing 3,000 feet he discovered that he could not pull the aircraft out of the dive as the controls were not working properly, nor could he throttle back the port engines as the throttle control rods were loose or severed. He gave the order to bail out. Flying Officer Alfred 'Paddy' Martin DFC the bomb aimer, and Flying Officer W K Bolton the navigator, and Sergeant W R Laws the wireless operator all went out through the forward hatch. Knight clipped on his pilot's parachute and then dived out himself. As Lashbrook tried to leave, the Halifax went into a spin. By pulling himself to the hatch and popping his parachute while leaning partially out of the Halifax, Lashbrook was pulled free by his parachute 'like a champagne cork out of a bottle'. He was at less than 1,000 feet and made a heavy landing 100 yards from the wreckage of his burning Halifax. So swift had been his decent that he saw Knight floating down a few hundred yards away. Knight and Neill were both taken prisoner but Lashbrook and three other members of the crew evaded capture.[13]

Leutnant Norbert Pietrek of 2./NJG4, who had completed his night fighter pilot training in January, returned to Florennes airfield in southern Belgium in his Bf 110F-4 with claims for two bombers, the first of which, was a Lancaster. Pietrek and Otto Bauchens his *Bordfunker* had been ordered to patrol in *Himmelbett* box *Kater* ('Tomcat') near their airfield. Pietrek chased the Lancaster until it crashed into a hill on the banks of the River Meuse. As he headed for a radio beacon Bauchens tried to make radio contact with *Oberleutnant* Brockmüller, their *Jägerleitoffizier* (*JLO*, or GCI-controller) but jamming prevented the *Bordfunker* from re-establishing contact. Nonethless Pietrek, open-mouthed, unexpectedly spotted an enormous 'barn door'. It was a Stirling.

A-Apple on 214 Squadron, flown by Flying Officer D E James RCAF, had taken off from Chedburgh at 21.50. While they were flying at 9,000 feet in bright moonlight and good visibility just south of St-Quentin, a Bf 110 was seen approaching on the starboard beam at the same level at a range of 800 to 1,000 yards. James immediately began corkscrewing, starting with a diving turn to starboard and shortly afterwards Sergeant Eric Markham Lee the rear gunner reported a 110 coming in to attack from astern. Almost at once the Bf 110 was seen attacking from the port beam and level. The 110 opened fire and hit the wings of the Stirling, apparently with no serious effects, but it seems probable that the turret hydraulics may have been damaged, as the rear turret became unserviceable after a 2–3 second burst had been fired. Lee was dead. James jettisoned his bombs and continued evasive action, picking up speed by diving, and at times the Stirling reached a speed of 300mph. The 110 opened fire at 800 yards and then came in very close, almost colliding with the Stirling. A stream of bullets passed through the window between James and the navigator; the mid-upper turret was damaged and the centre section and rest position riddled. The intercom and all electrical services failed. The mid-upper gunner fired all his ammunition in two or three long bursts. Pietrek pressed home his attacks and fired many bursts of tracer and HE shells at the Stirling. *A-Apple's* Nos 5 and 6 starboard wing tanks were holed and petrol was leaking out, and there was a fire beyond the starboard outer engine, with burning petrol coming from the trailing edge of the wing. Two engines were out of action. Pietrek and Otto Bauchens were completely exhausted and the Stirling was no longer a threat, so Pietrek broke off. It was thought by the crew that it was because the night fighter was out of ammunition but it was quite clear to Pietrek that the 'Tommy' would not make it home. Sure enough, it got as far as Crèvecoeur-le-Grand in the Oise and James gave the order to abandon the aircraft. Two of the crew were taken prisoner but James and four others evaded capture and returned to England.[14]

Pietrek's claim was confirmed but he did not receive confirmation for the Lancaster that crashed. It had come down in the area of a neighbouring *Himmelbett* box and was awarded to another fighter pilot who claimed a Lancaster in the area around that time.

Next day, Ron Read, who had gone on leave to Torquay a week after 'Groupie' Whitley went missing, returned to London:

On the way I read about the raid the night before on Pilzen. 'They had lost 36 aircraft, the highest loss to date.' Phew! 'That's a bit hot', I thought. When I arrived home on Saturday evening there was a telegram that had arrived that afternoon from Pam Finch. It said: 'MORTY MISSING LAST NIGHT 16th ON PILSEN.'

'Oh Hell! Morty gone! It was a shock and yet not more than I had feared. I was somehow expecting it. I felt that he was going to go the minute he told me he was married. He may have gone anyway but I had felt he was tempting fate, marrying in mid-tour. I know in his heart, he thought so too. I had a couple of day's leave left but I went back to Linton the next day. I wanted to find out what I could and to screen Morty's effects. It was customary for a close friend to do this, just in case there were any articles that might have been embarrassing to the family. The return journey on Sunday seemed slow and dragging. I had a lot of time to think. As ever, one felt there was always the chance that he and the crew would have bailed out and would turn up eventually as prisoners of war. That was a standard palliative for friends and family. It saved the immediacy of the alternative. When I arrived, I received a few tentative looks and words of sympathy. Close friends were worried about how I would take it. I got what details were available. Pilzen should have been a 'Piece Of Cake'; a long flight into Southern Europe, well away from the heavy defences. The 'Wingco' [Wing Commander Gerry Warner] had chosen to go himself. The Pilzen trip cut a swathe through the Linton aircrews, probably because they were in the second wave once more; a terrible waste. Apart from Morty there were five others missing: Flight Lieutenant 'Paddy' Dowse DFC, a pleasant Irishman on 78 Squadron on his second tour [Dowse and his crew had returned to the Squadron in February 1943 after having been interned in Spain after a raid on Italy in November 1942] and three sergeants and crews from 76. It was our worst night to date – a total of six crews or 42 bods. I knew few of them personally, as many were replacements for recent casualties. There were lots of new faces in the mess now.

Seven of the empty beds belonged to Bill Illingworth's crew, one of the replacements for recent casualities on 78 Squadron. Their Halifax, *K-Kathleen*, was lost without trace. Edwin Thomas, who had written his last letter to his mother on 8 April, would write no more letters home. Instead she would receive the dreaded telegram informing her that her son had been killed.

Ron Read cleared up Morty Mortensen's things the next day, with a sympathetic padre:

I didn't tell him that Morty went because he'd forsaken our pact with the Devil. He wouldn't have appreciated it, though Morty would. There were no skeletons in Morty's effects and they were sent off to his new wife. I sat down and wrote her a sympathetic letter, with as much cheer as I could find in it. Then set out to get on with life. I had seen quite a few of my friends go and it was an accepted aircrew tenet, that we put our lost friends behind us and forgot them as quickly as possible. Although he had been my closest friend for a year and a half, I was determined to adhere to this philosophy. I reasoned that Morty was a good pilot and if anyone could have made it he could. If he hadn't, well he was as aware as we all were, of what could happen. He'd often philosophized on the *'If you can't take a joke'* joke. Unfortunately it was now on him. No doubt we should learn in due course what had happened. Meanwhile life had to go on and it was just as well to embrace that old secret aircrew belief, 'Whoever it happens to; it won't be me.'[15]

News was received a few weeks later with a letter from a PoW camp from Mortensen's wireless operator Sergeant 'Steve' Stevens. After the Halifax had been hit by the combined fire of a Bf 109 and a Bf 110[16] five of the crew bailed out. Meanwhile, the aircraft was getting lower and by the time they were all out it was too low for Morty to jump. He and Sergeant Donald Alfred Pitman were killed in the ensuing crash. 'Typically Morty and typically a pilot's end' wrote Ron Read. 'It had happened before and would happen many more times. Now to forget it; there was plenty to get on with.'

There was brighter news. Flight Lieutenant Paddy Dowse and crew who had been shot down by a Bf 110 had survived and were prisoners of war. So too were three injured members of Flight Lieutenant Arthur Hull's crew, whose Halifax had been shot down over France by a night fighter on the Frankfurt raid on 10/11 April. Hull was found dead in the wrecked cockpit of *V-Victor* but Group Captain John Whitley and three others had evaded capture. 'Groupie' Whitley changed out of his uniform and flying clothing and into the civilian clothes he had carried with him and walked and bicycled across France, aided by the *Comète* line, to the Pyrenees.[17] He arrived in Spain on 12 May, returned home and was awarded a well-deserved DSO.[18]

Two days after the raids on Pilzen and Mannheim, Flying Officer Geoffrey Willatt, a bomb-aimer/navigator who was born in Nottingham in 1911 and had volunteered for the RAF after the disaster at Dunkirk, returned from his 48-hour honeymoon at the George Hotel in Stamford to discover that he had missed the carnage. Willatt had married Audrey, a teacher, on 14 April. When he returned the adjutant told Willatt that there had been many losses. After operations with Coastal Command, he and the rest of his crew, led by Sergeant Alan Angus Robertson, a 20-year-old Scot who had started his training as a barrister, had been posted to 106 Squadron in 5 Group in April 1943. After learning to fly Manchesters at Swinderby Robbie Robertson's crew were posted to Syerston, a pre-war permanent RAF station, straddling the main road (the Fosse Way, just south of Newark), where the crew's real operations began with 106 Squadron. Willatt recalls:

Our crew came from very diverse backgrounds. Frank Cawley was a very friendly though rather shy Canadian navigator. Arthur Edwin Taylor, our English wireless operator, was older; perhaps about thirty. Moseley was the English flight engineer. Sergeant Freddy Tysall, the mid-upper gunner, was a chirpy Cockney, and Merle Routson, the American rear gunner, a brash American from Bethlehem. The Canadian and American had volunteered for flying in Canada with the RAF. Tysall had to have all his remaining teeth extracted and complained that, until his false teeth appeared, he would find it impossible to bite off the thread while doing mending! At first I was the only officer on the crew but soon Robertson was commissioned. The others were sergeants. I'm sure Robbie was an excellent pilot, as he proved over and over again, but like me he often made rather bumpy landings. He at first found it difficult to mix with the others, during which time I became a sort of 'buffer' between him and some of them. We practised first (on Lancasters) on 22 April and flew various cross-country trips to get used to aircraft handling, navigation and practice bombing. We once flew over the Isle of Man where a radar pulse was directed vertically from Douglas. My open-shuttered camera fixed beneath the aircraft was supposed to pick up the radar pulse. We couldn't see anything as we were in cloud and there was no trace on the camera film. Various other long-distance trips were taken with taking-off and landing by day and night.

There had been very heavy losses of aircrew in bombing raids over Germany at this period of the war and Syerston had suffered as much as other stations. During my period of operations, for instance, I knew of no crew lasting the full tour of 30 operations; personnel changed over and over again. This gave a pervading feeling of tension and insecurity. It was then very probable that each crew, after taking off for a raid, would not come back. Acquaintances, familiar in the Mess for a few days, just disappeared. Unlike life in the Army in the front line, with constant danger to everyone, existence on a bomber station was unsettling; safe in England or even at home for a few hours and then over Germany in extreme danger the next night or nights. This life or 'half-life' had a severe effect on some people. We were all frightened of course and this was quite natural and had to be faced. I never was quite sure whether the fact that I sweated profusely after dressing for a flight was due to fright or the excessive amount of clothing needed for the cold at great heights; probably both. I practised bombing on ranges in various parts of Lincolnshire, usually near the coast, during which time on one day trip after bombing, one of my bombs 'hung up', i.e. didn't come off the hook. I suggested to Robbie that we should fly again over the target and do a jerking movement but before we could do this, the bomb fell off and landed in a farmyard near the back door of the farmhouse, just as the farmer's wife was coming out. Poor thing – she slammed the door and disappeared! A practice bomb was small but heavy and contained a small explosive charge which emitted a puff of smoke. I'm afraid she would have been seriously hurt if hit.

I noticed a curious thing about bombs dropping: as I looked forward and down, the bombs, after dropping free, disappeared backwards out of sight and then, after a time, reappeared much lower, appearing to fall forward again as they approached the ground or target. The 'blockbuster' bomb was shaped like a dustbin and this behaved on being released in much the same way, only being completely un-dynamic it rolled over and over in the air. At night of course these events were only partly visible. Finally, after long cross-country trips in all weathers, day and night, as far as Cornwall, Wales and North Scotland, we were ready for operations; not however, before inadvertently flying over Invergordon where the Fleet was stationed. We soon cleared off after puffs of smoke mysteriously appeared round us! The Navy shoot first and ask questions afterwards.

On the night of 18/19 April, Bomber Command raided La Spezia again when 173 Lancasters and five Halifaxes were dispatched to bomb the dock-yards. Eight others laid mines off La Spezia harbour. On 467 Squadron RAAF 'Bill' Manifold, the 23-year-old Australian pilot of *V-Victory*, with a painted kookaburra dangling the head of Hitler from its beak on the side of his cockpit, flew close to Mont Blanc 'with its jagged ridges knifing up through the snow'. Navigator Tom Moppett left his table and maps, 'Rubbing his hands together, his eyes wide in the delighted expression we had come to know so well when his face was not covered by the oxygen mask.' Manifold had once said that finding a navigator was 'as important as finding a wife' and he had picked Moppett out because he had 'a cheerful disposition'. Back home his great pleasure had been hiking and skiing, even camping out in the snow of the Bogong High Plain.[19]

At the target the centre of the bombing was north-west of the aiming point but the main railway station and many public buildings were hit. One Lancaster was lost and it could have been more.

On 20/21 April, 339 bombers visited Stettin and at Rostock 86 Stirlings attacked the Heinkel factory. Eleven Mosquitoes on 105 and 139 Squadrons carried out a bombing attack on Berlin as a diversion for the bombers attacking Stettin. The Mosquito 'night nuisance' operations were also designed to 'celebrate' Hitler's birthday. The raid on Stettin, a target more than 600 miles from England, proved to be the most successful attack beyond the range of *Oboe* during the Battle of the Ruhr. Visibility was good and the Path Finder marking was carried out perfectly. Approximately 100 acres in the centre of the town were claimed as devastated. Thirteen Lancasters, seven Halifaxes and a Stirling failed to return.[20] At Rostock a smoke screen concealed the Heinkel factory and bombing was scattered. Eight Stirlings failed to return.

One aircraft that made it back against all odds was flown by Pilot Officer Walter Scott Sherk RCAF on 35 Squadron, who was awarded a bar to his DFC on the night of 20/21 April by getting his lamed Halifax bomber back to Graveley. He had three other Canadians with him, Flying Officer George Glover McGladrey, and Flying Officer Roy Morrison who was navigator, both of whom were awarded the DFC, and Sergeant D G Bebensee who received the DFM for his part in the operation. (All three men had been on Squadron Leader Denzil Wolfe's crew on the third and final 'thousand' raid in 1942). They were sent to attack Stettin, and when over the target area, were hit by falling incendiaries. One of these penetrated to just behind the pilot's seat and jammed the aileron and rudder controls. In a matter of seconds flame and smoke filled the cockpit and Sherk's clothing caught fire. The bomber's tail tipped up and the aircraft, already fairly low, began sliding down in an unpleasant dive, every instant becoming an easier target for the ack-ack gunners. At the control column Sherk tried desperately to regain control of the unmanageable machine, while behind him McGladrey fought hard to beat out the crackling flames. Before the flames could be subdued much of the navigational equipment was ruined and rendered useless. The sergeant struggled to free the locked controls. The four men were doing everything they could to prevent what seemed to be inevitable, a crash on Stettin. Their efforts were rewarded. To their great relief the Halifax suddenly became manageable, and Sherk levelled out and circled round, preparing to head for home. McGladrey finished putting out the fire and then Morrison tried his hand with what was left of his equipment. It took a great deal of ingenuity to plot accurate courses in the circumstances but Morrison had all the ingenuity required. The four Canadians ran a gauntlet of danger all the way to the North Sea coast, for there was the possibility that the controls might jam again. It had taken Bebensee three-quarters of an hour to fix them. A second jam might mean a different ending. However, the lame duck was home before dawn, minus a few feathers but otherwise undisturbed.[21]

On 26/27 April, Duisburg was raided by 561 aircraft, including 215 Lancasters, 135 Wellingtons and 119 Halifaxes, 17 of which were lost, ten of them to NJG1 operating over the Netherlands. This heavy raid was a partial failure. The Path Finders claimed to have marked the target accurately but most of the bombing fell in the north-east of Duisburg.

Two massive mine-laying operations took place on the nights of 27/28 and 28/29 April. On the first night 458 mines were laid off the Biscay and Brittany ports and in the Frisian Islands. One Lancaster which went to the 'Elderberry' region failed to return. The next night 167 aircraft laid 593 mines in regions 'Spinach', 'Geraniums', 'Tangerines', 'Sweet Pea' and 'Silverthorne'; off Heligoland, in the River Elbe and in the Great and Little Belts. Low cloud over the German and Danish coasts forced the minelayers to fly low in order to establish their positions before laying their mines. Much light flak was seen and 22 aircraft were shot down. It was the heaviest loss of aircraft while mine-laying in the war. At Newmarket, 75 New Zealand Squadron lost four Stirlings and their crews, probably all to *Kriegsmarine* flak. At Wickenby also, four Lancasters on 12 Squadron failed to return. At Leconfield 196 Squadron lost three Wellingtons and their crews. At Downham Market 218 Squadron lost three Stirlings, which were shot down in the 'Sweet Pea' region. Pilot Officer Richard David Roberts DFM and his crew of Halifax II *A-Apple* on 158 Squadron at Lissett near the Yorkshire coast, were an experienced crew nearing the end of their tour when they were lost without trace in the 'Silverthorne' area. Roberts had gained an immediate DFM during operations to Nürnberg in March 1943. One of his crew was Flight Sergeant William Edward Ernest Bethell Priddin RCAF, an American from Saugus, Massachusetts. Another American casualty was Flight Sergeant Robert Russell Gourde RCAF, from Longview, Washington, the rear gunner on the crew of Sergeant George Kenneth Alfred Smallwood RCAF on 419 'Moose' Squadron at Middleton St. George. They were lost without trace in the 'Silverthorne' area.

Gardening operations were carried out in collaboration with the Admiralty; in effect, the Admiralty said where the mines were to be dropped and the aircrews laid them. They did so under the most hazardous conditions and it was work which demanded navigation of the highest order, because the points specified by the Admiralty had to be found in darkness without the benefit of landmarks. Mine laying technique usually was a silent glide approach at wave level before the huge mines were dropped by parachute. Silence was essential because the operation usually meant an incursion into the enemy's heavily-defended coast area, where land batteries and flak ships were always at the ready.

Having to lay their mines in clear moonlight right in the middle of a German convoy was one of the most exciting mining incidents of the war which befell Australians engaged on this work. Two who took part were Flight Lieutenant H G M Robinson DFC, a wireless operator air gunner, and Flying Officer J E H Morris DFC, rear gunner. Of the eight Halifaxes on 76 Squadron assigned to the operation, two turned back with technical trouble, and of the others, only the aircraft carrying the two Australians came back, holed by flak in many places. The minelayers went over the 35-ship convoy three times in an effort to pin-point the area in which the mines were to be laid, hurdling the vessels at low level while the ships' guns sent up a hail of flak. The air gunners fired at everything they could get in their sights. Morris himself used 1,500 rounds that night. The captain of the Halifax – 'a quiet RAF kid named Sanderson' as Morris says – would not give up and at last the mines were laid in the spot assigned to them. It happened to be right in the middle of the convoy.

Essen was again the target on 30 April/1 May. Just over 300 bombers were dispatched and six Lancasters and six Halifaxes were lost. Cloud was expected over the target so a Path Finder technique based entirely on ten *Oboe* Mosquito sky markers was planned. This was not expected to give such good results as ground-marking but the plan worked well and 238 crews reported that they had bombed Essen, although there was no major concentration and bombs also fell on ten other Ruhr towns. Operations in the month of May then opened on the 4/5th with the first major attack on Dortmund, by nearly 600 aircraft – the largest 'non-1,000' raid of the war to date. The largest mining town of the Westphalia coal-field and the southern terminus of the Dortmund-Ems Canal, Dortmund's industries included iron, steel, engineering and brewing. One of the crews that took part was Pilot Officer Robbie Robertson's in 106 Squadron, as Geoffrey Willatt recalls:

In the morning before a raid there was always a test flight, during which each engine was shut off in turn and then restarted. It was a rather alarming feeling sometimes to see only one set of propellers turning but the others always did restart. I tested my guns and the rear gunner tested his and the wireless operator did his stuff. During the tests, we wandered all over Lincolnshire, keeping no navigational flight plan. It was quite easy to get lost but there were various landmarks to look for: Belvoir Castle, Fosse Way (dead straight), Grantham railway station, the Wash, Lincoln Cathedral, Newark with practically the whole town with a castle, on the east side of the river. Map reading was one of my jobs and I soon became familiar with these landmarks. Then came the great moment when we attended a briefing in the Operations Room. A large map showed the target and we were all briefed by the Chief Navigator and then in their turn the Squadron Leader and sometimes the Station Commander, the bombing officer and the intelligence officer. Our Station Commander was Group Captain [Francis Samuel] Hodder and our Squadron Commander was Wing Commander R E Baxter. After general briefing, we each had an individual briefing by our own 'trade' expert. I was told the details of my bomb load and in what order the bombs should be released. Once I had got the designated aiming point in my bombsight and had pressed the 'tit' the bombs would automatically fall in the correct order. They all had different shapes and weights. In order to land roughly in the same place, their different aerodynamics had to be accounted for by dropping them in timed sequence. Difference in weight, however didn't affect their terminal velocity of 33ft per second.

After briefing, we returned for a flight meal – probably the usual bacon and eggs, etc. Then we went by truck to the dispersal point, where our plane was waiting and the ground crew were carrying out the final bomb loading and fuelling the tanks in the wings. All the guns were armed, ready for use (two for me and four in the rear turret). Once we were all aboard, the final testing began. We were dressed in long-sleeved vests and long johns, with silk and leather gloves, leather helmet and harness over all, to which the parachute could be fixed if needed. The parachutes were hung on hooks ready to hand for each member of the crew. I was positioned sitting on a step in front and below the pilot with the Perspex nose in front of me, my guns above and in front and a rack on my right holding small tell-tale bulbs, which showed whether the various bombs were released or still hanging in the bomb-bay beneath. There was an axe, supposed to be for use in releasing hung-up bombs. When bombs did fall off they were automatically fused and unsafe and could only be exploded.

The wireless operator was testing his communications and the navigator his flight plan. The pilot and flight engineer ran up each engine in turn and held it at full throttle for a few minutes to make sure all was well, as shown by all the dials in front of them – several dials for each of the four engines, which all had to be synchronised. Eventually, all had been tested and the pilot waved the wheel chocks away and the ground crew with their starting battery stepped away. It was nearly always quite dark, of course, and all instruction signals must be made by radio or by flashing lights. We rolled gently forward out of our dispersal booth and along the concrete track to join the queue for take-off on the main runway. Twelve or twenty-four giant Lancasters queuing up, with deafening engine noises, generated quite an exciting atmosphere. Gradually, the line of planes in front took off and it was our turn to move forward. At the far end of the runway a red light would change to green, which was the signal for us to go.

As the green light appeared, the pilot or flight engineer pushed the four levers of the engines forward, keeping the wheel brakes on, until full throttle was obtained and the whole plane throbbing. Then the brakes were released and we surged forward with quite a violent thrust in our backs, increasing speed rapidly to get lift-off and flying speed before the end of the runway. Up and away we went. The runway finished at the edge of a drop to a river below and due to the great weight of the aircraft with petrol and bombs etc, there was usually quite a sickening drop before levelling out and beginning to climb. Our aerodrome wasn't far from the coast, so that by circling and climbing before leaving land we could obtain maximum height, usually 30,000 feet.

Having reached maximum height, we headed for the coast. Quite soon we were approaching Holland. Soon, I could see a large expanse of water which was the Zuider Zee, then again, surprisingly quickly, the flashes, flares and searchlights over the Ruhr, which was our destination. There was no need for any navigational course from the navigator; Robbie just steered straight for the brilliant fireworks ahead. I think that I had not been given a specific aiming point but had instructions to aim our bombs where there were the most fires, pillars of smoke and brightly lit areas where buildings had been set alight by incendiaries. There was a steady, breathtaking approach after opening the bomb doors, until my bombsight coincided with an area lit by many fires. I was lying on the floor with my eye fixed to the telescope-like bombsight. When the critical moment came, after the agonising few minutes of the run-in, I pressed the 'tit', calling out 'Bombs gone!' as the plane lurched upwards after shedding its load. The pilot immediately pushed the nose down to build up speed and we rushed forward out of the target area – an enormous relief to all of us. A few minutes later he asked the navigator for a course home. No answer. Then, after a few minutes, Frank came up with a vague and rather dreamy answer, which was really no help at all. Robbie decided arbitrarily to take a course for home and turned west towards the North Sea and England, calling out the course he had taken. Out of the target area and again over Holland, I saw the Zuider Zee again and the sea but as we droned on the flight engineer spotted one engine badly overheating. His job was to concentrate on all the dials (several for each engine) to detect any malfunctions. This engine became so hot that it could have burst into flames and it had to be doused with foam. Once dealt with in this way, it was impossible to restart it. An adjustment in flying altitude was necessary but then, without a bomb load, there was no real anxiety. However, a second engine began to misfire and had to be throttled back. When a third engine began to behave poorly, there was real danger of being unable to get home. It was possible, of course, that one or more of the engines had been hit by shrapnel from anti-aircraft fire, although we hadn't detected anything like that.

How could we maintain height and was it any use jettisoning guns or anything heavy? We needed every gallon of fuel and couldn't afford to lose any that was left. By this time, we were so low I could see the waves on the sea and we were not yet near the coast of England. Where we should arrive was unclear, because the navigator, we discovered, had recorded nothing on his flight plan since his written record of the time we arrived at the Dutch coast on the way out! We were involuntarily and gradually descending to a dangerously low level when the coast, perhaps Essex, appeared in front. Robbie asked our advice what to do and I said we should 'ditch' if we could find a sandy beach, which would probably mean shallow water. However, the decision was up to him and he decided to cross the coast and told the wireless operator to give the ultimate emergency call, 'Mayday', which meant a desperate situation and higher priority than SOS. Almost at once, a voice out of the blue said, 'Docking – emergency landing ground speaking. I will put up a canopy of searchlights. Land east/west immediately when you see the canopy.'

We had looked for 'pundits' and other ground lights which were usually visible and could help navigation over England but a German air raid over Norwich had caused all lights to be turned off. We could hear the 'squeakers' (warning of barrage balloons flying to intercept enemy bombers). The squeakers could only be heard by Allied aircraft. Up came a flood of searchlights and, after a brief half-circle, Robbie cleverly landed us on a very small grass landing strip. A truck appeared with the local RAF officer in charge and a guard for our 'plane. Drinks, supper and beds were provided, with a lift back to our station in the morning. A marvellous piece of quick emergency help and full marks to the officer in charge at Docking, as well as to Robbie, who had brought us back safely!

The initial Path Finder marking at Dortmund was accurate but some of the backing-up marking fell short. Half of the large force did bomb within three miles of the aiming point and severe damage was caused in central and northern parts of Dortmund. Over 1,200 buildings, including the old Rathaus, were destroyed and over 2,000 more including the Hoesch and the Dortmunder Union steel factories and many facilities in the dock area, were seriously damaged. The operation cost Bomber Command 42 aircraft, 11 of which either crashed or were abandoned in bad weather over England. It was one of the worst nights of the war as far as 101 Squadron at Holme-on-Spalding Moor were concerned. The squadron lost six Lancasters although only two could officially be described as 'missing', while a third was badly damaged by flak and crashed in Yorkshire while returning to base. Seven men died and another seven were injured in two of the four crashed aircraft. One of the dead was Sergeant Martin David Davis RCAF, an American from St. Anthony, Idaho. He was rear-gunner on the crew of Sergeant James Ronald Browning RNZAF, whose Lancaster crashed at Scorton near Richmond. Browning and two other crew members besides Davis were killed. Two other 101 Squadron Lancasters crashed on their return to base but there were no injuries to the crews. A Halifax II on 405 'Vancouver' Squadron RCAF at

Gransden Lodge was missing and two others crashed trying to land at Wyton and Graveley airfields. At Pocklington three Halifax IIs on 102 Squadron were missing.

One of these was *V-Victor* piloted by Flight Sergeant James Bowman of Durham who ditched 50 miles off Flamborough Head. Five members of the crew of seven were on their maiden operational bombing trip. Over Dortmund the Halifax had unloaded its bomb cargo, but had been badly shot up by the flak gunners. Three of its four engines had been put out of action and Bowman had tried to get home on the one remaining. But the aircraft had lost height and gone on losing more and when out in the North Sea the order to ditch had to be given. The Halifax sank and the crew set to work firing the rockets stored in their dinghy. Those rockets were spotted at six o'clock in the morning by the sharp eyes of Sergeant D A Workman, a Birmingham man, who was piloting a Hudson of Coastal Command which was out on patrol. The Hudson's navigator worked out the position of the marooned crew and radioed it back to base. The Hudson then began flying round and round the bobbing dinghy, watchful against the appearance of any German aircraft or *E-boat*. Workman was still watching over the Halifax men when another Hudson flew over. This aircraft had been dispatched by ASR Headquarters and it carried one of the new parachute lifeboats. The boat was dropped from about a thousand feet and floated gently down, landing less than twenty yards from the dinghy. Bowman said afterwards:

> I've never been so frightened in my life as when this great boat came sailing down towards us from the air – we were sure it was going to hit us, it dropped so close. However, it landed all right and we soon scrambled in. I could hardly believe my eyes when I saw the engines. We got them going in a few minutes and they carried us forward for several hours at about six knots. The Hudson flashed us our course and we had got within about ten miles of England when we were met by a naval vessel. We were given air protection nearly the whole way back.

Sergeant Harold Mock, the Halifax flight engineer, related afterwards how the crew of the ASR Hudson came to see the men they had rescued next day in hospital, where they were recovering from their adventure.

'Imagine my surprise,' he said, 'to find that the pilot was a chap I know well. He lives near me in Exmouth. That's what I call a pal.' Flight Sergeant A H Mogridge, the ASR Hudson pilot, shared that surprise. That smiling reunion in a hospital ward was a happy augury for the new service of aid and mercy for the east-flying bomber crews begun by the crews of the RAF Air-Sea Rescue squadrons.[22]

Squadron Leader Kenneth Holstead 'Bobby' Burns DFC, an American from Oregon, who had received the award of the DFC in February while on

61 Squadron, flew one of 97 Squadron's Lancaster bombers to Dortmund but lost the use of one engine on the outward flight. To continue offered the prospect of having to jink from night fighters and flak with a lagging aircraft that might at any moment become completely unmanageable. Burns continued, got to the target, 'pranged' it and returned to Bourn, that dead engine still giving no sign of life.[23]

Geoffrey Willatt concludes:

After the disastrous trip to Dortmund, Frank Cawley the navigator confessed that he was so frightened that he literally had been unable to put pencil to paper or use his navigation computer after leaving the English Channel. The result was a posting away for him and off operations – probably home to Canada because he was after all, a volunteer in the RAF. We regretted losing such a nice, friendly person and were very sorry for him.

On 12/13 May there was a trip to Duisburg-Ruhrort for 572 bomber crews. In all, 238 Lancasters, 142 Halifaxes, 112 Wellingtons and 70 Stirlings were detailed for the operation. Not all of them reached the target. A 75 Squadron Stirling crashed on take off at Newmarket, injuring the pilot and one of his crew. The others on board were killed. Ontario-born and Toronto-educated Flight Lieutenant Douglas Julian Sale's Halifax on 35 Squadron was shot down near the small Dutch town of Haaksbergen in Gelderland province near the German border by *Oberleutnant* August 'Gustel' Geiger of III./NJG1, flying a Bf 110.[24] The 29-year-old pilot was blown out of the aircraft when it exploded and he landed in a pine tree. Four of his crew were taken into captivity and the two others were killed. Sale evaded capture and he soon made his way south, travelling through Belgium and France to Andorra where he arrived on the night of 25/26 June after having walked and cycled over 800 miles without once being supported by any of the escape lines. Sale and a French companion crossed into Spain and he left Gibraltar on 5 August and on his return to England he was awarded the DSO for his escape.

Thirty-five aircraft were lost on the Duisburg operation and three crashed in England. Worst hit was 51 Squadron at Snaith which lost four Halifaxes and one that crashed on return. *J-Johnny*, flown by Pilot Officer George William Locksmith, that went down over Holland was heard by Miss Waal-Witkamp, a seven-year-old schoolgirl living in a farmhouse with her parents and family in Beemster. Her mother prayed that it would pass over the top of the farmhouse. As if in answer to her prayers the Halifax's engines roared, emitting greater flames that caused the aircraft to lift itself over the farmhouse and crash into the boggy marshland adjacent to the canal embankment. There was no explosion so it was assumed that it had been unladen. After the crash German troops who had been following the descent, arrived and ordered the Dutch family to remain indoors. Later they gave the Waal-Witkamps torches and large sandbags and, with other people in the area, ordered them to search the crash site and fill the bags with any human remains that they found. Several bags were filled, which were then placed in larger bags. The Germans laid them overnight on the embankment of the Amsterdam-Den Helder canal, known locally as 'the ditch'. Piter Wezel, a 15-year-old farmhand in Jist, was attending to cattle at the crash site and he saw the rear section of the Halifax lying above the marshy ground with two bodies lying therein, one white and one burned black. Two high ranking German officers arrived and proceeded to sift among the exposed wreck-age, the front section having buried itself five metres into the marshy ground. Finding a collection of souvenirs, the officers rebuked the Army guards and confiscated the articles. At this time a German Army lorry arrived to take the two dead air crew to Amsterdam cemetery. Until her death Mrs. Waal-Witkamp always had tears in her eyes when she thought of what the pilot had done that night to save her family.

Whereas the thousand bomber raid on Cologne had taken ninety minutes, concentration at Duisburg-Ruhrort was so controlled that delivery of more than 1,500 tons of HE and incendiaries, more than was dropped on Cologne in the thousand-bomber raid, was made in half that time. Zero hour was fixed for 2 o'clock. The first flares and bombs went down dead on time. The last aircraft was winging home 45 minutes later. Flight Lieutenant Dennis Percival Puddephatt of Brighton gave a graphic description of the raid as viewed from his Halifax on 77 Squadron:

We arrived at the beginning and watched the bursts of high-explosive bombs making a continuous pattern. It was a grand night for the job. There was very little cloud and the moonlight showed up the country. Even without the flares which were dropped we could easily have identified the target. The Rhine was very clear; we followed it part of the way, till I saw the finger-shaped docks of the port at Duisburg-Ruhrort. When the attack started searchlights were trying to work in cones and there was one cone with about thirty beams in it. But very soon they split up as more and more bombers came in. It looked as if they just couldn't manage to concentrate on any one aircraft. There seemed to be a thundering regiment of bombers behind and around us. We could see dozens of them and away in the distance I saw fighters attacking one of them and tracer bullets streaking across the sky. As we turned away the place was filled with fires. When we were over the Zuider Zee on the way home, about 150 miles from Duisburg, the rear-gunner could still see them blazing. I shall never forget all those coloured lights – the explosions, flares and fires. And there were 'scarecrows' which Jerry seemed to be sending up to frighten us. They burst with a red explosion and then red and green stars poured out. It often burst near a bomber and did no harm.[25]

Sergeant R van Eupen from Wellington, New Zealand, a Stirling pilot, recorded his impression of the end of the raid. He was one of the last to arrive:

> There was one very large area of fire and we bombed this. But all round it there were other areas where the flames had got well hold. The only thing I could see in detail in this sea of fire was a large tower – perhaps a gasometer – standing out amongst the smoke and silhouetted against the flames.

Geoffrey Willatt recalls:

> As before, with the Dortmund raid, all hell was let loose but this time there was some cloud. Then I saw the target quite suddenly, with only a few minutes to go before bombing. This time, we'd navigated all the way, dropped our bombs and uneventfully navigated home without any emergencies. On landing, we taxied to our dispersal point and were taken by truck for debriefing. Debriefing consisted of questioning in detail by an intelligence officer on anything we had seen on the trip there or back and we also gave a description of the appearance of the target. Then breakfast and bed but I always found it difficult to sleep afterwards.

On 13/14 May, 442 aircraft, 135 of them Halifaxes, were detailed to bomb Bochum, a highly industrialized and an important transport centre for the entire Ruhr. Another 156 Lancasters and 12 Halifaxes set off on a long eight hour round trip to bomb the Skoda armaments factory at Pilzen again. One of these was *W-Willy*, a 57 Squadron Lancaster flown by 23-year-old Pilot Officer Jan Bernard Marinus Haye who was making his 23rd bombing operation. Born at Pehalongon in Java of Dutch parents who divorced in 1929, he attended school in Hilversum and The Hague. After his mother remarried in 1938 and went to live in England he visited her on holidays and from 1939 he went to schools there. 'Dutchy', or 'Bob' as he was known in the family because he considered himself more English than Dutch, took off from Scampton at 11.37 hours to attack Pilzen, carrying one 4,000lb HC bomb and five 1,000lb bombs. After leaving England the engine temperatures were a little high and the aircraft was climbing badly, with the result that the Dutch coast was crossed at 17,000 feet instead of 20,000 feet as intended. Apart from running a little warm, the engines appeared to be functioning perfectly.

The raid on Bochum at the eastern side of the central Ruhr started well, but after 15 minutes what were believed to be German decoy markers drew much of the bombing away from the target. Twenty-four bombers were lost, 13 of them Halifaxes. Sergeant Gerald Herbert Dane MID and the crew of *J-Johnny* on 78 Squadron had left Linton-on-Ouse at 23.39 hours. Sergeant R G Goddard the navigator recalls:

The aircraft was slow on this trip, only 145 IAS, possibly because this was the first trip with the mid-upper turret. Five to ten miles south of Cologne at 20,000 feet the revs on the starboard engine dropped and it cut out. The pilot feathered the propeller. It was not possible to maintain height on three engines and after a 5,000 feet height loss the bombs were jettisoned live. It was decided to make for the nearest point on the English coast by a route that missed enemy defences. Sometime later a jar was felt in the aircraft and the pilot said that the port outer engine was on fire. [They had been attacked by a night fighter flown by *Leutnant* Heinz Wolfgang Schnaufer of II./NJG1]. Dane ordered the crew to prepare to abandon and pressed the Graviner switch. The fire went out and the pilot said that there might not be a need to bail out. Two or three minutes later the engine caught fire again and the pilot ordered the crew to abandon the aircraft. From the bomb aimer's position the fire appeared to be coming from around the engine, and the flames, which were a reddish colour, were licking back to about half chord of the main plane.

Goddard was first to abandon the aircraft, the bomb aimer and wireless operator were preparing to follow. At the time Goddard left, the aircraft was at a height of 10,000 feet and was diving steeply but still just about under control. The fire was spreading fast towards the centre of the aircraft. Dane and Sergeant Jim Body, his second pilot, were killed. The others, with the exception of Goddard, escaped the aircraft but were taken prisoner.[26]

Wing Commander Don Smith DFC MID was surprised at the number of searchlights he encountered. A veteran on the Happy Valley run, he had never previously seen so many as on this night. 'They were everywhere, in some places unbroken walls of them.'

Smith had taken command of 76 Squadron after Leonard Cheshire left in April.

We were in the early part of the raid and it was obvious by the way the searchlights waved about at Cologne, Duisburg and Düsseldorf that they had no idea where the attack was going to develop. It was as light as day and the whole Ruhr valley seemed to be lit up by the moon and the searchlights. When we flew through them they almost blinded us. Near Bochum there must have been about fifteen large cones, with between thirty and forty beams in each. The lights would wave about until they found somebody. Then all the beams in the area would fasten on to that aircraft and shells would be pumped up the cone. We could see bombers held like that a long way ahead.

Smith would fly the maximum 20 trips, 16 on German targets, and remain at Holme-on-Spalding Moor until the end of December, when he received the DSO. He was then posted to instruct at an Operational Training Unit.[27]

Returning from Bochum five more bombers were lost in crashes in Norfolk and Suffolk. A Wellington crashed north-west of Winterton on the Norfolk coast, a Lancaster crashed further inland at RAF Coltishall and a Halifax ditched off Great Yarmouth.

218 (Gold Coast) Squadron at RAF Downham Market had detailed two crews for mine laying duties, the remaining 14 for Bochum. Of these, three aircraft returned early due to mechanical problems. Of the remaining crews most claimed to have attacked the primary target. None however were able to identify any ground details apart from the river; all bombed on Green TI markers dropped by the preceding Pathfinders. Nevertheless the returning crews reported a fairly concentrated attack, with lots of fires and smoke. One squadron crew bombed a last resort target. While landing at Downham Market at 04.55 hours Sergeant Bill Carney's Stirling swung off the flare path and crashed into the Watch Office and Operations Block. Tragically, two crewmen on another 218 Squadron crew who had disembarked from their aircraft and were about to enter the building for interrogation, were struck by Carney's Stirling and fatally injured. The Stirling was a write-off.[28]

G-George, captained by Sergeant T J Nichols, had taken off for Bochum at 00.25 hours. Shortly after crossing the Belgian–German border, the aircraft was attacked by a night fighter and badly damaged by cannon fire. The rear gunner, Sergeant John Salisbury Howard from Oldham, was killed in the attack. Nichols and his remaining crew were successful in bringing the badly damaged bomber home. Due to shortage of fuel, Nichols was diverted to RAF Chedburgh. While attempting to land it was discovered that the undercarriage and flaps were u/s, and when trying to make a belly-landing at 04.00 hours, all four engines cut out. The aircraft hit a tree and crashed on the edge of the airfield. As the Stirling broke up, five of the crew were flung clear of the wreckage. Nichols was severely injured, having sustained a broken left femur and severe shock. He was admitted to the West Suffolk Hospital at Bury St Edmunds, dangerously ill. Three of the other men, bomb aimer Sergeant James Philip Vaughan Hargest from Brecon, American mid-upper gunner Sergeant Scott Grover Cleveland RCAF and wireless operator Sergeant Thomas Arthur Jamieson, a Londoner from Wandsworth, all received multiple injuries and were killed in impact. Flight Engineer Sergeant Donald Wurr from Hull received multiple wounds in the crash and died shortly afterwards after being admitted to Hospital. Pilot Officer E G Pierce RNZAF, the crew's navigator escaped from the wreckage with a sprained left ankle and emotional shock. He was admitted to the Station Sick Quarters at RAF Chedburgh for 48 hours.[29]

Another of the Lancaster crews that took part in the raid on Pilzen was that of Robbie Robertson's, as Geoffrey Willatt recalls:

The Skoda factory was being used by the Germans because their war production in Germany was damaged severely by Allied bombing and they thought it would be difficult for our bombers to reach it after flying so far over their territory, vulnerable all the way to night fighter attacks. We had prepared for this trip, practising bombing a mock target on Lincolnshire marshes near the Wash, where there was a lake, stream and terrain similar to the actual area seen on approaching the armaments factory at Pilzen. Briefed to fly south over France as a 'blind' with a few planes bombing a French target to draw off enemy fighters, we had a turning point onto an easterly leg. The turning point was as busy as Clapham junction, with aircraft whizzing by, above and below and very dangerously near to us. I wonder how many collisions actually occurred! After an endless trek overland, during which, I could see and usually identify rivers (these were always visible provided there wasn't thick cloud), we arrived near the target and searched for the narrow stream, small lake and factory.

All were plainly visible and I bombed from only 10,000 feet, as it was said the anti-aircraft defences were light. I could see debris flying upwards in all directions and reported this at debriefing on our return to base. The usual high-level reconnaissance next morning by camouflaged, unarmed Spitfires showed the whole or most of the raid to have been a costly mistake. The Germans had cunningly covered over the stream and lake and built a flimsy mock factory some distance away from the real one. In England we adopted similar and other diversionary tactics to disguise places like Liverpool Docks. Our scientists were also able to 'bend' enemy radar direction signals from occupied Norway and France. On one raid, their bombers were thereby diverted to bomb the Irish Sea! Curiously, on the Pilzen raid, some of our bombers, through faulty navigation, had actually bombed the real factory.

Squadron Leader 'Bobby' Burns DFC, the American on 97 Squadron who a few nights earlier had got his Lancaster home from Dortmund with one dead engine, was 200 miles distant from Pilzen when he ran into a thick curtain of flak. His Lancaster was hit and the air-speed indicator rendered unserviceable. Burns again went on, bombed the target and got back to Bourn. He was awarded a bar to his DFC.

Nine aircraft failed to return from the raid on Pilzen. It took the total for the number of bombers missing to 33, of which all except six were shot down by *Nachtjäger* over Holland, Belgium and Germany. Six heavies were credited to *Hauptmann* Herbert Lütje, *Staffelkapitän* 8./NJG1. One of the three Halifaxes that he shot down on their return leg from Bochum was flown by Flight Lieutenant Dennis Puddephatt of 77 Squadron, who had given such a graphic description of the raid on Duisburg-Ruhrort a few nights earlier. All the crew were killed.[30] Lütje's first three claims were for Pilzen-bound Lancasters. Just after turning into the second leg of the track and about five miles before crossing the coast of the Dutch mainland, 'Dutchy' Haye, the 57 Squadron Lancaster pilot, noticed a white flare shot up behind *W-Willy* to about the height at which it was flying. It was a very dark night with no cloud. After crossing the Friesian Islands 'Dutchy', as was his normal custom, flew on a weaving course of about 15 to 20° each side of his track. But two or three minutes after midnight, just before crossing the German border, he flew straight and level to check his DR compass. When he had been flying straight and level for about two minutes he suddenly saw white tracer passing the nose of the aircraft from dead astern about 30° below level and heard shells hitting the aircraft. His attacker was Herbert Lütje. Haye believed that the enemy fighter might have been following the Lancaster unseen all the way from the point at which the white light was seen. As soon as the bomber was hit he pulled back the stick to make a starboard peel-off but almost immediately he felt the rudder bar suddenly go completely free and the rudder became serviceable. He accordingly side-slipped out of the peel-off down to about 16,000 feet and then noticed that the aircraft was on fire and flames were coming from the underside of the fuselage and the bottom of the main-planes below the inboard fuel tanks.

Lütje had fired only one burst and was not seen at all by any of the crew. 'Dutchy' ordered Warrant Officer C F Saville the bomb aimer to jettison the bombs at once and this he did, but the fire continued just as fiercely as before. He then ordered the crew to abandon the aircraft. During this time the aircraft became very nose-heavy and he had to keep turning back the elevators. The aileron control alone remained unaffected. The intercom also gradually became unserviceable. Flight Sergeant Roy Betteridge the flight engineer handed 'Dutchy' his parachute and he saw the bomber and flight engineer go past him and bail out. The navigator shouted something in the Dutchman's ear but he was unable to catch what he said and as the aircraft was becoming more and more out of control Haye waved to Warrant Officer J A Redgrave, the 24-year-old navigator from Enfield, Middlesex to get out at once. Redgrave and Stan Allison the Canadian WOp then bailed out. Meanwhile 'Dutchy' had to keep turning back the elevator control and he noticed that Fred Gilliver the mid-upper gunner standing behind him without his parachute. He shouted to him to get his parachute and get out. But by this time he had turned back the elevators as far as possible and the Lancaster suddenly went into a steep dive and the stick was useless. The fire had spread rapidly and the inside of the bomber was filling with smoke and flames. It was also blazing up round the engines but they continued to run satisfactorily. The IAS was then 250 and rising and about two minutes after *W-Willy* had been hit 'Dutchy' was forced to abandon the aircraft, which was then at about 10,000 feet and he jumped from the forward escape hatch.[31]

'Dutchy' successfully evaded capture in his native land and reached Amsterdam on foot and by bicycle where he received help from the Dutch Underground. On 30 May he assumed the identity of and used the papers of fellow Dutchman Rudolf Franz Burgwal, who had gone to England in 1941. He hid in the Burgwal family house in The Hague for the next eight weeks. During that time he met and fell in love with 22-year-old Elly de Jong, one of the Underground workers a few doors away. On 14 July, Haye and Pilot Officer Alfred Hagan, a Halifax bomb aimer who had been shot down on his first bombing operation on the night of 21/22 June, were told that an attempt would soon be made to get them to England. Finally, on 26 July Haye reluctantly said goodbye to Elly and he and Hagan and eight other Dutchmen sailed to England on a barge. Two days later and ten miles off the Thames Estuary the main engine broke down and the outboard gave only intermittent help, but they were picked up by HMS *Garth*. The barge was abandoned and sunk by the destroyer's guns. On returning to Scampton Haye discovered that four of his crew had survived to become prisoners of war but Gilliver and 'Curly' Williams the rear gunner had been killed. 'Dutchy' eventually returned to operations, flying on 83 (Path Finder) Squadron until the end of the war. After VE Day he returned to Holland to find Elly de Jong. She and other members of the Underground had been betrayed and arrested and sent to Ravensbrück concentration camp under sentence of death. Elly was transferred to Mauthausen from where she was liberated before the sentence could be carried out. On 8 November 1945 she married her RAF pilot and they lived happily together for over fifty years.[32]

Happy endings were a great fill-up and did much to improve morale. After the Dam Buster's raid on the night of 16/17 May the news gave everyone in Bomber Command and the country a tremendous lift when the results were known. Behind the headlines it was a different story, as Gwen Thompson, a WAAF telephone operator stationed at Scampton recalled.

On the night of 16 May the switchboard was swamped with calls. Many senior figures sporting 'scrambled egg' (gold braid) on their hats had arrived at the base. We knew then that something significant was happening. The Dam Busters had bombed the Möhne, Eder and Sorpe dams in Germany, causing wide spread havoc and great loss of lives on both sides. We had to send out 56 telegrams to the next of kin, which had been received from the local GPO at Skegness. Those young crews gave so much. For their families, it was a pyrrhic victory.

On 25 May Dick Richardson' crew on 218 Squadron at Downham Market were called out to do an ASR op. Jimmy Morris recalls.

The CO had received a call from an 8th Air Force squadron for us to search for a B-17 down in the North Sea. We took off about 06.00 hours in really nice weather and spent about seven hours flying over the North Sea. After a long time, Tom Harvey the WOp said he was getting a signal and gave the Skipper a course to set. We reached the target but could not identify anything because of a low sea mist. So, Tom sent a signal to the nearest ASR base which resulted in a B-17 crew being rescued from the sea. The Yank CO sent a nice thank you letter to 218 Squadron. It was an interesting op, seeing all the things floating around in the North Sea, but thank God we didn't meet any Jerry fighters. A mine-laying trip to Bordeaux became my last op on 218 Squadron, having then completed a total of 31 operations. I went on leave for two weeks and on my return to 218 I was shocked to see mostly new faces in the aircrew mess, the squadron having lost about ten kites while I had been away.

Nasty things happen in wartime.

Notes

1. *If You Can't Take A Joke* by S/L Ron Read DFC (December 1995).
2. See *Bomber Command* by Max Hastings (Pan 1979).
3. Halifax II JB871 MP-V.
4. D/R being dead reckoning navigation on a time and distance flown basis with an allowance made for possible drift.
5. *Feldwebel* Karl Gross and his *Bordfunker, Unteroffizier* Geck of 8./NJG4 flying a Bf 110G-4 from Juvincourt were guided onto the tail of the bomber by the ground radar of *15./Ln. Regiment 203*, and in a single long burst of cannon fire Gross shot DT775 down; his sole victory of the war. Whilst serving in 11./NJG6, Gross was KIA in a crash at Urzenici, Rumania, on 11 July 1944, cause u/k.
6. Halifax DT775 crashed in a field at Anoux near Briey (Meurthe-et-Moselle) in East France, where it burned out. Sgt Jack Adams and five of his crew bailed out safely and all were PoW. Sgt Joe Enwright, a married man with a small daughter, was KIA by cannon fire and his body was found near the remains of his rear turret the next day. Of the ten 78 Squadron crews who returned to Linton on Ouse

from Frankurt, six were shot down on ops 16 April–15 July 1943). 22 aircraft FTR from Frankfurt.

7. See *If You Can't Take A Joke* by S/L Ron Read DFC (December 1995) and *Flying Into the Flames of Hell* by Martin W Bowman (Pen & Sword, 2006).

8. Wilson was killed on 12/13 May when his 57 Squadron Lancaster was shot down on the operation to Duisburg and crashed at Maasiniel in Holland. Five of his crew died with him.

9. *Thundering Through The Clear Air: No. 61 (Lincoln Imp) Squadron At War* by Derek Brammer (Toucann Books, 1997). F/O Max Chivers was awarded the DFC for his gallantry and leadership. All of the crew of ED717 QR-S *S-Sugar* qualified to become members of the Goldfish Club. (With the support of the Messrs P B Chow & Co., makers of ASR equipment, a badge showing a winged goldfish flying over two waves was given to those whose lives were saved by Mae Wests and rubber dinghies.) In all, four Lancasters were lost and three more, either damaged or in mechanical difficulties, flew on to land at Allied airfields in North Africa. 175 Lancasters and 5 Halifaxes returned to Spezia on 18/19 April to bomb the dockyard but the centre of the bombing was NW of the AP. The main railway station and many public buildings were hit. One Lancaster FTR. 8 further Lancasters laid mines off La Spezia harbour. Finally, in August 1943, Milan and Genoa and Turin were bombed on one night by 1, 5 and 8 Groups and this was followed by individual bombing raids to Milan and Turin when the second award of a VC was gained during raids on Italy. On 16/17 August attacks on Italian cities, that had begun in June 1940, were finally concluded.

10. *The Bomber Command War Diaries: An Operational Reference Book 1939–1945*. Martin Middlebrook and Chris Everitt. (Midland 1985).

11. At much the same time a Hurricane of 504 Squadron flown by Sgt Ray Holmes crashed in Buckingham Palace Road. Holmes, who was last to attack the Dornier and who believed it was aiming for Buckingham Palace, reported that his wing had 'struck something' during the attack. Holmes landed by parachute in Hugh Street, Pimlico.

12. *218 Gold Coast Squadron Assoc Newsletter No. 48*, November 2007. Wing Commander Donald Teale Saville DSO DFC was born in 1903 at Portland in New South Wales. In 1928 he transferred from the RAAF to the RAF on a short service commission and by the end of 1941 was an acting Squadron Leader and flight commander on 458 Squadron RAAF. Between August and December 1942 he commanded 104 Squadron in Malta, his last operational post before arriving to command 218 Squadron. Squadron Leader Geoff Rothwell DFC was shot down flying a Stirling IV on a 138 Squadron SOE operation from Tempsford on 8/9 September 1944. He was taken prisoner.

13. Bolton was captured in Paris on 18 September. Laws successfully evaded with G/C John Whitley. Wally Lashbrook and 'Paddy' Martin were flown home from Gibraltar to Bristol in a Dakota on 21 June. Lashbrook was awarded the DFC. Martin was awarded the DFC later. See *RAF Evaders: The Comprehensive Story of Thousands of Escapers and their Escape Lines, Western Europe, 1940–1945* by Oliver Clutton-Brock (Grub Street 2009)

14. One of them, Sgt William George Grove, was later commissioned and was KIA flying with XV Squadron on the trip to Berlin on 24 March 1944.

15. *If You Can't Take A Joke* by S/L Ron Read DFC (December 1995).

16. Possibly *Feldwebel* Paul Faden of 11./NJG4 who claimed a Halifax south of Bitburg at 03.07 hours. Mortenson's Halifax II (HR659 EY-A) crashed near Trier.

17. See *RAF Evaders: The Comprehensive Story of Thousands of Escapers and their Escape Lines, Western Europe, 1940–1945* by Oliver Clutton-Brock (Grub Street 2009)

18. Whitley's successor, G/C D E L Wilson, an Australian who had been mainly engaged in training and had no experience of operations. What made him very unpopular was his attitude in his first couple of briefings, telling crews, most all veterans of many ops, how they should 'press on' more and not be slow to attack the heavy Ruhr targets. At a party W/C Gerry Warner and the new 76 Squadron Commander, W/C Don Smith, suggested that Wilson should try an op. He did go for the trip and the 'chop' on 22/23 June 1943 on the raid on Mulheim when he flew with P/O Carrie's crew, one of whom was killed, the rest being taken prisoner. Wilson was sent to *Stalag Luft III* where he became the Senior British Officer, replacing G/C Herbert Massey DSO MC after he was repatriated to Switzerland on 11 April 1944. See *Flying Into the Flames of Hell* by Martin W Bowman (Pen & Sword, 2006). AVM John Whitley became AOC 4 Group in February 1945, succeeding AVM Roddy Carr.

19. *Never A Dull!* by Bill Manifold (published privately, 1986). F/L 'Bill' Manifold DFC* finished his tour with a trip to Leghorn on 24/25 July 1943. He and his crew were then posted to 156 Squadron in August. *Flying For Freedom* by Tony Redding (Cerberus 2005).

20. *The Bomber Command War Diaries: An Operational Reference Book 1939–1945*. Martin Middlebrook and Chris Everitt. (Midland 1985).

21. *Bombers Fly East* by Bruce Sanders (Herbert Jenkins Ltd 1943). F/O's George McGladrey DFC RCAF and Roy Morrison DFC RCAF and Sgt D G Bebensee DFM were KIA on the night of 13/14 July 1943. Their pilot, S/L Denzil Wolfe DFC, with whom they had flown on 419 Squadron in 1942, and two other crew members were killed also. F/Os D J Smith RNZAF and D M Clarke RCAF were taken prisoner.

22. *Bombers Fly East* by Bruce Sanders (Herbert Jenkins Ltd)

23. See *Bombers Fly East*.

24. *Hauptmann* Geiger was KIA with his *Bordfunker* Feldwebel Koch on 29 September 1943, shot down by a Beaufighter of 141 Squadron. He had 53 victories and had been awarded the *Ritterkreuz with Eichenlaub*.

25. 'Scarecrow' shells were said to be anti-morale shells, fired in the path of a bomber stream to dishearten the crews. They represented aircraft being blown up. As they burst nearby, they showered flaming oil and petrol, together with the Path Finder flares and colour signals carried by RAF aircraft; in fact all the symptoms of an exploding aircraft. Briefings referred to the probability of 'scarecrows'. Having been briefed, crews would report that 'scarecrow were active tonight'. They saw them often and said how realistic they were. Crews wondered how the Germans could portray an exploding aircraft so accurately. At the end of the war, when German anti-aircraft personnel were interrogated, it was discovered that they had no such thing in their armoury. The 'scarecrows' were real RAF aircraft blowing up.

26. Dane's was one of three 78 Squadron Halifaxes shot down by night fighter *Experten*. JB924 flown by Flight Sergeant Richard Edward Bragg (KIA) was destroyed by *Hauptmann* Helmut Lent of IV./NJG1. Dane's brother, F/O Eric John Dane, the flight engineer on S/L Harold 'Jock' Swanston's crew on 103 Squadron, was KIA on the Mailly-le-Camp raid on 3/4 May 1944. Chorley.

27. See *Bomber Command* by Max Hastings (Pan 1979).

28. See *Flying Into The Flames of Hell* by Martin W. Bowman (Pen & Sword 2006)

29. P/O Pierce eventually returned to operational flying with 218 Squadron. On 10 August 1943 he was transferred. along with other crews of 'C' Flight. to form 623 Squadron at RAF Downham Market. Pierce became navigator to P/O G L Jenkins DFC, who had flown his first operation on 13/14 May 1943 to Bochum as a 2nd pilot to Sgt Hoey, whose crew were one of those who returned early due to engine problems. While leaving the target area over Nuremburg on 28 August 1943, Stirling III *H-Harry* was attacked by a night fighter. Jenkins began a corkscrew to port when they were immediately fired on by the rear gunner of a Halifax bomber. Fire broke out in the port wing and the order to abandon was given. Jenkins tried to hold the stricken bomber while the crew bailed out and crashed with the aircraft. Pierce spent the remainder of the war at *Stalag Luft III* Sagan. 218 'Gold Coast' Squadron Newsletter No. 31 November 2004.

30. JB892, which crashed into woods near Noordsleen at 02.52 hours. This followed JB966 on 405 'Vancouver' Squadron RCAF, which he shot down at 02.25 hours and it crashed near Oud Avereest. He shot down JD113 on 419 'Moose' Squadron RCAF at 02.45 hours and this Halifax crashed at Dalen.

31. Ten minutes after shooting down ED667, which crashed at Albergen, 7km ENE of Almelo, Holland, Lütje claimed R5611 on 106 Squadron at Rossum/Weerselo. Then Lancaster W4305 on 44 Squadron went down between Bevergern and Hörstel.

32. See *Shot Down and on the Run: True Stories of RAF and Commonwealth aircrews of WWII* by Air Commodore Graham Pitchfork (The National Archives, 2003 & 2007) and *RAF Evaders: The Comprehensive Story of Thousands of Escapers and their Escape Lines, Western Europe, 1940–1945* by Oliver Clutton-Brock (Grub Street 2009). Two weeks after being credited with the six victories, *Hauptmann* Herbert Lütje was awarded the *Ritterkreuz* and he was appointed *Kommandeur* of IV./NJG6 in Rumania. He ended the war as *Kommandeur* of NJG6 with 50 victories.

CHAPTER 6

Mary of the Golden Hair

Alone she waited, clad
In WAAF's uniform, Her sad
Blue Eyes stared in disbelief
Eyes that could not hide her grief

Gazed as though to draw apart
The unrelenting cloud. 'Depart
Cumulus. Let him find his base
Let me look once more upon his face.'

But the Signals WAAF already knew
There was no hope for him or his crew.
Had heard his last despairing call:
'Mayday, Mayday, Mayday.' That was all.

Jim Brookbank

The Flight Commander showed his face around the crew room door. 'Ah there you are,' he said, 'I'm putting you on with Wing Commander Parselle tonight – briefing is at 14.00 hours.' After the briefing Gilbert Hayworth and all the other pilots on 207 Squadron at Langar, Nottingham, in 5 Group knew that their target for the night of 23/24 May 1943 after a nine-day break in Main Force operations, was Dortmund in the Ruhr Valley area of Germany. Bomber Command detailed 829 aircraft to go to the region so sarcastically nicknamed 'Happy Valley' for what would be, except for the 1,000 bomber raids of 1942, the largest raid of the war. No less than 343 of the aircraft involved were Lancasters and the rest comprised 199 Halifaxes, 151 Wellingtons, 120 Stirlings and 13 Mosquitoes. There would be no element of surprise in their favour. A hot reception from countless radar controlled 88mm guns was an absolute certainty. Strong forces of experienced night fighters would also be out hunting for unwary bombers.

Feeling less like a hero than ever before, Hayworth collected and checked his numerous items of equipment: escape and evasion pack, flying suit, boots, helmets and headphones, microphone, goggles and parachute harness – but he could not find his knife, which had been missing for some days, and the mystery vexed him considerably. 'After all, one never knew when a good knife would be urgently required' he thought and he could not borrow one. Nobody would ever lend anything to the short-lived aircrew personnel. His questions to other flying crew members brought ribald responses and suggestions of a quite unhelpful nature. There was one item that Hayworth always carried, as he recalls:

Almost as old and famous as Lincoln Cathedral itself is the dear old Lincoln Imp – a mediaeval stone carving of a grotesque legendary demon which shelters within those hallowed walls. Reproductions of this grinning monster have always been on sale in the Lincoln area. One moonlit night at a spot not far from the Cathedral, Mary of the golden hair pressed one such tiny brass emblem into my hand. 'Keep him for luck,' she whispered. She knew that I was back on my second tour of bombing operations with Avro Lancasters but for many weeks the golden bauble just languished in my flying locker, quite unheeded. Something that I had expected then came to pass. Geoff Woodward my regular pilot and buddy became tour expired and departed from our bomber squadron. That meant that I was once more what was loosely referred to as a 'spare body'. The thought struck me that perhaps some symbol of good luck was a requisite and necessary item and I suddenly determined to take it along with me in the future. A Lincoln Imp would surely be a change from ordinary tokens such as rabbit feet, locks of hair or silk stockings, the like of which were currently much in favour as good luck charms. I rejected the thought of suspending him around my neck with ordinary string and persuaded a young lady in the parachute section to part with a length of strong silk cord. In a very short space of time that little figure became my closest companion.

Carrying all my weighty gear I started off on my way out to our aircraft and as I passed an open window the Squadron Signals Leader shouted, 'Have a good trip!' I peered in, saw that the blighter was using my knife to sharpen a pencil and promptly claimed it. 'Sorry old boy honestly didn't know it was yours, it was kicking around the crew room floor you know.' It was a relief to get it back as I already had a nasty foreboding about the forthcoming flight. The feeling was strengthened when our flight engineer overtook me and said 'We're having to change aircraft; the Wing Commander's Lancaster has a dud starboard outer engine and he's quite peeved about it because we now have to take *J-Jig* instead.' I groaned at this news for *J-Jig* was the oldest kite on the unit. What actually made her 'old' was the fact that she was the only aircraft not yet fitted out with any of the latest electronic equipment, which had cunningly been developed to foil the enemy radar and had proved effective in reducing casualty rates.

J-Jig still possessed amidships a certain antique item called a rest bed, originally provided for the comfort of incapacitated men but now universally regarded as a criminal waste of a space that could be far more profitably employed in the housing of electronic wizardry. And so it came to pass that at the appointed hour I was airborne in *J-Jig* as she took up her allotted station in the midst of nearly a thousand bombers heading for *Nazi* Germany. We had strict instructions to fly a set route at a specified height as part of a system designed to swamp the enemy's defences as efficiently as possible. Aircraft which failed to comply usually met with disaster, a fact we never lost sight of for a moment. Eventually we were dutifully attacking Dortmund and experiencing the familiar welcome from anti-aircraft fire. I directed the Wing Commander's approach to the aiming point where we had first to drop our 4,000lb high explosive 'Cookie' and then follow with hundreds of small incendiary bombs. To obtain our target photograph it was necessary to hold a straight and steady course for a short interval but once that was done we turned away on the course that was to take us home.

I was responsible for the additional task of scattering propaganda leaflets on the target area. These were supplied in neat bundles secured by string and after being untied were dispatched from the large nose escape hatch. I invariably performed this duty in a fair amount of haste and partly to give good measure but also to keep the inside of our bomber tidy and unencumbered, I used to dump the lengths of string as well. Oddly enough on this one occasion I failed to do so I think it must have been because I wanted to get that escape hatch closed very rapidly. We were being particularly bothered by gunfire and manoeuvring violently and there was a real danger of falling through it. This was soon to prove to be a providential omission. Jerry was on to our aircraft with no mistake about it. A never-ending succession of bright flashes and loud bangs made it quite obvious that we were a selected individual target. There were many long and weary minutes of this ordeal and just when we felt that we had managed to get clear of the heavily-defended target zone a final and fearfully loud bang was followed by the rattle of shell fragments on our aircraft. One of those fragments shattered the transparent roof hatch immediately above the pilot's head and away it went. The damage itself was comparatively minor but the consequences were serious, no hatch meant that the pilot was engulfed in an icy blast of air which continually raced over his head and shoulders and filled the inside of our aircraft.

The outside air temperature was about minus 25° Celsius, a deep freeze temperature, the blast velocity must have been about 280 mph. Our cabin hearing system was nullified and we did not require any spelling out of the details of our very unpleasant and threatening situation. Our Skipper would shortly be too frozen to retain proper control. If he reduced height sufficiently we could reach a zone where the air temperature would be merely around freezing point but that was no sort of remedy for our plight. We would then be separated from the main bomber stream and we all knew perfectly well that the Germans had a skilled and specialized watching service for the detection of separated aircraft. By this stage of the war they were renowned for their ability to destroy all such lame ducks, especially in the Ruhr Valley. So there we were; no hope if we stayed at our present height and no hope if we went to a lower height. Wing Commander Parselle did not utter a word but we sensed what was in his mind, he was getting ready to tell us to take to our parachutes while the going was good and leave him to try his luck for a little longer. Abandoning by parachute was not an attractive proposition, it is not easy to land at night without injury and there was more than a slight danger of being lynched by the local populace. The very best of the various consequences that might befall us would be the prolonged hardship and misery of an indefinite stay in a bleak prison camp. Across my mind floated a brief thought of all those at home nicely tucked away in snug little beds.

Ah beds! I then remembered the rest bed with its canvas cover 5 feet long and 4 feet wide; could I possible make it serve as a wind-break? Passing my clasp knife across to the air signaller I explained what was wanted. He was nearest to the rest bed and in double quick time he had that cover slashed off. I removed my gloves to obtain freedom of action and groped around the floor for the lengths of string which I knew to be lying around somewhere. To each corner of the canvas I fastened pieces of string and then I embarked on the task of closing that awful gap in the roof canopy. I did not expect it to be easy but neither did I expect it to be so agonizingly arduous. Although I am a six-footer with a long reach I found that I was hampered in a most exasperating manner because my oxygen mask was remorselessly dragged away from my face as I strove to reach suitable points of attachment for the front end of the sheet.

At heights approaching 20,000 feet a deprivation of oxygen produces fainting and unconsciousness within 10 to 15 seconds but I knew that I could rely on the elastic face bands of my oxygen mask to snap the mask back into position to revive me whenever I collapsed. Nevertheless it was a nightmarish experience because three or four times I had to endure a most unpleasant sequence of events. The sequence began with a short and frantic struggle to get one or two knots completed and ended with a blacking out and a collapse downwards and backwards. All this to the accompaniment not only of a freezing torrent of air but of the direct and unimpeded noise of our four Merlin engines which alone tended to paralyze the mind and render clear thinking difficult. At long last I did succeed in fastening the two front corners of the canvas exactly where I wanted them to be.

The job of securing the rear of the cover should have been easy because everything was more accessible and my oxygen supply was not troublesome as far as I can recall. What caused my heart to sink was the discovery that at the fourth and final corner the cord was just too short and there was no more twine to be found. I felt like throwing in the towel so to speak and then I remembered my Lincoln Imp. With hands that were well nigh frozen I fumbled through my flying clothing until I was able to reach his retaining cord and slash it free. That piece of parachute cord was ample and in a very short space of time my brain wave had become reality, our primitive windbreak was in position and functioning as required. I do not pretend that it was perfect but it certainly transformed what had been a howling gale into something that was little more than an uncomfortable draught. We were able to maintain altitude and stay within the protection of the main bomber stream and arrived back at base without further incident.

Zero hour had been timed for 01.00 with the attack to take place between 00.58 and 02.00. As an aid to navigation 11 *Oboe* Mosquitoes dropped yellow TIs at a key turning point. They then went on to drop three red TIs in salvo on the aiming point, with 33 backers-up dropping green TIs on the centre of the reds. The first wave of 250 aircraft comprised the best crews from all Groups, with all remaining non Lancasters in the second wave and the Lancasters in the final wave, with PFF aircraft at the head of each wave. The Path Finders marked the target exceptionally accurately in cloudless conditions and the ensuing attack went according to plan. Seven hundred and fifty-four bombers dropped 2,042 tons of bombs – the biggest bomb load ever dropped anywhere in a single night – and large areas in the centre, north and the east of Dortmund were completely devastated. Almost 2,000 buildings were destroyed and many industrial premises were hit, in particular the large *Hoeschstahlwerke* (Hoesch steel works), an important centre for the German war industry, and which ceased production. German records agree that the attack was accurate and in addition to extensive damage to houses a large number of industrial premises were destroyed or damaged.

Ground defences in the target area and night fighters on the return route put up a strong opposition, and 38 aircraft, 18 of them Halifaxes, failed to return. Eight Lancasters, six Stirlings and six Wellingtons were also lost. Sergeant Ray Foster, rear-gunner in a Lancaster, was startled to see the starboard wing of another Lancaster flash by in front of his own tail-plane. The tip of the bomber's wing passed between the trailing edge of another bomber's main-plane and the leading edge of its tail-plane. 'I could have shaken hands with the bomb-aimer in the other Lancaster,' said Foster. Flight Lieutenant H C Lee, of Felixstowe, piloting another Lancaster, made his attack late in the raid but before then had circled round the target for nearly an hour, awaiting his 'turn.' He was startled just as much as Sergeant Foster. 'As I made my attack,' he said later, 'a Stirling came streaking out only fifty feet above us and we were bumped by its slip-stream. By this time it was difficult to believe that it was a real town below; the place was so covered with fires and smoke.'

A Wellington on 431 'Iroquois' Squadron RCAF, which had just dropped its bomb load on Dortmund when it was hit by flak, was very fortunate. There was a terrific gust of air and the tail gunner and pilot vanished into the dark, and then the bomber went into a spin. Of the three men left on board only Flight Sergeant Stuart Sloan, bomb aimer, had done any flying and he had never handled a Wellington. Sergeant George Parslow, navigator and Flying Officer John Bailey, WOp/AG, stared at the wheeling mass of flame below and did not relish the idea of bailing out into the inferno and so they decided they would try to fly the crippled bomber home, a distance of some 300 miles. Bailey recalled:

It was all very Heath Robinson. Sloan grabbed the controls and somehow managed to right us. We were down to 2,000 feet and every gun seemed to be on us, not to mention searchlights. Parslow and I bunched round him and we tried to think up everything we knew about piloting. We flew by conference. Sloan was grand. He got the plane well up again and even managed to dodge the flak and searchlights. Thank goodness night fighters did not spot us! We were pretty shaky about the question of landing but Sloan was the calmest of the three. In fact, he was working up to a splendid landing when the starboard engine cut out. Even that did not rattle him. Somehow he got us down [at Cranwell]. He did nothing worse than overshoot the runway by a few yards. And nobody got hurt.[1]

Three of the missing Wellingtons were on 166 Squadron at Kirmington. At Ingham too, no word was received from HZ582 on 199 Squadron, which was one of 18 Wimpys that had taken off from the base, at 23.11 hours. Sergeant Horace William Austin, the 20-year-old pilot from London had an uneventful flight across the North Sea and the Netherlands but then the port engine of the Wellington stopped and the bombing had to be done on one engine. The Wellington left the target area and started back for England. They made it to the Brabant province in the Netherlands.

In the village of Veulen near Venray, *Oberleutnant* Walter Knickmeier
was on duty at his command station behind a radar screen on which the
bombers and night fighters could be observed as light dots. Steadily he
gave flight directions on the radio to 24-year-old *Oberleutnant* Manfred
Meurer of NJG1 who was airborne in a Bf 110 from the airfield at Venlo.
Guided by Knickmeier, Meurer soon found the slow flying Wellington.
Meurer approached the Wellington *von hinten unten* to the right, pulled
up and fired his cannon and machine guns at the unprotected fuselage and
wings of the slow flying British bomber, which caught fire immediately.
(*Oberleutnant* Meurer's total this night was two Wellingtons and a
Lancaster.) After Meurer's attack on HZ582, Austin made a turn above
Nistelrode and started flying in the direction of the village of Schaijk,
looking for a field to land the crippled aircraft in. In the early hours of
that Monday night, Toon van Duren was awakened by the noise. He sat
up in bed and said 'What is happening outside?' to his son Harrie, who
slept in the same bed. Toon looked at his alarm clock; the time was just
past 2am. They jumped out of bed, put on their trousers and went
outside in their wooden clog shoes. They looked into the sky and saw an
aircraft on fire coming from the south. A tail of smoke was visible behind
the aircraft.

Between Nistelrode and Schaijk, Austin ordered his crew to abandon
the aircraft. He was flying now towards the north-east. Doug Keevers, the
Australian navigator, was able to reach the trapdoor and he was first
out of the aircraft. He landed safely in Schaijk in a meadow behind the
farmhouse of Jan van de Bogaert along the Udense Dreef. He had been
wounded in his upper leg and had to be carried into the farmhouse of
Driek Verstegen whose son Harrie cycled over to Doctor Langendijk
in Schaijk and asked for medical help. He went also to the presbytery
and requested help from the curate, but Harrie was stopped in the
Schutsboomstraat by a police officer who asked him why he was out
after curfew. Harrie told him in confidence that he was getting help for a
wounded parachutist and Meulenberg telephoned the *Wehrmacht*. Later
that morning Keevers was taken prisoner.

Austin stayed at the controls so that all members of the crew could bail
out. Many local village people went outside to see what was happening
in the sky. Cornelis van der Heiden could see the flames and expected
that the pilot was looking to land. Above the Zandstraat the aircraft made
a turn towards the west, and John Last, the air bomber, who was badly
wounded in the leg during the attack, bailed out. He landed next to a
cornfield in pain and needed medical treatment urgently. He was given
something to drink at the farmhouse of Driek Verstegen before Doctor
Langendijk and the curate arrived around 3 o'clock and gave him first
aid. The Englishman showed a map and asked where he had landed. He
knew that he was in safe hands because on the wall was a picture of

Queen Wilhelmina. After a short while Last was confronted by a German officer and some soldiers. He was arrested and taken to hospital.

Austin apparently decided to make an emergency landing because air gunner Ralph M Costello and Arthur Herbert, the 23-year-old WOp, from Darleston, were too badly wounded to bail out. He turned 180° and skimmed over the roof of the farmhouse of Harrie Kusters before crashing in front of the farmhouse of Toon van Duren, shedding wheels and parts of the aircraft as it exploded. Austin was flung out of the aircraft when it hit the ground. His body was found nearby the wreck in a small dry creek. Blue coloured flames were visible at the front of the farmhouse and on the roof, which was sprayed with burning kerosene. Toon van Duren feared that the three members of the family in the farmhouse would not survive. Father and son ran to the farmhouse and shouted to Aunt Kee, the unmarried sister of Toon, and the two girls, Toos and Pieta: 'Get out, get out, we are burning down'. All three women got out, still in their night clothing. The van Duren family would have had no roof over their heads and no place to live if the neighbours had not taken them in. The village of Schaijk had good fortune that no local civilians died that night.

In Dortmund 599 people were killed, 1,275 injured and the bodies of 25 other people were never found. Toos and Pieta van Duren never forgot the night of the Wellington crash. For 55 years they and their brother Bert and sister Cisca would visit the graveyard in Uden and lay flowers on the airmen's graves.[2]

On the morning after the raid there came more congratulations and another promise from the Commander-in-Chief, addressed to all the crews in Bomber Command. 'In 1939 Goering promised that not a single enemy bomber would reach the Ruhr,' Sir Arthur reminded them. 'Congratulations on having delivered the first 100,000 tons on Germany to refute him. The next 1,000,000, if he waits for them, will be even bigger and better bombs, delivered more accurately and in much shorter time.'

After returning from Dortmund, Gilbert Hayworth had taken 'jolly good care' to retrieve his little Imp before leaving the aircraft and going off for a 'lovely operational breakfast' after which he thankfully went to bed and fell asleep before his head reached the pillow. Eventually he was roused by the duty runner who gave him his stock phrase 'You're on again':

I did not need to ask what it was that I was on. I was required to get down to the hangar and prepare for another bombing trip. To my astonishment I could make no reply, being quite speechless from an abominably sore throat, not only that, my neck and shoulders were painfully stiff and I had various other aches and pains all being the consequences of the night's ordeal. My services were dispensed with and I stayed in bed. Being thus provided with an opportunity to ruminate it was impossible not to think of my timely decision to carry the Lincoln Imp, the happy recovery of my clasp knife and my very unusual failure to dump all those odd bits of string. What would have happened if I had been without a knife or if I had jettisoned the string or if I had not been wearing the Imp on the parachute cord? I was still in bed when all the squadron aircraft took off with fresh loads and as I listened to the roar of the engines I wondered who had taken my place with the Wing Commander. He was unlucky whoever he was; the 4,000lb bomb exploded high over Germany and all the crew died except [sic] the Wing Commander.[3] Protected by his armoured seat he discovered that he was sailing through the sky still strapped to it. After releasing himself he parachuted to earth and became a prisoner of war until the end of hostilities. He returned home and subsequently rose to rank of Air Vice Marshal. He was about the only officer of air rank who ever called me 'Pal'.

Robbie Robertson's crew on 106 Squadron at Syerston had another worry – the behaviour of their American rear gunner, Merle Routson, as Geoffrey Willatt recalls:

Every time we flew, he complained of watering eyes which obstructed his vision. The MO could find no reason for this but he was taken off flying temporarily and a replacement provided. Flying Officer Ronald Reginald Shadbolt DFC was a very pleasant character and fitted in well with the rest of the crew. On our next trip, Merle was standing at the end of the runway giving the thumbs-up sign, in company with many others, as we taxied for take-off. The following day, when we all went to Nottingham for the evening, Merle said he'd been posted back home to America. After an evening on the town, we all went to see him off at the railway station. As the train started, he pulled me close and said in my ear, 'That's what lighter fuel in your eyes does for you.' I wonder whether, by doing this, he'd permanently damaged his eyesight and what excuse he gave on arriving back home? I heard of another aircrew member sitting up all night gazing into a naked electric light bulb. I found it hard to blame people like this and quite understood why. They were no good anyway for the job in hand. A few days leave followed, which Audrey and I spent in the Cotswolds at Chipping Camden. This was a second honeymoon, to compensate for the previous one of only 48 hours. It was a wonderful feeling to be away from southern England, which had aerodromes everywhere and tanks, troops and guns being trundled about on many roads.

On the night of 25/26 May, 759 bombers were dispatched to bomb Düsseldorf. 27 bombers were lost,[4] 21 of which were due to night fighters. The raid was a failure due to the difficulty of marking in bad weather. I./NJG1 at Venlo destroyed ten bombers, including Wellington X Z-*Zebra* on 431 'Iroquois' Squadron RCAF flown by Sergeant Bob Barclay. Sergeant Ken Dix, navigator, had misgivings from the off:

I was concerned when I saw that our flight path took us one and a half miles north of the German night fighter base at Venlo. I said they could orbit their beacon and pick off bombers behind the main stream but no route change was made. On the runway the port engine would not start and the other bombers went off. As a specially selected crew usually we were the lead machine. We carried 4,000lb of incendiaries to drop within less than ten seconds of the flares from the Path Finder Force aircraft going down on the target; usually from as near to 18,500 feet as we could reach with a full bomb load. But it was 22 minutes before we got the port engine going. So it left us well behind the main stream of bombers. The machine did not climb well enough and had not enough speed so we flew to Hornsea on the coast and flew across the North Sea to Ijmuiden. Then we headed between the flak zones of Soesterberg and Hertogenbosch on our way to the Track Indicator Markers laid by the Path Finders. We had just seen it and were on the correct track when Sergeant Harry Sweet in the rear turret shouted, '*FIGHTER!*' He immediately fired his four Browning machine guns.

At the same time as Harry Sweet opened fire, the fighter, a Bf 110 flown by *Oberleutnant* Manfred Meurer, *Staffelkapitän*, 3./NGJ1, fired his cannons and he hit the Wellington along the starboard beam from the tail as Bob Barclay took evasive action. Ken Dix continues:

The cannon shells had hit hard. They stopped just by my *Gee* radar set. The voice intercom failed and then our flashing intercom buttons also went off. Sergeant Michael Charles Jeffries, the WOp/AG, was behind the main spar ready to launch the flare for our picture after the bombing run. He was killed. The aircraft was blazing with the port engine hit and on fire. We were spinning round and down. I managed to get my chest chute into my new harness. I couldn't go back to Sergeant Jeffries because of the fierce flames driving me back. I went to the cockpit. The front hatch was open but Flying Officer Bert Bonner the bomb aimer and Bob Barclay had bailed out. They could have tried to contact us but the system had been hit. I had flown the aircraft when we were on exercises and I had also been on a pilot's course in Florida before becoming a navigator, so I decided to try and fly the Wellington back to base. I got into the pilot's seat and the Wellington at first answered the controls. I turned to fly northwest back to England then dived to try and put the flames out. It was going well when suddenly the control wires, hit by cannon fire, broke. I had no control so reluctantly I had to bail out. I pulled the ripcord and the turning Wellington just missed me. I saw it hit the ground.[5]

When Essen was subjected to a Main Force raid by 518 aircraft on 27/28 May, 23 bombers failed to return. Minor operations were flown on the night of 28/29 May, when 34 crews, some of them undoubtedly flying their first op, sowed mines off the Friesians.

On the moonless night of 29/30 May, Bomber Command flew one of the most significant raids of the Battle of the Ruhr. The area bombing of the Barmen north-eastern end of the long and narrow town of Wuppertal involved 719 aircraft in five successive waves. The town, which had been formed in 1929 by the union of the adjacent towns of Elberfeld and Barmen in the Upper Wupper Valley, was within easy *Oboe* range, and 11 of the Mosquito markers were dispatched. Sergeant Harry Barker, the bomb aimer on Flying Officer John Overton's crew on 218 (Gold Coast) Squadron at Downham Market recalls:

During the briefing the target was designated a dormitory town serving the factories of the Ruhr and it was clearly intended to destroy housing to disrupt the workers' production. We had a job to do and at that time bombing attacks on our own cities created a demand for retaliation. For my part I did not dwell on the damage and death resulting from our attacks. Instead I pictured the scenes shown in the press of Coventry and London burning. We were expected to hit back and that was what we did.

At the same briefing were 31-year-old pilot Flight Sergeant William Arthur Mathias Davis RAAF, who with his original crew had arrived at Downham Market on 24 March from their conversion courses. Five of the original crew were on their third flight on *A-Able*, their usual aircraft, which had been badly shot up over France on 22 May and had made an emergency landing at RAF Tangmere. The rear gunner, Flight Lieutenant Officer Leslie Abbiss, aged 41, and Sergeant Thomas Dixon the navigator, aged 22, were new to the crew. The two original members they replaced were sick. The rest of the crew comprised 21-year-old Sergeant James Bramble, the mid-upper gunner, 22-year-old Sergeant George Grant, the flight engineer, Sergeant William Howes, the 29-year-old bomb aimer, and the WOp, Sergeant Thomas Portrey, aged 30. As *Able* took off at 23.05 hours on Thursday 29 May to take part in a bombardment of Wuppertal, shortly afterwards, at 23.51 hours, 20-year-old *Leutnant* Heinz-Wolfgang Schnaufer and his *Bordfunker Leutnant* Baro took off in a Bf 110 night fighter from the Luftwaffe airfield at St-Trond in Belgium.

Sixty-two of the bombers turned back early with technical problems. One of the 292 Lancasters was piloted by Pilot Officer Robbie Robertson on 106 Squadron, as Geoffrey Willatt recalls:

> It was the custom to paint miniature bombs on the fuselage of one's own aircraft – ours was identified by the letter 'S for Sugar' – adding one for each bombing trip. I undertook to do this and, at the insistence of the crew, I also painted Superman above the bombs. Over the target at Wuppertal, which was chiefly obscured by cloud, I was about to release my bombs when I spotted another Lancaster immediately above us with its bomb doors open. I shouted to the pilot for a quick shift of direction and then dropped my bombs, through clouds, which were a vivid red from the fires beneath. One of my jobs was map reading. It was comforting in a way to be doing something rather than flying straight ahead and presenting a 'sitting duck' target to the enemy, who flew alongside a raiding force, picking off any stragglers.

In all, 150 individual aircraft were plotted on the *Würzburg* radars flying through the *Himmelbett* boxes in eastern Belgium, in which 13 Bf 110Gs and three Do 217s of II./NJG1 at St-Trond patrolled during the course of the night. For the loss of three aircraft and two aircrew killed, six II./NJG1 crews scored 11 victories, three of which (two Stirling IIIs and a Halifax) were credited to Schnaufer and Baro. At 02.22 hours, flying at 14,800 feet above the small village of Schaffen-Diest in Belgium, *A-Able* on 218 Squadron was intercepted and shot down by Schnaufer, who reported his encounter:

> At 23.51 hours on 29 May I took off for a night operation in the area of *Lurch* [a *Himmelbett* station just to the north of Liège]. At about 00.35 hours I was directed on to an in-flying enemy aircraft at an altitude of 3,500 metres. It was located on the *Fu SG 202* [*Lichtenstein* airborne radar] and after further instructions [from *Leutnant* Baro] I made out a four-engined bomber at 00.45 hours, about 200 metres away above and to the right. I attacked the violently-evading bomber from behind and below at a range of 80 metres and my rounds started a bright fire in the left wing. The blazing enemy aircraft turned and dived away steeply, hitting the ground and exploding violently at 00.48 hours; the position of the crash was 1.5 kilometres to the south of Belven, 5 kilometres north-west of Eupen, map reference 6134.

Able crashed and exploded adjacent to the *Luftwaffe* airfield at Schauffen. The crew of seven was blown to pieces. The remains of the crew were placed in three coffins. Having found two identity discs near the crash site, those of Sergeant Bramble and Sergeant Portrey, the Germans named the coffins accordingly and named the third coffin as 'the remains of three unknown'. At the time the Germans thought there was a crew of five on board *Able* and not in fact the seven who crewed the aircraft. The remains of the crew were buried at the village cemetery at Schaffen. The committal service was taken by the *Luftwaffe* padre of the neighbouring airfield and a photograph of the service was taken at the request of the Padre and a copy given to the grave digger. There was a story circulating at the time of the crash that two crew members had bailed out; it was not until the Casualty Inquiry Report was published on 9 July 1945 that the story was finally laid to rest. Until then the crew's families had remained in hope that two of the crew might be alive.[6]

Wuppertal had never experienced a major raid before and being a Saturday night, many of the town's fire and air raid precaution officials were absent. Six hundred bombers dropped 1,822 tons of bombs on the Barmen district and a large fire area started in the narrow streets of the old town centre. About 4,000 houses were burned to the ground and 2,450 to 3,400 people died as a minor firestorm raged. Around 118,000 people were made homeless. Since the previous month had been a dry one, the level of water in the Wupper River was now low. As a result the meagre force of 150 firemen and about a thousand volunteers had initially to depend on supplies from the emergency static water tanks positioned around the town. Once these were exhausted the fire crews had to connect their hose lengths together for distances of up to four miles to draw up the necessary water. It took almost eight hours to put out the fires. Soon after 03.15 hours a reinforcing fire-fighting unit from Bochum managed to get through to the devastated area around the town hall and was able to clear an escape route through which more than 2,000 people were led to safety. The railway station, two power stations, two gasworks, a waterworks and five out of the six major factories all suffered serious damage. The high explosive bombs and fires devastated more than three-fifths of Barmen; the area of severe damage covered almost 700 acres, or somewhat greater area than that blitzed in London during the entire war. In the absence of any appreciable 'creep-back' the south western end, Elberfeld, suffered little more than superficial glass and roof damage.[7]

Thirty-three bombers were lost, three more crashed on landing, 60 bombers returned with serious damage caused by flak and two after they were hit by night fighters. Six of the aircraft returned with damage caused by incendiary bombs falling from above. Twenty-two of the missing bombers had been shot down by *Nachtjäger*. Of the remaining losses, seven were attributed to flak and the other four to 'causes unknown'.

Two of the eight Stirlings that were missing were on 218 Squadron but John Overton's crew returned safely to Downham Market. Sergeant Harry Barker concludes:

> The raid on Wuppertal was at times a bit scary; we saw flak and searchlights for the first time and our trip lasted 4 hours 25 minutes. I remember the rewarding breakfast we had on return of bacon and egg and then getting back to our billet for six or seven hours sleep. When I awoke and had my lunch in the sergeants' mess, I wandered off on my own and lay down on the warm turf outside our hut. It was beautiful day, a bright blue sky and birds were singing ... It all seemed so unreal.

In all, 167 *Nachtjagd* victories were recorded in May. By the early summer of 1943 there was only one effective tactical measure available to Air Marshal Harris and his staff officers to counter the German night fighter defence. This was the saturation of the German GCI system by concentrating the RAF bomber routes through relatively few GCI *Räume* (boxes) or through *Gebiete* (zones) in which few or no GCI stations existed. In 1942, when the RAF began attacking targets within a period of 30 minutes, the narrow night fighter zone in the west was quickly penetrated and at the same time, only a few fighters came into contact with the bomber stream. Flak, emplaced in single batteries, was unable to cope with the concentrated attacks by the RAF. The carefully practiced system of concentrating several batteries' fire on a single target broke down because so many aircraft appeared over the target at the same time. As a result of all this the night fighter zone in the West had to be rapidly increased in depth and extended to Denmark in the north and to eastern France in the south. Operational control had to be developed whereby two or more night fighters could be brought into action in any one night fighter area at the same time. In addition, bombers over the target had to be attacked by fighters as well as flak, which had to be consolidated into large batteries and concentrated at the most important targets. Above all, accuracy had to be increased by developing a large number of radar range finders.

In June, the *Himmelbett Nachtjagd* claimed a record 223 victories, one of the highest loss rates of the month being achieved on 11/12 June when 44 aircraft failed to return, 29 of which were shot down by German night fighters. It was a very bright moonlight night when 76 aircraft set out for Münster, and 860 heavies, including for the first time, more than 200 Halifaxes, took off to bomb Düsseldorf, administrative centre of the Ruhr. The Münster operation was really a mass H_2S trial and the raid, which lasted less than ten minutes, was accurate and much damage was caused to railway installations and residential areas of the city. Just five aircraft were lost. Thirty-nine losses notwithstanding, the operation to Düsseldorf did not go entirely to plan. An *Oboe* Mosquito that inadvertently released a load of TIs 14 miles north-east of the city caused part of the Main Force to drop its bombs in open country. A curious haze made visibility difficult at Düsseldorf but 130 acres were claimed destroyed. It was estimated that over 1,200 people were killed, 140,000 were bombed out and scores of other buildings and 42 war industries were destroyed or seriously damaged. Five of the 14 Lancasters lost were from 12 Squadron at Wickenby, which reported the worst loss rate suffered by the squadron in a single night for the whole of 1943. Only three men survived from the 35 missing air crew. At Snaith three Halifax IIs on 51 Squadron were missing. *Y-Yorker*, flown by Flight Sergeant J H Collins, was hit by anti-aircraft fire from a British convoy in the North Sea while homebound and was ditched in the water about ten miles off Sheringham on the Norfolk coast. The local lifeboat went out but all the six survivors were rescued by another vessel. Flight Sergeant Jimmy Anderson's crew were all killed when their Halifax crashed in Holland.

The crew of *D-Donald*, which was shot down by flak, had better luck. Flight Sergeant K J S Harvey the pilot, his American flight engineer Flying Officer D S Roberts USAAF, and the rest of the crew survived and they were taken into captivity. Three Wellington X crews on 429 'Bison' Squadron RCAF and nine other Wimpys failed to return. A Canadian Wellington on 431 'Iroquois' Squadron RCAF, which landed safely at Oulton airfield in Norfolk collided with a Halifax on 427 'Lion' Squadron RCAF while taxiing and took the 'Iroquois' Squadron's total losses to three.

Warrant Officer Norman Francis Williams DFM*, a Halifax rear gunner on 35 Squadron in the Path Finder Force, was awarded an Australian CGM for his courage and amazing fortitude as during the attack on Düsseldorf. The decoration made him Australia's most decorated flying NCO. Williams' Halifax had just begun its bombing run when he saw a fighter's guns blazing out of the mist on the port quarter and slightly above. He swung his guns up and fired at the flashes. The Halifax pilot dived evasively and then Williams 'felt as though the world fell on top of him.' Another fighter had come up underneath as the bomber banked over and had delivered a heavy burst of fire. Williams was hit in the stomach by a cannon shell and in the legs and thighs by machine gun bullets. His rear turret was riddled and the turret put out of action, as was one gun on the port side. A machine gun bullet also furrowed the back of the RAF mid-upper gunner's head, temporarily blinding him. A shell pierced the starboard wing and set the rubber of the self-sealing petrol tank alight and blazing petrol began to stream from the wing, making the Halifax visible for miles. Temporarily paralysed from the waist down and in great pain, Williams continued to direct his pilot. He managed to see the second fighter for the first time as it broke away to port but lost sight of it again almost at once. Then the guns of both fighters blazed out of the mist simultaneously. Williams returned their fire as they attacked again and again. During these attacks he asked the bomb aimer to relieve the mid-upper gunner and was giving him instructions as well as directing his captain's evasive manoeuvres. Just as the bomb aimer got into action both fighters came in together on the port side, one very close. The Halifax turned away, bringing the second fighter into the line of fire. Williams opened fire and the enemy blew up: for a moment there were two flaming pieces in mid-air and then many pieces cascading down all over the sky.

When the first fighter had been shot down there was five minutes' silence and the crew thought the other had been frightened off. They got the bomb aimer out of the mid-upper turret to drop the bombs, while the wireless operator, who had been giving first aid to the wounded mid-upper gunner throughout the fight, went into the turret. Suddenly the second fighter came in again, attacking four or five times from different positions. Both Williams and the wireless operator returned fire, Williams continuing to direct his captain. The Australian was still paralysed down one side but had the strength to raise and lower himself on his elbows. The fighter began to come in directly behind, where Williams could get his guns on to it. It came in firing but its tracer streamed below the Halifax. Williams waited and then pressed the button and the German's guns stopped. It passed under Williams' turret fifteen yards away and he fired into it until his guns reached the limit of their range. After it had gone past, pieces of it were left behind in the sky. Other members of the crew saw it reel over and go down, with pieces still flying off, until it was out of sight. The crew estimated that the fighters had between them made 30 to 40 different attacks. It was over. The crew checked their position and found themselves ten miles off course. The fire in the wing had died down; the pilot dived and managed to put it out and they set course for base. Despite his wounds Williams refused to leave the rear turret and he directed the bomber through the defences on the coast. The Halifax flew through the guns and lights without further trouble and started across the North Sea. A flak ship there opened fire but scored no hit. Once clear of the coast, members of the crew tried to get Williams from the turret but the doors had jammed and they could not move him. The pilot made a masterly crash-landing at base, where Williams was chopped from the turret and, with the mid-upper gunner, taken to hospital, where he stayed for two months. Williams' laconic comment when they told him of his CGM was that 'anyone of the other chaps should have received it.'

On 12/13 June, 24 of the 503 aircraft raiding Bochum were destroyed by flak and fighters. The raid took place over a completely cloud-covered target but accurate *Oboe* sky-marking enabled all 323 Lancasters and

167 Halifaxes to cause severe damage to the centre of the city, such that 130 acres were destroyed. Geoffrey Willatt recalls:

> Nearing the target, we were astonished to see a large orange-coloured moon in front. It obviously wasn't actually the moon, so we weaved to avoid it. It realigned itself and several times it barred our way but finally disappeared. We were questioned exhaustively at debriefing but never heard whether Intelligence came up with an explanation. I think they concluded that we'd suffered from collective hallucination. I still think it was either some clever new anti-aircraft device or a flying saucer. Our next trip, to Oberhausen, on the night of 14/15 June was a 'boomerang'. Shortly after take-off one of the engines failed. We radioed for instructions and were told to circle over the North Sea until most of the fuel was used up, lightening the all-up load for re-landing. Sometimes in such circumstances it was necessary to jettison bombs in the sea. In either case, it was imperative to lose weight because, in theory, it would otherwise be impossible to re-land with a full load of bombs and petrol without the whole thing blowing up on impact. (However, on another trip, to Wuppertal on 24/25 June immediately after take-off two engines became faulty and, without hesitation Robbie turned back and re-landed with a sickening thump – a frightening experience but there was no alternative. This time, there was a spare aircraft which we climbed into and we set off again).

Oberhausen was cloud-covered but once again the *Oboe* Mosquito sky-markers were accurate. Seventeen of the 197 Lancasters despatched failed to return.[8] It would have been more but for the fortitude and perseverance of the bomber crews. *Minnie The Moocher*, a Lancaster on 61 Squadron piloted by Sergeant A H Moores of Bromley in Kent made the journey to Oberhausen with a 4,000lb 'cookie' in the bomb-bay. Moores knew what the east-flying bombers could expect from the Ruhr defences in the days following the great attack on the Möhne dam. Happy Valley had not changed, except for the worse. Thirty miles from the target *Minnie* was attacked by night fighters. They smashed the Lancaster's rear-turret and holed the fuselage badly and when they disappeared they left behind a disturbing reek of cordite, which gave Moores the impression that his aircraft was on fire somewhere in the region of the bomb-load. But in about ten minutes, if the great bomb did not explode before that time, he could drop the 4,000-pounder where it was scheduled to go. He decided to take a chance. He could have jettisoned the big bomb there and then or he could have ordered the crew to bail out. He would have been justified in any action he took to save his own life and the lives of his crew but he saw the fires of burning Oberhausen ahead. That decided him.[9]

Flying Officer Robert Owen Van Note from Warrensburg, Missouri, pilot of *A-Apple*, a 9 Squadron Lancaster, was on his 30th and final operation of his tour. The American, who had attended the University of Colorado before enlisting in the RCAF in March 1942, was flying *A-Apple* for the 20th time. They bombed the target, but at 01.54 hours in bright moonlight at Soesterburg at 23,000 feet, *A-Apple* was intercepted by a twin engined enemy fighter. *Boozer*, a passive warning device, which gave a visual identification of both *FuG 202* used by German night fighters, and *Würzburg* transmissions, showed 'Yellow'.[10] Van Note began a moderate weave for about ten minutes. Sergeant Dale the rear gunner reported an enemy aircraft 500 yards astern flying the same course as the Lancaster. On instruction from Dale, Van Note carried out a diving turn to port and the enemy aircraft followed the bomber down. At 400 yards both the rear and mid-upper gunners fired bursts that appeared to enter the fuselage of their attacker. Van Note then started a barrel corkscrew and the enemy fighter broke away to the starboard quarter, from which direction it made another attack, firing short bursts with cannon and machine guns, although the tracer passed well above them. The rear and mid-upper gunners fired long bursts and the tracer was seen to enter the enemy aircraft, which broke away in a dive and was not seen again. No damage was sustained by the Lancaster. In total the two gunners had fired 1,450 rounds with no stoppages. Van Note and his crew had completed their tour.[11]

Minnie the Moocher also got back to base. Moores told his story the following day:

My bomb aimer, Sergeant J D Cushing, whose home is at Ealing, told me that there were two Junkers 88s below. The next thing I heard was the rear-gunner open up with a four-seconds burst. I think it was then that he was hit, because I heard nothing more and the intercom was cut off. The wireless operator, Sergeant Norcliffe, a Halifax man, thought that we were on fire and in looking for the flames knocked off his oxygen tube. He was so dazed that he said to me, 'Are you the pilot of this aircraft?' We all believed that there must be a fire owing to the overpowering reek of cordite. Actually it came from an enemy shell and I was expecting our 4,000lb bomb to go off at any moment. But I was determined not to jettison the bomb after the distance we had flown. So we carried on to the target and when our full load had gone down I heaved a sigh of relief. I was amazed to find that the aircraft could still fly true and level. I turned for home. We hit the coast right where we wanted to. When our badly damaged Lancaster touched down at base we found that the rear-gunner had been killed by a cannon shell. It had smashed one side of the rear-turret. There were holes as big as coconuts in the fuselage and both starboard propellers had been hit. Luckily they had continued to function.

But Minnie, apparently, had not been labelled moocher lightly. She had mooched home not much more than 50 per cent operational. She had the one characteristic that all moochers have in common – she had arrived.

The work of training had its dangers and its heroes. There were grave risks in flying around a blacked-out England, piloted by a pupil. An act of courage in training operations over England on 16 June 1943 cost the life of Flight Sergeant Mervyn Byron Fettell, an Australian instructor at 27 OTU Litchfield, although it saved his crew. Fettell was captain of a Wellington engaged in one of his last night exercises, a triangular course from Lichfield to Norfolk and Bristol. At 10,000 feet the Wellington and a Lancaster collided. The Wellington's starboard engine became detached, a large hole was made in the bottom of the fuselage near the flare chute, all the electrical equipment failed and the impact forced the forward entry hatch open. Fettell ordered the crew to abandon the aircraft and with the utmost coolness checked over the equipment of two of his crew before they bailed out. He then assured himself that the remainder of his crew were preparing to abandon the aircraft. Then Fettell discovered that his own parachute was missing – it had apparently fallen out when the bombers collided. Although he knew now that he must remain in the aircraft, he continued, with cool courage, to supervise the fitting of the parachutes and harness of the remainder of the crew, all of whom made safe descents. Fettell then tried to land the aircraft but he overshot, crashed into some trees near Bibury, seven miles northeast of Cirencester and was killed. The Lancaster also crashed, killing all seven on board.

Fourteen Lancasters were lost from a force of 202 Lancasters and ten Halifaxes of 1, 5 and 8 Groups that raided Cologne on 16/17 June. The marking for this raid was not by *Oboe* but by 16 heavy bombers of the Path Finders fitted with H_2S. Air Vice Marshal Don Bennett recalled that:

So far as the Main Force bombers were concerned, we detailed the method [of marking] by three codenames. These were 'Newhaven' for ground marking by visual methods, when the crews simply aimed at the Target Indicators (TIs) on the ground; 'Parramatta' was when we ground-marked using H_2S only, owing to bad visibility or broken cloud; and finally 'Wanganui', which was pure sky-marking when Main Force crews were required to bomb through these sky-markers [parachute flares to mark a spot in the sky if it was cloudy] on a required course which we detailed … The names … were chosen very simply. I asked one of my air staff officers, Squadron Leader Arthur Ashworth: 'Pedro, where do you come from?' And he replied: 'From Wanganui'. I then said: 'Just to keep the balance with New Zealand, we will call the blind ground marking by the name of 'Parramatta'.

Then, looking for a third name for visual ground marking, Bennett pressed the bell on his desk and summoned Corporal Ralph, his little golden haired WAAF confidential clerk who sat outside his door and tried to guard him. 'When she came in I said: "Sunshine, where do you live?" And she replied, "Newhaven". Thus it was that these famous codenames were born.'

Another PFF innovation was the post of 'Primary Blind Marker,' who had the responsibility of making a run over the target and releasing his markers entirely by radar methods. The equipment used enabled the navigator to see a 'picture' of the ground when he was above cloud. All bombing attacks at night above cloud-covered targets were carried out by using this method, the marking aircraft dropping sky flares which the main force used as an aiming point.

The target area at Cologne on 16/17 June was cloud-covered and some of the Path Finder aircraft had trouble with their H_2S sets. The sky-marking was late and sparse and the bombing of the all-Lancaster Main Force was thus scattered. Several hundred aircraft approached Cologne but because of the bad weather, only the first 100 bombed, the remainder turning back. Most of the damage in Cologne was to housing areas with 401 houses destroyed and nearly 13,000 suffering varying degrees of damage. Three of the missing Lancasters were on 156 Squadron at Warboys, one of which was believed shot down by flak in Belgium. The Lancaster III flown by Pilot Officer Robert Ballantine Miller, which crashed in the vicinity of Mönchengladbach, took all the crew to the deaths. Two days later all seven crew, including Technical Sergeant Eastman G Fisher, the rear gunner, a graduate of Brandon College in Manitoba, were buried in the Städtfriedhof. There they remained until after the war when they were reinterred at the Rheinberg War Cemetery.

On 19/20 June, 290 aircraft of 3, 4, 6 and 8 Groups took off to bomb three targets, the Schneider armaments factory, the Breuil steelworks at Le Creusot, and the electrical-transformer station at Montchanin. Twenty-six of the H_2S-equipped Path Finders tasked with releasing flares at Le Creusot were to fly on to drop flares over the target at Montchanin. By the light of these flares a further 26 Lancasters of 8 Group were to bomb the target. At Snaith, 20 Halifaxes on 51 Squadron were waiting to be bombed up for the raid when an explosion took place in the bomb dump at about 13.30 hours. Incendiaries caught fire and all personnel were forced to take cover until 17.00 hours. During this time a large number of bombs exploded, killing 18 people. Transport was rushed to RAF Holme to obtain replacement bombs and 14 Halifaxes were bombed up in time for the operation. Soon after take-off *V-Victor* on 77 Squadron at Elvington crashed south of Heslington near 4 Group HQ. All the crew were killed.

The Main Force crews were detailed to make two runs from between 5,000 and 10,000 feet, dropping a short stick of bombs each time, but the smoke from the many flares that were dropped obscured the targets and results were poor. All crews bombed within 3 miles of the centre of the target but only about one fifth managed to hit the factories. Many bombs fell in residential areas. At Montchanin most of the attacking crews mistook a small metals factory for the transformer station and bombed this target instead. A few crews did identify the correct target but no bombs scored hits on it. Two Halifaxes failed to return from the raid on Le Creusot.

The following night 56 Lancasters of 5 Group and four Path Finder crews on 97 Squadron in 8 Group flew the first shuttle raid to North Africa, during which they carried out an attack on the Zeppelin Works at Friedrichshafen on the north shore of the Bodensee (Lake Constance), the south shore of which is in Switzerland. The Master Bomber was Group Captain 'Slosher' Slee, who had led the Le Creusot operation, and his deputy was the Australian Wing Commander Cosme Gomm. In addition there were two controllers, either of whom could take charge of the proceedings in the event of an emergency. The force took off late in the evening of 20 June and over France they progressively lost height down to 10,000 feet as they passed Orléans and then lower still to between 2,500 and 3,000 feet. After crossing the Rhine they began to climb to their attack altitude which was 5,000 feet for the Path Finders and 10,000 feet for the 5 Group aircraft. Cosme Gomm took over the control of the operation after Slee's Lancaster lost an engine. At the target Pilot Officers D I Jones and Jimmy Munro released a string of flares parallel to and on either side of the Zeppelin sheds.[12] Flak was heavier than anticipated and Gomm ordered the Main Force up to 10,000 feet. Jones later reported that he had to abandon one marking run because it was impossible to hold his Lancaster steady in the concussions from the exploding bombs. John Sauvage put down a green TI just north of the factory and this was followed by a green TI dropped accurately by Flight Lieutenant Eric E 'Rod' Rodley, a survivor of the Augsburg low level raid. More TIs were dropped along the shoreline around the two pre-designated points so that rest of the Lancasters could bomb indirectly. After the attack, all except one of the Lancasters, which had been driven off track by thunderstorms, orbited the target to form up before heading south for airfields at Maison Blanche and Blida in Algeria. All arrived safely but 'Rod' Rodley had a scare after a TI hung up, and when he was far out over the Mediterranean and had lost height, the barometric fuse operated and the candles ignited. His first inclination that all was not well was when he saw the red glow beneath his aircraft. Thinking he was under attack Rodley took evasive action while Sergeant Duffy the flight engineer, checked for damage. The bomb bay was a mass of flames but Duffy quickly jettisoned the blazing remains into the sea.

Six of the Lancasters were damaged by flak, one beyond repair but considerable destruction was caused to the factory. A confused array of *Nachtjagd* fighters patrolled the Florennes-Juvincourt area in vain, waiting for the return of the bombers, who in fact flew home a few nights later, bombing La Spezia en route.

On 21/22 June, before the moon period was over, 705 aircraft[13] attacked Krefeld just inside Germany near the frontier with Holland, in good visibility. The German radar stations, *Tomtit*, 15 miles north-east of Brussels, and *Hamster, Butterfly, Gorilla, Beaver, Robin* and *Wasp* further north, went on the alert immediately. Each station's *Freya* radar spotted and tracked incoming aircraft and the *Würzburg Riese* (Giant *Würzburg*) determined the exact range and height when the aircraft came closer. The *Würzburg Riese* was then used to direct fighter aircraft against the incoming bomber. By 01.10 hours the radar stations to the North were all busily directing their fighters onto incoming bombers, but at *Tomtit Leutnant* Kühnel and the men of XIII Company, 211th Luftwaffe Signals Regiment, searched in vain for a contact and *Unteroffizier* Deller and his six-man crew could see nothing on the screens of the second *Würzburg Riese*.

In order to saturate the German fighter defences along the route of the attack, the bomber crews kept together in a concentrated 'stream'. The period from 01.49 to 01.57 hours at the target was allocated to the 98 Stirlings, which comprised the third wave. One of the Stirlings was *G-George*, flown by Pilot Officer William Golder Shillinglaw RAAF on 218 Squadron, who had taken off from Downham Market in the three-quarters full moon at 00.15 hours with more than six tons of HE and incendiaries. The Australian's crew was quite cosmopolitan and included Flying Officer Rhoar Helvard a Dane, Sergeant Raymond Percy Goward and Flight Sergeant Douglas Joseph Ashby-Peckham RNZAF.[14] Sergeant Patrick Desmond McArdle the navigator busied himself with the route. Over the North Sea, Sergeants Thomas Reginald Lunn in the nose, Arthur Edward Gurney in the mid-upper and Edgar Desmond Hart in the rear turret each fired a short burst to test their guns.

Shillinglaw crossed the French coast but then strayed over Belgium on the way to the target. Orbiting overhead radar station *Tomtit* in a Bf 110 was *Leutnant* Heinz-Wolfgang Schnaufer of *Stab* II./NJG1. Schnaufer had been scrambled from St-Trond airfield near Brussels at 00.54 hours. The crew of *Tomtit*'s long-range *Freya* radar observed a lone aircraft, which, if it maintained its present course would come within range of the giant *Würzburg Riese* radar. Now, at 01.20 hours Schnaufer received a radio warning from *Leutnant* Kühnel of a *Kurier* approaching from the west. At 01.26 hours, as Schnaufer flew west to intercept, *Tomtit* picked up the in-flying Stirling on the giant GCI radar and Kühnel informed *Leutnant* Baro, Schnaufer's *Bordfunker*.

'*Kurier* range 34 kilometres, height 4,300 metres, bearing 285 degrees.'

Baro picked out the target on his radar screen and gave Schnaufer a running commentary on the unsuspecting bomber crew's movements. Finally, at 01.30 hours and 500 metres away to the right and above, Schnaufer caught sight of the flames from the *Viermot*'s engine exhausts. He pulled in closer and recognized it as a Short Stirling. As he closed in underneath the bomber he was seen by one of the Stirling's gunners and Shillinglaw hurled his aircraft into a violent corkscrew in an effort to shake off the attacker.[15] *Unteroffizier* Deller watched the blips almost merge on the radar screen in front of him. Outside on the roof of the building *Unteroffizier* Schellenburg, duty watch-keeper, peered into the night sky waiting for an explosion, which would signal an *Abschuss*. Schnaufer attacked the violently evading enemy aircraft and he reported: 'It caught fire in the fuselage and the wings and continued on, burning. Then it went into a vertical dive and crashed.' As dawn broke *Leutnant* Kühnel set off to look for the crash site to verify Schnaufer's 13th victory. He found confirmation three kilometres northeast of Aarschot. The rudder and rear turret were found 1,500 metres from the wrecked aircraft. All seven crew lay dead in the wreckage of the burnt out Stirling. They were removed for burial at Langdorp churchyard.

A total of 44 aircraft were lost, 38 of them due to *Himmelbett* night fighters operating mainly over the southern provinces of the Netherlands.[16] The Path Finder aircraft produced an almost perfect marking effort, ground markers dropped by *Oboe* Mosquitoes being well backed up by the Path Finder heavies. In 53 minutes, 619 bombers dropped 2,306 tons of bombs on the markers, more than three quarters of them achieving bombing photographs within three miles of the centre of Krefeld. The whole centre of Krefeld – approximately 47 per cent of the built-up area – was burnt out and over 5,500 houses were destroyed and 72,000 people lost their homes. Twenty thousand of these were billeted upon families in the suburbs, 30,000 moved in with relatives or friends and 20,000 were evacuated to other towns.[17]

On 22/23 June, when 565 bombers raided Mülheim, 578 people were killed and 1,174 were injured in the twin towns of Mülheim and Oberhausen. Post war the British Bombing Survey Unit estimated that this single raid destroyed 64 per cent of Mülheim. Thirty-five bombers, 12 of them Halifaxes, failed to return. Four of the Halifax Vs were all from 427 'Lion' Squadron RCAF at Leeming. One of them was *P-Pampers*, flown by Pilot Officer George Austen Cadmus RCAF, a native of Buenos Aires: hence the clever pun on the word 'pampas'. His parents, who lived at Reepham in Norfolk, were notified of his death a few days later. None of the crew in fact survived. Eight Lancasters also were lost. A 207 Squadron Lancaster flown by Flying Officer Philip Gerard Herrin that took off from Langar crashed near Cologne with the loss of all the crew, including Flying Officer Georges Kleinberg, who had been a Doctor-at-Laws at the University of Brussels. Four Wellingtons, including two on 429 'Bison' Squadron RCAF at East Moor were lost, one of which, was flown by the CO, 22-year-old Wing Commander Joseph Logan Savard DFC RCAF, who was killed along with the rest of his crew. Of the 11 Stirlings lost, four were from 75 New Zealand Squadron at Newmarket Heath. Only five men survived from the 28 crew members on the four aircraft. WO2s Robert Ernest Tod DFM and Richard Douglas Tod, twins from Canada on Flight Lieutenant Thomas Fraser McCrorie's crew, were among the dead. The Stirling was shot down into the Ijsselmeer by *Oberleutnant* Lothar Linke of IV./NJG1. The Tod twins were laid to rest in Medemblik General Cemetery.[18]

Flight Sergeant Frank Mathers RAAF on 77 Squadron piloted back to Elvington a Halifax II which, although crippled by flak, with one turret smashed, two engines out of action, short of petrol and losing height, shot down an attacking Bf 110 as it limped home across the Channel. For this epic flight the pilot was awarded the Conspicuous Gallantry Medal, which is extremely rare and ranked in status second only to the VC. Mathers' bomber had been first hit over Mülheim just as the bomb doors closed, by a burst of heavy flak, which set alight the starboard engine. The flight engineer feathered the propeller and the fire went out but almost at once the port inner engine was hit, caught fire and it too, had to be feathered. Then the starboard aileron control was shot away, other equipment was put out of action and three of the petrol tanks holed. Two of them drained completely. The Halifax was losing height steadily as Mathers flew back through the fierce Ruhr defences. He ordered everything moveable to be jettisoned to lighten the aircraft and his crew set to work with axes, chopping out first the seats and cushions, the oxygen bottles and the navigator's table, then all the instruments that could be spared. Finally the mid-upper turret was dismantled and some of the guns went overboard but by the time the coast was reached the bomber was still descending. It was down to 1,500 feet when the Bf 110 attacked. It came in from the stern and the first burst went through the rear turret, past the pilot's seat and out through the front. The crew's first intimation of the danger was when tracer bullets ripped through the fuselage. A bullet knocked a piece of equipment, about to be jettisoned, out of one airman's hand and through the hatch. Flight Sergeant William Fisher Speedie, the rear gunner, in the only complete turret saw the fighter closing in and fired one short burst as it climbed up. Then a burst from the enemy shot all his four guns out of action. As Speedie coolly repaired them the Bf 110 closed in again and again. The Halifax was hit again, this time the bullets passing so close to the gunner that a piece of his Mae West was torn off at the shoulder.

In the meantime the intercommunication system had been shot away and Mathers was cut off from the rear turret. He continued to take what evasive action was possible on his two remaining engines, knowing when the 110 was attacking only by its tracer tearing into the wings and fuselage of the Halifax. He imagined by his silence that Speedie had been killed but at the enemy's third attack the rear gunner was ready, and as the fighter closed in dead astern he delivered a burst from all four guns. Two of the guns failed again but Speedie went on firing with the other two as the Messerschmitt came right under his sights. There was a sudden explosion in the enemy aircraft's cockpit, it swerved off and lost height and the rear gunner followed it down with his fire until it hit the sea and burst into flames. By then the Halifax was down to 400 feet but by superb airmanship Mathers managed to straighten it and maintain height. As he struggled on to reach the English coast Sergeant Edward George Owen French, the wireless operator, kept in touch with base, obtaining directions and calling for assistance for an emergency landing. By the time the coast was crossed the petrol gauges showed zero and Mathers called up the nearest airfield. At a signal he went down to land. He could not lower the damaged undercarriage, and with no petrol left to stay in the air, a belly-landing had to be made. This he made with great skill and the battered Halifax finally slid smoothly to a standstill with every member of the crew safe.[19]

Wuppertal was the destination for 630 aircraft on 24/25 June when Elberfeld, the other half of the town (unharmed on 29/30 May) was the target, the Barmen half of the town having been devastated. The Path Finder marking was accurate and the Main Force bombing started well, but the creep-back became more pronounced than usual and 30 aircraft bombed targets in more western parts of the Ruhr. Post-war estimates were that 94% of the Elbefeld part of Wuppertal was destroyed on this night [20] Altogether, 34 aircraft were lost. Ten of these were Halifaxes and 10 were Stirlings, including one that ditched off Orford Ness. Eight Lancasters and six Wellingtons were also lost and another Stirling crashed at Chedburgh on return.

Warrant Officer P C Andrews' Halifax crew on *C-Charlie* on 405 'Vancouver' Squadron RCAF at Gransden Lodge were flying their fourth operation in five nights. Before joining 405, Warrant Officer Gordon Tisbury the rear gunner, and Sergeant Glyn 'Jock' Jones the navigator from Troon in Scotland, had flown many ops together on Larry Copenhaver's crew on 424 'Tiger' Squadron. Larry was an American and had trained on A-20 Havocs before joining the Canadian Squadron. Tisbury was born in Twickenham and was working at Warner Brothers at Teddington, hoping to become a cameraman. He had enlisted in the RAF at Chiswick, West London, aged 17, on 24 June 1940 after he managed to convince the recruiting sergeant that he was 18 and wanted to fly. He was told that they were not recruiting aircrew at that time but that he could join RAF ground defence, a new section being formed to defend airfields against air and ground attacks, and then try to re-muster into aircrew. Within a week he was committed to the RAF and was sent to Blackpool for initial training. Tisbury and Jones flew about ten ops with Copenhaver before the crew was split up.[21] It was a massive blow to them all, as they had formed a very close bond. Tisbury and 'Jock' Jones were posted to 432 Squadron and after flying three ops were then posted to 405 Squadron.

Finding themselves off course, *C-Charlie* was picked up by enemy radar, being out of the main group. Realising they were on their own and with warning bleeps coming from their alarm system indicating that another aircraft was within a thousand yards of them, they braced themselves for an attack. After a moment of sheer numbing terror as the German fighter closed in and opened fire, Sergeant Joseph Wendelin Kucinsky RCAF, the 23-year-old American tail gunner from Wilkes Barre, PA, shouted to the pilot to turn starboard. Those words were his last, as almost immediately he and Sergeant Charles Price RCAF were hit by a burst of 8mm and 20mm gunfire and they were killed. The left tail unit and both starboard engines were set on fire.

Warrant Officer Gordon Tisbury's intercom and oxygen connections above his head were blown away. He tried to make contact with the rest of the crew as instructed but in the darkness and with the aircraft lurching, by the time he had reached the forward cabin the rest of the crew had bailed out. He made his way back to the fuselage to find his parachute, which was stored next to the mid upper turret. Managing to get his parachute on, Gordon found the escape hatch and jumped, but owing to the trauma and lack of oxygen, blacked out as soon as he left the aircraft. When he came round he was on the ground in a field of potatoes with a sprained ankle. A group of children arrived on the scene and ran off after seeing him only to return with a German police officer who drew his revolver. Stories were rife at the time throughout the RAF about airmen being lynched by German civilians and he felt very worried. After telling the German that he was not armed and owing to the fact that he was unable to stand, the German said something to the children and they ran off and returned with a man pushing a wheel barrow. Tisbury was dumped in this and wheeled down to the local village and a police cell.[22]

Just 24 hours later 473 bombers took off to attack Gelsenkirchen, the first time since 1941. A Halifax crashed just after take-off from Leeming after developing a swing. The target was obscured by cloud and five of the 12 *Oboe* Mosquitoes found that their equipment was unserviceable so regular and accurate marking was not possible. Geoffrey Willatt on 106 Squadron recalls. 'Over Gelsenkirchen we'd been told to await radio instructions at the target. As we approached a voice said, "I am about to fly low over the target – aim at me." And there he was, passing the target far below and silhouetted against the ground fires. We learnt afterwards that the voice was Group Captain Cheshire's.'[23]

The raid was a failure and bombs fell on many other Ruhr towns, including Solingen, 30 miles from Gelsenkirchen. Thirty-one aircraft failed to return, and *E-Easy*, a Lancaster on 61 Squadron, which was badly damaged by flak, was abandoned over Lincolnshire while trying to reach Syerston. *G-George*, flown by Pilot Officer Eric Charles Hughes, was the second of two Stirlings on 218 Squadron that was lost.[24] It came down at Lichtenvoorde in Holland just after 01.15 hours. A night fighter did the damage. Flight Lieutenant Alister Boulton the navigator, who was a New Zealander and the sole survivor, did not know how he found an escape hatch and was unconscious on the way down. Wounded and burnt, he did not see the ground, but he felt his wrist break on landing. A voice said, 'You must be prepared to die.' Boulton thought that it must be a German about to finish him off but happily it was a Dutchman who explained much later that Boulton was so badly injured that he thought he would have bad internal injuries as well and he was preparing the airman for his death![25]

All told, Bomber Command lost 275 bombers shot down in June 1943.

Cologne was subjected to three consecutive heavy raids in late June and early July. On 28/29 June, 608 heavies were dispatched. Geoffrey Willatt recalls:

By this time there was a specific aiming point for each target. In this case it was Cologne Cathedral, next to the bridge over the Rhine and the main railway station. The cathedral was clearly visible and my flash photograph automatically taken when the bombs, in theory, landed, showed I had got an aiming point on the building. As we returned at dawn over the Channel, I could see a 'V' formation of boats below. We went down to have a look, causing them to scatter like frightened fish. I'm sorry perhaps to have scared British MTBs doing something useful. We crossed the coast of England and headed for Lincolnshire and home. The runway at Syerston was marked distinctly by three yellow soda lights on one side in contrast to the other white runway lights. After getting permission to land, lining up and descending, to our horror we saw another aircraft landing immediately beneath us. Robbie pulled back the joystick and put on full throttle. Although our wheels were already lowered, a very dangerous accident was just avoided. We found out later that Newton nearby, operated by Poles had also recently used the same identification lights. The usual procedure on arriving over home base, to avoid collisions, was that returning planes 'stacked' on the circuit, one above the other and separated by perhaps 500 or 1,000 feet in height, until each in turn was given permission to land, often a very dreary wait! All we wanted was a quick landing, debriefing and bed. Dickie Fairweather was the navigator replacement for the wretched Frank, who had been sent home to Canada. Dickie was a delightful bloke, British Honduran and an excellent navigator. He had been ill in hospital while his original crew had been shot down. He was full of bright ideas. Unlike other navigators, who paid little attention to astro-navigation, he often took sextant shots of the stars or moon – particularly useful checks when the ground was obscured by cloud. He said the Germans couldn't interfere with *them*. Flying blind in cloud (no stars or moon visible) one night, after a long silence, Dickie said, 'Robbie, change course onto 274.' After heading onto this reading, Robbie asked why. Dickie said, 'Just my jungle instinct.'

Twenty-five bombers failed to return. One of these was *A-Apple*, a Halifax on 35 Squadron flown by Flight Lieutenant Nelson Alexander Cobb DFC RCAF who was killed. All seven men in his crew bailed out and were captured, although Flying Officer M A Sachs, the tail gunner, was cornered by an irate mob who believed that he was the pilot. Flight Sergeant Roy MacDonald, mid-upper gunner on the 35 Squadron crew of Flight Lieutenant T H Lane DFC RCAF, who were shot down on Krefeld on 21/22 June and all taken prisoner, met Sachs in *Stalag Luft VI*. 'They gave him a hell of a beating. They took his boots and then proceeded to hammer his face in with them. He was still sort of jumpy when I met him. He told me that they then took him out to a lorry in which there were five or six dead RAF aircrew and drove him straight through the outskirts of Hamburg where he said there was a body hanging up at virtually every intersection. I don't suppose you could blame the Germans really. There were a lot of people in England who felt pretty much the same.'[26]

Flying Officer Eugene L Rosner USAAF and his crew on 106 Squadron returned to Syerston having completed their 18th op. Following interrogation after the Cologne trip and a bacon and egg breakfast, they all tidied up and headed off on nine day's leave that all the crews were due every six weeks. On returning a week later Rosner told them he would be returning to London to re-muster in the USAAF. He had been pestering the American authorities for weeks to get a transfer to the 8th Air Force. He promised to get the crew some more leave while he was away. Two days later he returned from London wearing the uniform of a 1st Lieutenant. He had been accepted by the USAAF but he was to complete his tour of operations with the RAF.[27]

Geoffrey Willatt continues.

A group of civilian scientists came to test their inventions in flight. One of them had an artificial leg and was very scruffy – a typical mad scientist. His appearance exactly fitted the character in Nigel Balchin's novel *The Small Back Room* and he may well have been the role model. I don't know what his black box contained but he squatted with it on the floor, saying he'd just invented it and gave Robbie instructions to fly at different altitudes. We were allowed prior to a raid again to Cologne on 3/4 July to use the usual morning flight test to make a trip to another station, where Robbie, as a trainee-barrister, helped to defend an airman at a Court Martial.

Twenty-six Lancasters on 460 Squadron RAAF were drawn up at Binbrook, where the Aussies had decamped in May 1943, for the attack on Cologne. The aircrews and most of the ground crews were at their evening meal when, suddenly, at 18.00 hours an alarm came. Through an electrical short circuit the entire bomb load on DV172 had been released and had fallen to the ground, where the incendiary part of the load was burning fiercely beneath the aircraft. Up went the 4lb incendiary clusters with the 500lb HEs roasting in the centre of the inferno. Two shocked maintenance crewmembers inside the bomber leapt out and tried to roll the 4,000lb bomb away from the mass of burning incendiaries. They saw it was hopeless and ran for safety. They had covered 400 yards when the 4,000lb Cookie and the 500lb bombs exploded, scattering the incendiaries among other aircraft. The two airmen were blown to the ground but escaped with shock. Then R5745, the Lancaster next to DV172, burst into flames and two minutes later its load, which included another 4,000lb bomb and three 1,000lb bombs, exploded, wrecking the bomber, throwing still more incendiaries among the aircraft and setting fire to starter trollies. Before the second Lancaster exploded, Group Captain Hughie Edwards vc DSO DFC, the first Australian air VC, who had taken command of RAF Binbrook on 18 February, claimed that he was driving at 50mph when he was passed by one of the ground crew on foot. Some airmen claimed that they were passed by 20-year-old Pilot Officer Roberts Dunstan, the Australian one-legged air gunner! In half an hour two Lancasters were destroyed and seven made unserviceable. The runways were then cleared and 17 Lancasters left for Cologne.[28]

Altogether, 653 bombers were dispatched. The aiming point was that part of the city situated on the east bank of the Rhine where much industry was located. Path Finder ground marking was accurately maintained by both the Mosquito *Oboe* aircraft and the backers-up, and the Main Force was able to carry out another heavy attack on the cathedral city. Twenty industrial premises and 2,200 houses were destroyed and 72,000 people were bombed out. Thirty-one bombers failed to return, a dozen of them being claimed by the *Nachtjagd Versuchs Kommando* (Night Fighting Experimental Command), which was allowed for the first time to operate over a burning city above the height at which the flak guns reached. This type of night fighting was hastily introduced under the command of *Ritterkreuzträger Oberst* Hans-Joachim 'Hajo' Herrmann, a bomber pilot and one of the foremost blind flying experts in the *Luftwaffe*, who had been agitating for a long time without success for permission to practice freelance single-engined night fighting. Hermann had reasoned that by the light of the massed searchlights, Path Finder flares and the flames of the burning target below, the freelance, single-engined *Wilde Sau* (*Wild Boar*) FW 190 and Bf 109 pilots could easily identify enemy bombers over a German city. By putting a mass concentration of mainly single-engined fighters over the target, his pilots could, without need of ground control but assisted by a running commentary from a *Centraler Gefechtsstand* (Central Operational Headquarters) visually identify the bombers and shoot them down.

Nine of the 10 Halifaxes that were lost were claimed by night fighters. *B-Baker*, a Path Finder on 35 Squadron, was claimed by *Hauptmann* Siegfried Wandam of I./NJG5 who died within the hour, killed by return fire from one of the bombers. Eight Lancasters and eight Wellingtons were also lost. One of the five Stirlings that failed to return was a 149 Squadron aircraft at Lakenheath piloted by Flight Sergeant George Cozens DFM of Upper Norwood. In April he and his navigator, Flying Officer Ernest Redman DFC of Wembley, had received their awards for bringing their Stirling home from Rostock after their aircraft was hit by incendiaries dropped by other aircraft, which wrecked the navigator's cabin and the front turret. One of the 30lb incendiaries dropped clean through Redman's chart and out through the floor while he was writing his log. This time there was no happy ending for the two Londoners and four other members when their Stirling crashed at Geetbets in Belgium. One of the crew evaded and another was taken prisoner. In addition to these losses, two Wellingtons on 432 'Leaside' Squadron RCAF crashed in Kent and two Halifaxes on 76 Squadron crash landed at Hartford Bridge and near Ashtead in Surrey. A Stirling overshot on return to West Wickham and another Stirling, which was forced to turn back, veered off the runway at Lakenheath.

Bomber crews were not aware yet of the new danger posed by the *Wild Boars* but they had more than enough to concern them for the present. Willatt recalls:

There was always the fear that we could be 'coned' over enemy territory. They had radar-controlled searchlights which, once fixed on an aircraft, would follow it whatever avoiding manoeuvre it took. Then the other nearby searchlights would pick it up and the night fighters would arrive to shoot it down. This happened to us. We were lit up in dozens of blinding lights and there seemed to be no avoiding the inevitable fate. Robbie said, 'Going down' and the nose jerked downwards, giving that sinking feeling one gets in a fast lift: straight down and gathering speed but it seemed agonisingly long before the lights dropped away. We were then flying very fast and had reached a dangerously low level – tearing over an island, followed by the North Sea. We found out from our log that we'd been in imminent danger of hitting the ground on the island of Sylt, just off the German north coast.

Over 200 aircrew lost on the Cologne trip were now listed as missing, presumed killed, but there was always a chance that a loved one might have survived and was a prisoner of war. WAAF Aileen Walker trudged tearfully along the lane from RAF Waddington to the local railway station clutching a box. At the station the rail-man could see that Aileen had been crying. She handed the box over and apologised for the box being wet. A few weeks earlier Aileen had been entrusted with 'Red' Wakeford's little dog 'Sniffer' but his master and his crew of K-King had failed to return from the Cologne raid on the night of 3/4 July. Aileen had intended to cycle to the railway station with the dog but she could not get the box balanced on her bicycle and had had to walk. Aileen had wanted to keep 'Sniffer' and her mother in Nottingham wanted him as well, but the dog had to go to Wakeford's mother in Torquay in Devon. Flight Lieutenant John Alfred Wakeford DFC, educated, a big man with a great mop of red hair, had been the first officer Aileen had served in the mess at Waddington. It was her first lunch and she walked through the door of the dining room with two plates of soup expecting perhaps a dozen or twenty airmen but there seemed to be hundreds and they all gave her wolf whistles, which they always did with a new WAAF. Aileen put the soup down in front of Wakeford and nearly spilled it all over him. He asked if she was all right. She put the other soup down and walked out and kept walking until she was in the 'ladies'. The sergeant in charge persuaded her to go back in with more soup and to 'give them back what they gave you'. Regaining her composure Aileen returned. Without looking around, Wakeford said, 'Aileen, I'm bringing a dog back from leave and when I go on ops I'm taking that bomb aimer with me, the one you're going out with, so you can look after my dog.'

That bomb aimer was Sergeant Harold Joseph 'Harry' Hawkridge, 20 years old from Harehills, Leeds. But in June their relationship had cooled. After bombing the Zeppelin sheds at Friedrichshafen, 9 Squadron had flown on to North Africa and when 'Red' Wakeford's crew and the rest came in, everyone except Hawkridge were carrying bunches of bananas. No one had seen a banana for years. They were like treasure. Alec Backler, Wakeford's 22-year-old wireless operator from Burnage had brought some for Aileen's WAAF friend Muriel. They were very close, unlike Aileen and Harold. Aileen said to Harold, 'Well, if you can't be bothered to bring me some bananas back, I can't be bothered to see you anymore. He said, 'I've sent you something a lot better than bananas but you'll have to wait for it, just a couple of weeks.'

Aileen was setting up the tables in the dining room when a letter came for her. It had stamps and postmarks all over it and it was in Harold's hand writing, postmarked 'Algiers'. Aileen shouted, 'Muriel! They're alive!' But when she opened the envelope it said that by the time she got it, Harold would be on leave at home. Hawkridge wrote that he had kept his distance long enough. He was coming back for her and they were going to be married. Aileen was reading this and he was dead. And still she was not finished with the tears because a few days later there was a little box in the post and it was from Harold's mother. The letter thanked her for making her son's last hours happy ones and she hoped that Aileen would accept this necklace as a small token.

Wakeford's Lancaster had been shot down in flames by a Luftwaffe night fighter and had crashed in the Rhine, where the Germans found two bodies, WAAF Muriel's boyfriend Alec Backler and Sergeant George Dohaney, the Canadian rear gunner. Of the rest of the crew, no trace was ever found. The only other officer in Wakeford's crew was the observer, 20-year-old Flying Officer Reeves, an American from Oneida in Madison County, New York State. Like his pilot, he had been given an expensive education, and had moved to Canada with his mother when his parents divorced. In November 1941 Reeves volunteered for RCAF service. His first name was Jonah. Aileen remembered that it did not sound too lucky.[29]

By July 1943 Peter Bone was undergoing training in Canada. A year earlier it was with relief that he received his call-up papers to report to the Aircrew Reception Centre in London, on 24 August 1942, five days before his twentieth birthday:

My friend, six months older than I, received his papers the same day. Geoff Willis and I were soon separated at the Aircrew Reception Centre, firstly by our surnames and then by the doctor. He was a kindly senior officer whose faded wings indicated he had possibly been a World War I pilot. Astigmatism would, he said, make it difficult for me to judge my height in landing a plane. 'Awfully sorry laddie' he said apologetically, 'but we just don't have that many aircraft for you to practice on.' It was just as well. It didn't take me long to realize I wasn't of the right stuff to be a fighter pilot. So, I was put down for navigator training. I had only a general idea of what that might entail but in my youthful enthusiasm; that was fine by me. After months of feeling that I had overstayed my welcome in Civvy Street where, it seemed, only the very young and the elderly were still at home, I welcomed the opportunity to experience new adventures. But my first few weeks weren't particularly adventurous. We were billeted in requisitioned blocks of luxury apartments near London's Regent Park Zoo. Geoff had, I discovered later, been accepted for pilot training and was billeted elsewhere. These apartments had been stripped of all their luxury furniture and fittings and we slept in bunk beds, four to a room. At 05.45 every morning I was awakened by the noisy arrival of the corporal who had the misfortune to be held responsible for our every movement. He made it clear from the beginning that he would brook no nonsense. To underline his intention, he banged an iron bar on the end of each metal bed, setting up reverberations calculated to dislocate the spine. But he was a fair man and we got to actually like him.

We were issued our uniforms which, by guess or by gaily seemed to fit, more or less, and boots, which had at first felt like concrete blocks. We were given lists of equipment that we had to draw from stores and were introduced for the first time to the phraseology unique to the British military: 'Socks, airman, for the use of ... gasmask, airman, for the use of ... housewife, airman, for the use of'. That last item caused a lot of hilarity until it was explained that a housewife in the RAF was a needle, a reel of cotton and a packet of wool. Darn it!

We marched everywhere. When we marched to the Zoo cafeteria, which had also been requisitioned by the RAF, was it my imagination that a hyena laughed at us as we passed his cage?

Once my badly blistered feet recovered, I began to enjoy the route marches through London. It was physically liberating and we became more proficient and drew admiring glances from passersby. Montgomery's push at El Alamein in North Africa had been successful. It was the first good news from the war fronts in three years and we basked in the reflected glory of our 8th Army. But more importantly, I was beginning to take pride in being a member of His Majesty's Royal Air Force. I was making new friends, with Bill from Portsmouth, Sid from Cardiff, Harold from Glasgow. Most of us had never been away from home before and we relied on each other for companionship. Weekends were free from Saturday noon, however, and I was lucky to be able to get home quickly on passes, in particular, for my twentieth birthday. But we were anxious to get going. Drill and route marches were all very well we said but dammit; we had volunteered to fly. However, many thousands of would-be aircrew were already in the pipeline of training that all had to go through before we were deemed ready for war. Being caught up in the process of training was like being in a parade. You are marching along briskly when you realize that somewhere ahead things have come to a halt. You mark time for a while and then the parade moves forward again.

So it was throughout our training. Every so often we would be shunted into what was called a holding unit, where the emphasis was on physical fitness and discipline. Drill, route marches, obstacle courses; more drill and so on. I found I enjoyed the feeling of well-being as we evolved from a bunch of ungainly rookies into a squad able to snap to attention as one man. A split-second response to a command would condition us, they said, to obey an order to bail out without question. We grumbled of course but it made sense and we got stuck into it. And there was another incentive. 'Play ball with me', said our instructors and 'I'll play ball with you'. That made more immediate sense. We played ball.

We were glad however, when in late 1942 we entrained for a pretty little seaside resort on the red cliffs of South Devon, in Britain's West Country. This would be our home for the next three months. We were billeted in what had been small family hotels before the RAF had requisitioned them. I shared, with three other trainees, a room overlooking Babbacombe Bay. Below the cliff was a small beach but access to it by an almost vertical cliff rail tram was blocked off, because the beach was mined. On sunny days it was a picture postcard scene but as winter approached, the Gulf Stream brought many days of wet weather. Most of our training, however, took place in classrooms and my abiding memory of Babbacombe is of marching from one classroom to another, clad in oilskins to protect us from the incessant rain. In the darkness of early morning and late afternoon, our corporal would head the procession swinging a red lamp to warn motorists of our approach. In the classrooms we learnt about the theory of flight, the rudiments of air navigation, aircraft recognition, bombing techniques, gunnery, the internal combustion engine and the Morse code. Out on the cliffs on fine days we learned semaphore and skeet shooting and did physical training and drill in a local park.

And there was the little theatre on the front where, in happier days, concert parties had entertained holiday-makers twice nightly. Now we filed into it for lectures such as the one by the Medical Officer, who, with the aid of colour photographs, described graphically what we could expect if we failed to take precautions when assailed by a sudden rush of blood to the crotch, as he delicately put it. I threw myself into all this new knowledge with gusto. There was never any need for heavy-handedness on the part of our instructors. We treated them with respect and they reciprocated. The tone was set on the first day, when our navigation officer, who I think had been a school teacher, entered the classroom with a friendly 'Good morning, gentlemen'. We were a happy bunch and it was common-place for us to sing popular ditties such as *She'll be coming round the mountain when she comes* and *I've got sixpence, jolly, jolly sixpence*, as we marched from one class to another.

This sounds too much like the seven dwarfs singing *Heigh ho, as off to work we go*, so I should add that we were well aware of the progress of the war and it wasn't just the papers that reminded us that there was a war on. Occasionally we would see a Focke-Wulf 190 fighter-bomber streak in under our radar at nought feet to achieve complete surprise and drop a bomb on the Navy at nearby Teignmouth. The RAF hospital on the road down to Torquay was bombed with some loss of life and one morning as we drilled in Carey Park, a FW 190 came out of nowhere to spray us with bullets. We dived into bushes and amazingly no-one was hit. The *Luftwaffe* certainly knew we were there. But now, in early 1943 the US Army Air Force stationed in Britain and after several months of small attacks in occupied France, began sending increasing numbers of its Fortresses and Liberators ever deeper into Germany.

We were still a long way from seeing action in the air. On graduation day we were under no illusions: this war was going to be a long, hard struggle. This was only the end of the beginning! It was at Babbacombe that I met up again with Geoff Willis. It was pleasant to walk down the hill into Torquay to see a film and have a slap-up tea of beans on toast or Welsh rarebit on Saturday afternoons. As the final examinations approached, we would quiz each other on aircraft recognition or the internal combustion engine. We were in different squadrons so I didn't see him at all during the week. We both passed our courses, after which our ways parted again. For me, it was another holding unit. More drill, route marches and obstacle courses. Here there was a rather bad-tempered senior officer who seemed to be either suffering from an ulcer or a permanent hang-over. To be whacked smartly on the thumb by his baton on a bitterly cold day for not pressing them to the seams of one's trousers in the slow march was no laughing matter. On the next holding unit we paraded for a roll-call every morning but this was no ordinary roll-call – it was to designate where each trainee would go for advanced training under the Commonwealth Air Training Plan. The governments of Canada and Rhodesia had set up air bases in their respective countries to give elementary flying experience to would-be pilots and navigators in more stable climatic conditions and far from enemy interference. I would be sent to Canada with some of my friends I had come to know well. I knew a little about Canada from my schooldays, its prairie wheat fields, the Fraser River teeming with salmon and the Rocky Mountains and I had enjoyed the first of the war films, *The Forty-Ninth Parallel*. And oh yes, I knew it was cold there but that was about all.

Another troop train took us one night to Greenock in Scotland. No bands played. There was no-one to see us off. We filed silently up the gangplank of a huge ship, its grey camouflage blending into the chill, misty darkness. It was only when we were on board that we were told we were on the *Queen Elizabeth*. Conceived as Britain's latest crack transatlantic liner to capture the coveted Blue Riband from France's *Normandie*, she had been secretly launched in 1940 in battleship grey and had already carried thousands of servicemen and women all over the world without mishap, unescorted and relying on her speed to out-manoeuvre *U-boats*. We slipped quietly out of Greenock before dawn early in June 1943 and steamed slowly around the top of Northern Ireland into the open Atlantic. Apart from chronic sea-sickness the crossing was for me uneventful. We had to do look-out duty on the gun-platforms in four-hour shifts, when the Navy gunners enjoyed recounting lurid stories of being torpedoed by *U-boats*. We didn't know that there were no *U-boats* within hundreds of miles because Hitler had just ordered them to the Mediterranean to shore up the faltering Italians now that an Allied invasion of Sicily seemed imminent. One morning we caught glimpses of the New York skyline through the early mist. As it cleared I spotted the Statue of Liberty. America! We docked alongside the capsized *Normandie*, which had caught fire at its moorings at the beginning of the war.

There was no time for sightseeing, however. We were whisked off the *Queen Elizabeth* on to a troop train that took us up into Canada, to another holding unit at Moncton, New Brunswick, there to join thousands of other RAF personnel destined to take courses under the Commonwealth Air Training Plan. While administration made sense of all the paperwork, we were left much to our own devices. But we were soon on the move again. Another train, headed by a monster engine of Canadian Pacific Railways, took us via Montreal to Winnipeg. On its arrival that warm July morning, we were initiated into that unique North American neighbourhood ritual, the 'Welcome Wagon'. While a military band played, local matrons plied us with buns, coffee and lots of smiles. It was all rather overwhelming. Only a few weeks earlier we had left a grey and battered Britain under cover of darkness and in the greatest secrecy. These good people seemed to be unaware there was a war on. What we had forgotten of course was that just a year earlier, a thousand Canadian soldiers had died on the beaches at Dieppe and that 2,000 more were now in prisoner-of-war camps and receiving letters and Red Cross parcels from 'the folks back home', just like these Winnipeggers who were now welcoming us so warmly. Certainly I was soon to learn that 'a stiff upper lip' wasn't the sole prerogative of the British during the *Blitz*.

In short order I found myself with about thirty other would-be navigators at No. 5 Air Observer School attached to Winnipeg Airport. We would take our elementary air navigational exercises in yellow twin-engined training aircraft. But first we went back to school for ground exercises that were a little more advanced than the ones

I had sailed through at Initial Training Wing six months earlier. We were free at weekends after Saturday noon and soon located important landmarks like the movie theatres, the YMCA and, for some but not for me, the beer parlours and dance halls. I had given my girlfriend back home an RAF brooch and life was full and exciting enough without complicating it with a romance that could be only short-lived. Furthermore, I had never learned to dance, so, with a few like-minded trainees, I explored a city that never seemed to sleep. Even at midnight, Winnipeg was ablaze with light from gaudy neon signs that decorated most shops and to sit on a stool at a drug store soda counter and order a double milk shake was, for me, the icing on the cake after seeing the latest Judy Garland movie. A greater contrast with blacked-out and rationed Britain was hard to imagine.

One sunny Sunday afternoon a fellow trainee and I were strolling through Assiniboine Park when a pretty teenage girl came over and asked us if we would like to join in a ball game. Mary was with her parents and young brother. We said we would and did. Before the afternoon was over we were invited to spend the occasional week-end with the family. Soon, Tom Handley and I were catching the streetcar out to the East Kildonan Loop. Mr. Hooper was a high school principal and a rather reserved, austere man. By contrast, his wife was cheerfully outgoing and I took to her right away. Alan was fourteen and in the Air Cadets. We learned that two older sons by a first marriage were already in the Royal Canadian Air Force. George was a mid-upper gunner in Lancasters operating over Germany, while Gordon was an air gunner on Catalinas based in Ceylon. I began to notice that Mary was looking at Tom a great deal and it was soon evident that things were getting serious. As I felt I was already 'spoken for' I had no problem with that.

What I did have a problem with were my navigation air exercises. I enjoyed the daylight map-reading exercises; lying in the nose of the aircraft with a map and identifying landmarks as they moved slowly beneath. I was captivated by the checkerboard landscape: acres upon acres of ripening grain under the prairie sun, the long straight rural roads, the occasional rail track punctuated with grain elevators standing like sentinels every few miles with a nearby town's name painted in large white letters on the side. It was all so different from the rumpled patchwork quilt of the English countryside I had loved to explore on my bicycle in my late teen years. The night exercises were my undoing. We would-be-navigators were required to work out the estimated time of arrival, ETA over a town somewhere ahead on our route. This was usually a large circle, at the centre of which was Winnipeg, nearly always visible through the haze like a twinkling pin cushion. After working feverishly with my rule and set-square for, I was painfully aware, much longer than my colleagues, I would hand a piece of paper to the pilot. These pilots were on contract from Canadian Pacific Airlines and some had probably been bush pilots. They were used to flying by the seat of their pants. They wore lumberjack shirts and baseball caps and some smoked foul-smelling mini-cigars and probably, they were bored stiff. On receiving my ETA the pilot more often than not looked at it dispassionately, slowly removed his mini-cigar from his mouth and growled 'We passed it ten minutes ago, bud!' Needless to say, this couldn't go on and before long I was summoned to the Chief Instructor's office. It was a short, friendly interview. I just wasn't navigator material. I knew that and was relieved to be 'washed out' of the course in November. 'Has worked hard but has been unable to cope with the work' was the official verdict. I was posted to Brandon to yet another holding unit to be 'remustered' to another aircrew trade. But the bomb aimers' course had a nine months' waiting list and it was clear that the powers-that-be weren't going to let me be unproductive for that long. 'How about air gunner?' the officer suggested brightly. 'We're always short of air gunners, you know'. I probably did know but didn't want to think about it. So, I didn't ask why and the officer didn't elaborate. 'Well, that's settled then. You'll be on the next gunnery course. Good luck, laddie! NEXT!'

I began my course at No. 3 Bombing and Gunnery School at McDonald near Portage La Prairie and just south of Lake Manitoba. The training aircraft were single-engined Fairey Battles, which had been massacred in the Battle of France in 1940. Hurriedly withdrawn, they had been shipped across the Atlantic to train future bomb-aimers and air gunners. It was now winter and Christmas 1943 was rapidly approaching. Tom Handley, my former buddy on the navigation course and I kept in touch with the Hooper family and were happy to accept their invitation to spend Christmas with them. On Christmas Eve we arrived to find the family in shock. The telegram had just arrived to say that George, who had never returned in November from a bombing operation on Düsseldorf in the Ruhr, was now confirmed dead. Mary took Tom and me aside and asked us not to say a word when the other guests arrived. So there was much laughter as we played party games and sang carols and popular songs around the piano. I don't recall now how I felt but both Tom and I must have grown up a little without realizing it that Christmas Eve.[30]

On the prairies in winter it was often 30 below. Standing at the corner of Portage and Main waiting for a street car to take us out to the East Kildonan Loop on a bitter Saturday afternoon was an endurance test for Tom and I. 'Oh wait 'till next winter', said the locals encouragingly. 'Your blood will be thicker by then'. But at the height we would-be gunners flew – probably about 5,000 feet – it was even colder. The escape hatch cover in the floor of the fuselage was usually missing and the frigid air was painful to the face. Then the two Browning machine guns would freeze up. We wore thick flying suits of course, including helmets and gloves and when the guns inevitably stopped firing we were required to clear the stoppage without removing our gloves. How we managed to do this delicate operation wearing thick bulky gloves I cannot remember but we did somehow. One trainee ignored the instruction and his fingers immediately froze to the metal. I think he failed the course.

It was difficult at times to tell which was the snow covered ground and which were the snow-laden clouds. We went up, two to an aircraft, to fire rounds of .303 ammunition at a drogue towed by another aircraft. Target practice on the ground is one thing. But when one is firing from a moving platform at a drogue towed by another platform that is being deliberately flown at varying speeds in poor visibility, the chances of hitting the drogue, let alone the bulls-eye on it, diminish rapidly. Exercises were frequently re-scheduled because of 'white-out' conditions or aircraft unservice-ability. We used to joke that the old aircraft needed five hours of maintenance, more string and adhesive tape, for every hour in the air. My final exercise was cancelled because of a blizzard and I graduated in March 1944 with an average assessment, although I suspect I came nearer the bottom of the course than the top. I now realized of course that I wasn't cast in the mould that produced fighter pilots, or bomber pilots for that matter. I had come down to earth but I knew I still had a small but vital part to play in aircrew.

Every morning, as we had entered the flight office, I couldn't avoid seeing the chalked reminder on the blackboard. 'You are here to learn to kill'. Well, yes, I understood that, of course, that's what guns are for but I was far from getting my feelings round the concept. But I would cross that bridge when I came to it and in my youthful innocence, that bridge was still somewhere in the future. I would take each day as it came. The war was going well on the whole. North Africa had been cleared of Germans and now that Sicily had been taken, Allied troops were punching their way up Italy despite strong resistance. Italy had surrendered and had re-entered the war on the Allied side. There was much speculation that the long-planned landings in Northern France would come in the near future. So here I was; waiting for orders to join a troop ship at Halifax, Nova Scotia. My tunic now bore the half-wing of an air gunner and three sergeant's stripes. For better or worse, Hitler, here I come! But as we were given a few days' leave, I decided to join several fellow graduates in a trip to New York, of which I had had a tantalizing glimpse nine months earlier. Among them was Frank

Broome, who had arrived at the Gunnery School at about the same time I did after being washed out of a pilot's course in Florida. Frank was 20 but he looked like a teenager. He had been a junior draughtsman and loved all things technical. He had been bitterly disappointed that he would never fly a Spitfire and was still quite cynical about this abrupt turn of events but he had gradually accepted his fate and had buckled down like the rest of us to the intricacies of the .303 Browning machine gun.

Now, *en route* to New York by train for pre-embarkation leave I realized that my companions were looking forward to a hectic few days of pubbing, dancing and girl-chasing, whereas I wasn't. I still had my girlfriend back home who was still wearing, I hoped, an RAF brooch. So while the others went boozing and then to dances, I struck out on my own and 'did' New York as thoroughly as I could in the few days I had. After our whirlwind days of sight-seeing, it was goodbye to New York, New York. From Montreal I had to return to Moncton, New Brunswick, our last holding unit before embarking at Halifax for the return Atlantic crossing to Liverpool. I had been there only three days before I met up again with my friend Geoff whom I had not seen for three months. He had been taking more advanced flying training. It was good to reminisce about those seemingly far-off days when we would pack sandwiches and a bottle of lemonade into our saddle-bags and set off on a Sunday morning for a day's cycling through the country lanes of Kent and Sussex. That had been only a few years ago, when we were still teenagers. Now we were suddenly young men and ready – well, almost ready, to go to war.

Notes

1. Sloan received an immediate award of the Conspicuous Gallantry Medal, was commissioned and posted to pilot training. John Brian Godfrey Bailey and George Charles William Parslow received immediate awards of the DFC and DFM respectively. They later became part of the crew of W/C John Coverdale MID, the Squadron CO, but were lost without trace with Coverdale on a Wellington X on the 21/22 June 1943 raid on Krefeld, one of 44 aircraft that FTR. Sgt (later F/L) Sloan became a Halifax pilot on 158 Squadron and flew on ops from January 1945 to the end of the war.
2. *218 Gold Coast Squadron Assoc Newsletter No. 40* March 2006.
3. Sgt R E H Hood-Morris also survived and was taken prisoner. The other six crew died. W/C T A B Parselle was captured in Paris and imprisoned at Fresnes Prison from 20 July to 28 August 1943 after which he was moved to *Stalag Luft III* for the rest of the war. Post war he became commandant of the RAF College, Cranwell.

4. 3.6% of the force despatched. II./NJG1 crews returned with eight victories, including *Major* Walter Ehle with four. His attack near Jülich on Halifax II JB837 of 77 Squadron flown by Sgt Richard Lewis resulted in a massive explosion, which not only downed the Halifax but also two Stirling IIIs, EF361 of 7 Squadron flown by F/L Joseph Francois Exavier Gillies Berthiaume RCAF (all KIA), and EH887 of 218 Squadron, flown by Sgt Norman Sidney Collins (KIA).

5. Wellington X HE990, which crashed at Venray NW of Venlo, was the first of 3 RAF bombers Meurer shot down on 25/26 May. Dix and Barclay PoW. Meurer went on to claim Lancaster III LM320 on 100 Squadron, at Vlodrop, and Lancaster III W5001 on 207 Squadron, at Neerbosch. On 20/21 January 1944 *Hauptmann* Manfred Meurer, *Kommandeur* I./NJG1, and his *Funker, Ritterkreuzträger Oberfeldwebel* Gerhard Scheibe in He 219A-0 'Owl' G9+BB were hit by debris from their 2nd victim of the night and they crashed to their deaths, 20 km E of Magdeburg. In less than 2 years Meurer had claimed 65 *Nachtabschüsse* (night victories) (including 40 *Viermots* and 2 Mosquitoes) in 130 sorties.

6. Colin Howes, writing in the *218 Gold Coast Squadron Assoc Newsletter, No. 49*, February 2008. Schnaufer's second victory was another 218 Squadron Stirling, flown by P/O Stanley Gordon Allan RAAF (all KIA). The third, a Halifax II on 35 Squadron, was flown by F/O Ronald Hoos. (Hoos and 5 of his crew KIA. 1 PoW).

7. *Battle Over the Reich* by Alfred Price. (Ian Allan Ltd 1973)

8. Among those lost, 49 Squadron at Fiskerton were missing three Lancasters, as were 460 Squadron RAAF at Binbrook. P/O Kenneth McCulloch and his crew on 619 Squadron were shot down by *Hauptman* Hans-Dieter Frank. All the crew died. Frank's final victory total was 55 and he was killed with his crew in a mid-air collision with a Bf 110G-4 on the night of 27/28 September 1943. It is very likely that the collision was caused by an attack by W/C J R D 'Bob' Braham of 141 Squadron. Frank ejected from the *Uhu* and landed safely but he was choked to death by the cable of his radio helmet, which he had omitted to disconnect and which compressed and crushed his larynx. His *Bordfunker, Oberfeldwebel* Erich Gotter was either thrown from the aircraft or he bailed out without the aid of his ejection seat, which was found in the wreckage with the seat harness undone. Frank was posthumously awarded the *Eichenlaub*.

9. Adapted from *Bombers Fly East.*

10. *Boozer*, which was fitted to Stirlings on 7 Squadron in late 1942, was a simple system that used a series of coloured lights to indicate which type of enemy radar was tracking the aircraft: a yellow light warned the crew of AI radar and a red light warned of *Würzburg* ground radar. By early 1943 *Boozer* was a triple channel system and it was

intended to be installed in all Bomber Command aircraft, but in the event distribution remained limited.

11. In August the American Skipper and his navigator would receive DFCs. 'Van' transferred to the USAAF with the rank of captain, serving on attachment with the Air Ministry on strategic planning. He married his fiancée, Miss Marjorie Sullivan of Lincoln, and in October he became the first American officer to receive his DFC from HM King George VI. Post-war, Van Note worked in USAFE Intelligence. He died in November 1954 after a long illness. See *No Need To Die: American Flyers in RAF Bomber Command* by Gordon Thorburn (Haynes Publishing 2009)

12. F/L James Francis Munro DFC RCAF was KIA on the operation to Berlin on 22/23 November 1943.

13. 262 Lancasters, 209 Halifaxes, 117 Stirlings, 105 Wellingtons and 12 Mosquitoes.

14. Sgt R E Ashby-Peckham was the sole survivor on a 75 Squadron RNZAF Wellington that crashed near Stapleford, Cambridgeshire on an Air Test on 10 January 1941.

15. 218 Gold Coast Squadron Assoc Newsletter No. 51

16. 17 Halifaxes, 9 Lancasters, 9 Wellingtons and 9 Stirlings. Twelve of the losses were on the Path Finders: 35 Squadron lost six out of its 19 Halifaxes that took part in the raid.

17. *The Bomber Command War Diaries: An Operational Reference Book 1939–1945*. Martin Middlebrook and Chris Everitt. (Midland 1985).

18. See *RAF Bomber Command Losses of the Second World War, Vol.4 1943* by W R Chorley (Midland 1996).

19. Only 110 Conspicuous Gallantry Medals (Flying) were awarded in WWII. When it was instituted in November 1942 it was to right the anomaly that existed between officers and NCO airmen in that there was no equivalent to the DSO, which was awarded to commissioned officers only. Nothing existed for the non-commissioned airmen between the DFM and the VC. *In Action With the Enemy: The Holders of the Conspicuous Gallantry Medal (Flying)* by Alan W Cooper. (William Kimber 1986). P/O Frank Mathers CGM RAAF was KIA on the night of 5/6 September 1943 on the operation on Mannheim.

20. *The Bomber Command War Diaries: An Operational Reference Book 1939–1945*. Martin Middlebrook and Chris Everitt. (Midland Publishing 1985).

21. Larry was transferred to the USA forces on 10 January 1944.

22. Andrews, 'Jock' Jones, Flight Sergeant W Kingsley RCAF and Sgt F Bowker were also taken into captivity.

23. Willatt also recalls: 'After the war and through a mutual friend, we went to a Memorial Service in London for a friend's daughter. She had worked for G/C Cheshire, when he ran the Cheshire Homes for sick and dying people. She had started homes in various parts of the

world and died almost as soon as she retired. G/C Cheshire gave an address in her honour. After the service I spoke to him and told him that the last time I'd heard his voice was over Gelsenkirchen (as described). He said, "It had to be done" and that was all. He had flown with enormous courage throughout the war in the air and was a great leader. In peace time, his charitable inspiration was outstanding.'

24. The other was *W-William*, flown by Squadron Leader D M Maw, which crashed in Holland. All the crew were taken prisoner.

25. *218 Gold Coast Squadron Association Newsletter No. 17* edited by Margery Griffiths.

26. *The Bombing of Nuremburg* by James Campbell (Futura 1973).

27. *The Lancaster at War* by Mike Garbett and Brian Goulding (Ian Allan 1971).

28. See *Legend of the Lancasters*. When he was 17 Dunstan had joined the Australian Imperial Forces, went into battle with the 6th Division and on 15 January 1941 he was hit in the right knee by a shell fragment. His right leg was amputated after five operations and he was sent back to Australia. After 7 months in hospital he was discharged with an artificial leg. He urged the authorities to let him join the RAAF and despite his disability he was accepted in June 1942. His first operation was an attack on Düsseldorf on 11 June and he finished his tour with an attack on the same target on 3 November. He would take his crutches with him in the air and when he had to go aft would crawl there on one leg. At the end of his tour he received the DSO, the only Australian air gunner to win this award. He was a gunnery instructor when the war ended.

29. See *Bombers First And Last* by Gordon Thorburn (Robson Books, 2006).

30. Peter Bone adds. 'I suspect that the quiet courage displayed by that sturdy Canadian family was a factor, through perhaps unacknowledged at the time, in my decision to emigrate to Canada in 1959 and to become a Canadian citizen.'

Index

Alexander, Squadron Leader George W. 3
Allcock, Squadron Leader G. M. 93–94
Anderson, Bill 64, 74–75, 83–84
Augsburg 5
Austin, Sergeant Horace William 198–200

Bailey, Flying Officer John 198, 232
Bardney 106–107
Barker, Flying Officer Harry 123–124, 203
Barmen 203, 217
Barnes Flying Officer W. G. DFC 3–4
Barron, Wing Commander DSO* DFC DFM 48
Barton-Smith, Sergeant Hugh 24
Bateman, Pilot Officer Don 115
Battle of the Ruhr, start of 129
Becker, Ludwig 143–144
Bennett AC1 25–26
Bennett Sergeant (later Squadron Leader) Tom 'Ben' 27–28, 42–48
Bennett, AVM Don 22, 211–212
Berlin 103–107, 110, 112, 125–127, 137–138, 144, 172
'Betty's Bar' 150
Binbrook 21, 25, 102, 221, 233

Blida 213
Bochum 132, 138–140, 182–184, 186, 208–209
Bone, Peter 224–232, 235
Bottesford 100
Bourn 24
Bowman, Flight Sergeant James 179
Breighton 113, 159, 166
Bremen Thousand Bomber Raid 95
Bremen 2–3, 26
Brookbank, Jim 193
Brooks, Pilot Officer Ron 23
Buechler, Flight Sergeant Maurice Emanuel RCAF 31–32
Burns, Squadron Leader Kenneth Holstead 'Bobby' DFC 179–180, 185
Burtt-Smith, Sergeant Jim 9–12
Bushby, John 5–6, 74–76

Cadmus, Pilot Officer George Austen RCAF 215
Carter, Flying Officer Gordon Henry Francis DFC* RCAF 120–121
Cawthorne, Sergeant Charles 100–101
Charlwood, Sergeant Don 40, 103, 111–113, 123
Chedburgh 39, 168, 184–185, 217

Chell, Pilot Officer David 67
Cheshire, Group Captain Leonard
    VC DSO DFC* 84, 183,
    234–235
Child, Norman 24–25, 28–29,
    63–64
Chivers, Max 156–158
Churchill, Winston 1, 117, 135
Collard, Wing Commander R. C.
    DFC 21
Cologne 41, 116–117, 121, 181,
    183, 211–212, 219–221, 223
Coltishall 20, 184
Cook, 'Syd' 112
Cooke, Flight Lieutenant
    Grimwood C. DFC DFM
    94–95
Corbett, Ray 70–73
Coryton, AVM Alec 41
Crapp, Pilot Officer Errol RAAF
    128–129
Croft 101, 163
Cutty Sark 142

Dalton 119
Dam Busters' raid 187–188
Dane, Sergeant Gerald 183–184,
    191
Daniels, Wing Commander
    Sidney Patrick 'Pat' DSO DFC*
    83
Danzig (Gdansk) 5–6
Davis, Flight Sergeant William
    Arthur Mathias RAAF
    203–205
de Jong, Elly 187
Dennison, Pilot Officer B. C. 135
Dimbleby, Richard 106
Dix, Sergeant Ken 202–203
Dixon, Sergeant John 15–16
Dixon-Wright, Wing Commander
    Frank 9, 15
Docking 178
Dortmund 178–182, 185, 193–198,
    200

Dortmund-Ems Canal 34
Downham Market 38–39, 67–68,
    88, 130, 133, 162, 184, 188,
    191, 203, 206
Dowse, Flight Lieutenant 'Paddy'
    67, 169–170
Driffield 117
Duffield, Sergeant John 121
Duisburg 6–9, 26–28, 137, 151, 173
Duisburg-Ruhrort 90–93, 180–182,
    186
Dunstan, Pilot Officer Roberts
    221, 235
Düsseldorf 21, 30–31, 113–114,
    202, 206–207, 235

East Moor 30, 130
East Wretham 84
Edwards, Group Captain Hughie
    VC DSO DFC 221
Elberfeld 203, 217
Elsham Wolds 40, 54, 84, 95,
    111–112, 127, 141
Elvington 213, 216
Emden 115, 141
Emmerich 141–142
Essen 4, 30–31, 102–103, 113,
    129–132, 135–136, 142, 175,
    203

Fallersleben 88, 93
Fereday, Sergeant Baden 9, 12–15
Fettell, Flight Sergeant Mervyn
    Byron 211
Finchingfield 39
Fisher, Pilot Officer Alfred Ernest
    137–138
Fiskerton 119
Frankfurt 23, 28, 34, 107, 112, 119,
    151
Freestone, Flight Lieutenant
    Stanley 124–125
Friedrichshafen 213–214
Frizzell 'Frizzo' 10
Furner, Jack 95–100

Gdynia 129, 137
Geiger, *Oberleutnant* August
    'Gustel' 138, 180
Gelsenkirchen 218–219
Genoa 58–61, 65, 68–69, 72
Gibson Wing Commander Guy
    81, 106–107
Giddings, Mary 79–80, 83
Gildner, *Oberleutnant* Paul 123,
    143
Gill, Pilot Officer Alan 24
Gilmore, Squadron Leader
    Edward Gerard DFC RCAF
    118–119
Glass, Squadron Leader Ray DFC
    132–133
Goddard, Sergeant R. G. 183
Goebbels, Josef 125, 142
Goering, Hermann 200
Gomm, Wing Commander
    Cosme 213
Gransden Lodge 179
Graveley 22, 90, 173, 179
Griggs, Sergeant Frank RAAF 2–3,
    48
Grimsby 128, 139

Hall, Sergeant Geoffrey 163–165
Hamburg 16, 21, 116, 119, 146
Harris, Sir Arthur 1–2, 8, 99, 103,
    105, 125–126, 136, 200, 206
Harsh, Flying Officer George R.
    RCAF 34–39, 51
Hartford Bridge 222
Hawes, Flight Sergeant Bill 8
Hawkridge, Sergeant Harold
    'Harry' 223–224
Haye, Pilot Officer Jan Bernard
    Marinus 'Dutchy' 182–183,
    186–187
Hayworth, Gilbert 193–197,
    200–201
Hazard, Sergeant Ivan Henry 122
Herrmann, *Oberst* Hans-Joachim
    'Hajo' 222

Heslington Hall 101
Himmelbett operations 204, 206,
    215
Hobbs, Sergeant Arthur 106–107
Hockaday, Sergeant Neville
    RNZAF 4, 6–9, 16–17, 19–21
Holden, Wing Commander
    George DFC 71
Holme-on-Spalding-Moor 62, 71,
    88, 178, 184, 212
Holmes, Sergeant John 29–30
Holmes, Sergeant Ray 189
Howells, Sergeant Jim 9
Hull, Flight Lieutenant Arthur
    156, 170
Hurst, John Anderson 53–57,
    84–85, 133

Icklingham Marshes 39
Ingham 198
Irvin Parachute Co 146

Johnson, Arthur 'Johnnie' 23
Johnstone, Flying Officer R. D.
    131–132

Kassel 24
Kiel 41, 142–143
Kinloss 117
Kirmington 138, 198
Kleinsman, Hendrik 24
Knacke, *Oberleutnant* Reinhold 31
Krause, *Leutnant* Hans 138
Krefeld 214
Kropf, Flying Officer Lorne
    32–33, 51
Krupps Works 31, 132
Küthe, *Unteroffizier* Helmut 114,
    123

La Spezia 156–158, 172, 189
Lakenheath 3, 80, 135, 222
Langar 67, 120, 193
Lashbrook, Squadron Leader
    Wally DFM 167

Le Creusot 41–48, 212–213
Leconfield 130
Lemon, Squadron Leader P. C. 'Cheese' DSO DFC 22
Lent, *Hauptmann* Helmut 'Bubi' 13
Lichfield 211
Lincoln Cathedral 126, 175, 194
Lincoln 4
Linton-on-Ouse 62, 70, 73, 101, 149, 156, 169
LMF 146–147
Locksmith, Pilot Officer George William 180–181
London 89
Lorient 113–114, 119, 122–123
Lütje, *Hauptmann* Herbert 186, 192

Maddern, Sergeant Geoff 40, 102–103, 112
Mahaddie, Squadron Leader Thomas Gilbert 'Hamish' 117–118, 135, 144
Maison Blanche 213
Mannheim 95
Mannheim-Ludwigshafen 163
Marham 9
Martin Pilot Officer John A. DFC 70
Massey, Group Captain Herbert DSO MC 190
Mathers, Flight Sergeant Frank RAAF 216–217
McCubbin, Flying Officer Jimmy 37, 142–143
Melbourne 33, 65, 67
Mellor, Flight Sergeant Gordon 39–40
Meurer, *Oberleutnant* Manfred 199, 202
Middleton, Rawdon Hume RAAF 79–83, 108
Milan 62–64, 121–122, 189
Mildenhall 79, 81–83, 150
Minnie The Moocher 209–211

Mock, Sergeant Harold 179
Moir, Flying Officer Colin 'Col' 86–88
Moores, Sergeant A. H. 209–211
Morris, Jimmy 38–39, 61–62, 76–77, 133–134, 188
Mortensen, Flight Lieutenant Edward George 'Morty' 150, 169–170
Moss, Sergeant Leonard 24
Mulheim 215
Mullock, Major MC 58–59
Munich 33, 94, 112
Münster 24, 206–207
Murray Flight Sergeant William Frederick RCAF 32
Musselwhite, Pilot Officer Leslie James 31–32

Newmarket Heath 26, 84, 93, 126, 216
Nienburg 88
North Luffenham 59
Nuremburg 132

O'Donoghue, Squadron Leader Charles 141–142
O'Riordan, Flying Officer Clifford Timothy 158–159
O'Shaughnessy, Flight Sergeant T. G. 90–93
Oakington 16, 22, 94, 117, 133,
Oberhausen 209, 215
'Oboe' device 109–110
Osborn, Squadron Leader Richard DFC 113–114
Osnabrück 40
Oulton 207
Overton, Flying Officer John 203, 206

Parselle, Wing Commander 193, 196, 232
Path Finder Force 22–23, 26, 30, 33, 40, 142

Pietrek, *Leutnant* Norbert
167–168
Pilzen 165–169, 185–186
Pipkin, Flight Lieutenant L. C. 27
Pocklington 35, 84–85
Porter, Sergeant James 40–41
Powdrell, Squadron Leader
Walter Harry 121
Puddephatt, Flight Lieutenant
Dennis Percival 181–182, 186

Rae, Sergeant Bill 57–60
Ragg, Betty 107–108
Raymond, Sergeant Robert
104–106
Read, Flight Lieutenant Ron DFC
150, 156, 168–170
Reed, Sergeant 'Stan' 151–156
Robb, Sergeant Angus 129–130,
146
Robb, Sergeant Ian 95
Robertson, Sergeant Alan Angus
'Robbie' 170, 175, 177, 185,
201, 204, 221
Robinson, Operation 41–45
Robinson, Wing Commander
Basil Vernon DSO DFC 69–70,
78
Rodley 'Rod' 213
Rostock 172, 222
Rothwell, Squadron Leader Geoff
126, 130–131, 145–146,
159–163, 189
Rowling, Flying Officer 'Paddy'
89–90
Rufforth 67, 120
Russell, Huia 19–20, 80

Saarbrücken 33, 49–50
Saville, Wing Commander
Donald Teale DSO DFC 189
Saxelby, Squadron Leader Clive
'Sax' 27
Scampton 4–5, 45, 63, 85, 107, 127,
187–188

Schnaufer, *Leutnant* Heinz
Wolfgang 183, 204–205,
214–215
Scorton 178
Scunthorpe 139
Searby, Squadron Leader John
71–72
Sewell, Sergeant Horace A. W. 2
Shepherd, Flying Officer Ian
James RNZAF 15
Sherk, Pilot Officer Walter Scott
RCAF 173
Shillinglaw, Pilot Officer William
Golder RAAF 214–215
Sidwell, Pilot Officer Leslie 16–19
Skellingthorpe 4
Slee, Wing Commander 'Slosher'
42–43, 213
Sloan, Flight Sergeant Stuart 198,
232
Smith, Squadron Leader Don DFC
MID 30–31, 190
Smith, Wing Commander Don
183–184
Snaith 131, 180
Solingen 219
Soltau 90
Spafford, Flying Officer
Frederick M. 'Spam' DFC DFM
RAAF 52
Stettin 172–173
St-Nazaire 137
Storey, Flying Officer Anderson
106–107
Stradishall 2–3, 25
Stuttgart 74–76, 134, 160–161
Swinderby 4, 100
Syerston 94, 106, 156, 171,
219–220
Sylt 26

Thomas, Roy 107–108
Thomas, Sergeant Edwin 149–150
Thompson, Flight Lieutenant
Fred DFC 117, 135

Thompson, Gwen 187–188
Thompson, Walter 117, 135
Timperley, Sergeant 'Tim' 60, 139–140
Tisbury, W/O Gordon 217–218
Tomyn, Steve 163, 165
Topcliffe 32, 56, 135
Tudor, Wing Commander 'Mary' 4–5
Turin 69–71, 80–82, 84–86, 119, 189

Upper Heyford 42

Van Note, Flying Officer Robert Owen 210, 234
Verran, John 121–122, 126–127, 137

Waddicar, Flight Sergeant 2, 48
Waddington 4, 25, 31, 33, 88, 90, 115, 137, 223
Wakeford, Flight Lieutenant John Alfred DFC 223–224
Walker, Aileen 223–224
Walker, Group Captain Clive 'Gus' 109
Waltham (Grimsby) 25, 28, 57, 60, 128
Warboys 67, 112
Warner, Wing Commander Gerry 169, 190

Waterbeach 99
Weatherall, 'Bob' 8, 48
Webber, Keith 112–113
Whitley, Group Captain John Rene AFC 149–151, 156, 168–169, 190
Wickenby 119, 207
Wilhelmshaven 4, 22, 30, 123
Willatt, Flying Officer Geoffrey 170–172, 175–178, 180, 182, 185, 201, 204, 209, 218–223, 234
Williams, W/O Norman Francis DFM* 207–208
Wilson, Flying Officer Victor Albert 157
Wilson, Group Captain D. E. L. 190
Wismar 33
Wood, Pilot Officer Kemble RAAF 88
Wooden Horse, escape 109
Woodhall Spa 59, 89
Wuppertal 203–206, 209, 217
Wymeswold 129
Wyton 22, 65, 75, 179

York 150
Young, Sergeant John Charles Harley 'Bull' RAAF 122–123

LE	9/13
MA	01/13